COMPUTER SIMULATION

Edited by **Dragan Cvetković**

Computer Simulation
http://dx.doi.org/10.5772/65134
Edited by Dragan Cvetković

Contributors

Andrey Grigoriev, Joachim Van Der Herten, Tom Van Steenkiste, Ivo Couckuyt, Tom Dhaene, Andreja Rudolf, Slavica Bogović, Beti Rogina-Car, Andrej Cupar, Simona Jevšnik, Zoran Stjepanovič, Helena Gabrijelcic, Dejana Javoršek, Nika Bratuž, Tanja Nuša Kočevar, Dejan Jovanovic, Ivan Pribicevic, Jianqiang Lin, Jianqun Lin, Ling Gao, Huibin Lin, Yutian Lin, Yilin Ren, Marcin Hojny, Mildreth Alcaraz-Mejia, Raul Campos-Rodriguez, Marco Caballero-Gutierrez, Aida Huerta Barrientos, Yazmin Dillarza Andrade

Published by InTech
Janeza Trdine 9, 51000 Rijeka, Croatia

Publishing Process Manager Nina Kalinic
Technical Editor SPi Global
Cover InTech Design team

First published June, 2017
Printed in Croatia
Legal deposit, Croatia: National and University Library in Zagreb

Additional hard copies can be obtained from orders@intechopen.com

Computer Simulation, Edited by Dragan Cvetković
p. cm.
Print ISBN 978-953-51-3205-9
Online ISBN 978-953-51-3206-6

For EU product safety concerns:
IN TECH d.o.o., Prolaz Marije Krucifikse Kozulić 3, 51000 Rijeka, Croatia,
info@intechopen.com or visit our website at intechopen.com.

Meet the editor

Dragan Cvetković graduated in Aeronautics from the Faculty of Mechanical Engineering, University of Belgrade, in 1988. In the Aeronautical Department he defended his doctoral dissertation in December 1997. So far he has published 61 books, scripts and practicums about computers and computer programs, the aviation weapons and flight mechanics. He has published a large number of scientific papers in the country and abroad as well. Since 20th March 2007, he had been working at the SINGIDUNUM UNIVERSITY in Belgrade as an assistant professor. Since 1st October 2013, he has been working as the Dean of the Faculty of Informatics and Computing at the Singidunum University, Belgrade. He became a Full Professor in the field of Informatics and Computing in March 2014.

Contents

Preface

Information technologies have changed people's lives so much that now it is almost impossible to imagine any activity that does not depend on the computer in some way. Since the invention of the first computer systems, people have been trying to take advantage of computers in order to solve complex problems in various areas. With the development of the industry, there was a need for a PC in the calculation of the building and automotive construction. Traditional methods of calculation have been replaced by computer programmes that had the ability to predict the behaviour of structures under different loading conditions. In this way, expensive experiments, tests and examinations had been replaced by cheaper and more powerful computational methods that do not require the destruction of the structure to determine its capacity.

Fortunately, computer programmes allow such problems to be solved, in the first place by making the simulation of the real system and after that by performing its realization in practice. Computer simulation or a computer model has the task to simulate the behaviour of an abstract model of a particular system. Computer simulations have become a useful part of mathematical modelling of many natural systems in physics, quantum mechanics, chemistry and biology and then in economic systems, psychology and social sciences, as well as in the engineering process of new technologies, in order to gain a better insight into their way of working and behaving.

Computer simulations are different from computer programmes that run a few minutes, because the simulation can be run on the local network and can last for hours or if it is a demanding simulation, it can last even for days. It can be said that, probably, the simulation can be exceeded (or perhaps even imaginable) by methods that can be solved using a pencil and a paper.

Nowadays, computer simulations are used to solve problems in all spheres of life. Meteorological forecasts, the calculation of rainfall, water flows in rivers, underground water flow and oil exploitation are just some of the areas that cannot be imagined without computers. One of the most interesting computer applications is the simulation of processes in the human body. Modern software solutions enable the calculation of muscle fatigue in certain activities, the deposition of fat in the blood vessels, the risk of cancer and so on. In the future, these programmes will be able to allow the realization of virtual surgeries and to predict the effects of surgery before they are performed in reality.

Chapters are listed in a logical order, but they can be arranged differently, depending on the point of view. The first chapter provides an overview of the development of a novel agent-based simulation model of socio-environmental innovation diffusion in the RENDRUS network based on complex adaptive systems approach. The second chapter shows the study about rendering of colours with three rendering engines and based on changes in the brightness of the object background. In the review part of the third chapter, advanced methods that enable visualization at micron resolution, methods used in 3D visualization workflow and methods used for research purposes are presented. The fourth chapter deals with computer simulation of different textile forms. In the fifth chapter, modelling and computer simulation of microbial growth and metabolism kinetics, bioreactor dynamics and bioreactor feedback control are made to show the application methods and the usefulness of modelling and computer simulation methods in optimization of the bioprocess technology. Chapter 6 presents experimental problems related to research aiming at obtaining data necessary to formulate a physical model of deformation of steel containing a zone consisting of a mixture of the solid and the liquid phases. Chapter 7 presents an idea of constructing a scientific workshop focused on high-temperature processes, based upon a concept of integrated modelling combining the advantages of computer and physical simulations. Surrogate models provide an appealing data-driven strategy to accomplish these goals, for applications including design space exploration, optimization, visualization or sensitivity analysis, and these models are dedicated to the eighth chapter. High-frequency and microwave electromagnetic fields are used in billions of various devices and systems. Design of these systems is impossible without detailed analysis of their electromagnetic field. Most microwave systems are very complex, so analytical solution of the field equations for them is impossible. Computer simulation of high-frequency electromagnetic fields is shown in the ninth chapter. Chapter 10 proposes the modelling of the task allocation problem by the use of Coloured Petri Nets. The proposed methodology allows the construction of compact models for task scheduling problems. The PROMETHEE method, as a mathematical model for multi-criteria decision-making, is one of the ideal methods used when it is necessary to rank scenarios according to specific criteria, depending on whom the ranking is applied to. Chapter 11 presents various scenarios whose ranking is done according to defined criteria and weight coefficients for each of the stakeholders.

I would like to express my sincere gratitude to all the authors and coauthors for their contribution. The successful completion of the book *Computer Simulation* has been the result of the cooperation of many people. I would especially like to thank the Publishing Process Manager Ms. Nina Kalinić for her support during the publishing process.

Dragan Cvetković
Singidunum University
Faculty of Informatics and Computing
Belgrade, Republic of Serbia

Chapter 1

Modelling and Simulation of Complex Adaptive System: The Diffusion of Socio-Environmental Innovation in the RENDRUS Network

Aida Huerta Barrientos and

Yazmin Dillarza Andrade

Additional information is available at the end of the chapter

http://dx.doi.org/10.5772/67740

Abstract

Socio-environmental innovation is a process of social change that implies both the participation of agents on social and environmental initiatives and the generation and diffusion of relevant information, which lead social transformations for collective benefit. During the diffusion of socio-environmental innovations through a communication network, the information is created and shared among participants until mutual understanding is reached. In the case of National Network for Sustainable Rural Development (RENDRUS) network, getting innovations adopted is very difficult by people in rural communities due to the lack of effective communication channel. This study aims to develop a novel agent-based simulation model of socio-environmental innovation diffusion in the RENDRUS network based on complex adaptive systems approach. First, the conceptual model of socio-environmental innovation diffusion in the RENDRUS network based on complexity approach is developed. Then, an agent-based simulation model is implemented using Netlogo software, followed by the simulation model analysis and the design of plausible simulation scenarios. The simulation results illustrate how S-curve emerges from the interrelationships between agents considering endogenous and social cohesion effects. The conclusions argue that more social cohesion and popularity of socio-environmental innovations between small rural producers and their organizations, governmental institutions, academic institutions and the knowledge society corresponds to less time to adopt socio-environmental innovations.

Keywords: complex adaptive systems, modelling and simulation, socio-environmental innovation, diffusion

1. Introduction

As Sagarpa [1] explains, the Mexican National Network for Sustainable Rural Development (RENDRUS) network is a knowledge network for collaborative learning from producer to producer that contributes to diminishing the territorial inequality since it allows producers to know their own experiences. As Sagarpa [1] points out, the RENDRUS network contributes to food security through the development of capacities in rural communities, as well as the incorporation of new technologies that allow producers to establish areas for improvement in their productive, organizational and business processes. In this direction, the incorporation of innovations, the adoption of applied technology and the incorporation in the processes of extension to universities in rural areas led to the establishment of links between producers, their organizations and the knowledge society to generate sustainable rural development in Mexico.

On the one hand, according to Quiroga and Barrera Gaytan [2], the socio-environmental innovation is a process of gradual change through action research in localized territories, which implies that a set of actors, based on their own interests, mission and capacity, participate in specific activities (scientific, technological, environmental, cultural, organizational, financial and commercial) whose orientation is not only to give a creative answer to linked problems of rural development and conservation of natural resources but also to generate learning that lead to the autonomy of the actors and structural transformations that are reflected in the collective benefit. Following Ref. [2], the socio-environmental innovation seeks to generate a flow of relevant information through channels and networks of interaction, promote the process of generation and diffusion of innovations and emphasize as central aspect the interconnection of these channels and networks. On the other hand, as Rogers [3] states, the diffusion of innovation is a communication process through certain channels over time among the members of a social system, where participants create and share information with one another in order to reach a mutual understanding. As described by Rogers [3], from the late 1920s to the early 1980s, the nine major diffusion traditions were anthropology, early sociology, rural sociology, education, medical sociology, communication, marketing, geography and general sociology; the problem faced was the research designs that consisted mainly of correlational analysis on data gathered in one-shot surveys of respondents (adopters and/or potential adopters of an innovation). More recently, the complex adaptive system (CAS) approach was used to analyse the spread of an innovation through a complex social system. The concept of complex adaptive system was introduced in 1967 by Walter Buckely to define a system in which large networks of essential components, without central control and simple rules of interaction between the network components, give rise to complex collective behaviour, sophisticated information processing and adaptation via learning and evolution. Derived from the interactions between CAS and the environment, the internal state of CAS changes through time-forming trajectories that may or may not converge to certain regions of its state space such as the attractors and repulsors, depending on the function they perform. In the study of CAS, it is interesting to know its emergent properties, those that arise at higher structural levels and are due to the interactions between the elements at a lower structural level. The approach of modelling and simulation has been used to better understand the dynamic and evolution of CAS. As suggested by Viale and Pozzali [4], complex adaptive system research can teach us a series of useful lessons, especially those features necessitating the consideration of innovation systems as a complex adaptive system because studying the dynamics of innovation is a complex task.

As Yilmaz [5] points out, from the complexity perspective, the innovation is conceptualized as a CAS phenomenon that occurs at different scales, including individual, group and organizational levels. For instance, at the collective level, innovation can be conceptualized as global property that emerges from the local interactions of actors within a CAS, which influence one another in response to the influence they receive. In this direction, Yilmaz [5] suggests that in a study of CAS it is necessary to know structural and behavioural conditions, for the emergence and sustainment of innovation. As reported by Yilmaz [5], the benefits of abstracting a conceptual model of collective innovation based on the CAS perspective are as follows:

- The empirical understanding of innovation is improved through a formal agent-based simulation model testbed by making it possible to explore particular types of observed regularities via simulation scenarios.
- Agent-based simulation models can be used as computational laboratories for the discovery of organizational designs that are conducive to innovation.
- Agent-based simulation acts as theory generation enabler by facilitating a better understanding of innovation complex dynamics over a full range of feasible configurations and behaviour of complex social systems.

In the study of diffusion of innovations based on CAS perspective, Rogers et al. [6] explores the actual and potential hybridization of these two system theories, relying on illustrations from historical to practical applications of the diffusion of innovation model credited by Rogers [3], particularly the STOP AIDS communication campaign in San Francisco, USA. Modelling the diffusion of environmental innovations not only helps understanding diffusion processes but also enables researchers to develop scenarios of future use of these innovations, therefore indicating possible ways towards a more sustainable future, as Schwarz [7] stated. In the case study of the RENDRUS network, there is much interest in the diffusion of socio-environmental innovations in territories because it is one way to more sustainable use of natural resources. This chapter presents a novel agent-based simulation model of the diffusion of socio-environmental innovation in the RENDRUS network based on the CAS perspective in order to understand the diffusion process in the network for achieving sustainable rural development. The study is of relevance because obtaining an innovation and best practices in the value chain adopted is often very difficult to people in territories. Additionally, we consider that CAS approach gives a better basis for understanding the diffusion of socio-environmental innovation as an evolutionary network of functional elements that interact exhibiting characteristics of a complex adaptive system. An important aspect of the resulting simulation model is that it provides an analytical tool to support the decision-making of governmental institutions towards sustainable rural development in Mexico.

The chapter is divided into five main sections. In Section 2, the conceptual for diffusion of socio-environmental innovation in the RENDRUS network based on CAS approach is developed. In Section 3, the agent-based simulation model for diffusion of socio-environmental innovation in the RENDRUS network is implemented using Netlogo software. The agent-based simulation model analysis and the design of plausible simulation scenarios for achieving sustainable rural development in Mexico are presented in Section 4. The concluding remarks are drawn in Section 5.

2. A conceptual model for diffusion of socio-environmental innovation in the RENDRUS network based on CAS perspective

2.1. Conceptual model development

According to Sayama [8], the various modelling approaches can be put into the following major families:

- *Descriptive modelling*. In this approach, modellers try to specify the state of a system at macro-level at a given time point, capturing what the system looks like. This can be done taking a picture, creating prototypes such as physical models or using quantitative methods such as statistic models.
- *Rule-based modelling*. In this approach, modellers try to come up with dynamical rules at micro-level that explain the observed macro-behaviour of a system. The modelling methodologies mainly used are cellular automata, network models, agent-based models and dynamical equations.

2.2. Agent-based modelling and simulation (ABMS)

CAS perspective concerns with elements called agents that learn or adapt in response to rule-based non-linear interactions with other agents generating the behaviour and the hierarchical structure of a CAS; particular combinations of agents at one level become agents at the next level up [9]. As the result of the non-linear interactions, the agents are able to cooperate and evolve, improving in certain cases their fitness over time [10]. In the mid-1990s, the ABMS computational approach was recognized by Holland as a foundational methodology to the study of CAS [11]. ABMS is a form of computational modelling whereby a phenomenon is modelled in terms of agents and their interactions [12] using the bottom-up perspective in the sense that the system behaviour that we observe in the model emerges from the bottom of the system by the direct interrelations of the agents from the basis of the model [13]. So, it is possible to understand the simple interaction rules between agents at local level. The definition of a space scale is fundamental in ABMS, while the time scale varies in discrete steps. From the computational perspective, the software that is used to program agents has its origins in the areas of Artificial Intelligence, especially in the subfield of Distributed Artificial Intelligence [14, 15], whose objective is the study of agent's properties and the design of networks of interaction between them. It was suggested by Wooldridge and Jennings [16] that computational agents are typically characterized as follows:

- *Autonomy*: the agents had direct control of their actions and their internal state.
- *Social skills*: the agents interacted with other agents through a computational language.
- *Reaction*: agents were able to perceive their environment and respond to it. The environment could be the physical world, a virtual world or a simulated world that includes other agents.
- *Proactivity*: because the agents reacted to their environment, they themselves had to take the goal-oriented initiative.

In general, the environment of agents is interpreted in terms of a metaphorical vocabulary of beliefs, desires, motives and emotions, which are generally applied more in the description of people. The agent´s attributes typically modelled are knowledge and beliefs, inferences, social models, representation of knowledge, goals, planning, language and emotions. According to Macal and North [17], an agent-based model contains the following four elements (see **Figure 1**):

- Agents, their attributes and environment.
- Relationships between agents and the rules of interaction.
- A connectivity network that defines how and with whom agents interact.
- Agent´s environment that interacts with agents, interchanging information.

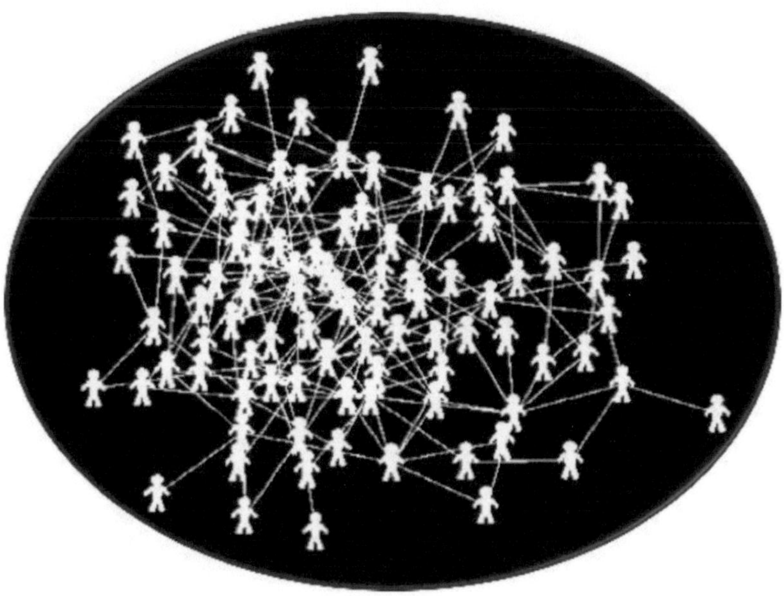

Figure 1. A network of elements in a typical agent-based model.

2.3. The RENDRUS network modelled as a CAS

The RENDRUS network conceptualized as a CAS presents the following characteristics (see **Figure 2**):

- *Multiple key heterogeneous agents.* Small rural producers and their organizations, governmental institutions, academic institutions and the knowledge society.
- *Different structural levels.* At micro-level, the RENDRUS network is constituted by rural producers interacting with one another, and with governmental and academic institutions, while at macro-level, the collaborative learning emerges for leading to the autonomy of rural producers and the structural transformations, which are reflected in the collective benefit.
- *Intrinsic diversity among its key agents.* Small producers from the 32 Mexican federal states are product of the exposure of their own experiences within a socio-economic, cultural and environmental context. So, the incorporation and adoption of new socio-environmental innovations, in order to establish areas for improvement in productive, organizational and business processes, are determined by local requirements.
- *Functional dynamics.* The RENDRUS network is an open system that exchanges relevant information containing producer´s experiences, with the complex environment. In order to survive (increasing the participation of rural producers and governmental and academic institutions), the RENDRUS network has to adapt itself to new conditions imposed by the environment, adjusting its functional units through the modification and selection of new socio-environmental innovations.

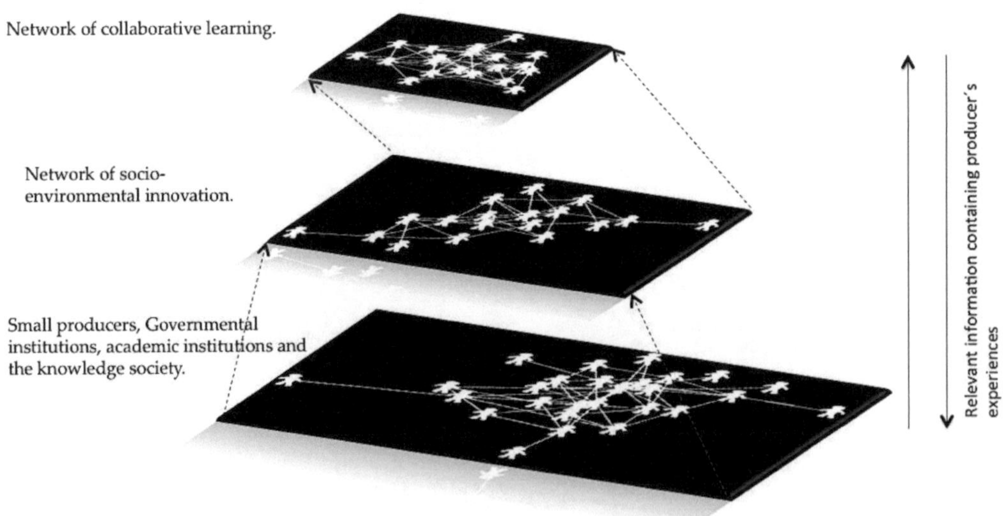

Figure 2. The conceptual model of the RENDRUS network based on CAS approach.

- *The impact of the social structure*. The interactions between members of the RENDRUS network are not random but are rather limited by social networks, both internally and externally. The social structure and socio-cultural interactions between members have a crucial effect on the process of evolution of the adoption of socio-environmental innovations. In this case, the principle of the social structure is based on the community.

2.4. The diffusion of socio-environmental-innovation model in the RENDRUS network based on CAS approach

The diffusion in the RENDRUS network is the process by which socio-environmental innovation is communicated through certain channels (meetings, Internet, etc.) over time among rural producers and their organizations, governmental institutions and academic institutions. In this case, when new answers to complex problems regarding sustainable rural development emerge from the interactions between rural producers and governmental and academic institutions and these are diffused and adopted or rejected by rural producers, some alterations occur at functional and structural level of the RENDRUS network, originating a social change due to the activation of peer networks about such socio-environmental innovation in the next four areas: transformation of primary, agricultural and livestock production, rural industry and marketing, rural non-agricultural services and handicrafts, and rural extension.

Following Ref. [3], we present the five attributes of socio-environmental innovations of the RENDRUS network as follows:

- *Relative advantage*. The degree to which rural producers perceive the socio-environmental innovation as being better than the practice it supersedes. The exchange of innovation-evaluation information between rural producers of the RENDRUS network, using the communication network, lies the diffusion process.
- *Compatibility*. The degree to which the socio-environmental innovation is perceived by rural producers as consistent with the existing socio-cultural values, past experiences and specific needs of potential adopters.
- *Complexity*. The degree to which rural producers perceive the socio-environmental innovation as relatively difficult to understand and use.
- Trialability. The degree to which the socio-environmental innovation may be experimented with on a limited basis.
- *Observability*. The degree to which the results of the socio-environmental innovation are visible to other rural producers.

In summary, socio-environmental innovations of the RENDRUS network that are perceived as relatively advantageous, compatible with existing socio-cultural values, beliefs and experiences, relatively easy to adapt, observable and divisible for trial, will be adopted more rapidly by rural producers.

As discussed by Bass [18], in the literature, two models for how innovations diffuse through social systems are recognized: endogenous and exogenous. On the one hand, in the endogenous diffusion model, how fast an innovation spreads is a function of its own popularity between the members of the social system. Following Ref. [18], in this case the proportion of the social system that has adopted the innovation over time starts out slow, slowly builds to a critical mass, where it achieves exponential growth, and finally levels off as it saturates the social system. The model, as seen in **Figure 3**, is a bell-shaped curve that shows the data about the general endogenous diffusion process on a frequency basis, whereas the s-shaped curve shows the same data on a cumulative basis [3]. On the other hand, in the exogenous diffusion model, potential adopters respond directly to exogenous effects.

From the CAS perspective, both variety and reactivity are necessary for the diffusion of an innovation [6]. Variety refers to the diverse population for emergence and adaptation and it is necessary for information exchange that takes place between an innovation sender and an innovation receiver, whereas reactivity refers to the sensitivity to change where only those populations with adaptability to change can survive at the higher fitness thresholds that occur during cascading mutation/extinction [6]. The information exchange between an innovation sender and an innovation receiver is a critical process in the diffusion of socio-environmental innovation in the RENDRUS network. It means that more information about best practices and new technology corresponds to less uncertainty on rural producer perceptions about relative advantage, compatibility and complexity of innovations, creating better conditions to the emergence and adaptation. The diffusion of socio-environmental-innovation model in the RENDRUS network based on CAS approach contains the following four elements (see **Figure 4**):

- *Heterogeneous agents*. Small rural producers and their organizations, governmental institutions, academic institutions and the knowledge society. The agents (*ag*) have two attributes: the number of neighbours having already adopted the socio-environmental innovations (*an*) and a random threshold for adoption (*rt*) with a normal distribution $N(100,25)$ to satisfy the heterogeneity condition. The Bass model [18] allows evaluating the evolution of both endogenous and exogenous diffusion as follows:

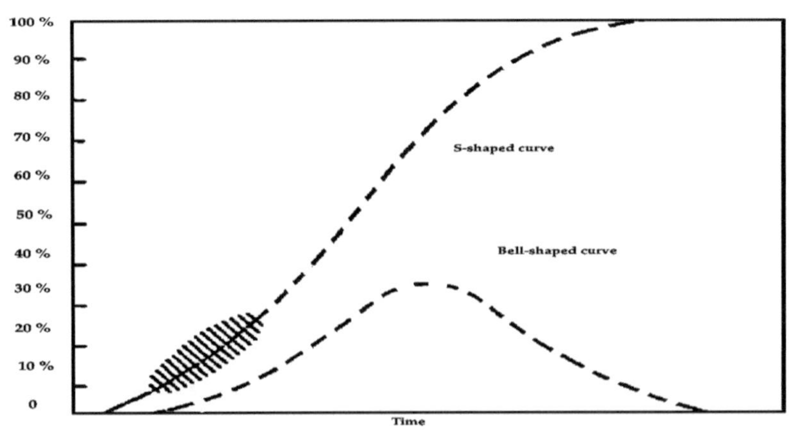

Figure 3. The endogenous diffusion model of an innovation over time by members of a social system, adopted from Ref. [3].

http://dx.doi.org/10.5772/67740

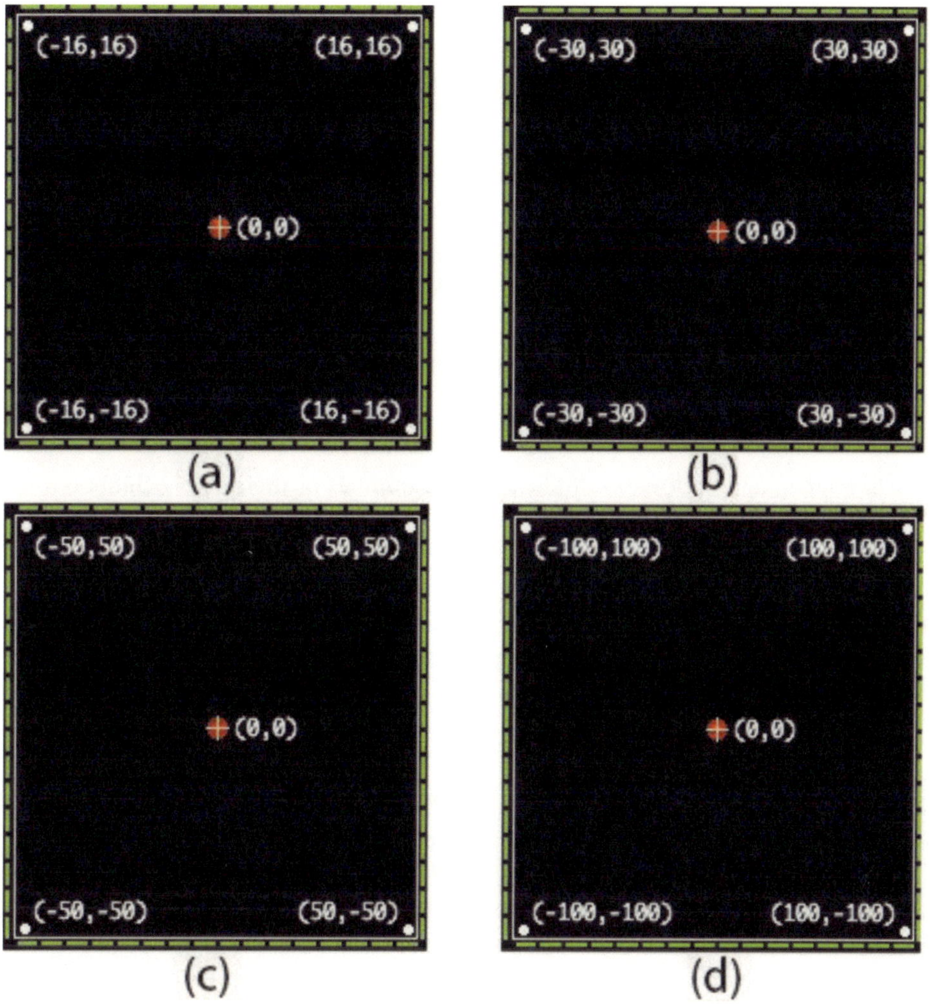

Figure 4. The Netlogo grid based on four different values for MAX-PXCOR and MAXPYCOR, (a) MAX-PXCOR = MAXPYCOR = 16 with a total of 256 patches, (b) MAX-PXCOR = MAXPYCOR = 30 with a total of 900 patches, (c) MAX-PXCOR = MAXPYCOR = 50 with a total of 2500 and (d) MAX-PXCOR = MAXPYCOR = 100 with a total of 10,000 patches.

$$f_t = (p + q\,F_t)(1 - F_t), \quad (1)$$

where F_t describes the proportion of potential adopters having already adopted the innovation, p coefficient refers to the exogenous effect, and qF_t coefficient indicates the endogenous effect at time t. The endogenous diffusion model is a special case of Eq. (1) when $p = 0$. Additionally, one mechanism assumed by endogenous diffusion models is contagion, whereby those who have adopted the innovation directly promote the innovation to those with whom they are in contact [19]. In this study, we use a variant of endogenous diffusion model based on threshold called information cascade, whereby the number of prior adoptions is a source of credible information. The importance of threshold models is the aggregation of popularity [20].

- *Rules of interaction.* Agents interact with their neighbours and the decision for adopting socio-environmental innovations depends if *rt* value is less than a non-linear function evaluated in terms of the number of adopters (*na*), the endogenous effect (*ee*) and the social cohesion between agents (*sc*) whose range can be dynamically updated to revise the *rt* of an agent, as follows:

$$rt \; < \; ee * \left(\frac{na}{ag}\right) + (an * sc) \tag{2}$$

- *A connectivity network.* The network is built generating each agent from 0 to 4500. Once an agent is created (old agent), a new referred position is searched for five neighbours, to create the new agent.
- Agents interchange information indicating the number of their own neighbours having already adopted the socio-environmental innovations (prior adoptions).

3. Agent-based simulation model for the diffusion of socio-environmental innovation in the RENDRUS network

3.1. Netlogo simulation software

Netlogo software, first developed in the late 1990s by Uri Wilensky, is a general-purpose agent-based modelling language used worldwide that provides a graphical modelling environment [21], freely available on the Netlogo website (https://ccl.northwestern.edu/netlogo). As Wilensky [22] explains, it is an extension of the Logo language in which user controls a graphical turtle by issuing commands, and it includes a grid of patches, each patch is a cell computationally active. Turtles and patches are self-contained objects with internal local state. In Netlogo models, time passes in discrete steps, called ticks. Netlogo allows to scale space and time, such as 1 m^2 = 1 patch and one tick can represent a minute or a day, and so on. The grid can be adjusted using the MAX-PXCOR (horizontal direction) and MAXPYCOR (vertical direction) in two-dimension (2D), to create a larger or shorter world keeping the view a manageable size on the main screen, for a total of MAX-PXCOR * MAXPYCOR patches. **Figure 4** illustrates the Netlogo grid with different MAX-PXCOR and MAXPYCOR values, where the worlds wrap both horizontally and vertically. As seen in **Figure 5**, the grid can be visualized in 2D and three dimension (3D).

3.2. The agent-based simulation model implementation

Our agent-based simulation model implemented in Netlogo software produces four artificial worlds, each populated by 1000, 2000, 3000 and 4500 heterogeneous agents, respectively. In order to ensure that the simulation parameters are realistic, we base our agents upon RENDRUS network data about small rural producers available on the RENDRUS website

http://dx.doi.org/10.5772/67740

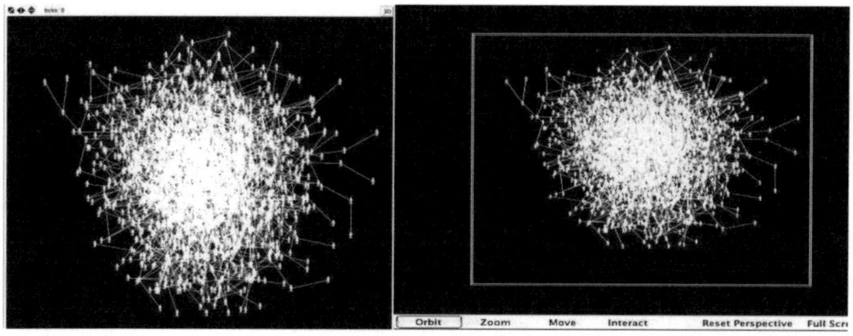

Figure 5. The Netlogo grid including turtles and patches in 2D and 3D. Netlogo grid space of patches in (a) 2D and (b) 3D.

(http://rendrus.extensionismo.mx/rendrus/rendrus). The artificial worlds created vary in the following experimental factors: (a) endogenous and (b) social cohesion effects. We use them to study the rate of adoption, as the relative speed with which socio-environmental innovations are adopted along time. The endogenous effects refer to the popularity of socio-environmental innovations, based on the relative advantage that rural producers perceive from the socio-environmental innovation as being better than the practice it supersedes. The popularity increases when the results of the socio-environmental innovation are visible to other rural producers, whereas social cohesion effects represent the compatibility perceived by rural producers about the innovation as consistent with the existing socio-cultural values, past experiences and specific needs of potential adopters. **Table 1** shows the endogenous and social cohesion effect's numerical values used in the simulation model.

The time variable allows us to plot the number of RENDRUS members adopting the socio-environmental innovation along time. In this model, each 'tick' from Netlogo represents 1 day in the time scale. The simulation model starts with one agent who has already adopted the socio-environmental innovation. The simulation model ends after 1200 simulation days (ticks). As can be seen in **Figures 6–9**, the proportion of adopters starts out slow due to the interactions between heterogeneous agents then, slowly builds to a critical mass growing exponentially, and finally the number of adopters saturates the artificial world that represents the RENDRUS network.

3.3. Agent-based simulation model validation

As Wilensky and Rand [12] explains, simulation model validation is the process of determining whether the implemented simulation model corresponds to some phenomenon in

Simulation parameter	Lower value	Upper value
Endogenous effects (*ee*)	10	20
Social cohesion effects (*sc*)	30	50

Table 1. The range of simulation parameters.

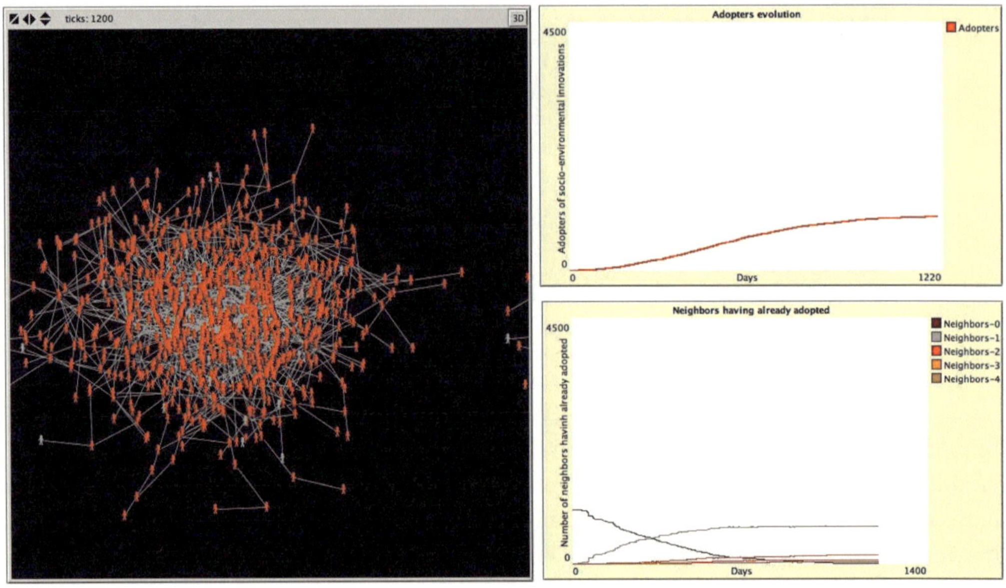

Figure 6. An artificial world populated by 1000 heterogeneous agents, *ee* = 10, *sc* = 30.

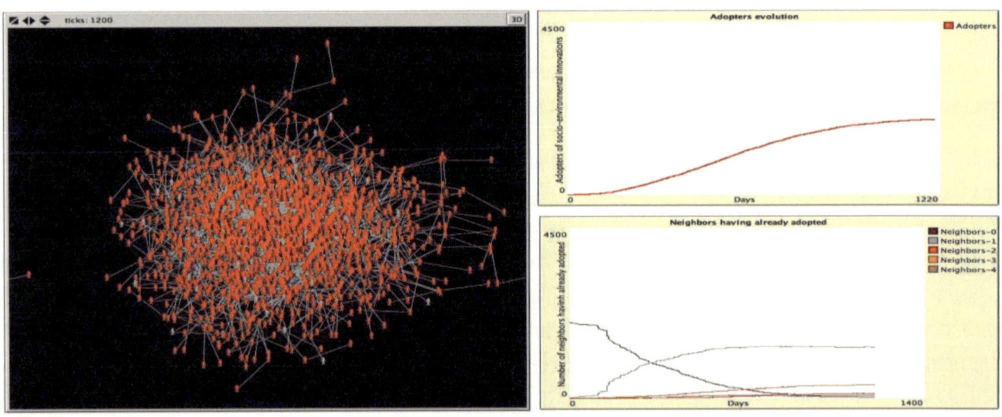

Figure 7. An artificial world populated by 2000 heterogeneous agents, *ee* = 10, *sc* = 30.

the real world. Our agent-based simulation model was validated using the dynamic technique called sensitivity analysis. Through it, values of simulation parameters are systematically changed over some range of interest and the simulation model's behaviour is observed [23]. This technique allows identifying the simulation parameters to which the simulation model behaviour is very sensitive. The simulation parameter considered to carry out the sensitivity analysis is the social cohesion effect (*sc*). In this case, the agent-based simulation model is executed considering two values for this parameter: 20 and 50. The artificial world considers 4500 heterogeneous agents. The endogenous effect (*ee*) is fixed on 10. The simulation model ends after 1200 simulation days (ticks). The simulation results are illustrated

http://dx.doi.org/10.5772/67740

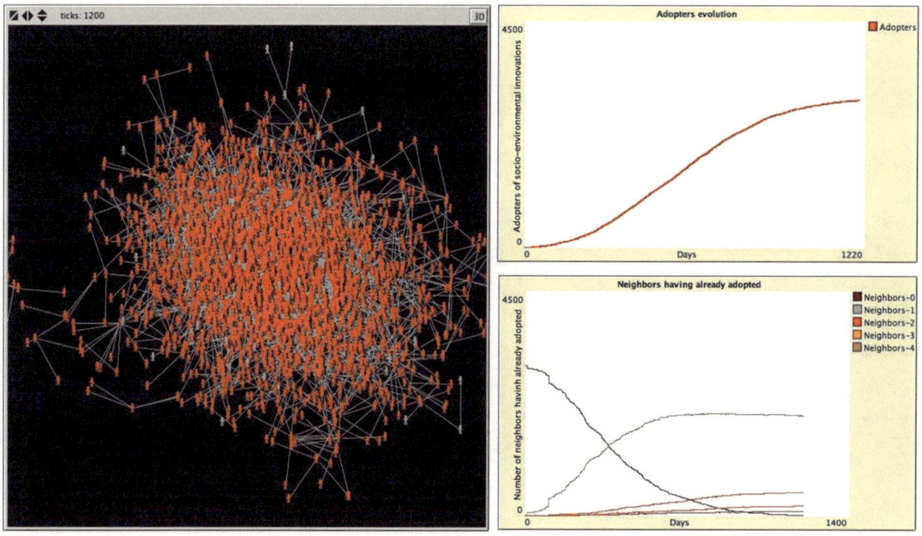

Figure 8. An artificial world populated by 3000 heterogeneous agents, *ee* = 10, *sc* = 30.

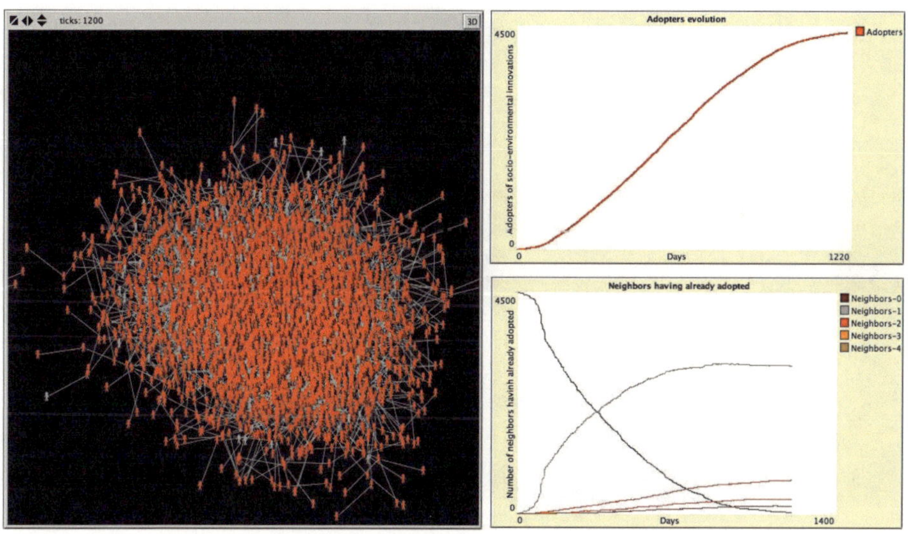

Figure 9. An artificial world populated by 4500 heterogeneous agents, *ee* = 10, *sc* = 30.

in **Figures 10** and **11**. As can be seen in **Figure 10**, the proportion of adopters reaches near 50% of the total population in 1200 ticks. In this case, the rate of adoption, as the relative speed with which socio-environmental innovations are adopted along time, is very slow. On the contrary, as can be seen in **Figure 11** the proportion of adopters starts out slow then, grows exponentially, and finally just in 298 ticks the number of adopters saturates the artificial world. Therefore, more social cohesion among agents in the RENDRUS network corresponds to less time to adopt socio-environmental innovations and *vice versa*, and less

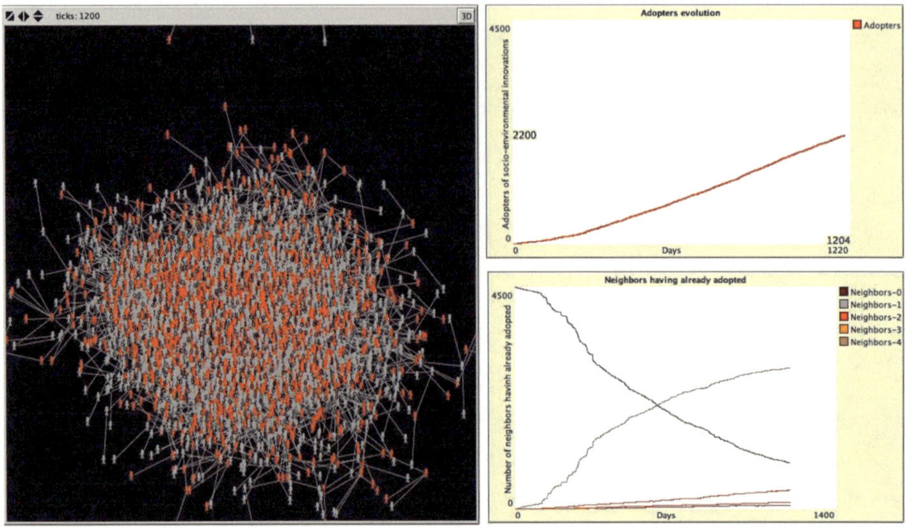

Figure 10. An artificial world populated by 4500 heterogeneous agents, *ee* = 30, *sc* = 20.

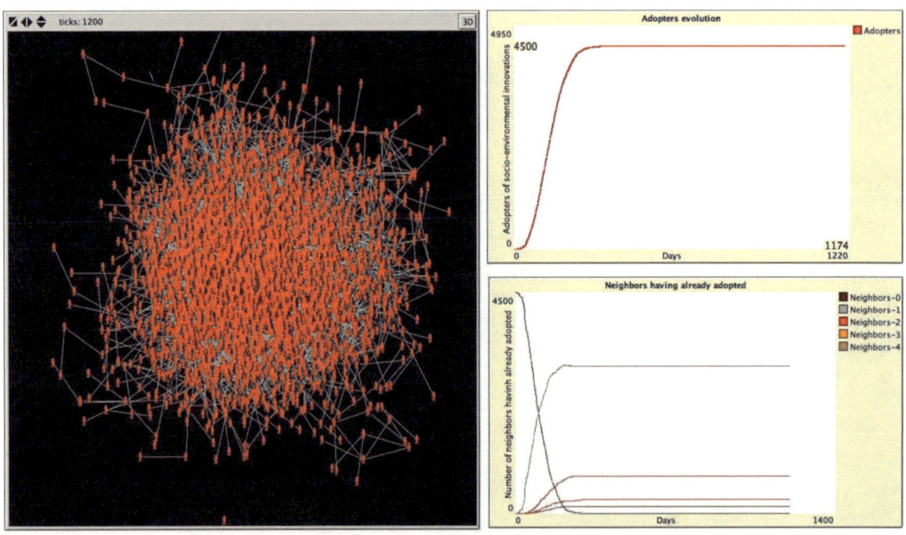

Figure 11. An artificial world populated by 4500 heterogeneous agents, *ee* = 10, *sc* = 50.

social cohesion corresponds to much more time to the adoption. In this case, the innovation adoption is very sensitive to the social cohesion of the RENDRUS network.

3.4. Agent-based simulation model verification

As Wilensky and Rand [12] explains: simulation model verification is the process of making sure that the simulation model has been correctly implemented on a computer using simulation software. In Netlogo software, the compilation and execution processes that prepare the model to run happen behind the scenes and require no intervention by the user; however, syntax and

http://dx.doi.org/10.5772/67740

other coding errors that cause runtime errors during compilation and execution process interrupt the simulation [24]. In this phase, we eliminated the 'bugs' from the code so the model was correctly implemented, free of errors.

4. Agent-based simulation model analysis

4.1. Designing plausible simulation scenarios for achieving sustainable rural development in Mexico

Sustainable development is a process of change in which the exploitation of resources, the direction of investment, the orientation of technological development and institutional change are made consistent with both future and present needs [25]. Mexico is a country committed to addressing sustainable development, as demonstrated by the actions undertaken over the last few years [26]. For instance, in 2001 the Mexican Congress approved the Law on Sustainable Rural Development, on which the sustainable rural development is defined as the improvement of social welfare and economic activities in the territory specified outside the urban centres considered in accordance with the applicable provisions, ensuring the permanent conservation of natural resources, biodiversity and ecosystem services in that territory. Another tangible result is the National Network for Sustainable Rural Development (RENDRUS) that promotes a series of annual meetings for exchanging and evaluating successful experiences between rural producers, seeking a process of collective learning at different levels. In this context, we consider the design of plausible simulation scenarios essential for a better diffusion of socio-environmental innovations through the RENDRUS network in order to improve the social welfare in rural areas, ensuring the permanent conservation of natural resources, biodiversity and ecosystem in such areas.

Scenarios were introduced over 50 years ago firstly by Herbert Kahn as a means to overcome the limits of reductionist thinking in response to the difficulty of creating accurate forecasts. In scenarios, the notion of wholly predictable futures of a system is rejected and instead the alternative futures that explore the paths to each, emphasizing the need to attend to disruptive change as normal, are seen [27]. Plausibility-based scenarios described by Schoemaker [28] are useful approaches in situations characterized by increasing uncertainty and complexity. According to Peterson et al. [29], in order to build scenarios, it is important to specify what is known and unknown about the system's dynamics then, the alternative ways that the system could evolve must be identified. After that, a set of scenarios is built, through which our current thinking about the system should be expanded. Following Ref. [29], the dynamics of scenarios must be plausible; neither nature nor the agents involved in the scenario should behave in implausible ways. The most important part of a scenario's plausibility is likely to be the behaviour of agents. In this direction, the behaviour of small rural producers and their organizations, governmental institutions, academic institutions and the knowledge society could improve the diffusion of socio-environmental innovations through the RENDRUS network. Our simulation model considers that agent's behaviour is influenced by the *rt* parameter (the random threshold for adoption). The *rt* indicates the popularity of the socio-environmental innovations. **Table 2** shows the range of simulation parameters for plausible simulation scenarios.

Simulation parameter	Lower value	Upper value
Endogenous effects (*ee*)	10	10
Social cohesion effects (*sc*)	50	50
Random threshold for adoption (*rt*)	*N*(50, 15)	*N*(70, 15)

Table 2. The range of simulation parameters for plausible simulation scenarios.

4.2. Analysis of plausible scenarios

Figure 12 illustrates the evolution of adopters over time. We observe that the proportion of adopters starts out fast forward then, grows exponentially and finally just in 15.6 days (ticks) saturates the artificial world.

As seen in **Figure 13**, the proportion of adopters starts out slow then, grows exponentially and finally just in 88.5 days (ticks) saturates the artificial world. Therefore, more popularity of socio-environmental innovations (*rt*) among small rural producers and their organizations, governmental institutions, academic institutions and the knowledge society corresponds to less time to adopt it by the RENDRUS network considered as a whole.

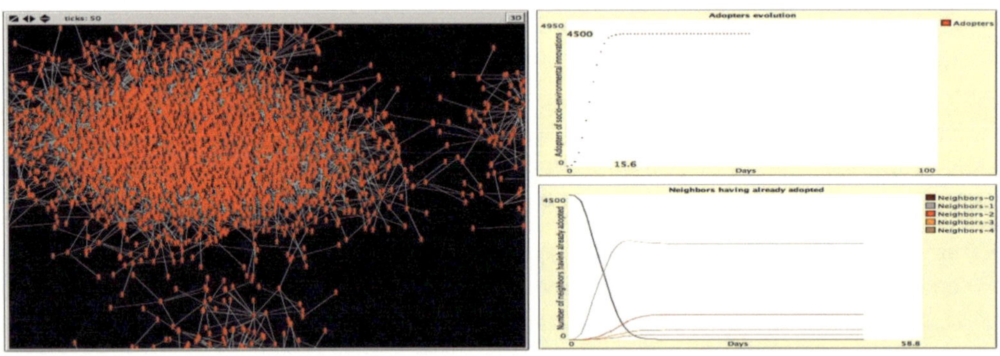

Figure 12. Artificial world populated by 4500 heterogeneous agents, $ee = 10$, $sc = 50$, $rt \sim N(50, 15)$.

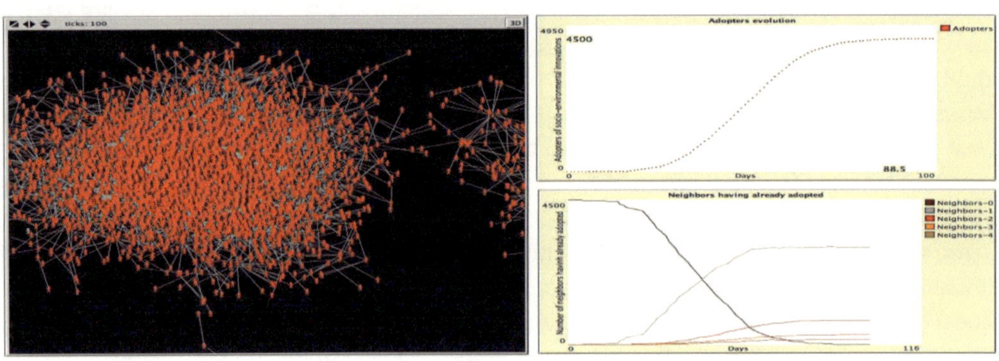

Figure 13. Artificial world populated by 4500 heterogeneous agents, $ee = 10$, $sc = 50$, $rt \sim N(70, 15)$.

http://dx.doi.org/10.5772/67740

5. Concluding remarks

The socio-environmental innovation is defined as a process of gradual social change through action research in localized territories, whose orientation is not only to give a creative answer to linked problems of rural development but also to generate learning that lead to the autonomy of the actors that is reflected in the collective benefit. The RENDRUS network is a governmental initiative to establish links between producers, their organizations and the knowledge society to generate sustainable rural development in Mexico. This chapter presented a novel agent-based simulation model of the diffusion of socio-environmental innovation in the RENDRUS network based on the CAS perspective in order to understand the diffusion process in the network. Modelling and simulating the socio-environmental innovation diffusion is important because it helps us understand the use of innovations that can support the sustainable rural development. From the simulation results, we observed on the one hand that more social cohesion among small rural producers and their organizations, governmental institutions, academic institutions and the knowledge society corresponds to less time to adopt socio-environmental innovations, and on the other hand that more popularity of socio-environmental innovations among them corresponds to also less time to adopt it. In conclusion, the diffusion of socio-environmental innovation to contribute to the sustainable rural development in Mexico depends upon a deep understanding of the interactions among rural producers and their organizations, governmental and academic institutions.

Author details

Aida Huerta Barrientos[1,2]* and Yazmin Dillarza Andrade[1]

*Address all correspondence to: aida.huerta@comunidad.unam.mx

1 Faculty of Engineering, National Autonomous University of Mexico, Mexico City, Mexico

2 The Complexity Sciences Center, National Autonomous University of Mexico, Mexico City, Mexico

References

[1] Sagarpa [Internet]. 2016. Available from: http://rendrus.extensionismo.mx/rendrus/

[2] Quiroga C A, Barrera Gaytan J F. Evaluar la innovación socioambiental? In: Bello Baltazar E, Naranjo Piñera E J, Vandame R, editors. La otra innovación para el ambiente y la sociedad en la frontera sur de México. Mexico: El Colegio de la Frontera Sur; 2012.

[3] Rogers, E M. Diffusion of innovations. London: Collier Macmillan Publishers; 1983.

[4] Viale R, Pozzali A. Complex adaptive systems and the evolutionary triple helix. Critical Sociology. 2010; **36** (4).

[5] Yilmaz L. Innovation systems are self-organizing complex adaptive systems. Association for the Advancement of Artificial Intelligence. 2008.

[6] Rogers E M, Medina U E, Rivera M A, Wiley C J. Complex adaptive systems and the diffusion of innovations. The Public Sector Innovation Journal. 2005; **10** (3): 2–26.

[7] Schwarz N. Agent-based modeling of the diffusion of environmental innovations. An empirical approach. In: Proceedings of the 5th International EMAEE Conference on Innovation; 17–19 May 2007.

[8] Sayama H. Introduction to the modeling and analysis of complex systems. New York: Open SUNY Textbooks; 2015.

[9] Holland J H. Complexity, a very short introduction. New York: Oxford University Press; 2014.

[10] Huerta-Barrientos A, Flores de la Mota I. Modeling sustainable supply chain management as a complex adaptive system: the emergence of cooperation. In: Krmac E, editor. Sustainable supply chain management. Croatia: InTech; 2016. DOI: 10.5772/62534

[11] Holland J H. Hidden order: how adaptation builds complexity. USA: Perseus Books; 1995.

[12] Wilensky U, Rand W. An introduction to agent-based modeling. Cambridge: The MIT Press; 2015.

[13] Miller J H, Page S E. Complex adaptive systems. An introduction to computational models of social life. Princeton: Princeton University Press; 2007.

[14] Bond A H, Gasser L. Readings in distributed artificial intelligence. Los Altos, CA, USA: Morgan Kaufmann; 1988.

[15] Chaib-draa B, Moulin B, Mandiau R, Millot P. Trends in distributed artificial intelligence. Artificial Intelligence Review. 1992; **6**: 35–66.

[16] Wooldridge M, Jennings N R. Intelligent agents: theory and practice, Knowledge Engineering Review. 1995; **10**: 115–152.

[17] Macal C, North M. Introductory tutorial: agent-based modeling and simulation. In: Proceedings of the Winter Simulation Conference, December 2011. p. 1456–1468.

[18] Bass F M. A new product growth for model consumer durables. Management Science. 1969; **15**: 215–227.

[19] Rossman G. The diffusion of the legitimate and the diffusion of legitimacy. Sociological Science. 2014; **1**: 49–69.

[20] Granovetter M. S. Threshold models of collective behavior. American Journal of Sociology. 1978; **83**: 1420–1443.

[21] Dorner D. The logic of failure: recognizing and avoiding error in complex situations. New York: Basic; 1997.

[22] Wilensky U. GasLab: An extensible modeling toolkit for exploring micro-and-macro-views of gases. In: Roberts N, Feurzeig W, Hunter B, editors. Computer modeling and simulation in science education. Berlin: Springer Verlag; 1999. p. 151–178.

[23] Banks J. Handbook of simulation: principles, methodology, advances, applications, and practice. Georgia: John Wiley & Sons, Inc; 1998.

[24] Stigberg D. An introduction to the Netlogo modeling environment. In: Westervelt J D, Cohen G L, editors. Ecologist-developed spatially explicit dynamic landscape models, modeling dynamic systems. New York: Springer; 2012.

[25] World Commission on Environment and Development. Our common future. Oxford: Oxford University Press; 1987.

[26] Huerta-Barientos A, Lara-Rosano F. An initiative of Mexican Government towards sustainable rural development and innovation: The national network RENDRUS case. In: Lasker G E, Hiwaki K, editors. Sustainable development and global community. Ontario: The International Institute for Advances Studies in Systems Research and Cybernetics (IIAS); 2016.

[27] Wilkinson A, Kupers R, Mangalagiu D. How plausibility-based scenario practices are grappling with complexity to appreciate and address 21st century challenges. Technological Forecasting & Social Change. 2013; **80**: 699–710.

[28] Schoemaker P J H. Multiple scenario development: its conceptual and behavioral foundation. Strategic Management Journal. 1993; **14** (3): 193–21.

[29] Peterson G D, Cumming G S, Carpenter S R. Scenario planning: a tool for conservation in an uncertain world. Conservation Biology. 2003; **17** (2): 358–366.

Chapter 2

Rendering Techniques in 3D Computer Graphics Based on Changes in the Brightness of the Object Background

Nika Bratuž, Helena Gabrijelčič Tomc and
Dejana Javoršek

Additional information is available at the end of the chapter

http://dx.doi.org/10.5772/67737

Abstract

Maintaining accurate colour constancy and constant colour appearance are only a few challenges one must conquer in a modern day digital three-dimensional (3D) production. Many different factors influence the reproduction of colour in 3D rendering and one of the most important is certainly rendering engines. In our research, we have studied rendering of colours with three rendering engines (Blender Render, Cycles and Yafaray) of an open source 3D creation suite based on changes in the brightness of the object background from 20 to 80%. In one of these cases, colour of the object was adapted to the lighter background using the colour appearance model CIECAM02. With the analysis of colour differences, lightness and chroma between colours rendered using different rendering engines; we found out that rendering engines differently interpret colour, although the RGB values of colours and scene parameters were the same. Differences were particularly evident when rendering engine Cycles was used. However, Cycles also takes into account the object background. Numerical results of such research provide findings, which relate to the respective environment, and also these certainly demonstrate the successful implementation of the colour appearance model CIECAM02 in the 3D technologies and, in our opinion to other software packages for 3D computer graphics.

Keywords: 3D computer graphics, rendering engines, Blender Render, Cycles, Yafaray, CIECAM02

1. Introduction

The creation of static image in three-dimensional (3D) computer graphic pipeline involves: object modelling, texturing, definition of materials and shading algorithms, illumination, camera setting and rendering. Exact algorithmic description and sampling of light (and consequently colour) for calculation of final rendering are possible only with the consideration of the basis of radiometry. Radiometry presents the set of mathematic tools, rendering algorithms for description of electromagnetic weaving and light phenomena [1]. The fundamentals of these algorithms are complex and multi-layered; however, for visually accurate 3D CG (i.e. computer generated) imagery, the understanding of the basic reflectance models should be at least understood and implemented in the workflow. In general, the reflection of light can be described with two functions, i.e. BRDF—bi-directional reflectance distribution function and BSSRDF—bi-directional scattering-surface reflectance distribution function [2–4].

The BRDF function was defined by researcher Nicodemus [2] half a century ago and today its application is also well anchored in modern 3D computer graphic solutions. In general terms and as well-known from colourimetry, the mathematical abstraction of BRDF considers parameters of lights source, 3D model with defined textures and materials and the observer (virtual camera), therefore the function could be implemented on all types of 3D object surfaces. In dependence of the angle and the direction of the incident light, the function calculates the radiance value from the 3D object's surface in the observer's direction. Similarly as BRDF, BTDF—bi-directional transmittance distribution function is also defined, calculating the portion and disposition of transmitted light. Based on mathematical foundations of both BRDF and BTDF functions, the BSDF—bi-directional scattering distribution function for the light scattering phenomena on the surfaces and in the materials was also determined [4].

The requirements for achieving photorealistic renderings and description of all optical phenomena in 3D virtual space with different visualization technologies also demanded the development of the function BSSRDF [4]. With BSSRDF, the specific reflectance phenomena in translucent materials with higher portion of light scattering are described. Therefore, the so-called subsurface light transport defines the higher amount of light scattering between the starting point where the light is entering the material and (from the entrance's point of view) very distant exit point. With the implementation of this function, the issues of visualization of natural materials such as skin and wax were solved.

Reflectance models (shading algorithms) as the derivatives of the above-mentioned functions represent the definition of type of interactions between material and light. Regarding their mathematical definition and results of their application on the objects, shading algorithms can be used as: (1) models for diffuse surfaces when they describe the surfaces with partial of total diffuse light reflectance; (2) models for surfaces with specific optical properties (metals, anisotropic materials); and (3) models for specular reflective and transitive surfaces, describing the total and partial specular reflectance and/or transmittance [5–8].

The most basic BRDF function is implemented in Lambert reflectance model, defining entirely diffuse surfaces. This model includes a lot of physical and mathematical simplification; however, it is still adequate for opaque and mat surfaces in CG visualizations [5].

Further, the Phong empirical model was developed with very basic level of consideration of lightning, observer (angle, distance) and normal direction for the calculations of reflected radiance at a surface point. Specular reflection in this specular model is calculated as an exponential function of a cosine function [9].

The further developments in 3D rendering brought new solutions and advanced simulations (mathematical interpretations) of objects during rendering. Models named Oren-Nayar, Torrence-Sparrow, Blinn and models for anisotropic surfaces discuss the object surfaces as an organization of a large number of very small, differently oriented surfaces called microfacet.

With the calculations of light phenomena on a large number of small diffuse surfaces, the Oren-Nayar model [5] describes the partially diffuse material surface (which can include also some specular areas in dependence of incident light). On the contrary, Torrence-Sparrow model [6] was developed for metallic surfaces with specific highlights and shadows. The calculations in this model are performed for a large number of completely specular (metal) surfaces.

Blinn's approach to reflectance calculations involves the mathematical model including exponential averaging of normal vectors' disposition on small surfaces of 3D object. The exponential factors included in Blinn's model determine very rapid changes of normals of smooth object surfaces, while these changes are small for diffuse and relief surfaces [7]. The limitation of Blinn's model is the calculation of symmetrical reflection only, whereas as in nature and in 3D CG imagery many surfaces have asymmetrical light reflections. This has brought to the development of models for specific surfaces. Ashikhmin and Shirley [8] presented the BRDF model for objects with anisotropic surfaces (polished metal, hair and cloth). In this model, the properties of a reflected light in a defined surface point are changed in dependence of the rotation of observation around the defined point.

When considering mathematical description, models for specular and transmissive surfaces are in general simpler as above-mentioned models. The cause of their simplicity can be found in the non-complex interactions between light and material, both in geometrical and physical sense. In these models, both functions BRDF and BTDF calculate specular reflectance of the light rays so that the incident light on the surface is scattered in a specified angle (on totally specular surfaces the angle of incident light rays is identical to the angle of reflected light). When specular transmission occurs, the Sneller law and Fresnel equation are implemented in calculations [10].

Illumination in 3D space can be defined as direct and indirect (any process, which simulates indirect lighting, is also referred as global illumination). The principles of both types of illumination and consequently their equations are different, so that for direct illumination only the illumination directly from light sources is taken into account. In contrast, during the integration of indirect illumination, besides direct light sources, all the objects (background) in the scene are also considered as secondary light sources and different light interactions from all surfaces (materials) are performed and calculated. Rendering engines involve one or more often a set of rendering techniques, which algorithms translate all the data about 3D geometry, textures, materials, illumination and camera (observer) in 2D images.

During last decades, indirect illumination was a subject of various researches [11–15]. Each rendering engine uses its own combination of rendering algorithms and methods and with the implementation of different variations of the functions BRDF, BTDF and BSDF, includes also its own derivation of light transport equation (LTE) [10].

Path tracing was introduced by the researcher Kajiya [11] and is still used in the modern solutions as a version of ''single-direction'' path tracing or bi-directional path tracing [16]. This technique is based on Monte-Carlo equation for light transport. The paths of scattered light rays are generated with the gradual tracing from starting point in the camera and ending point in light sources. The basic parameter of this technique is path sampling that demand a very large number of samples for the quality and accuracy of image generation in one pixel. Rendering times are consequently very consuming. Namely, unsuitable number of samples usually results in rendering ''errors'', i.e. more often noise.

Instant global illumination [13] implements the principle of tracing a lower number of light rays from the light source and re-constructs a defined number of point light sources (so-called virtual light sources) in the positions (points), where the path of rays intersect the scene object and background. In the further procedure, the integrator calculates the radiance of objects surface on the intersecting points, taking into account virtual light sources and laws of indirect illumination.

Beside above-mentioned techniques, the methods of photon mapping and particles tracing are also frequently implemented in the work-flow. These techniques were developed by Jansen [12]. These techniques also use simplifications in calculations with systematic distortions of statistical data during sampling. In rendering procedure, they introduce systematic error into the radiance approximation. The basic idea is to construct a path from lights, where every vertex on the path is treated as sample of illumination. The calculation of optical phenomena (reflection, refraction, transmission, scattering) is performed for every object's surface in the space, considering the optical and colour properties of all objects. The method is proceeded in two phases. In the first phase, the photon map is generated, whereas in the second the variation of ray tracing occurs.

The peak of the development in rendering methods is unbiased rendering techniques. Here, the simplifications and distortions in calculation of final rendered images are minimal [15]. Among these techniques, at least Monte Carlo light transport should be mentioned. The Monte Carlo's method involves bi-directional path tracing of light rays, with the starting point in the observer (camera) and ending point in light source(s). The paths are processed with the modification of paths of rays and with the consideration of indirect illumination also in the parts of the scene, which are excluded from calculations within the other rendering techniques [17].

Even though the general rendering algorithms are known, exact solutions that are implemented in software packages are not open source, neither and apart from Cornell box used for user's testing, there are no standardized method available for objective testing of renderings and visualizations [18]. In fact, considering opinions of the developers, the photorealism in CG imagery was already achieved. However, it must be noted that in some references visual perception of photorealism is actually considered from observers' point of view. Namely, some of the references state that photorealistic accuracy cannot be achieved without perceptual cues that yet remain unsolved [19, 20].

International Commission on Illumination CIE (fr. Commission Internationale de l'Eclairage) established the basis of colourimetry already in the beginning of twentieth century. Nowadays, these bases are also the fundamentals of different derivatives of numerical evaluation of colours [21]. Nevertheless, the accuracy of these fundamentals can be severely discussed [22].

Namely, the results of many researches presented that the perception of colour is not depending only on the observer, stimuli and light source but also on viewing conditions, media where the colour is observed (display, computer display, mobile phones) and specific conditions for each media (overexposure or glare) [23–25]. Besides, the studies demonstrated that cultural context and psychological aspects too have significant influence on the perception of colour [23, 26]. As a result, the application of colourimetry started to spread in different areas and many researches experimented various influences and conditions on colour perception [27–29], including the studies of the colour appearance models [30].

As a definition of the technical committee CIE TC1-34, the colour appearance model is capable to predict perception properties of colour, such as lightness, chroma and hue [31]. Developed by International Commission on Illumination CIE, CIECAM97s was an important step to formation of uniform colour appearance model and is a foundation of actually used CIECAM02 [27, 30, 32, 33]. This simple colour appearance model performs the bi-directional calculations on a large number of data bases and is also, due to its simple structure, practical and applicable on different areas [34, 35]. The model can be used for colour transforms [31], as a connection space in colour management [36, 37], for calculation of colour differences [38, 39], for colour rendering predictions depending on different illumination sources and for definition of metamerism [30, 40]. In our research, the CIECAM02 model was used for calculation of colour transforms during the colour changes of background of a defined object.

In the last decade, the perception of colour and surface properties in 3D generated scenes were analysed with different methods and experiments. The studies of illumination and material influence on renderings revealed that observers perceive the colours that are reproduced in renderings differently as they are predicted by algorithms of various rendering methods [41–43].

Xiao and colleagues [41, 42] demonstrated that by different illumination conditions, there are differences in colour perception between graphical simulations of matte disks and specular spheres. Yang and colleagues [44, 45] presented an expanded study of the correlation between colour perception of surfaces and illumination cues. In these researches, colour constancy was depending on the number of light sources, especially in colour perception of highlights. Meanwhile, the perception of total surface specularity and the perception of the background were discovered not to be so relevant during the observations. In addition, other authors have analysed many aspects of colour constancy and colour perception in 2D and 3D scenes [46–49].

So far, in 3D computer-generated imagery, only preliminary researches about the preservation of uniform colour perception of objects in different observation and illumination conditions were published [50, 51]. Therefore, the review of the references showed that the colour appearance model that would facilitate the prediction of perceptual colour properties as lightness, chroma and hue was still not implemented in 3D virtual space.

In the presented research, we have studied rendering of colours with three rendering engines (Blender Render, Cycles and Yafaray) of an open source 3D creation suite based on changes in the brightness of the object background from 20 to 80%. In one of these cases, colour of the object was adapted to the lighter background using the colour appearance model CIECAM02. One of the main goals of the research was the implementation of the colour appearance model CIECAM02 in the 3D technologies.

2. Experimental

2.1. Methods

2.1.1. Defining test setups

To compare different rendering engines, a simple scene was setup in Blender open source 3D creation suite. Scene was composed from background, object, light source and camera (**Figure 1**). Three rendering engines were used, namely Blender Render, Cycles and Yafaray. Yafaray is an open source Monte Carlo ray tracing engine used for generating realistic images with metropolis ray tracing. Yafaray is used in form of add-on and can generate realistic images using path tracing, bi-directional path tracing and photon mapping. Blender Render is physically non-objective rasterization engine that geometrically projects objects to an image plane without advance optical effects. Cycles is objective, physically unbiased rendering engine that employs path-tracing algorithm. Firstly, a simple grey chart was used to calibrate the scene, since different settings are applied to different rendering engines regarding light intensity. RGB values for each rendering engine were measured to provide repeatability among different rendering engines. Colour management was turned off to achieve accurate RGB values. In Blender software, colour management is not entirely equivalent to colour management used in other professional graphic applications.

Background and object in **Figure 1** are composed of diffuse material with intensity 1 without specular of mirror component. Object was in the shape of a sphere. Diffuse shading model was set to Lambert shader for Blender Render and Yafaray. Cycles only supports BSDF that is composed of Lambert and Oren-Nayar shading model. Camera with automatic settings was set in front of the object at the distance of 10 units and light source was set directly behind the camera. A reflector was set as white light and cone with 120° beam angle of the beam and constant fall-off. Light intensity was changed with rendering engine to achieve repeatability and was 1 for Blender Render, 4000 for Cycles and 14 for Yafaray. Rendering engine settings were as follows: image size was set to 800 × 800 pixels in an 8-bit sRGB colour space, amount

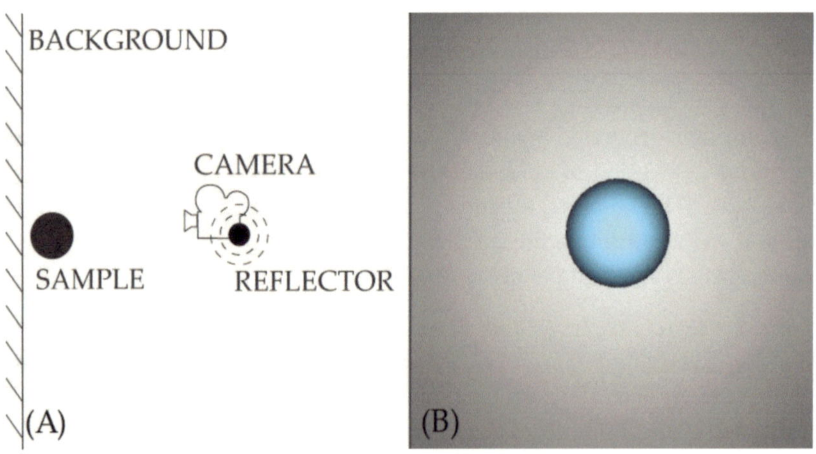

Figure 1. Schematic representation of scene setup in Blender software (A) and rendered image (B).

http://dx.doi.org/10.5772/67737

of anti-aliasing samples per pixel was set to 8 with Gaussian reconstruction filter, all shading options were on, including ray tracing, tile size was set to 64 × 64 units. Rendering was carried out by central processing unit (Intel i7 4770).

Input colours were in the range of RGB = [0, 0, 0] to RGB = [255, 255, 255] with interval of 25.5 units per channel, adding up to 1331 samples. Background was defined as 20 and 80% lightness, meaning RGB20 = [51, 51, 51] for 20% lightness and RGB80 = [204, 204, 204] for 80% lightness. In **Table 1**, important characteristics of each scene element are presented for all rendering engines.

		Blender Render	**Cycles**	**Yafaray**
Object	Colour	1331 colour samples		
	Material	Surface	Diffuse	Glossy-diffuse
	Diffuse	Lambert	BSDF (Lambert in Oren-Nayar)	Lambert
	Amount	1	/	1
	Specular	Off	Off	Off
	Other effects	Off	Off	Off
Background	Colour	RGB20 (20% lightness) and RGB80 (80% lightness)		
	Material	Surface	Diffuse	Glossy-diffuse
	Diffuse shading	Lambert	BSDF (Lambert in Oren-Nayar)	Lambert
	Intensity	1	/	1
	Specular shading	Off	Off	Off
	Other effects	Off	Off	Off
Light source	Lamp	Spot		
	Colour	White		
	Intensity	1	4000	14
	Shape	Cone with 120° beam angle		
Camera	Focal length	35 mm		
	Settings	Auto		
Render settings	Dimensions	800 × 800 pixels		
	Colour space	sRGB		
	Depth	8 bit		
		PNG		
	Colour management	Off	/	/
	Anti-aliasing	Gauss, 8 samples		

Table 1. Rendering engine settings for object, background, light source and camera and general rendering settings.

2.1.2. Colour adaptation with CIECAM02 colour appearance model

Above-mentioned input colours were imported to Blender software as input values RGBi on RGB20 background, as input values RGBi on RGB80 background and as adapted values RGBa on RGB80 background (**Figure 2**). This presents a set of images that will be later used for evaluation. Also, simultaneous contrast can be observed between input colours on RGB20 and RGB80 backgrounds.

Adapted colour was calculated with CIECAM02 colour appearance model as presented in **Figure 3**. From input RGBi values, XYZi values were calculated and used to calculate appearance correlates lightness J, chroma C and hue h, via reverse models adapted XYZa and RGBa were calculated. Following parameters were used in both directions: luminance of the adapting field was set to L_A = 16 cd/m^2 and white point to D65 and surroundings was set to average. Relative luminance of the background was Y_B = 20% for input colours and Y_B = 80% for adapted colours.

2.1.3. Evaluation

Next to input RGBi values and adapted RGBa values, lightest colour RGBs and average colour RGBp on spherical object on rendered image were also obtained. CIELAB values were also

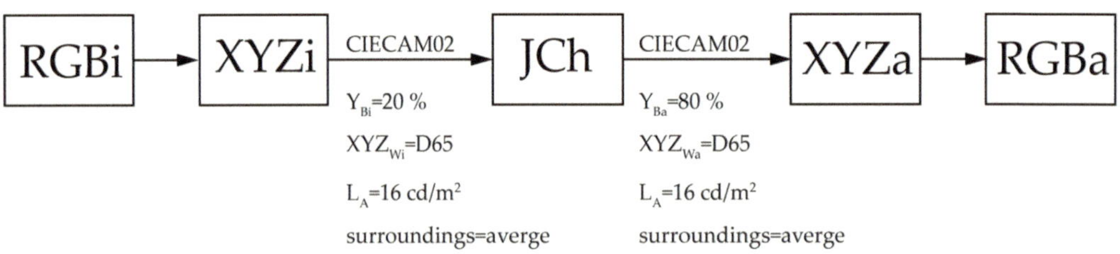

Figure 2. A set of images for colour RGBi = [51, 77, 179] for Cycles rendering engine. From left to right follow input colour RGB on RGB20 background, as input colour RGB on RGB80 background and as adapted RGB colour on RGB80 background.

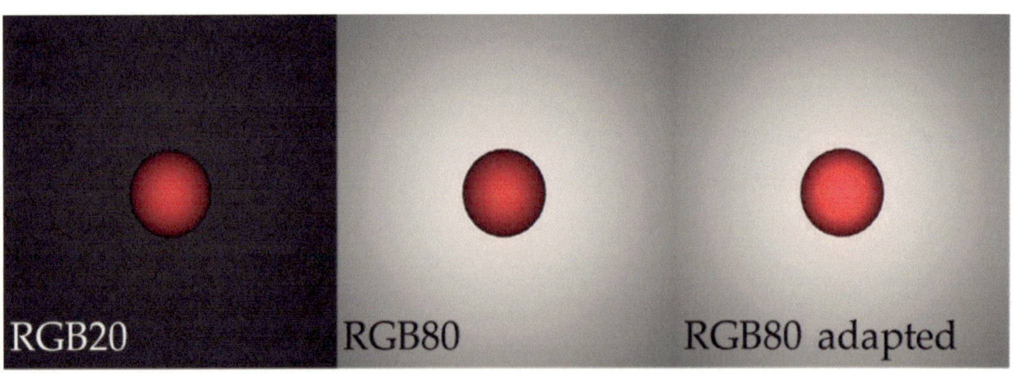

Figure 3. Adaptation workflow, marking 'i' stands for input and marking 'a' for adapted colours.

calculated for each sample of input and adapted RGB values and graphically presented in aforementioned sets. Colour difference ΔE_{00} was calculated between pairs of values, namely between (1) input colour RGBi on RGB20 background and input colour RGBi on RGB80 background and (2) input colour RGBi on RGB20 background and adapted RGBa colour on RGB80 background.

3. Results and discussion

3.1. Colour difference between input and adapted values

Firstly, average colour difference ΔE_{00} between input colour RGBi on RGB20 background and input colour RGBi on RGB80 background (without adaptation) and input colour RGBi on RGB20 background and adapted RGBa colour on RGB80 background was calculated. Results are presented in **Table 2**. It was expected that colour difference would be zero between input colours RGBi on both backgrounds, since input value was actually the same. Despite the fact, there was slight difference between read values for Cycles rendering engine. It can be concluded that in that case, background slightly affects the rendered colour. Average colour difference between input RGBi and adapted RGBa values was greater than zero considering that input value was adapted to different background, thus the colour is slightly changed. Smallest colour difference was obtained for Blender Render, followed by Yafaray. Greatest colour difference was calculated for Cycles.

3.2. Colour difference between input and rendered values

Next, colour difference ΔE_{00} between values that were input into Blender and values that were obtained from rendered images (as lightest colour RGBs and average RGBp colour on spherical object) was calculated for input colours on RGB20 and RGB80 background and adapted colours on RGB80 background. The results are presented in **Table 3**.

It can be noted that colour difference between input and rendered colour on RGB20 and RGB80 remain roughly the same due to the fact that the input colour in the setting was the same between all pairs, which can be deducted from **Table 2**, where colour difference was zero for Blender Render and Yafaray, means background does not affect colour for those two rendering engines.

Rendering engine	**Colour difference ΔE_{00}**	
	20–>80%	**20–>80% CIECAM**
Blender Render (BR)	0	3.28
Cycles (CY)	1.67	6.29
Yafaray (YF)	0	4.42

Table 2. Average colour difference ΔE_{00} between input colour RGBi on RGB20 background and input colour RGBi on RGB80 background (without adaptation) and input colour RGBi on RGB20 background and adapted RGBa colour on RGB80 background.

		Colour difference ΔE_{00}		
		Input RGBi on RGB_{20} background	Input RGBi on RGB80 background	Adapted RGBa on RGB80 background
	Rendering engine	Rendered RGBi on RGB20 background	Rendered RGBi on RGB80 background	Rendered adapted RGBa on RGB80 background
RGBs	Blender Render	3.66	3.66	28.65
	Cycles	10.34	10.85	28.98
	Yafaray	9.11	9.11	34.62
RGBp	Blender Render	0	0	33.11
	Cycles	10.63	10.63	32.83
	Yafaray	9.78	9.87	37.86

Table 3. Average colour difference ΔE_{00} between input and rendered colours for lightest RGBs and average colours RGBp.

Next, a difference between colour difference of lightest RGBs and average RGBp colour on the sphere can be noted. Values vary less than 10% for Cycles and Yafaray, but there is a great difference between lightest and average colour for Blender Render, obviously there is no difference between average RGBp input and rendered colour on both backgrounds. Also, notable difference is present when comparing lightest colour RGBs rendered with Cycles, confirming that Cycles does somehow takes background into account when rendering light colours.

In contrast, colour difference between adapted and rendered adapted colour is high. Colour difference is higher for average colour and lightest colour, which is consistent with non-adapted colours. Values here vary for more than 10%, most for Blender Render, which is quite opposite from non-adapted colours. Presumably, adapted colour is treated differently than non-adapted colour by rendering engines.

3.3. CIELAB evaluation

CIELAB colour values were calculated for all colours and lightness L*, a* and b* co-ordinates of lightest RGBs and average RGBp colours and presented graphically. Following from left to right, input colour RGBi on RGB20 background, input colour RGB on RGB80 background and adapted colour RGBa on RGB80 background are presented in each figure with lightness L* on *y*-axis and sample on *x*-axis.

In **Figures 4** and **5**, a specific grouped pattern can be noted, which is created due to sample selection algorithm, where colours follow in batches from darkest to lightest. Charts for non-adapted colours remain the same but there is increase in lightness of adapted colours, which is a result of adaptation to darker background. This effect can be clearly seen in lower parts of the chart where darker colours resided. In **Figure 5**, samples are set lower on the chart, since lightness L* of average colours is lower, but despite the fact, the effect of adaptation can be seen in darker colours.

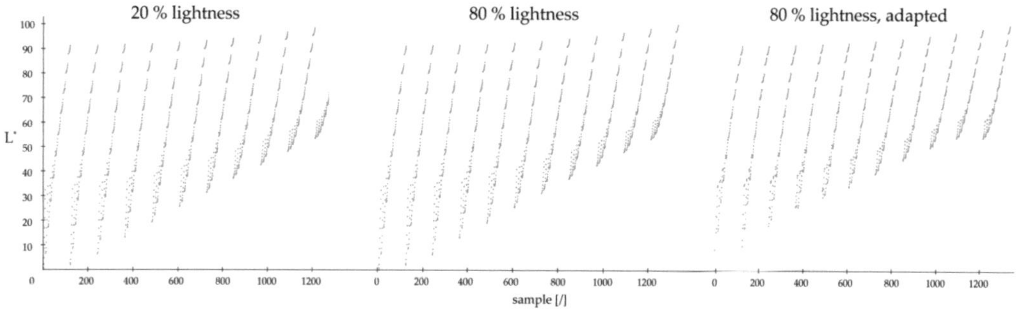

Figure 4. Lightness L* of lightest RGBs colour for each sample for Blender Render.

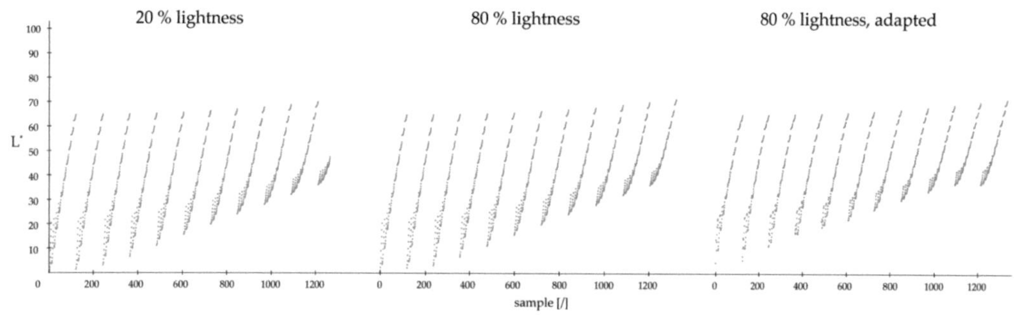

Figure 5. Lightness L* of average RGBp colour for each sample for Blender Render.

In **Figures 6** and **7**, a* and b* co-ordinates for each sample for Blender Render are shown. In **Figure 6**, where a* and b* co-ordinates for lightest RGBs colour are presented, it can be observed that colour space roughly matches sRGB gamut. All renderings took place in sRGB colour space. For adapted colours, there is condensation of samples along lines running from the centre.

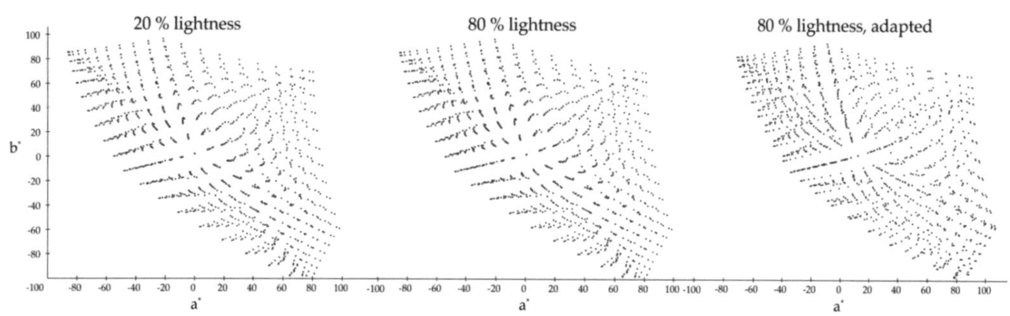

Figure 6. a* and b* co-ordinates of lightest RGBs colour for each sample for Blender Render.

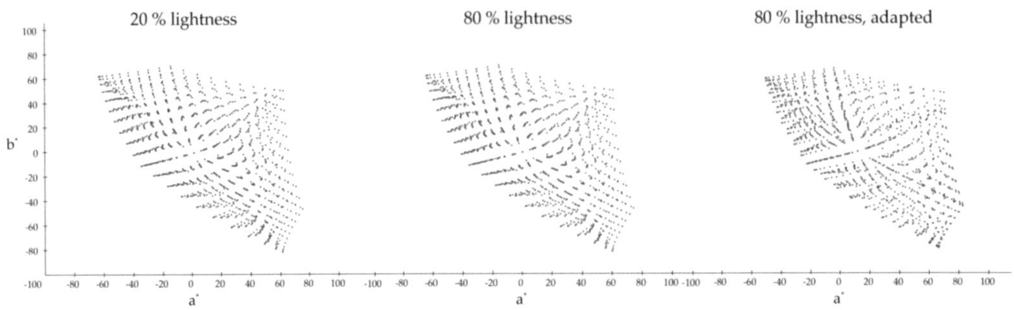

Figure 7. a* and b* co-ordinates of average RGBp colour for each sample for Blender Render.

In **Figure 7**, where a* and b* co-ordinates for average RGBp colour are presented, it can be observed that gamut is smaller than for lightest colours. Again, condensation can be visible for adapted colours.

In **Figure 8**, lightness L* of lightest RGBs colour for each sample rendered with Cycles is shown. In comparison with Blender Render, samples are grouped in parts were lightness is higher, so the arrangement of samples is different. Lightness does not grow constantly as in case of Blender Render. There is a jump when RGB values go over 125. Here, samples are scattered in lighter regions, meanwhile for Blender Render, there is scattering in darker regions. Lightest colours have higher lightness L* in comparison to Blender Render and CIECAM02 makes colours lighter to achieve constant colour appearance.

In **Figure 9**, lightness L* of average RGBp colour for each sample for Cycles is presented. Lightness chart is similar as in case of Blender Render, but the jump in lightness for colour with RGB over 125 is still visible, but not to such extent. The effect of adaptation can still be visible.

Some outstanding phenomena can be observed in **Figure 10**, where a* and b* co-ordinates of lightest RGBs colour for each sample for Cycles are presented. Adapted colours are grouped in a few groups along the lines emerging from the centre. In this case, largest colour difference was obtained in **Table 3**. In **Figure 11**, where a* and b* co-ordinates of average RGBp colour for each sample for Cycles are shown, this anomaly cannot be observed to such extent. Based

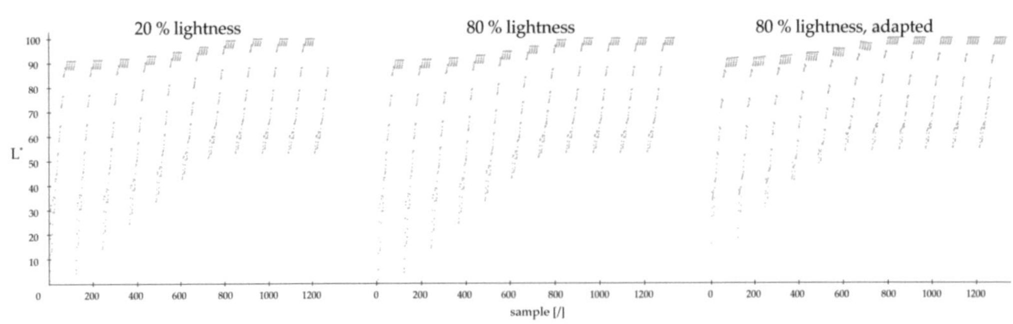

Figure 8. Lightness L* of lightest RGBs colour for each sample for Cycles.

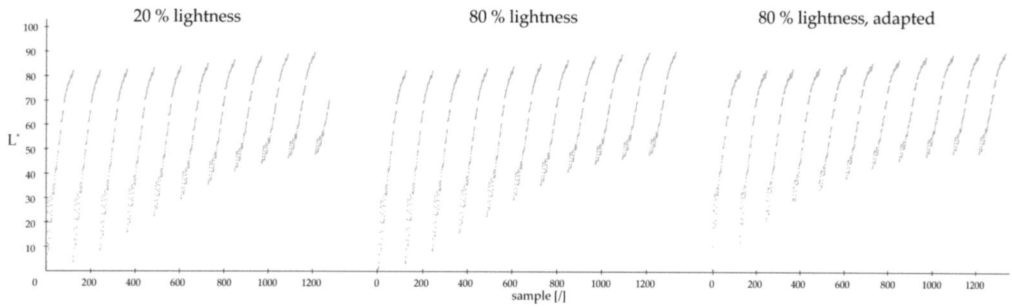

Figure 9. Lightness L* of average RGBp colour for each sample for Cycles.

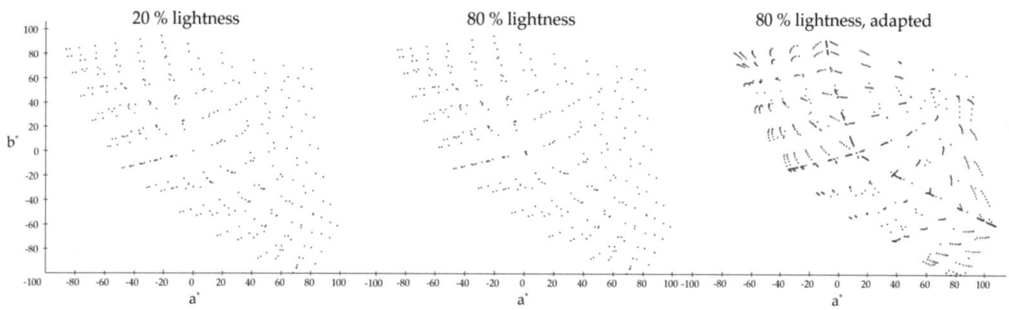

Figure 10. a* and b* co-ordinates of lightest RGBs colour for each sample for Cycles.

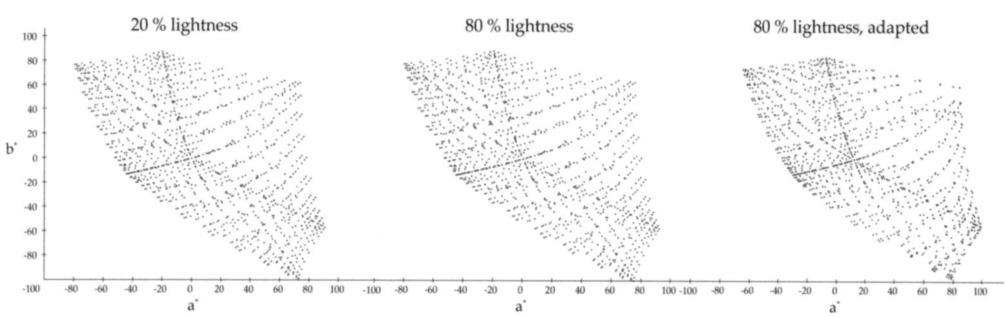

Figure 11. a* and b* co-ordinates of average RGBp colour for each sample for Cycles.

on this observation and colour differences, it can be concluded that lighter colours are treated differently by Cycles than darker colours. Gamut of both charts still resembles that of sRGB colour space.

The results for Yafaray are presented in following figures. In **Figure 12**, lightness L* of lightest RGBs colour for each sample for Yafaray is presented. If compared to Blender Render, there is again more scattering in lighter regions, same as for Cycles. In addition, the jump in lightness for colours with RGB higher than 125 can be visible too. Adaptation effect can also be visible,

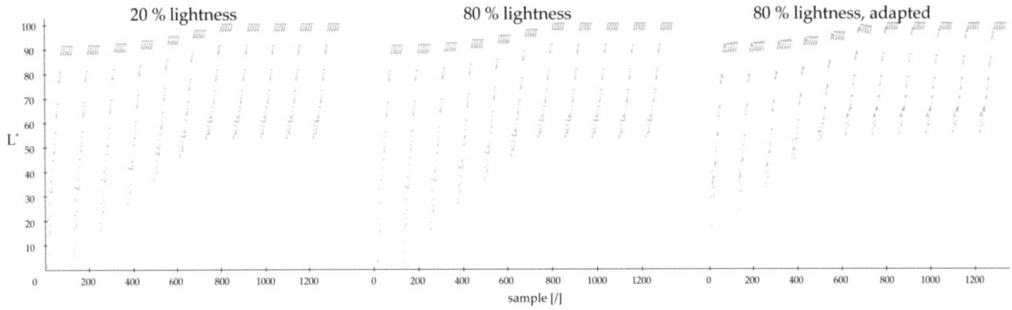

Figure 12. Lightness L* of lightest RGBs colour for each sample for Yafaray.

same as in previous instances. Lightness L* of average RGBp colour obtained for each sample for Yafaray is similar to those of Cycles (**Figure 13**). Again, adaptation affects lightness of colours but not as notable as for lightest colours.

In **Figure 14**, a* and b* co-ordinates of lightest RGBs colour for each sample for Yafaray are presented. Again, gamut matches sRGB colour space. In comparison to Blender Render, samples are condensed into groups for input colours too, meanwhile adapted colours are similar to Cycles, and even though it is not reflected in colour differences. In **Figure 15**, a* and b* co-ordinates of average RGBp colour for each sample for Yafaray are shown. Again, there is difference between input and adapted colours but not as pronounced as in previous case.

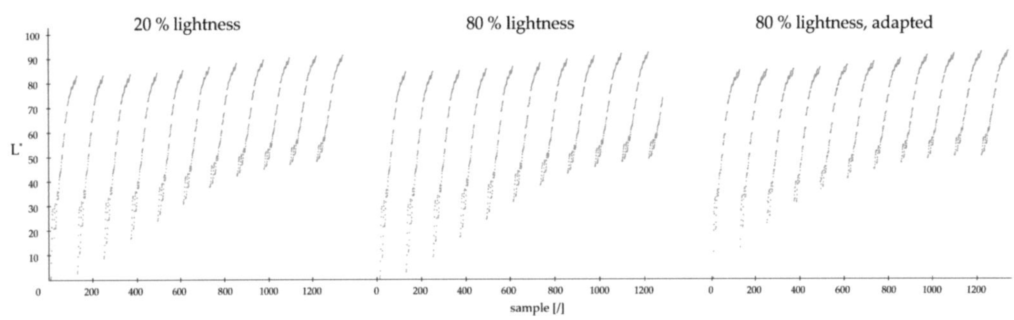

Figure 13. Lightness L* of average RGBp colour for each sample for Yafaray.

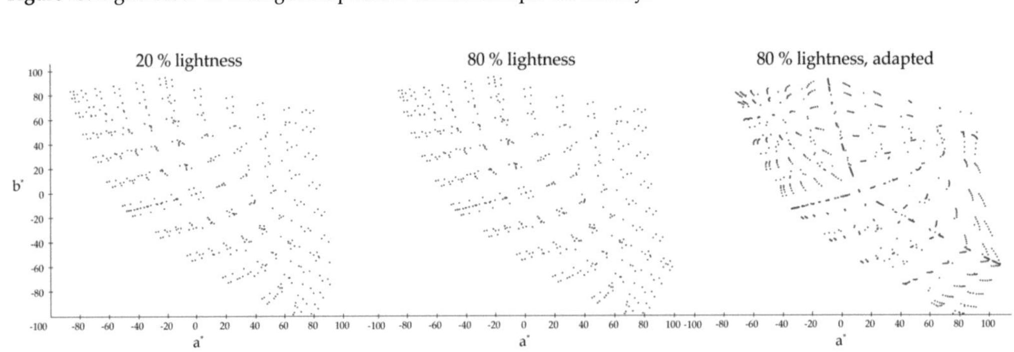

Figure 14. a* and b* co-ordinates of lightest RGBs colour for each sample for Yafaray.

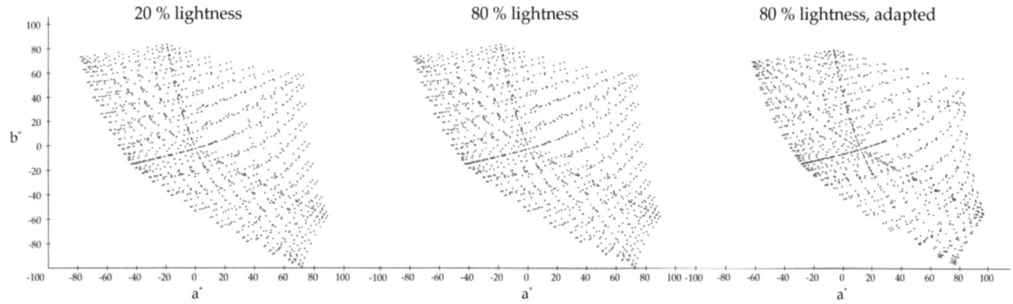

Figure 15. a* and b* co-ordinates of average RGBp colour for each sample for Yafaray.

By comparing CIELAB values, it can be concluded that rendering engines do not treat all colours equally. Even though Cycles and Yafaray do not apply same shading algorithms, yet results are surprisingly similar. It was ascertained that colour differences are largest for Cycles and same fact was confirmed by the analysis of CIELAB values. Moreover, there is a notable influence of the background on rendered colour for Cycles.

3.4. Relationship between L*s and L*p

In **Figures 16–18**, the relationship between lightness of lightest colour L*s in the image (on *x*-axis) and average colour L*p in the image (on *y*-axis) is presented in sets for input colour on RGB20, input colour on RGB80 and adapted colour on RGB80. In **Figure 16**, this relationship is presented for Blender Render. It can be seen that this relationship is quite linear and roughly follows $y = 0.7x$ function. Lightness L*p is lower than L*s, which was expected due to the fact that shading (therefore darkening) is applied on an object. It can be observed that this relationship is uniform for lighter colours; meanwhile grouping can be observed for darker colours. It can also be noted that when adaptation is carried out, colours shift towards lighter colours. This shift is most visible in the range of darker colour with L*s = [0–10]. The same phenomenon was observed previously when analysing CIELAB values.

In **Figure 17**, this relationship is presented for Cycles. It can be observed, that this relationship is not linear, colours are scattered and their position is depending on colour. Again, darker

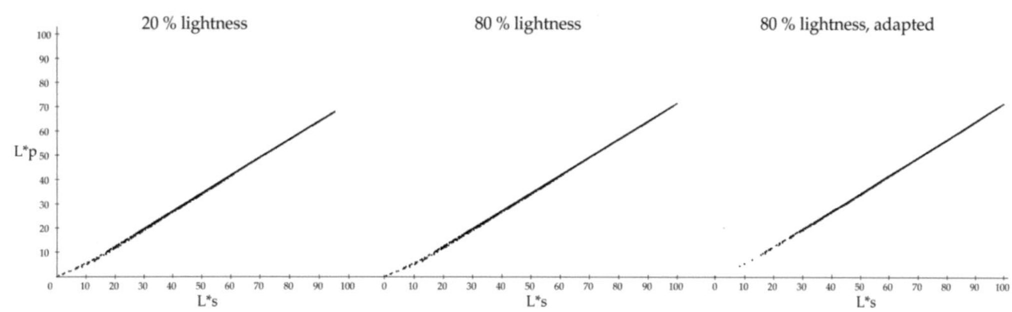

Figure 16. Relationship between lightness of lightest colour L*s in the image and average colour L*p in the image for Blender Render.

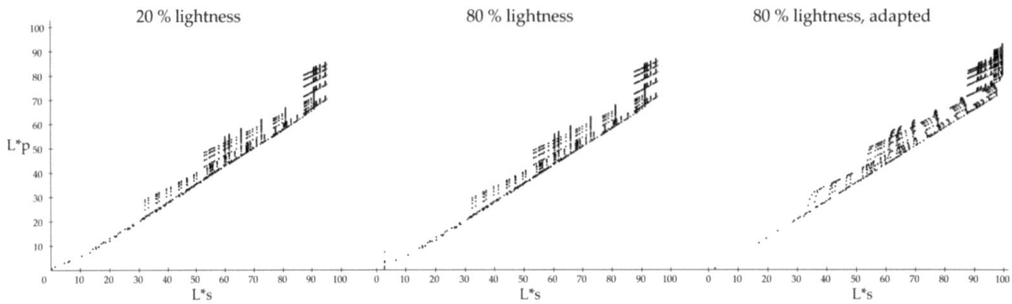

Figure 17. Relationship between lightness of lightest colour L*s in the image and average colour L*p in the image for Cycles.

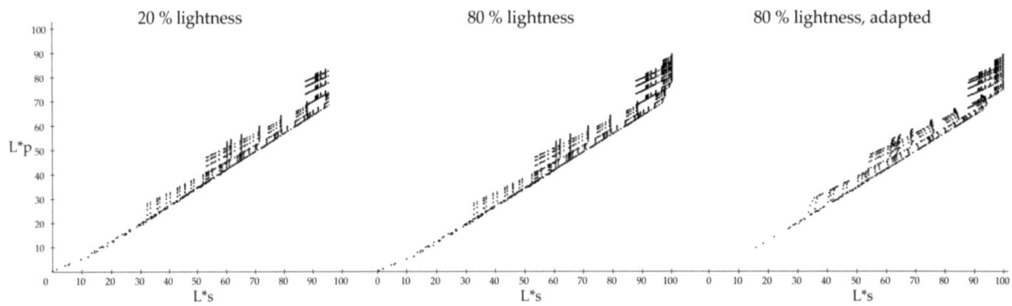

Figure 18. Relationship between lightness of lightest colour L*s in the image and average colour L*p in the image for Yafaray.

colours are grouped, meanwhile lighter colours scatter in groups depending on lightness and is most notable in range L*s = [90–100]. Interestingly, despite contiguous growing of scattering, there is quite uniform range of L*s = [80–90]. For adapted colours, a colour shift is again visible, but in this case it is dependent on lightness. The distance of the shift depends on lightness, this is visible in range of L*s = [30–40]. In this range, lighter colours are shifted more than darker, which is contrary to previous conclusions.

In **Figure 18**, this relationship is presented for Yafaray and it can be observed that results are similar to those for Cycles and are in accordance with CIELAB values analysis. Only difference is visible for lightest colours, they seem to be less scattered as for Cycles. Again, adapted colours shift towards lighter colours with some non-linear shifts, similar to Cycles.

After analysing the relationship between lightness of lightest colour L*s in the image and average colour L*p in the image for all rendering engines, it can be concluded that Blender Render shades colours linearly, meanwhile the shading is more complex in case of Cycles and Yafaray and that it depends on individual colours or colour groups. For those two rendering engines, it was noted that the colours separate into groups. Shading of darker colours inclines towards linear, meanwhile shading pattern of lighter colours cannot be easily defined. A notable difference was perceived between input colours on lighter and darker background. Relationship was the same in case of Blender Render, meaning that it does not consider background. In contrast, the relationship changed for Cycles and Yafaray, meaning that those two rendering engines do consider background and/or surroundings when rendering image. This phenomenon was not observed for Yafaray when analysing CIELAB values.

3.5. Relationship between C*s and C*p

In **Figures 19–21**, the relationship between chroma of lightest colour C*s in the image (on *x*-axis) and average colour C*p in the image (on *y*-axis) is presented in sets for input colour on RGB20, input colour on RGB80 and adapted colour on RGB80. In **Figure 19**, this relationship is presented for Blender Render and it can be observed that similarly to previous section is quite linear with some deviation in regions with lower chroma. Chart is even more uniform in terms of chroma after adaptation.

In **Figure 20**, chroma relationship is presented for Cycles and it can be observed that the relationship is still quite linear for input colours but more spread meaning that Cycles does not treat colours based on chroma. After adaptation, chroma of darker colours decreases and chroma of lighter colours increases, again depending on original colour.

In **Figure 21**, this relationship is presented for Yafaray and again similarities with Cycles can be observed. Likewise Cycles, relationship remains linear for input colours but colours are spread along *y*-axis. In contrast with Cycles, region with lower chroma C*s < 10 is also covered and after adaptation, chroma in darker regions increases.

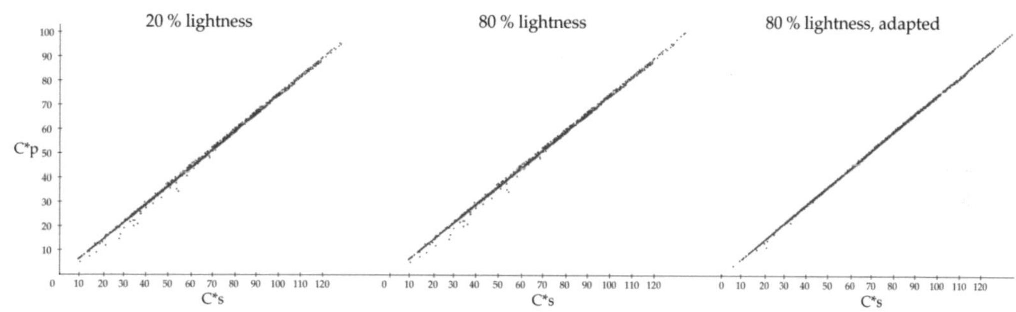

Figure 19. Relationship between chroma of lightest colour C*s and the image and average colour C*p in the image for Blender Render.

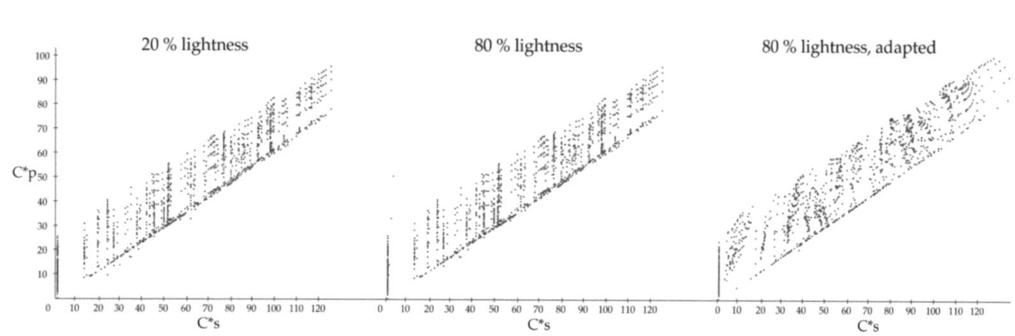

Figure 20. Relationship between chroma of lightest colour C*s and the image and average colour C*p in the image for Cycles.

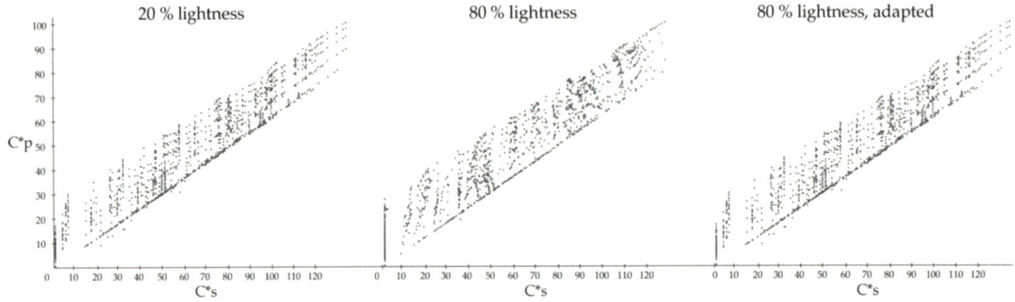

Figure 21. Relationship between chroma of lightest colour C*s and the image and average colour C*p in the image for Yafaray.

Again, Blender Render shades colour uniformly based on chrome unlike Cycles and Yafaray where shading is complex and depending on each colours. In comparison with lightness relationship, colours were not divided in groups but spread more equally. Similarly, difference noted between input colours on lighter and darker background was again visible for Cycles and Yafaray, but not as much as lightness. It can be concluded that chroma affects shading too. Chroma of adapted colours is shifted but not in same directions as lightness and not in same way for all rendering engines.

3.6. Relationship between Rs and L*p, Gs and L*p and Bs and L*p

Finally, relationship between each RGB component of lightest colour (Rs, Gs and Bs on *x*-axis) and lightness of average colour L*p (on *y*-axis) was graphically presented. *z*-axis was introduced to avoid overlapping. Charts are presented in sets for input colour on RGB20, input colour on RGB80 and adapted colour on RGB80.

In **Figure 22**, this relationship is presented for Blender Render. It can be observed that charts are the same for input colour on RGB20 and RGB80 background. The effect of adaptation is visible in terms of lightness and RGB values and that there are some anomalies in darker regions of R and B component which was observed in preliminary research. It can also be observed that CIECAM02 effects lightest colour only minimally.

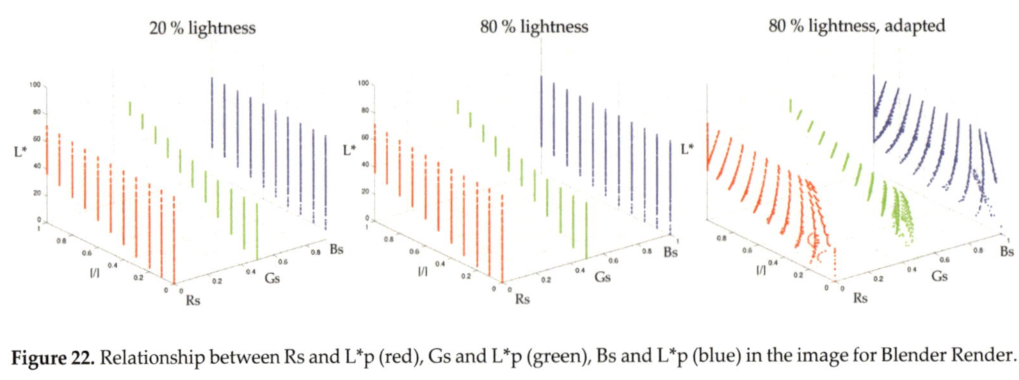

Figure 22. Relationship between Rs and L*p (red), Gs and L*p (green), Bs and L*p (blue) in the image for Blender Render.

http://dx.doi.org/10.5772/67737

In **Figure 23**, this relationship is presented for Cycles and compared to Blender Render, colours are differently grouped and cover wider range of lightness. There is a visible difference for input colour on RGB20 and RGB80 background, same as previous analysis. Again, there is notable difference between input and adapted colours and there are larger changes for darker colours when adapted.

In **Figure 24**, this relationship is presented for Yafaray and results are again similar to those for Cycles, the difference for input colour on RGB20 and RGB80 background is only minimal. Effects of adaptation are again similar to those for Cycles.

From the results, it could be concluded that Blender Render shades colours linearly, meanwhile shading for Cycles and Yafaray is more complex. Both rendering engines consider when rendering colour.

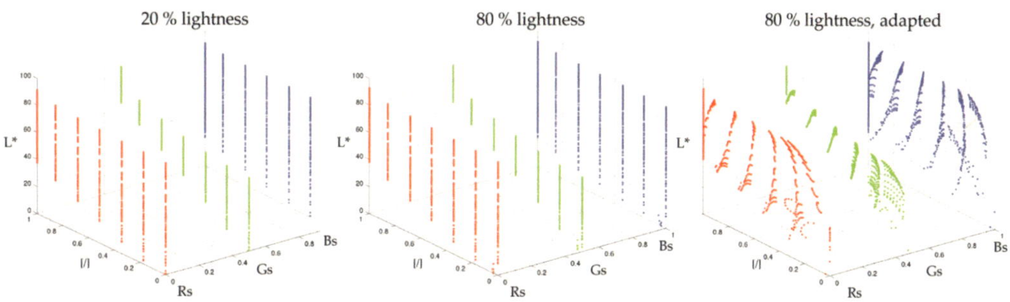

Figure 23. Relationship between Rs and L*p (red), Gs and L*p (green) and Bs and L*p (blue) in the image for Cycles.

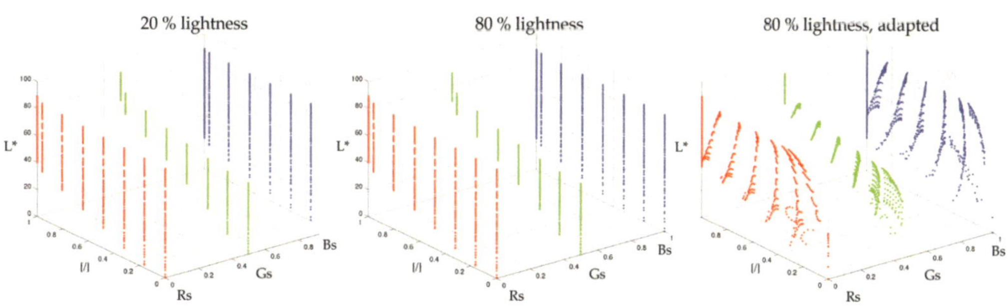

Figure 24. Relationship between Rs and L*p (red), Gs and L*p (green) and Bs and L*p (blue) in the image for Yafaray.

4. Conclusion

The process of producing 2D image from 3D mathematically described that space is very complex, since it depends on many factors that cannot be completely influenced by user.

One of these factors is certainly rendering of colour, and not only in the field of 3D technologies but also in the field of other computer graphics. Despite the progress and the availability of information and knowledge in this field, there is still no clear answer about colour perception, since this phenomenon is, besides physical factors also dependent on some other factors. With the emergence of new complex algorithms for rendering and visualization, the problem of colour reproduction has increased and, despite the established methods there are still no universal solutions to ensure constant colour appearance. Although the colour appearance models, more specifically CIECAM02, have been in use for many years, it has yet not been analysed and explored to ensure constant colour appearance in the field of computer graphics. Demonstration of successful implementation of the model CIECAM02 was possible only empirically, so it was necessary to determine how algorithms interpret colour during simulation and reproduction and also how rendering engines interpret colour on a 2D rendered image after setting the 3D scene.

For that purpose, in our research, we have studied rendering of colours with three rendering engines (Blender Render, Cycles and Yafaray) of an open source software Blender based on changes in the lightness of the object background from 20 to 80%. In one of the cases, colour of the object was adapted to lighter background using the colour appearance model CIECAM02.

With the analysis of colour differences, lightness and chroma between colours rendered using different rendering engines, we found out that rendering engines differently interpret colour, although RGB values of colours and scene parameters were the same. Differences were particularly evident when rendering engine Cycles was used. Results showed that Blender Render treats colour more linearly than other two more advanced rendering engines, Cycles and Yafaray, at least in case of lightness and chroma. In the case of Cycles and Yafaray, colours and change of their properties are considered non-linear, while shading varies depending on the colour and its properties. In addition, we found out that especially Cycles, due to the using of indirect lighting in the colour renderings, also takes into account the object background, since results were different when the background was changed without any adjustments to the colour.

Implementation of the CIECAM02 model in the colour rendering workflow of used rendering engines was successful, since its use in all three cases resulted generally in a better visual match (smaller colour differences) between pairs of stimuli at a controlled change in defined parameters. We have also found out that the quality and quantity of maintaining colour appearance depends on the principle of rendering engines operation and on lightness and chroma of a rendered colour.

The possibilities for further research to in-depth understanding of rendering engines and shading's influence on colour are possible in terms of integration of larger number of objects and backgrounds colours, and also the inclusion of visual assessment with a larger number of observers.

Author details

Nika Bratuž, Helena Gabrijelčič Tomc* and Dejana Javoršek

*Address all correspondence to: helena.gabrijelcic@ntf.uni-lj.si

Department of Textiles, Graphic Arts and Design, Faculty of Natural Sciences and Engineering, Chair of Information and Graphic Arts Technology, University of Ljubljana, Ljubljana, Slovenia

References

[1] McCluney R. Introduction to Radiometry and Photometry. 2nd ed. Norwood: Artech House Publisher; 2014. 240 p.

[2] Nicodemus FE. Directional reflectance and emissivity of an opaque surface. Applied Optics. 1965;**4**(7):757–776. DOI: 10.1364/AO.4.000767

[3] Bartell FO, Dereniak EL, Wolfe WL. The theory and measurement of bidirectional reflectance distribution function (BRDF) and bidirectional transmittance distribution function (BTDF). In: Proceedings of SPIE, Radiation Scattering in Optical Systems, Hunt GH, editor. Huntsville; 1980. pp. 154–160. DOI: 10.1117/12.959611

[4] Donner C, Lawrence J, Ramamoorthi R, Hachisuka T, Jensen HW, Nayar S. An empirical BSSRDF model. ACM Transactions on Graphics (TOG)—Proceedings of ACM SIGGRAPH 2009. 2009;**28**(3):1–10. DOI: 10.1145/1531326.1531336

[5] Nayar M, Oren SK. Generalization of Lambert's reflectance model. Petrovich L, Tanaka K, editors. In SIGGRAPH 94 21st International ACM Conference on Computer Graphics and Interactive Techniques; July 24–29 1994; Orlando, Florida, USA. New York, NY, USA: ACM; 1994. pp. 239–246. DOI: 10.1145/192161.192213

[6] Torrance KE, Sparrow EM. Theory for off-specular reflection from roughened surfaces. Journal of the Optical Society of America. 1967;**57**(9):1105–1114. DOI: 10.1364/JOSA.57.001105

[7] Blinn JF. Models of light reflection for computer synthesized pictures. In: SIGGRAPH '77 Proceedings of the 4th annual conference on Computer graphics and interactive techniques; July 20–22 1977; San Jose, California, USA. New York, NY, USA: ACM; 1977. pp. 192–198. DOI: 10.1145/965141.563893

[8] Ashikhmin M, Shirley P. An anisotropic Phong BRDF model. Journal of Graphics Tools. 2000;**5**(2):25–32. DOI: 10.1080/10867651.2000.10487522

[9] Phong BT. Illumination for computer generated pictures. Communications of the ACM. 1975;**18**(6):311–317. DOI: 10.1145/360825.360839

[10] Pharr M, Humphreys G. Physically based rendering: from theory to implementation. 2nd ed. Burlington: Morgan Kaufman; 2010. 1200 p.

[11] Kajiya J. The Rendering Equation. Wolfe R, editor. In: Seminal Graphics: Pioneering Efforts That Shaped The Field; New York, NY, USA: ACM; 1998.

[12] Jansen HW. A Practical Guide to Global Illumination using Photon Maps. Pueyo X, Schröder P, editors. In: Proceedings of the Eurographics Workshop on Rendering Techniques 96; June 7–19 1996; Porto, Portugal: Springer; pp. 21–30.

[13] Wald I, Kollig T, Benthin C, Keller A, Slusallek P, Debevec P, Gibson S, editors. Interactive global illumination using fast ray tracing. EGRW '02 Proceedings of the 13th Eurographics workshop on Rendering; June 26–28 2002; Pisa: Italy; pp. 15–24.

[14] Kurt M, Edwards D. A survey of BRDF models for computer graphics. ACM SIGGRAPH Computer Graphics—Building Bridges—Science, the Arts & Technology. 2009;**43**(2). DOI: 10.1145/1629216.1629222

[15] Kouhzadi A, Rasti A, Rasti D, Why NK. Unbiased Monte Carlo Rendering – A Comparison Study. International Journal of Scientific Knowledge. 2013;**2**(3):1–10.

[16] Lafortune, EP, Willems YD. Bi-directional Path Tracing. Santo HP, editor. In: Third International Conference on Computational Graphics and Visualization Techniques; December 5–10 1993; Alvor, Algarve, Portugal. Lisbon, Portugal: Association for Computing Machinery, Portuguese ACM Chapter; 1993. pp. 145–153.

[17] Veach E, Guibas LJ. Metropolis light transport. Owen SG, Whitted T, Mones-Hattal B, editors. In Proceedings of the 24th annual conference on Computer graphics and interactive technique; August 3–8 1997; Los Angeles, CA, USA. New York, NY, USA: ACM Press/Addison-Wesley Publishing Co.; 1997. pp. 65–76.

[18] Vidmar Ž, Gabrijelčič Tomc H, Hladnik A. Performance Assessment of Three Rendering Engines in 3D Computer Graphics Software. Acta Graphica. 2014;**25**(3–4):101–114.

[19] Ferwerda JA. Three varieties of realism in Computer graphic. Rogowitz BE, Pappas TN, editors. In: Proc. SPIE 5007, Human Vision and Electronic Imaging VIII, 290; August 20 2003; Santa Clara, CA, USA: SPIE; 2003. DOI: 10.1117/12.473899

[20] McNamara, A. Visual perception in realistic image synthesis. Computer Graphics forum. 2001;**20**(4):211–224. DOI: 10.1111/1467-8659.00550

[21] CIE technical report: Colorimetry. 3st ed. Vienna, Austria: Commission Internationale de l'Eclairage; 2004. 72 p.

[22] Fairman HS, Brill MH. Hemmendinger H. How the CIE 1931 color-matching functions were derived from Wright-Guild data. Color Research and Application. 1997;**22**(1):11–23. DOI: 10.1002/(SICI)1520-6378(199702)22:1<11::AID-COL4>3.0.CO;2–7

[23] Hurlbert A. Colour vision: putting in context. Current Biology. 1996;**6**(11):1381–1384. DOI: 10.1016/S0960-9822(96)00736-1

[24] Winawer J, Witthoft N, Frank MC, Wu L, Wade AR, Boroditsky L. Russian blues reveal effects of language on color discrimination. Proceeding of National Academy of Science of United States of America. 2007;**104**(19):7780–7785. DOI: 10.1073/pnas.0701644104

[25] Hunt RWG. The reproduction of colour. 6th ed. Chichester: John Wiley and sons; 2004. 702 p.

[26] Trstenjak A. Psihologija barv. Ljubljana: Inštitut Antona Trstenjaka za psihologijo, logoterapijo in antropohigieno; 1996. 494 p.

[27] Javoršek A. Preizkus modela barvnega zaznavanja CIECAM97s v standarnih pogojih [thesis]. Ljubljana: University of Ljubljana; 2004. 38 p.

[28] Süsstrunk S E. and Finlayson G D. Evaluating chromatic adaptation transform performance. In: Thirteenth Color Imaging Conference Color Science and Engineering Systems,

Technologies, and Applications; November 7–10 2005; Scottsdale, Arizona, USA. Society for Imaging Science and Technology; 2005. pp. 75–78.

[29] Xiao K, Wuerger S, Fu C, Karatzas D. Unique hue data for colour appearance models. Part II. Color research and application. 2013;**38**(1):22–29. DOI: 10.1002/col.20725

[30] Fairchild M. Color Appearance Models. 3th ed. Chichester: John Wiley and sons; 2013. 385 p.

[31] Bratuž N, Javoršek A, Javoršek, D. Barvne pretvorbe v CIECAM02 in CIELAB. Colour Transforms in CIECAM02 and CIELAB. Tekstilec. 2013;**56**(3):222–229.

[32] Luo MR, Hunt RWG. The structure of the CIE 1997 colour appearance model (CIECAM97s). Color research and application, 1998;**23**(3):138–144. DOI: 10.1002/(SICI)1520-6378(199806)23:3<138::AID-COL5>3.0.CO;2-R

[33] Fairchild M. Status of CIE color appearance models. Chung R, Rodrigues A, editors. In: Proceedings. SPIE 4421, 9th Congress of the International Colour Association, 550; April 2 2001; Rochester, NY, USA: SPIE; 2002. DOI: 10.1117/12.464726

[34] Li C, Luo MR, Hunt RWG, Moroney N, Fairchild MD, Newman T. The performance of CIECAM02. Chung R, Rodrigues A, editors. In: 10th Color Imaging Conference: Color Science and Engineering Systems, Technologies, and Applications; 2002; Scottsdale, AZ, USA: The International Society for Optics and photonics; 2002.

[35] Brill MH, Mahy M. Visualization of mathematical inconsistencies in CIECAM02. Color research and application, 2012;**38**(3):188–195. DOI: 10.1002/col.20744

[36] Specification ICC.1:2010: Image technology colour management – architecture, profile format, and data structure. Reston, VA, USA: International Color Consortium, 2010. 113 p.

[37] Tastl I, Bhachech M, Moroney N, Holm J. ICC Color Management and CIECAM02 [Internet]. 2005 [Updated: 2005]. Available from: http://www.hpl.hp.com/news/2005/oct-dec/CIC05_CIECAMICC_final.pdf [Accessed: 12. 9, 2016]

[38] Melgosa M, Trémeau A, Cui G. Chapter 3: Colour Difference Evaluation. In: editor, Advanced Color Image Processing and Analysis. New York: Springer Science+Business Media; 2013. pp. 59–78.

[39] Windows Color System [Internet]. 2014 [Updated: 2014]. Available from: https://msdn.microsoft.com/en-us/library/dd372446(v=vs.85).aspx [Accessed: 13. 9. 2016]

[40] Guay R, Shaw MQ. Dealing with Imaginary Color Encodings in CIECAM02 in an ICC Workflow. Chung R, Rodrigues A, editors. In: 13th Color Imaging Conference: Color Science and Engineering Systems, Technologies, and Applications; 2005; Scottsdale, AZ, USA: The international society for optics and photonics; 2005.

[41] Xiao B, Brainard DH. Surface gloss and color perception of 3D objects. Visual Neuroscience, 2008;**25**(3):371–385. DOI: 10.1017/S0952523808080267

[42] Xiao B, Hurst B, MacIntyre L, Brainard DH. The color constancy of three-dimensional objects. Journal of Vision, 2012;**12**(4):1–15. DOI: 10.1167/12.4.6

[43] Fleming RW, Dror RO, Adelson EH. Real-world illumination and the perception of surface reflectance properties. Journal of Vision, 2003;**3**(5):347–368. DOI: 10.1167/3.5.3

[44] Yang JN, Maloney LT. Illuminant cues in surface color perception: Tests of three candidate cues. Vision Research, 2001;**41**(20):2581–2600. DOI: 10.1016/S0042-6989(01)00143-2

[45] Yang JN, Shevell SK. Surface color perception under two illuminants: The second illuminant reduces color constancy. Journal of Vision, 2003;**3**(5):369–379. DOI: 10.1167/3.5.4

[46] Ruppertsberg AI, Bloj M. Reflecting on a room of one reflectance. Journal of Vision, 2007;**7**(13):1–13. DOI: 10.1167/7.13.12

[47] Ruppertsberg AI, Bloj M, Hurlbert A. Sensitivity to luminance and chromaticity gradients in a complex scene. Journal of Vision, 2008;**8**(9):1–16. DOI: 10.1167/8.9.3

[48] Guzelj A, Hladnik A, Bračko S. Examination of colour emotions on a sample of slovenian female population. Tekstilec, 2016;**59**(4):311–320. DOI: 10.14502/Tekstilec2016.59.311-320

[49] Hedrich M, Bloj M, Ruppertsberg AI. Color constancy improves for real 3D objects. Journal of Vision, 2009;**9**(4):1–16. DOI: 10.1167/9.4.16

[50] Bratuž N, Gabrijelčič Tomc H, Javoršek D. Application of CIECAM02 to 3D scene in Blender. Urbas R, editor. In: 7th Symposium of Information and Graphic Arts Technology; June 5–6 2014; Ljubljana, Slovenia. Ljubljana: University of Ljubljana, Faculty of Natural Sciences and Engineering, Department of Textiles; 2014.

[51] Bratuž N, Jerman T, Javoršek D. Influence of rendering engines on colour reproduction. Novaković D, editor. In: 7th International Symposium on Graphic Engineering and Design; November 13–14; Novi Sad, Serbia. Ljubljana: University of Novi Sad, Faculty of Technical Sciences, Department of Graphic Engineering and Design; 2014.

Chapter 3

Modelling and Visualisation of the Optical Properties of Cloth

Tanja Nuša Kočevar and Helena Gabrijelčič Tomc

Additional information is available at the end of the chapter

http://dx.doi.org/10.5772/67736

Abstract

Cloth and garment visualisations are widely used in fashion and interior design, entertaining, automotive and nautical industry and are indispensable elements of visual communication. Modern appearance models attempt to offer a complete solution for the visualisation of complex cloth properties. In the review part of the chapter, advanced methods that enable visualisation at micron resolution, methods used in three-dimensional (3D) visualisation workflow and methods used for research purposes are presented. Within the review, those methods offering a comprehensive approach and experiments on explicit clothes attributes that present specific optical phenomenon are analysed. The review of appearance models includes surface and image-based models, volumetric and explicit models. Each group is presented with the representative authors' research group and the application and limitations of the methods. In the final part of the chapter, the visualisation of cloth specularity and porosity with an uneven surface is studied. The study and visualisation was performed using image data obtained with photography. The acquisition of structure information on a large scale namely enables the recording of structure irregularities that are very common on historical textiles, laces and also on artistic and experimental pieces of cloth. The contribution ends with the presentation of cloth visualised with the use of specular and alpha maps, which is the result of the image processing workflow.

Keywords: 3D visualisation, cloth appearance model, porosity, specularity, image processing

1. Introduction

The development of three-dimensional (3D) modelling of cloth appearance is of great interest for various areas activity that requires precise and realistic visualisation of cloth surface, especially its optical characteristics. For some purposes—in fashion, in the automotive and film industries, in architecture, for the preservation and visualisation of cultural heritage and so on—detailed visualisations of fabrics are needed. There are certain characteristics of textile texture that are particularly challenging to visualise, such as the porosity of the structure, which can be very complex, for example, in the case of a lace structure, the translucency of fibres and the unevenness of cloth surface (e.g. in the case of worn materials). When visualising a textile material, both the purpose of the visualisation and the viewing distance have to be considered.

In the review part of the chapter, we present an overview of the methods used for cloth appearance, whereas in the final part of the manuscript, we put substantial focus on the visualisation of cloths with uneven surfaces, which is often the case in the visualisation of cultural heritage. We also present the results of our research, which includes a method of image processing to generate a specular and alpha map for the visualisation of cloth surface. A cloth surface with considerably uneven texture cannot be visualised with methods that generate even or patterned relief, while unevenness can be the result of fabric damage or use. Therefore, data should be obtained using a 3D scanning method or with photo documentation. For this purpose, it is extremely important to record information on a very large sample surface to obtain a distribution of structure irregularities. On the other hand, taking into account the wide range of possible applications, the model should not have excessively detailed topology.

2. Visualisation of the optical and constructional parameters of cloth

In computer graphics, the cloth modelling includes cloth geometry, cloth deformation and simulation and cloth appearance models. The basic idea of the last is the calculation of data to give a realistic appearance of the virtual representation from real-world data at the fibre, yarn and fabric levels [1, 2]. In real-world environments, the appearance of cloth depends on three main conditions: light source, the optical-reflective properties of the material and surface and the observer's visual perception [3]. These three conditions are also considered in mathematical computations for the graphic visualisation of cloth. The optical properties of cloth objects (at the level of the final cloth and at the micro level, i.e. yarns and fibres) are defined by their chemical and physical properties and yarn/fabric structures. In the virtual world, the optical properties of the objects are represented as mathematical abstractions, with a set of three types of data being the most important: geometrical data (object topology), image data (texture and maps) and data on electromagnetic wave and light phenomena (reflectance models and rendering algorithms).

Due to the multi-layered structure of textiles, the final calculation of optical phenomena on their surface is very complex, i.e. at all three levels (fibre, yarn and fabric), the actions of electromagnetic wave and light phenomena can be described with the equation: *incident light = portion of reflected light + portion of absorbed light + portion of scattered light + portion of transmitted light.*

http://dx.doi.org/10.5772/67736

For the final appearance, a particular optical phenomenon of the entire structural hierarchy at a constructional and compositional level should be taken into consideration to enable an accurate generation and evaluation of surface effects [4].

Cloth properties that contribute to visual appearance and are included in appearance-modelling are as follows:

1. optical properties (reflection, scattering, transmission and absorption)
2. porosity
3. colour (optical properties of fibres and yarns and constructional parameters)
4. texture and relief (type of weave, fibre and yarn construction parameters and finishing)
5. specific properties (anisotropy, yarns and fibres with special effects and higher translucency).

3. Advanced appearance models

Recently, Schröder et al. [5] and Khungurun et al. [6] have reviewed appearance models and categorised them into three main types of approaches: *surface and image-based, volumetric and fibre-based models* and the *explicit approaches of modelling*. It should not be overlooked that some methods implement the combination of fundamentals of different type of appearance models. The cues that Schröder et al. [5] systematically defined and analysed in the study were translucency, silhouette, light diffusion, the possibility of real-time rendering, scalability, integration scale and viewing distance.

3.1. Surface-based and image-based models

In surface-based models, different reflectance and texture functions *bidirectional reflectance distribution functions* (*BRDF*), *bidirectional scattering distribution functions* (*BSDF*), *bidirectional texture functions* (*BTF*), *bidirectional curve scattering distribution function* (*BCSDF*) and *bidirectional fibre scattering distribution function* (*BFSDF*) are implemented. Here, the fabric is represented as a two-dimensional surface (mesh, curve), what has as a consequence the limitations as incorrectness of presenting the 3D silhouette on micro- and macro-level and fabric edges. Moreover, when the simple shape-based approaches that include texture images and relief maps are implemented, there is an insufficient correctness of visualisation of optical phenomena on fibres level and missing accuracy of anisotropic shading [5, 6]. In general, surface-based models are scalable and used for far and medium viewing distance. They can reproduce translucency and can be implemented in real-time solutions; moreover, their integration scale is on the level of the composition [5].

The principle of *BRDF* and in general terms *BSDF* models [7, 8] is the simplification of reflectance and scattering presented as a function of four real variables that define how light is reflected (scattered) at a surface in dependence of optical properties of materials. The function, with the schematic presentation in **Figure 1**, presents the flow of *radiance* that is emitting from the 3D object in the direction of the observer, depending on the direction, angle of incident radiance and position. In the function $BRDF_\lambda$ $(\theta_i, \theta_r, \varphi_i, \varphi_r, u, v)$ and **Figure 1**, L_r is radiance, i.e. reflected radiance form material on space angle and projected surface, E_i is irradiance, i.e. intensity of incident light on surface of material, angles θ_i and θ_r are zenith angle between irradiance and radiance and normal vector on the surface (z); angles φ_i and φ_r are azimuth angles between orthogonal axis of irradiance and radiance; and u and v are position parameters.

In the researches, Ashikmin [10], Irawan and Marschner [11] and Sadeghi [12, 13] used surface representation of fabric geometry that included functions such as *BRDF*, *BSDF* and the collection of various texture data.

Ashikmin [10] presented a *microfacet BRDF* model that solves the modelling of shape of highlights and enables maintaining of reciprocity and energy conservation. The function was tested on various materials, including satin and velvet fabric.

Adabala et al. [14] used *weave information file* (*WIF*) to obtain weave pattern. This format involves threading information, the definition of threading of the warp threads and a lift plan (the weft pattern). The colour scheme for weave pattern is defined with pattern mix and the colour combination and colour information of warp and weft threads. In their research, three weave patterns (one grey scale map and two colour maps) were used. The focus was on both, cloth modelling for the distant and close-up viewing of the material and the development of reflectance models that covered the both viewing conditions. The *Cook-Torrance microfacet BRDF* model was employed. Transmission, transmission of light through gaps and colour bleeding through fibres were also considered and calculated.

Irawan [15] presented the goniometric measuring method of the *anisotropic BRDF* for four textile fibres and three weave patterns. Besides, he proposed a reflectance model defined on the basis of specular scattering from fibres composing yarns (consequently weave pattern). For the representation of the geometry, physical-based models and data-driven models BTF are

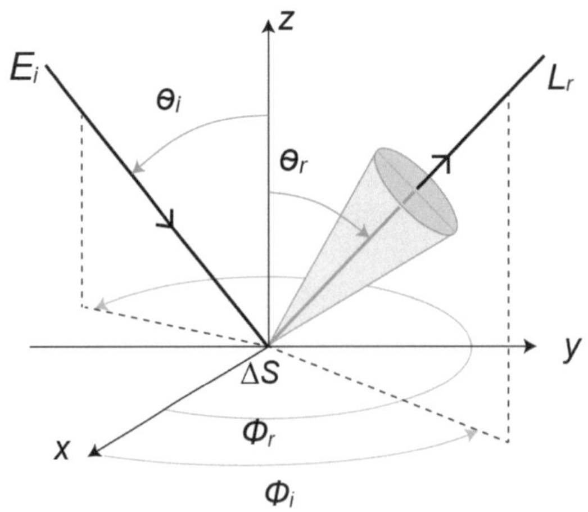

Figure 1. Schematic presentation of BRDF [9].

analysed and compared in his doctoral research. Here, the model for calculation of specular highlights in the texture and the BRDF of polyester lining cloth are presented. The results of the thesis presented the collection of fabric visualisations, in which photorealism, perhaps also due to some theoretical assumptions, can be discussed in comparison of the results of modern approaches.

The above-mentioned research continued with the publication of Irawan and Marschner [11] that presented the analysis of the specular and diffuse reflection from woven cloth mainly influencing the optical properties of the fabric. In their research, the procedural scattering model for diffuse light reflection, which calculates the reflection in dependence of texture, is proposed. The research was performed for the variety of fabric samples, including natural and synthetic fibres and staple and filament yarns. Different weave patterns were also included in the analysis (plain, satin and twill). The model is based on the analysis of specular reflectance of light from fibres and simulates the finest fabric surfaces. The model is not data-driven and includes physical parameters as geometry of the fibres and yarns and the weave pattern. The results in the experimental part are evaluated in comparison with high-resolution video of the real fabric and the *BTF* calculations of analysed fabrics were performed.

The *bidirectional texture function* (*BTF*) is an image-based representation of appearance as a function of viewing and illumination direction [16]. A BTF is a function of six variables and six-dimensional »*reflectance field* $L = L(x, y, \theta_i, \varphi_i, \theta_o, \varphi_o)$*, which connects for each surface point* (x, y) *of a flat sample and the outgoing to the incoming radiance in the direction* (θ_o, φ_o), (θ_i, φ_i), *respectively*« [17]. Dana et al. firstly introduced this function in 1999, when the new BTF-based workflow for CG representation of over than 60 different samples was defined. In their report, the samples were observed with over 200 different viewing/illumination combinations. With the involvement of BTF, the authors introduced a new surface appearance taxonomy as is presented in **Figure 2**, where the difference in surface appearance between fixed and varied viewing and illumination directions can be observed. At fixed viewing/illumination directions, reflectance is used at coarse-scale observation and texture at fine-scale observation, and at varied viewing/illumination directions, BRDF and BTF are used.

Sattler et al. [17] presented a method of determining the BTF of cloths and materials with similar reflectance behaviour including view-dependent texture-maps and using a principal component analysis of the original data. The novelty of their work was also the point light

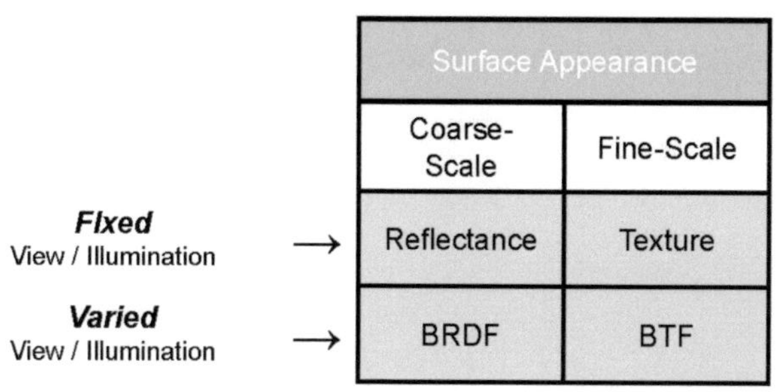

Figure 2. Surface appearance at fixed and varied viewing and illumination directions [16].

sources that enable smooth shadow boundaries on the geometry during the data acquisition. Besides, the system was sensitive to geometrical complexity and the sampling density of the environment map, on the basis of which the illumination could be changed interactively.

In the research of Wang et al. [18], the focus was on spatial variations and anisotropy in cloth appearance. The data acquisition device is presented in **Figure 3**. For the definition of the reflection of the light at a single surface point, they used a *data-driven microfacet-based BRDF*, i.e. a six-dimensional *spatially varying bidirectional reflectance distribution function (SVBRDF)* $\rho(x,i,o)$ [19]. In **Figure 3**, x is surface point, i is lighting direction, o is viewing direction, h is half-angle vector, n is upward normal direction, $\rho(x, i, o)$ is BRDF at surface point and Ω_+ is hemisphere of $\{h \mid h \cdot n > 0\}$. Besides, the microfacet *2D normal distribution function* (*NDF*) was implemented. In their research, the SVBRDF was modelled from images of a surface that was acquired from a single view. In their results, they confirmed the reliability of their method, which generates anisotropic, spatially-varying surface reflectance that is comparable with real measured appearance and was tested on various materials.

In some recent researches, the accuracy of BTF was discussed. In the review of appearance modelling methods by Schröder et al. [5] the explanation that the implementation of BTF can limit the appearance results is presented. Namely, the application of BTF can result in incorrectness of modelling of shadow boundaries. Some issues can occur also in the modelling of areas of high curvature that are not represented adequately when BTF is measured with the flat sample as a reference. Moreover, the reproduction of transparency and silhouette correctness are challenging with the use of this function.

The researches performed by Sadeghi and his colleagues [12, 13] present the appearance models for visualisation of microstructures. In the last part of the dissertation [12], after the presentation of the models for rendering rainbows and hair, appearance model for rendering cloth is introduced. Here, the focus were the measurements of BRDF of various fabric samples and yarns, which brought to the development of a new analytical BRDF model for threads. The method includes the measurements of profile of reflected light from various types of real yarns. After the measuring, the evaluation and comparison with the reflectance behaviour of the yarns that were predicted with the appearance model was performed, taking into account the fabric composition and yarn parameters [13]. A geometry of light reflection is calculated

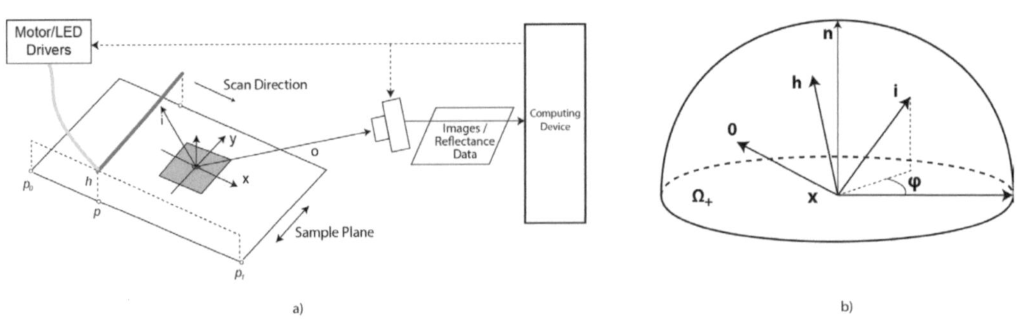

Figure 3. Data acquisition device and *microfacet-based SVBRDF* model [18].

http://dx.doi.org/10.5772/67736

from the cylindrical fibre, where longitudinal angles are computed regarding to the normal plane and the azimuth angles are calculated based on the local surface normal direction.

Iwasaki et al. [20] presented the research about interactive rendering (and interactive editing of parameters for scattering function) of static cloth with dynamic viewpoints and lighting. The method implemented micro cylinder model presenting weaving pattern and patch for calculation of light reflectance with the integration of environment lighting, visibility function, scattering function and weighting function. Their method includes the use of the gradient of signed distance function to the visibility boundary where the binary visibility changes.

3.1.1. Light scattering models for fibres

These models are geometric models of micro geometry that are combined with advanced rendering techniques (global illumination). Here, the micro geometry can be generated procedurally and optical properties of fibres have to be defined with the measurements. Two crucial parameter of fibres have to be considered: anisotropic highlights and translucency (**Figure 4**) [5].

The fundamentals of light scattering models for fibres that are used in various modern solutions were developed by Marschner et al. [21]. The calculations consider the fibres to be very thin and with long structures, which diameter is very small in comparison to viewing and lighting distance. Consequently, the fibres can be approximated as curves in the scenes and a far-field approximation and curve radiance and curve irradiance are implemented, resulting in bidirectional far-field scattering distribution function for curves *BCSDF* (*Bidirectional Curve Scattering Distribution Function*).

Zinke and Weber [22] upgrade the *BCSDF* in *Bidirectional Fibre Scattering Distribution Function* (*BFSDF*) that is a more general approach for light scattering from filaments. In their methods, different types of scattering functions for filaments were used and parameterized for the minimum enclosing cylinder, in which the *BFSDF* calculates the transfer of radiance (**Figure 5**).

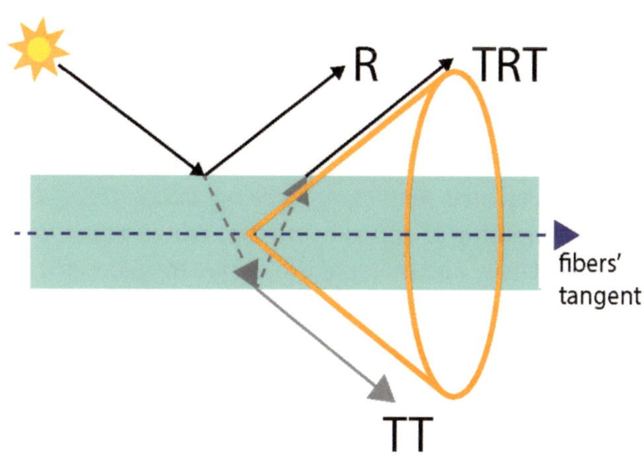

Figure 4. Light scattering from fibres, where R is surface reflection, TT is transmission and TRT is side reflection [5].

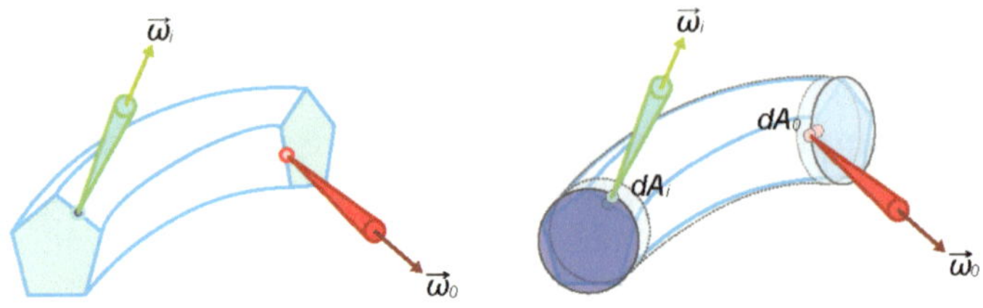

Figure 5. Scattering model from a fibre: *bidirectional scattering-surface reflectance distribution function* (*BSSRDF*) at the actual surface of the fibre—left and *bidirectional fibre scattering distribution function* (*BFSDF*) at the local minimum of the cylinder—right [5].

3.2. Volumetric models

Volumetric models consider certain unsolved issues of surface and image-based models by calculating the thickness and fuzziness of the fibres and yarns. The problems of consistent silhouettes and light diffusion in difficult-to-access object areas and accuracy of observation at medium distance are solved with various methods and their combination: with the use of volumetric light transport; the examination of microscopic structures and the processing of computed tomography (CT) data. Here, the fabric elements (fibres, yarns and cloth) are treated as a volume and light scattering models that are applied are, in many applications, explicit [5]. These models enable translucency, light diffusion and optimal silhouettes formations. Their results are scalable and, in dependence of a type of a model, can be integrated in details at yarn and fibre scale. For real-time solutions, they are not suitable and the viewing distance accuracy is usually medium, however in the modern solutions also medium to close.

In volumetric models, *light transport theory* is usually applied and the calculations for cloth include *energy transfers in anisotropic media*, i.e. *anisotropic light transport computation* occurs [23]. In isotropic media, the properties do not depend on the rotation and viewing angle, whereas in anisotropic media (fibres, hair), the optical properties depend on orientation.

Schröder et al. [5] define two types of volumetric appearance models of cloth, a *micro-flake model* and a *Gaussian mixture model* of fibres. In *micro-flake model,* the material is represented as a collection of idealised mirror flakes. Here, the basis of anisotropic light transport are applied, however volume scattering interactions and orientation of flakes are represented with a directional flake distribution. In *Gaussian mixture model,* fibre location and scattering events are calculated from statistical distribution of intersections between real fibres geometry. Light scattering is additionally calculated with *curve scattering models* (*BCSDF*). The mathematical calculations include the computing of defined yarn that is intersecting a voxel cell, for which a Gaussian directionality, density and material properties are generated.

Before the year 2000, there were only few investigations on the use of volumetric methods in the representations of anisotropic, structured media. First implementations were performed for knitwear and for fur [24, 25] and that was the beginning of the several researches in the last century.

Xu et al. [26] used the so-called *lumislice* (**Figure 6**), a modelling primitive cross-section of yarn that presents a radiance on the level of the fibres (occlusion, shadows, multiple scattering). The sequence of rotated and organised *lumislices* builds the entire structure of a knit-cloth.

In their work, Schröder et al. [27] introduced a concept called *local visibility* and used a *Gaussian mixture model* as the approximation of the fibre distribution. This parameter is able to predict self-shadowing and calculates the correlation between defined eye rays and shadow rays. It considers voxels and the size of a yarn cross section and is a fundamental of the function *bidirectional visibility distribution function* (*BVDF*). Besides, the authors presented an effective fibre density, which is calculated with the sum of contributions of line segments representing a cloth and intersecting with a certain voxel. The voxelized cloth was finally rendered with *Monte Carlo path tracing rendering technique*.

Zhao et al. [28] shortly reviewed the volume imaging technologies (CT, magnetic resonance and ultrasound) and discussed their limitation in the sense of their inability for acquiring data that represent direct optical appearance of the material. Besides, the volume rendering and volumetric appearance models are the focus of the paper's introductory part, discussing the complexity of developing the volumetric models that result in physical accuracy and the limitations of procedural methods, which do not consider and calculate the irregularities of cloth. The phenomena of fabric structural and yarn unevenness are crucial for the representation of the natural and organic appearance of cloths. The experiment introduced a method that combines acquisition of volume models, generated from density data of X-ray computed tomography (CT) scans and appearance data from photographs. The authors used a modified volume scattering model [29, 30] that describes accurately the anisotropy of the fibres. Due to the very small area that was scanned with CT, in which the result was a very detailed volume reconstruction at a resolution of singular fibre, the represented data have to be augmented and computed with the use of density and orientation fields in the volume that defines the scattering model parameters. Consequently, a highly detail volume appearance

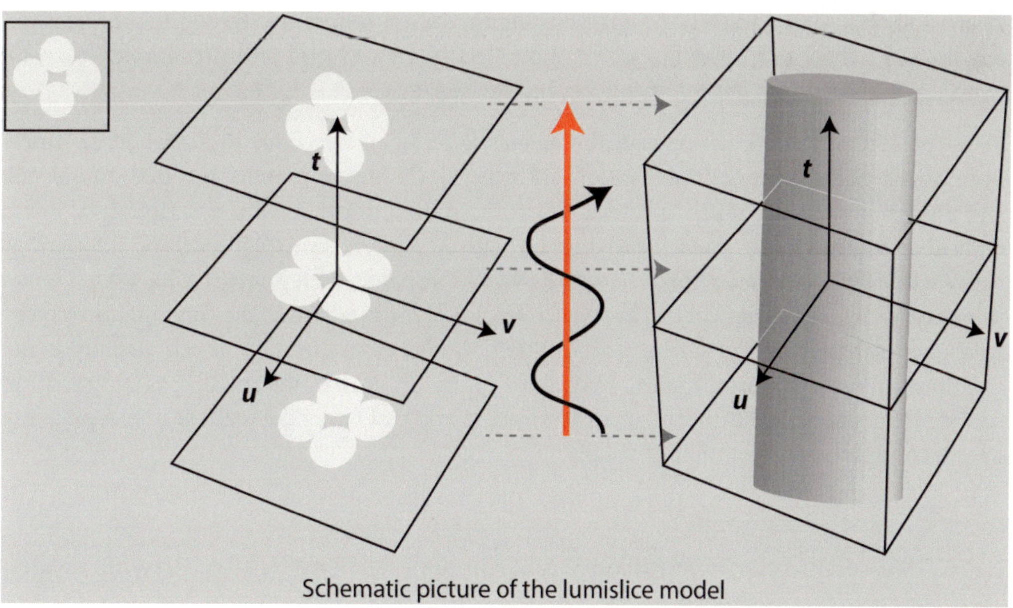

Figure 6. Generation of a volumetric yarn segment. The fluff density distribution in the upper left corner is rotated along the path of the yarn to yield a yarn segment [26].

model (including highlights and detailed textures) was created with this appearance matching procedure involving the density and orientation fields extracted from the 3D data. The rendering occurs after the definition of global optical parameters. Here, the photo taken under known but not controlled lighting was used and the optical properties were associated with the acquired volume so that the texture of the rendered volume matched the photo's texture. The procedure defines physically accurate scattering properties in the volume of the analysed material and visually and optically accurately describes the appearance of the cloth at the fibre geometry level (small scale) and at viewing from distance. Moreover, at small and large scale, the appearance of the fabric is natural due to the reconstruction of the irregularities at fibre, yarn and cloth level.

After the introduction of micro-CT imaging in volumetric appearance modelling of cloth, Zhao et al. [31] upgraded their research in the next years with the research that presented the cloth modelling process involving the CT technique and the expansion of its use on various fabric and weave patterns with the implementation of a *structure–aware volumetric texture synthesis method*. The process involves two phases: *exemplar creation phase* and *synthesis phase*. In the first phase, the volume data are acquired with CT scans of very small fabric samples describing the density information on a voxel grid, fibre orientation and yarns. The samples database is created with the procedure that tracks the yarns and their trajectories in the volume grid and segments the voxels so that they match the appropriate yarn and automatically detects the yarn crossing patterns. In the second synthesis phase, the input data are the collection of 2D binary data of weave pattern and 2D data describing the warp and weft yarns at yarn intersecting points. As a result, the output volume is generated that represents the fabric structure, which matches the output of the first phase (exemplars created in the first phase). Further, with the purpose to solve the complexity during the rendering of volumetric data, Zhao et al. [32] also introduced a precomputation-based rendering technique with *modular flux transfer,* where exemplar blocks are modelled as a voxel grid and precompute *voxel-to-voxel, patch-to-patch* and *patch-to-voxel flux transfer matrices*.

Recently, Zhao et al. [33] proposed the *automatic fitting approach* for the creation of procedural yarns including details at fibre level (**Figure 7**). CT measurements of cotton, rayon, silk and polyester yarns are taken as a basis for computation of procedural description of yarns. Optical properties of the yarns were defined with *Khungurn scattering model* [6]. Renderings occur with *Mitsuba renderer* [30]. The results were compared with photographs, which do on some areas include hairier parts. That was a success of the method, as the combination of very small samples involved in CT acquisition method and procedural approach, usually is not able to reproduce important fabric irregularities. By all means, the method is successful in solving the issue of replication of small pieces of fabric and offers the realistic non-replicating approach to the representation of details.

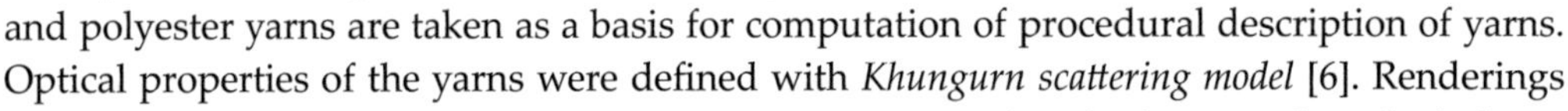

Figure 7. Presentation of the technique for automatic generation procedural representation of yarn including: (a) CT measurements, (b) fitting procedural yarns and (c) final rendering of textiles [33].

3.3. Fibre-based explicit methods

Fibre-based explicit models use representations with very accurate calculation of reflectance properties in intersecting point between light rays and actual fibres geometry and describe the fabric as a collection of individual discrete fibres represented with explicit geometry. These models are computationally very expensive and can be used for the most physically accurate simulations at fibre level accuracy and close viewing distances including the phenomena of translucency, optimal silhouettes and light diffusion. Usually, the results of explicit methods are not appropriate for real-time solutions [5].

Zhang et al. [34] proposed a solution for the scale-varying representations of woven fabric with the *interlaced/intertwisted displacement subdivision surface* (*IDSS*). The *IDSS* is capable to map the geometric detail on a subdivision surface and generate the fine details at fibre level. The model solves the issues of multiple-view scalability at inter- and intra-scale in woven fabric visualisation due to the implementation of interlaced, intertwisted vector displacement and a three-scale transformation synthesis.

Schröder et al. [35] presented a pipeline of cloth parameterization from a single image that involves a geometric yarn model and automatic estimation of yarn paths, yarn widths and weave pattern. Their *inverse engineering pipeline* includes input images and coarse optical flow field description, fine flow description of local yarn deformation, fine regularisation of image, output visualisation, the use of active yarn model that procedurally generates fibres, rendering with the setting of fibre and material parameters (**Figure 8**).

Khungurun [6] presented a fibre-based model including a *surface-based cylindrical fibre representation* on the basis of volumetric representation. The latter is the voxel array that involves a density of the material at a certain voxel and a local direction of the fibre at this specific voxel. The procedure of fibre geometry generation includes: volume decomposition, fibre centre detection, polyline creation and smoothing and radius determination. The entire pipeline includes: (1) a description of a scene geometry and a set of input photographs of a fabric that were acquired at different lighting and viewing conditions at a defined scene; (2) a development of a light scattering model; (3) the implementation of appearance matching that uses gradient descent optimisation to find optimised parameter values of scattering model and evaluates the differences between renderings and photographs with the objective function. The rendering occurs in extended version of *Monte Carlo path tracer*. Their research ends with the comparison of micro geometry constructed from CT scans with the explicit fibre-based method and concludes the analysis that both techniques are very successful in representation of cloths at micron level. In **Figure 9**, (a) fabric geometry creation and (b) appearance modelling pipeline are presented.

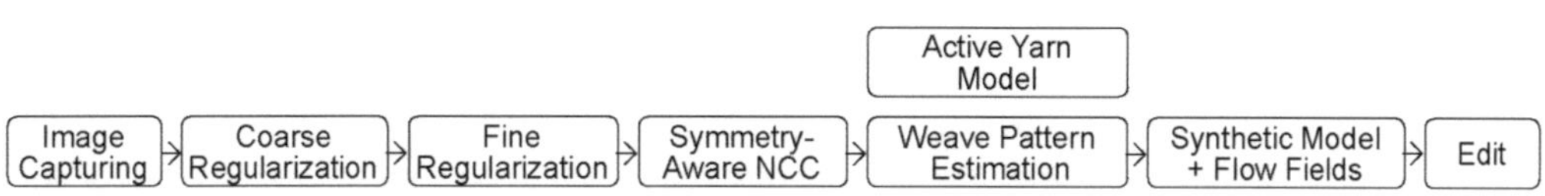

Figure 8. Inverse engineering pipeline for visual prototyping of cloth [35].

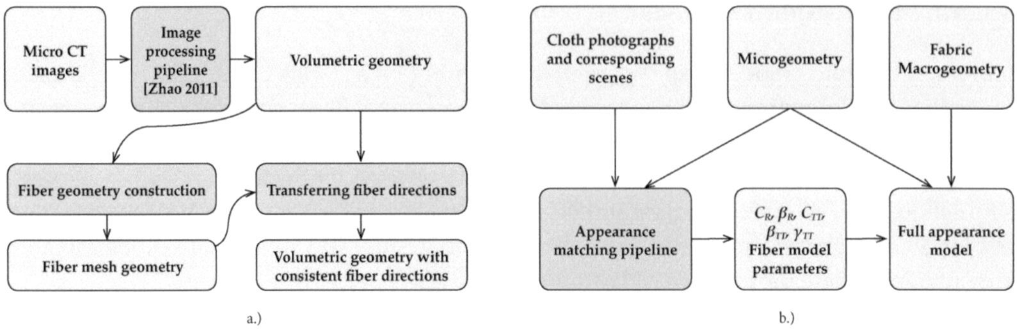

Figure 9. (a) A fabric geometry creation and (b) appearance modelling pipeline [6].

4. Texture-based reconstruction of the specularity and porosity of cloth

In the context of appearance modelling, mathematical appearance models were reviewed, but computationally less expensive techniques should not be overlooked. These latter techniques are firmly established in 3D animation workflow and in the production of static visualisations that include many objects on the scene, which can be viewed especially at medium and far distance.

4.1. Texture mapping

In 3D technology, texture mapping has been used for realistic visualisation of variety of surfaces for a very long time. Using that technique, 2D details of surface properties, i.e. 2D photographs that provide colour and texture surface information from a given object, are added to a 3D geometrical model. In the aspiration to visualise photo realistically, more than one image, respectively, map is needed. Realistic texture must illustrate the complexity of the material surface, what can be achieved using texture mapping without demanding 3D modelling of every detail [36].

Texture mapping is the method which applies texture to an object's boundary geometry, which can be a polygonal mesh, different types of splines or various level-sets. The polygonal mesh is the most suitable for the method, while texture is simultaneously covering the polygons of an object that can be triangles or quads. This process assigns texture coordinates to the polygon's vertices and the coordinates index a texture image and interpolated across the polygon at each of the polygon's pixel determine the texture image's value [37]. The 2D texture that is applied to polygons on the 3D model can be a tiling or a non-tiling image. Methods for computing texture mapping are often called *mesh parameterization methods* and are based on different concepts of piece-wise linear mapping and differential geometry [36, 37].

In UV mapping, defined parameters can be specified by a user, such as precise location of cuts respectively seams, where the 3D model unfolds into a mesh. A UV map can also be generated totally automatically or can be creating with combination of both.

The very first introduction of image texturing was in 1974 by Catmull [38]. He introduced the idea of tying the texture pattern to the parameter values. The method guarantees that the pattern rotates and moves with the object. It works for smooth, simple patterns painted on the surface but for simulation of rough textures it was not correct. Since then, the use of various texture mapping for defining different parameters of surface appearance was developed and is in use.

The map that is most commonly used is a *diffuse or a colour map* that gives surface a colour. Other maps can define *specular reflection, normal vector perturbation, surface displacement, transparency, shadows* and others.

Visualisation of roughed, wrinkled and irregular material, firstly introduced by Blinn [39, 40], can be implemented with the *bump mapping, i.e.* a texture function for creation of small perturbation of model's surface normals before using them in the intensity lighting calculations. With introducing bump map with its functions, roughness of the material can be visualised, although for best result of macroscopic irregularities they have to be modelled. The result of bump mapping is a material that is illusory bumpy, while the geometry of the model is not changed, therefore it is sufficient for shallow types of roughness. Images or maps for visualisation of bumps are greyscale and simulate surface's height, respectively white represent the highest parts or depth, black areas represent the lowest parts.

Where the observation of a rendered model is very close, realistic shading of bumpy surfaces provided with bump mapping is not appropriate while the surface profile does not reveal the realistic roughness and the occlusion effects of the bumps are not visible. In that case the use of a *displacement map* is necessary. A displacement map contains perturbations of the surface position. When using the displacement map, the geometric position of points on the surface is displaced. This technique is used to add surface detail to a model with the advantage that it has no limitations on bump height. The type of mapping can be considered as a type of modelling although computationally can be quite demanding [41].

A *normal map* can be used to replace normals entirely. The normal maps are used for adding details to a model without using more polygons. Geometry can be achieved on all three axes. Normal map should be an RGB image which gives three channels that correspond to the X, Y and Z coordinates of the surface normal. For creation of transparent, semi-transparent or even cut-out areas in the surface, a greyscale *alpha map* can be used.

Aliasing is the artifact that appears when using repetitive images, usually with regular patterns and with high resolution, or animations where the repetition period becomes close to or smaller than the discretization size. The result of such an artifact, where the texture pattern becomes comparable in scale to the raster grid is a moiré pattern that can be highly noticeable in visualised scenes [42].

Aliasing artifacts can be solved with the use of an anti-aliasing technique called *MIP mapping* [37]. In 1983, Williams [43] described the MIP mapping or pyramids which are pre-calculated and optimised sequences of images at a variety of different resolutions. The method is used to decrease the rendering time, to improve the image quality. At MIP mapping techniques the texture pattern is stored at a number of resolutions. By the process of filtering and decimation, images with high resolution are transformed into ones with lower resolution and that eliminates aliasing.

4.2. Work-flow for visualisation of irregular cloth surface

The review of the appearance modelling models revealed that the visualisation of natural appearance of cloth is still a challenge for procedural and computational approaches. The computer-based solution was presented in the research of Zhao et al. [28], however, the issues in representation of irregular cloth structure samples with morphologic, relief and texture data on the large scale that are crucial for visualisation of cloths demand a special attention. This is the case also of the historical and worn cloth that cannot be modelled procedurally with the methods for fibres, yarns and cloth appearance modelling, but with the accurate image-based techniques. Besides, in the cloth production, airy structures, as laces are extremely difficult to reproduce with ordinary 3D modelling techniques in software for 3D computer graphic and they can be computed with simulation algorithms only to some extend [44]. Special attention should be put also on visualisation of hand-made fabrics, artistic and experimental cloths often used in interior and in fashion design.

At micro level appearance modelling, virtual textile porosity is created as a result of interlacing threads into a textile structure and specularity as a consequence of computations of reflectance of shading algorithms. These models are suitable for visualising at close viewing distances or for predictive renderings, for example in the case of computer-aided design (CAD). Besides, porosity, specularity and other irregularities and structural phenomena, that are visible only when cloth is observed at far viewing distance, should not be overlooked. For instance, one should not obey the uneven distribution of organic volume formation in yarns structure that only after interlaced in the final cloth form a random pattern of manifestation.

The aim of our contribution was the analysis and reconstruction of cloth *specularity* (presenting total specular reflectance and partial reflectance) and *porosity* (presenting the translucency of cloth and, in technical terms, a void part of the textile's full volume) with the implementation of *image processing in the workflow* (**Figure 10**), generation of specular and alpha map (map for porosity) and the definition of the optimal application (mapping) on geometrical models. The image-based appearance modelling workflow for accurate visualisation of a worn cloth that had heterogeneous structure on a large scale was established, which originates from photo documentation (image information) of the material. It was crucial for this process to record information on a very large sample surface (microscopic analysis is hence not appropriate), where it was possible to record uneven structures and time-dependent deformation. The analysed sample was a part of the national costume from the Gorenjska region (100% cotton fabric, plain weave, warp density = 20 threads/cm, weft density = 15 threads/cm, Z yarn twist in warp and weft threads).

The review of the references showed that for the analysis and modelling of appearance of uneven textile surfaces, the use of image-processing methods and computationally less demanding virtual representation is sufficient [45, 46]. These workflows focus on the acquisition of specific data, i.e. optical [47–49] and constructional [50], and numerical approaches to extract meaningful information on different levels in dependence of the further data implementation. Following these foundations, various illumination conditions at photo acquisition (the combination of two diffuse, left and right, and one direct light) were analysed in the workflow of our research, followed by two phases of image processing (histogram equalisation and rolling ball algorithm). The processing phases were found to be crucial for the detection of specular and porous areas of interest. A special focus was on the study of the optimal threshold

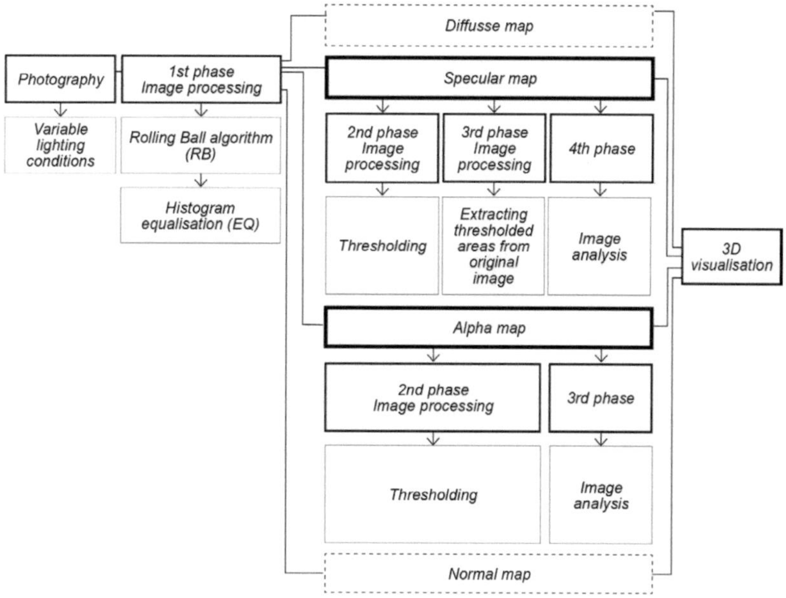

Figure 10. The workflow for visualisation of a worn cloth that has heterogeneous structure.

method, which enabled the creation of specular and alpha map. Here, the comparison of local and global algorithm techniques [51] was performed and the evaluation of the image analysis results of thresholded images, where different threshold algorithms were implemented.

For the porosity, the threshold was defined with three techniques: min. local point of a histogram, manual definition and *Yen* algorithm (which was selected on the basis of the image analysis among different ImageJ algorithms) [52].

The detection of specular areas was found to be significantly dependent on local and global threshold approach and *Percentile* algorithm was finally selected, as other algorithms resulted in threshold images that were unsuitable for further 3D visualisation [53]. Image analysis of detected porous and specular areas enabled the numerical evaluation of areas covered by pores and specular surfaces and the average size and the number of porous and specular areas. Within the image analysis of porosity, special attention was paid to the formation of connected and closed pores in the map for porosity. Here, the connected pores were treated as error, since this phenomenon is not possible to be present in the real fabric. Specular areas manifested different organisation and disposition in dependence of illumination, image processing phase and the type of thresholding algorithm. Further, for the implementation in 3D rendering, the defined specular maps were selected and used with the consideration of location of virtual lights and the specularity appearance of the real fabric.

Fabrics were visualised in 3D program Blender using four different maps, the diffuse map that was a photograph, the normal map, the specular and the alpha map. The last two maps were created and analysed through the workflow established in our research work. In **Figure 11**, the results of the workflow including variable (real and virtual) lighting conditions and image processing of specular and alpha maps on cloth visualisations are presented. On the left side

Figure 11. Left: Emphasised specular areas on cloth sample for diffuse ((a) and (b)) and direct ((c) and (d)) illumination during image acquisition and different positions of virtual lights, and right: (e) the visualisation of porosity with the phenomena of connected and closed pores.

of **Figure 11**, emphasised specular areas are presented for diffuse (a and b) and direct (c and d) illumination during image acquisition. The difference among the samples a and c versus b and d is visible due to different position of virtual lights during rendering, where the manifestation of specularity strongly depends on type of lights (diffuse versus direct). On the right side of **Figure 11**, the visualisation of porosity can be observed with the phenomena of connected and closed pores.

5. Conclusions

Our contribution is a comprehensive review of advanced and less-demanding methods for modelling of cloth appearance.

The models are classified as image-based, surface-based, volumetric and explicit and the advances in these computer-aided approaches and computations for cloth visualisation are discussed regarding their pipeline, procedure complexity and results implementation at fibre, yarn and cloth scale viewing conditions. In the second part of the chapter, a texture-based and image processing-based modelling of porosity and specularity of irregular cloth surface was introduced. For a realistic modelling and visualisation of a worn cloth with heterogeneous structure and surface on a large scale, a detailed image information of the sample was captured and corresponding image processing methods were applied. In the procedure, the definition and implementation of the optimal threshold algorithm was crucial and the results served as maps for image-based modelling. The maps were evaluated with the image analysis so that the pores and specular areas could also be numerically analysed before they were applied in a final 3D reconstruction. The contribution reviewed the importance of cloth appearance modelling in 3D computer graphic and presented the opportunities for further developments and implementations.

Author details

Tanja Nuša Kočevar and Helena Gabrijelčič Tomc*

*Address all correspondence to: helena.gabrijelcic@ntf.uni-lj.si

Department of Textile, Graphic Arts and Design, Faculty of Natural Sciences and Engineering, University of Ljubljana, Ljubljana, Slovenia

References

[1] Jevšnik S., Kalaoglu F., Terliksiz S., Purgaj J. Review of computer models for fabric simulation. Tekstilec, 2014, 57(4), pp. 300–314. DOI: 10.14502/Tekstilec2014.57.300–314.

[2] Magnor M. A., Grau O., Sorkine-Hornung O., Thebalt C. Digital Representations of the Real World. 1st ed., Boca Raton: CRC Press, 2015, pp. 225–238. DOI: 10.1201/b18154-30.

[3] McCluney R. Introduction to radiometry and photometry. 2nd ed., Norwood: Artech House Publishers, 2014, 470 p.

[4] Chen X., Hearle J. W. S. Structural hierarchy in textile materials: an overview. In Modelling and Predicting Textile Behaviour. 1st ed., Cambridge: Woodhead Publishing, 2010, pp. 3–37.

[5] Schröder K., Zhao S., Zinke A. Recent advances in physically-based appearance modeling of cloth. In: SIGGRAPH Asia Courses, Course Notes, Singapore, November 28–December 01, 2012, art. no. 12. DOI: 10.1145/2407783.2407795.

[6] Khungurun P., Schroeder D., Zhao S., Bala K., Marschner S. Matching real fabrics with micro-appearance models. ACM Transactions on Graphic, 35(1), 2015, pp. 1–26. DOI: 10.1145/2818648.

[7] Nicodemus F. Directional reflectance and emissivity of an opaque surface. Applied Optics, 1965, 4 (7), pp. 767–775. DOI: 10.1364/AO.4.000767.

[8] Bartell F. O., Dereniak E. L., Wolfe W. L. The theory and measurement of bidirectional reflectance distribution function (BRDF) and bidirectional transmittance distribution function (BTDF). In: Hunt G. H. (ed.). Proceedings of SPIE 0257, Radiation Scattering in Optical Systems, Huntsville, March 3, 1980, Vol. 257, pp. 154–160. DOI: 10.1117/12.959611.

[9] Ceolato R., Rivière N., Hespel L. Biscans B. Probing optical properties of nanomaterials. 12 January 2012, SPIE Newsroom. Available: http://spie.org/newsroom/4047-probing-optical-properties-of-nanomaterials. Accessed 10.1.2017. DOI: 10.1117/2.1201201.004047.

[10] Ashikmin M., Premože S., Shirley P. A microfacet-based BRDF generator. In: Proceedings of the 27th annual conference on Computer graphics and interactive techniques, New York: SIGGRAPH'00, ACM Press/Addison-Wesley Publishing Co., 2000, pp. 65–74. DOI: 10.1145/344779.344814.

[11] Irawan P., Marschner S. Specular reflection from woven cloth. ACM Transactions on Graphics (TOG), 2012, 31(1), art. no. 11. DOI: 10.1145/2077341.2077352.

[12] Sadeghi, I. Controlling the Appearance of Specular Microstructures. San Diego: University of California, pp. 131–176. Available: https://www.yumpu.com/en/document/view/13881324/controlling-the-appearance-of-specular-microstructures-computer-Accessed 10.1.2017.

[13] Sadeghi I., Bisker O., De Deken J., Jensen W. H. A practical microcylinder appearance model for cloth rendering. ACM Transactions on Graphics, 2013, 32(2), art. no. 14, pp. 1–12. DOI: 10.1145/2451236.2451240.

[14] Adabala N., Magnenat-Thalmann N., Fei G. Visualization of woven cloth. In: Eurographics Symposium on Rendering 2003, Switzerland: Eurographics Association Aire-la-Ville, Leuven, Belgium, June 25–27, 2003, pp. 178–185.

[15] Irawan P. Appearance of Woven Cloth, PhD thesis, Cornell: Cornell University, 2008, Available: https://www.cs.cornell.edu/~srm/publications/IrawanThesis.pdf, pp. 15–19. Accessed 10.1.2017.

[16] Dana J. K., Ginneken V. B., Nayar K. S., Koenderink J. J. Reflectance and texture of real-world surfaces. ACM Transactions on Graphics, 18(1), 1999, pp. 1–34. DOI: 10.1145/300776.300778.

[17] Sattler M., Sarlette R., Klein R. Efficient and realistic visualization of cloth. In: Dutre P., Suykens F., Christensen P. H., Cohen-Or D. L. (eds.). EGRW '03 Proceedings of the 14th Eurographics Symposium on Rendering, The Eurographics Association, Belgium — June 25–27, 2003, Switzerland: Eurographics Association Aire-la-Ville, 2003, pp. 167–177. DOI: 10.2312/EGWR/EGWR03/167-177.

[18] Wang J., Zhao S., Tong X., Snyder J., Guo B. Modeling anisotropic surface reflectance with example-based microfacet synthesis. In: Proceedings of ACM SIGGRAPH 2008. ACM Transactions on Graphics, Los Angeles, California, August 11–15, 2008, New York: ACM, 27(3), art. no. 41, pp. 1–9. DOI: 10.1145/1360612.1360640.

[19] Nicodemus F. E., Richmond J. C., Hsia J. J., Ginsberg I. W., Limperis T. Geometric considerations and nomenclature for reflectance. Monograph 161, National Bureau of Standards (US). Available: https://graphics.stanford.edu/courses/cs448-05-winter/papers/nicodemus-brdf-nist.pdf. Accessed 8.1.2017. DOI: 10.1109/LPT.2009.2020494.

[20] Iwasaki K., Mizutani K., Dobashi Y., Nishita T. Interactive cloth rendering of microcylinder appearance model under environment lighting, Computer Graphics Forum, 2014, 33 (2), pp. 333–340. DOI: 10.1111/cgf.12302.

[21] Marschner R. S., Jensen W. H., Cammarano M., Worley S., Hanrahan P. Light scattering from human hair fibers. In: ACM Transactions on Graphics (TOG) - Proceedings of ACM SIGGRAPH 2003, San Diego, California, July 27–31, New York: ACM, 22(3), 2003, pp. 780–791. DOI: 10.1145/1201775.882345.

[22] Zinke A., Weber A. Light scattering from filaments. IEEE Transactions on Visualization and Computer Graphics. 2007, 13(2), pp. 342–356. DOI: 10.1109/TVCG.2007.43.

[23] Jakob W., Arbree A., Moon T. J., Bala K., Marschner S. A radiative transfer framework for rendering materials with anisotropic structure. In: ACM Transactions on Graphics (TOG) - Proceedings of ACM SIGGRAPH 2010, Los Angeles, California — July 26–30, 2010, New York: ACM, 2010, 29(4), art. no. 53. DOI: 10.1145/1778765.1778790.

[24] Gröller E., Rau T.R., Straβer W. Modeling and visualization of knitwear, IEEE Transactions on Visualization and Computer Graphics, 1995, 1(4), pp. 302–310. DOI: 10.1109/2945.485617.

[25] Kajiya J. T., Kay T. L. Rendering fur with three dimensional textures. In: SIGGRAPH '89 Proceedings of the 16th annual conference on Computer graphics and interactive techniques, New York: ACM, 1989, 23(3), pp. 271–280. DOI: 10.1145/74333.74361, Available: https://www.cs.drexel.edu/~david/Classes/CS586/Papers/p271-kajiya.pdf.

[26] Xu Y. Q., Chen Y., Lin S., Zhong H., Wu E., Guo B., Shum H. Y. Photorealistic rendering of knitwear using the lumislice. In: SIGGRAPH '01 Proceedings of the 28th Annual Conference on Computer Graphics and Interactive Techniques, New York: ACM, 2001, pp. 391–398. DOI: 10.1145/383259.383303.

[27] Schröder K., Klein R., Zinke A. A volumetric approach to predictive rendering of fabrics. Computer Graphics Forum, 2011, 30(4), pp. 1277–1286. DOI: 10.1111/j.1467-8659.2011.01987.x.

[28] Zhao S., Jakob W., Marschner S., Bala K. Building volumetric appearance models of fabric using micro CT imaging. In: ACM Transactions on Graphics (TOG) – Proceedings of ACM SIGGRAPH 2011, Vancouver, British Columbia, Canada — August 07–11, New York: ACM, 2011, 30(4), article no. 44, pp. 98–105. DOI: 10.1145/2010324.1964939.

[29] Jakob W., Arbree A., Moon T. J., Bala K., Marschner S. A radiative transfer framework for rendering materials with anisotropic structure. In: ACM Transactions on Graphics (TOG) - Proceedings of ACM SIGGRAPH 2010, Los Angeles, California, July 26–30, 2010, New York: ACM, 29(4), art. no. 53, pp. 1–13. DOI: 10.1145/1778765.1778790.

[30] Jakob W. Mitsuba Documentation, Date of publication February 25 2014, date of update 16.7.2014, 2014, Available: http://www.mitsuba-renderer.org/releases/current/documentation.pdf, 249p. Accessed 17.1.2017.

[31] Zhao S., Jakob W., Marschner S., Bala K. Structure-aware synthesis for predictive woven fabric appearance. In: ACM Transactions on Graphics (TOG) - Proceedings of ACM SIGGRAPH, New York: ACM, 2012, 31(4), article no. 75. DOI: 10.1145/2185520.2185571.

[32] Zhao S., Hašan M., Ramamoorthi R., Bala K. Modular flux transfer: efficient rendering of high-resolution volumes with repeated structures. In: ACM Transactions on Graphics (TOG) - SIGGRAPH 2013 Conference Proceedings, New York: ACM, 2013, 32(4), art. no. 131. DOI: 10.1145/2461912.2461938.

[33] Zhao S., Luan F., Bala K. Fitting procedural yarn models for realistic cloth rendering. In: ACM Transactions on Graphics (TOG) - Proceedings of ACM SIGGRAPH, July 2016, New York: ACM, 2016, 35(4), art. no. 51. DOI: 10.1145/2897824.2925932.

[34] Zhang J., Baciu G., Zheng D., Liang C., Li G., Hu J. IDSS: a novel representation for woven fabrics. IEEE Transactions on Visualisation and Computer Graphics, 2013, 19(3), pp. 420–432. DOI: 10.1109/TVCG.2012.66.

[35] Schröder K., Zinke A., Klein R. Image-based reverse engineering and visual prototyping of woven cloth. IEEE Transactions on Visualization and Computer Graphics, 2015, 21(2), pp. 188–200. DOI: 10.1109/TVCG.2014.2339831.

[36] Heckbert P. S. Survey of texture mapping. IEEE Computer Graphics and Applications, November 1986, 6(11), pp. 56–67. DOI: 10.1109/MCG.1986.276672.

[37] Haindl M., Filip J. Visual Texture. Accurate Material Appearance Measurement, Representation and Modeling. 1st ed., London: Springer-Verlag, 2013, 284p. DOI: 10.1007/978-1-4471-4902-6.

[38] Catmull E. A Subdivision Algorithm for Computer Display of Curved Surfaces, PhD dissertation, Salt Lake City: University of Utah, 1974.

[39] Blinn J. F. Simulation of wrinkled surfaces. ACM SIGGRAPH Computer Graphics, ACM New York, 1978, 12(3), pp. 286–292. DOI: 10.1145/965139.507101.

[40] Max N. L., Becker B. G. Bump shading for volume textures, IEEE Computer Graphics and Applications, 1994, 14(4), pp. 18–20. DOI: 10.1109/38.291525.

[41] Cook L. R. Shade trees. ACM SIGGRAPH Computer Graphics, 1984, 18(3), pp. 223–231, ACM New York. DOI: 10.1145/964965.808602.

[42] Cant R., Shrubsole P. A. Texture potential MIP mapping, a new high-quality texture antialiasing algorithm. ACM Transactions on Graphics, 19(3), July 2000, pp. 164–184. DOI: 10.1145/353981.353991.

[43] Williams W. Pyramidal parametrics, ACM SIGGRAPH Computer Graphics, 1983, 17(3), pp. 1–11. DOI: 10.1145/964967.801126.

[44] Gabrijelčič T. H., Pivar M., Kočevar T.N. Definition of the workflow for 3d computer aided reconstruction of a lace. In: Simončič B. (ed.), Tomšič B. (ed.), Gorjanc M. (ed.). Proceedings, 16th World Textile Conference AUTEX 2016, June 8–10, 2016, Ljubljana, Slovenia, Ljubljana: Faculty of Natural Sciences and Engineering, Department of Textiles, Graphic Arts and Design, 2016, p. 8.

[45] Cybulska, M. Reconstruction of archaeological textiles. Fibres & Textiles in Eastern Europe, 2010, 18, 3(80), pp. 100–105.

[46] Hu, J., Xin, B. Visualization of textile surface roughness based on silhouette image analysis. Research Journal of Textile and Apparel, 2007, 11(2), pp. 8–20. DOI: 10.1108/RJTA-11-02-2007-B002.

[47] Havlová M. Model of vertical porosity occurring in woven fabrics and its effect on air permeability. Fibres & Textiles in Eastern Europe, 2014, 22, 4(106), pp. 58–63.

[48] Hadjianfar M., Semnani D., Sheikhzadeh M. A new method for measuring luster index based on image processing. Textile Research Journal, 2010, 80(8), pp. 726–733. DOI: 10.1177/0040517509343814.

[49] Jong-Jun K. Image analysis of luster images of woven fabrics and yarn bundle simulation in the weave - cotton, silk, and velvet fabrics. Journal of Fashion Business, 2002, 6(6), pp. 1–11.

[50] Swery E. E., Allen T., Piaras K. Automated tool to determine geometric measurements of woven textiles using digital image analysis techniques. Textile Research Journal, 2016, 86(6), pp. 618–635. DOI: 10.1177/0040517515595031.

[51] Kočevar T. N., Gabrijelčič T. H. Analysis of different threshold algorithms for definition of specular areas of relief, interlaced structures. In: Pavlovič Ž. (ed.). Proceedings, 8th International Symposium on Graphic Engineering and Design GRID 2016, Novi Sad, November 3–4, 2016, Novi Sad: Faculty of Technical Sciences, Department of Graphic Engineering and Design, 2016, pp. 297–304.

[52] Kočevar T. N., Gabrijelčič T. H. 3D visualisation of woven fabric porosity. Tekstilec, 2016, 59(1), pp. 28–40. DOI: 10.14502/Tekstilec2016.59.28–40.

[53] Kočevar T. N., Gabrijelčič T. H. 3D visualisation of specularity of woven fabrics. Tekstilec, 2016, 59(4), pp. 335–349. DOI: 10.14502/Tekstilec2016.59.28–40.

Chapter 4

Textile Forms' Computer Simulation Techniques

Andreja Rudolf, Slavica Bogović, Beti Rogina Car, Andrej Cupar, Zoran Stjepanovič and Simona Jevšnik

Additional information is available at the end of the chapter

http://dx.doi.org/10.5772/67738

Abstract

Computer simulation techniques of textile forms already represent an important tool for textile and garment designers, since they offer numerous advantages, such as quick and simple introduction of changes while developing a model in comparison with conventional techniques. Therefore, the modeling and simulation of textile forms will always be an important issue and challenge for the researchers, since close-to-reality models are essential for understanding the performance and behavior of textile materials. This chapter deals with computer simulation of different textile forms. In the introductory part, it reviews the development of complex modeling and simulation techniques related to different textile forms. The main part of the chapter focuses on study of the fabric and fused panel drape by using the finite element method and on development of some representative textile forms, above all, on functional and protective clothing for persons who are sitting during performing different activities. Computer simulation techniques and scanned 3D body models in a sitting posture are used for this purpose. Engineering approaches to textile forms' design for particular purposes, presented in this chapter, show benefits and limitations of specific 3D body scanning and computer simulation techniques and outline the future research challenges.

Keywords: textile forms, computer simulation techniques, 3D scanning, 3D body models

1. Introduction

The chapter entitled textile forms' computer simulation techniques is intended for raising awareness about the importance of modeling and simulation of different textile forms. Since textile objects are very common and omnipresent all-around us, the appropriate simulation techniques can be stated as a very important part of a wide area of computer simulation.

Textiles can be generally divided into linear (fibers, yarns, threads), two-dimensional (woven, knitted fabrics, nonwovens) and three-dimensional (garments, architectural textiles, some technical textiles) textile forms. Modeling and simulation of these forms can be extremely complex due to their visco-elastic properties and unique behavior when exposed to forces, even though relatively small ones, such as gravitational force.

The topics, referring to computer-based simulation of textile-based objects, have already been investigated by a number of researchers and authors. Many of them have developed or applied different methods and models for describing the structure and behavior of textile forms. However, there is still lack of newer publications, dealing with the intriguing phenomena, related to modeling and simulation of complex textiles, garments, and other textile forms.

The modeling and simulation techniques for woven and knitted fabrics and garments are discussed in view of accurate understanding of the relationship between the construction and behavior of textile forms as a key in engineering of textile forms' design for intended applications. Three approaches for modeling of textile forms are presented, i.e., geometry-based, physically based, and hybrid approach. Computer simulation of textile forms in interaction with the 3D objects and its importance for the development of specific, custom-designed garments are considered from the perspective of virtual prototyping on the 3D scanned body models.

The chapter introduces three case studies, related to recent advances in engineering approach to computer simulation techniques in the field of textile science. The first one deals with modeling and simulation of textile fabrics and fused panels based on finite element method. The second case study refers to simulation of garments using the sitting 3D human body models using one of the commercial 3D CAD packages. Topic of the third case study is connected with application of simulation techniques used for developing of a special form of protective clothing for sport aircraft pilots—the so-called antig suit.

2. Complex modeling and simulation techniques of textile forms

The visual appearances of the textile forms for both the real and the virtual are influenced by:

(a) the shapes of the three-dimensional (3D) textile forms determined by the corresponding two-dimensional (2D) pattern pieces and

(b) used textile materials that which behavior is influenced by their mechanical and physical properties.

The realistic behavior of textile materials in the virtual environment mainly depends on computer-based models of the textile materials. They are used for simulation of different textile forms such as tablecloths, flags, garments, shoes, etc. with the aim to study the behavior of textile materials in the virtual environment or to develop the complex shape of the textile forms, which consist of two or more pattern pieces.

The simulation techniques of textile forms should be stable and fast so that they can be applied in different environments, and interactive performance can be achieved [1].

To simulate textile forms, different modeling approaches are developed to model the structure of textile materials. These are either geometrical, physical, or hybrid models [1–3]. In the virtual environment, interactions between the textile forms and other 3D objects (collision detection and collision response) are of great importance, therefore, should be also computed. When the 3D shape of the textile form is computed, it could be rendered for visualization.

2.1. Geometrical models

The geometrically based approaches are used when the final shape of the textile form is needed without considering the dynamic process. They are simple and have low cost of computation [1].

In the computer graphics, the fabric simulations were first performed by using the geometrical models. These models represent simple geometrical formulations of the fabric without its physical and mechanical properties on local surfaces. Therefore, they are unsuitable for complex reproducible fabric simulation. They focused on appearance of the geometrical shape, particularly folds and wrinkles, which are presented by geometrical equations [1, 2].

The first attempt to the fabric simulation by using a geometrical model was presented by Weil in 1986 [2, 4]. He suggested a method for simulation of the hanging fabric as a mesh of points. The simulation of its shape was carried out by fitting of the catenary curves between the hanging or constraint points.

The research studies regarding the garments simulation by using the geometrical modeling can be found in 1990. A method for modeling of the sleeve on a bending arm was based on a hollow cylinder that consists of a series of circular rings and with a displacement of circular rings along the axial direction, the folds are formed [1, 2]. A method for designing of the 3D garment directly on a 3D digitized shape of the human body was presented by Hinds and McCartney [5]. They represented the garment as a collection of 3D surfaces (pattern pieces) of complex shape around the static 3D body, whose fit around panel edges with respect to body form may vary over the surface. A geometrical approach for modeling of the fabric folds on the sleeve was proposed by Ng and Grimsdale [6], where a set of rules was developed for automatic generation of the fold lines.

In general, the geometrically based simulation techniques are used for modeling of the fabric and garment drape. Therefore, they are effective in computing the shape of fabrics or garments. However, the geometrically based techniques usually do not take into account the dynamic interaction between the fabric/garment and the object, because they are difficult to be geometrically modeled [1].

Stumpp et al. [7] proposed a geometric deformation model for the efficient and robust simulation of garments. With this model a high stretching, shearing, and low bending resistance could be modeled, and the deformed region can be restored back to its original shape. Therefore, it can be used for modeling of the interaction between the fabric and other objects of different shapes. Researchers had represented the physically plausible dynamics of their approach with a comparison to a traditional physically based deformation model, **Figure 1**. The results show that the similar fabric properties can be reproduced with both models.

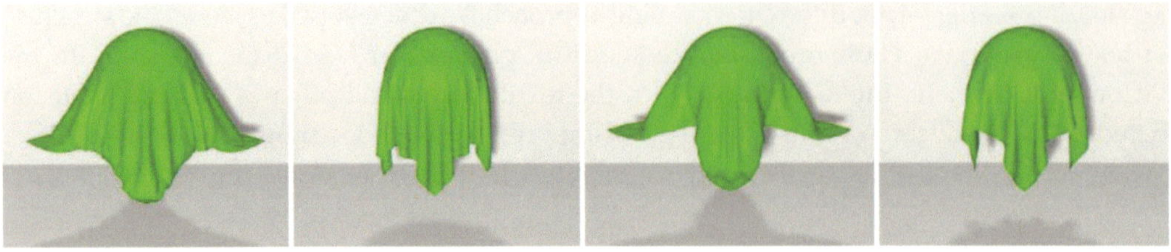

(a) (b) (c) (d)

Figure 1. Computer simulation of a fabric piece onto a sphere: (a, b) fabric draping by using the physically-based approach, (a, b) (c, d) fabric draping by using the geometrically-based approach [7].

2.2. Physical models

The physically based approaches are widely used for computing the mechanical behavior of textile forms. In addition, in physical-based methods, deformation is based on the structures and properties of textile materials. The structures and properties of textile forms have been investigated as highly flexible mechanical materials from the 1970s. Mechanical simulation intends to reproduce the virtual fabric surface with given parameters, which are expressed as strain-stress relationships and described by curves due to different degrees of simplification and approximation. Simple linear models can approximate these curves, whilst the nonlinear analytic functions (polynomials on interval-defined functions) are used for accurate models. In addition, the fabric mass per surface unit should be considered [3].

The physically based models are independent of geometrical representation. Therefore, with them it is possible to solve complex numerical problems by integrating various constraints. The special attention was been paid to simulation of large deformations of textile forms [1]. The behavior of textile material can be described by a complex system of mathematical equations (mechanical laws), which are usually partial differential equations or other types of differential systems. Analytical solutions, which are provided only for a limited class of simple equations and solve only simple situations, are not suitable for complex fabric simulations. Therefore, the numerical methods are implemented into a fabric simulation, which requires discretization, explicit computation of the physical values at precise points in space and time. Space discretization can be achieved through numerical solution techniques (models derived from continuum mechanics), or through the mechanical model itself, as in particle system models [3].

The first approach to simulation of the fabric and deformable surfaces introduces Terzopoulos et al. [1, 3, 7–9]. He obtained the motion of the object's points using the Lagrange's equations of motion that had been first discretized by a finite-element method. Therefore, there was a need to solve a large system of ordinary differential equations.

2.2.1. Particle-based approach

A particle-based system divides the object (fabric) into small particles on triangular or rectangular mesh. The points are defined as finite masses at the mesh intersections [2]. The number of points is defined according to the used problems and techniques. For example, a piece of fabric could be modeled as a two-dimensional arrangement of particles, which conceptually representing the intersection points of the warp and weft yarns within a fabric weave, thus can be plain, twill, satin weave, etc. [10].

The first particle systems for fabric simulation are based on a form of the mesh [11, 12]. By using this simulation approach, the fabric drape as a dynamic phenomenon was simulated very realistic on the table, on the sphere, etc. These types of simulations have already been reflected by the nonlinear behavior similar to continuum mechanics models. Their accuracy was limited for simulation of large deformations and required longer computation times. Furthermore, faster models based on spring-mass meshes were developed, and for computation were used to fast implicit numerical integration methods [3, 13]. In this modeling technique, an object is represented as a collection of mass points (circle particle) that are interconnected by structural, bend, and shear springs through a mesh structure. The mass points are interconnected by linear springs within the position and velocity at a certain time and mass [1, 10, 14]. The way the springs are connecting the particles (the topology of the object) and the differences in strength of each spring influence the behavior of the object as a whole. The different type of mesh topologies has been presented with respect to the connection between the mass and springs [15]. These are rectangular mesh that was first proposed in 1995 by Provot [16], **Figure 2(a)**, responsive mesh was described by Choi and Ko [17], **Figure 2(b)**, triangular mesh was presented by Selle et al. [18], **Figure 2(c)**, and the simplified mesh Hu et al. [19], **Figure 2(d)**.

2.2.2. *Finite-element approach*

The finite elements method (FEM) is widely used for mechanical simulation and numerical analysis. It is based on the usage of matrix algebra. The finite-element method was been developed in a particular scientific disciplines with a wide possibility of solving various problems in mathematics, physics, continuum mechanics, etc.

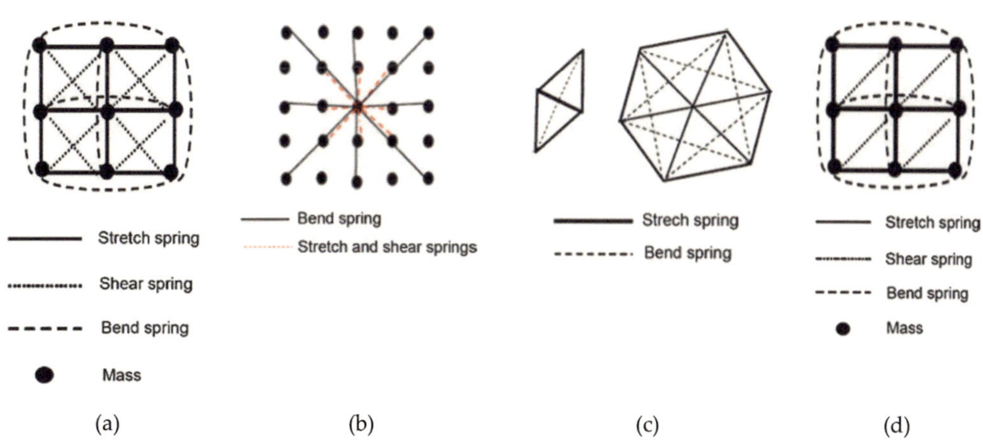

Figure 2. Mesh topologies of the mass spring model [15].

FEM is mainly used for application of elastic solid or shell modeling for mechanical engineering purposes, where linear elasticity and small deformations appears. Therefore, it is not so well adapted for fabrics, which is very deformable object. Early attempts to fabric modeling by using FEM showed high computation times [3, 20]. However, it was discovered that by using appropriate simplification and efficient algorithms the FEM is also usable in interactive graphics applications on the field of textile engineering [3]. The research studies regarding the finite element analysis applied to fabrics are well described in source [21].

For solving problems with FEM, it could use different computer programs such as ANSYS, ABAQUS.

Solving of the mechanical problems with finite element method proceeds in several steps [22]:

- discretization of the continuum,
- element equation,
- integration,
- boundary conditions,
- numerical analysis,
- interpretation of results.

For the analysis of problems using the finite element method, it is first necessary to create the so-called geometric model of the real problem. This step is followed by the discretization of a problem on one-, two- or three-dimensional elements, depending of the structure [22]. When building the finite elements mesh, we have to assure that the mesh fits the structure of the geometric body. The elements should be selected in a way that their shape suites the form of the body. Depending on their form, the elements are divided in liner, shell and volume elements, beam elements, membrane elements, spring, and damper elements and infinite elements, **Figure 3**.

Each finite element has a certain number of nodes, which determine the geometry and position of each individual element, **Figure 4**. The elements are interconnected via nodes and form a finite element mesh.

If we observe the displacement u in the element, we can see that, taking into account a generally designed and loaded model, it changes depending on the coordinates. This scenario is unknown in advance and is given in the form [24]:

$$\{u\} = \begin{Bmatrix} \mathbf{u} \\ \mathbf{v} \\ \mathbf{w} \end{Bmatrix} = \begin{Bmatrix} \mathbf{f(x, y, z)} \\ \mathbf{g(x, y, z)} \\ \mathbf{h(x, y, z)} \end{Bmatrix} \tag{1}$$

For any chosen finite element, Eq. (1) can be written in the matrix form [24]:

$$\{\mathbf{u}\} = [\mathbf{a}]\{\mathbf{c}\} \tag{2}$$

where $\{\mathbf{u}\}$ is the displacement vector in the element, $[\mathbf{a}]$ the matrix, $\{\mathbf{c}\}$ is the vector of constants.

The basic equation of the finite element specifies a link between the node forces, respectively, the vector of external loads {F} and nodal displacements {U} and is given as follows [24]:

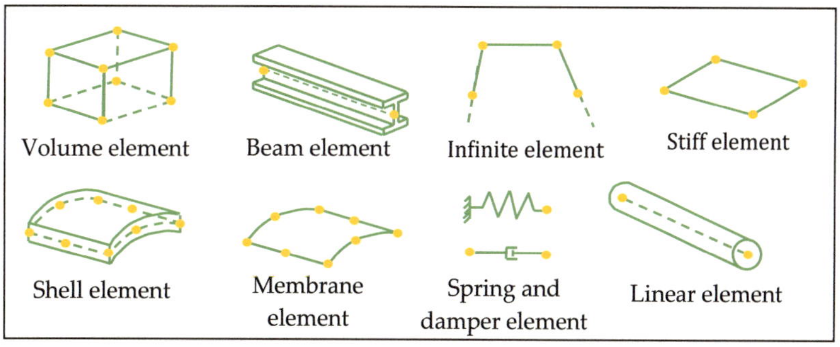

Figure 3. Types of finite elements [23].

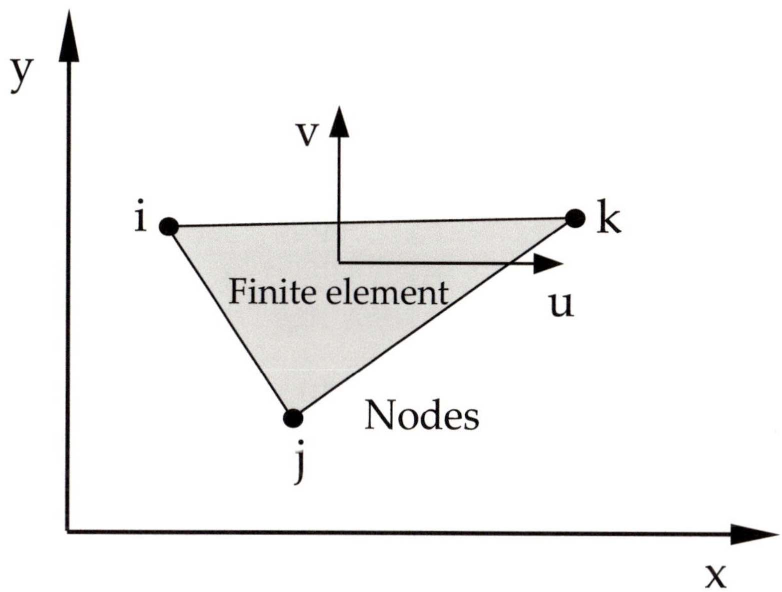

Figure 4. General description of the element.

$$\{\mathbf{F}\} = [\mathbf{K}]\{\mathbf{U}\} + \{\mathbf{F}^{\mathrm{T}}\} \tag{3}$$

where [**K**] is the stiffness matrix of the finite element, which depends on the shape functions of the used elements and on rheological parameters (Young's modulus, shear modulus, Poisson's number), and $\{\mathbf{F}^{\mathrm{T}}\}$ is the load vector, which takes into account the temperature of the load.

If the temperature by observing the construction load is neglected, the basic equation for the finite element is given as [24]:

$$\{\mathbf{F}\} = [\mathbf{K}]\{\mathbf{U}\} \tag{4}$$

The finite elements of a certain space occupy their local coordinate system, and therefore they must be transformed into a so-called common global coordinate system. This transformation of the equations of individual elements from the local coordinate system (x, y, z) in the global system (X, Y, Z) is effected by transformation matrices. The equation, which defines the rule of the transformation of the equation of a finite element from the local to the global coordinate system, is given in the following form [24]:

$$\{\overline{F}\} = [\overline{\mathbf{K}}]\{\overline{\mathbf{U}}\} \tag{5}$$

where $\{\overline{F}\}$ is the nodal forces given in the global coordinate system, $\{\overline{U}\}$ is the nodal displacements given in the global coordinate system.

The system, which is discretized into finite elements, has *e* elements and *n* nodes, **Figure 5**. The equation of the system is obtained by aggregating all the equation of the expression Eq. (5) for all the elements *e* in the total equation, symbolically given as [24]:

$$\mathbf{F} = \mathbf{K} \cdot \mathbf{U} \tag{6}$$

Aggregation takes place in a way to combine all the elements of the matrices belonging to the common node.

Vectors of nodal forces **F** and nodal displacements **U** are further written in the following form [24]:

$$F = \begin{matrix} \{\overline{\mathbf{F}}_1\} \\ \{\overline{\mathbf{F}}_2\} \\ \{\overline{\mathbf{F}}_3\} \\ \vdots \\ \{\overline{\mathbf{F}}_n\} \end{matrix}, \; U = \begin{matrix} \{\overline{U}_1\} \\ \{\overline{U}_2\} \\ \{\overline{U}_3\} \\ \vdots \\ \{\overline{U}_n\} \end{matrix} \tag{7}$$

where the submatrices $\{\overline{F}_i\}$ and $\{\overline{U}_i\}$ have such number of components as the degrees of freedom of a certain node.

K is the stiffness matrix consisting of n × n submatrices $\lfloor \overline{K}_{rs} \rfloor$ and is determined based on the stiffness matrix of individual elements, when they are divided into submatrices that belong to

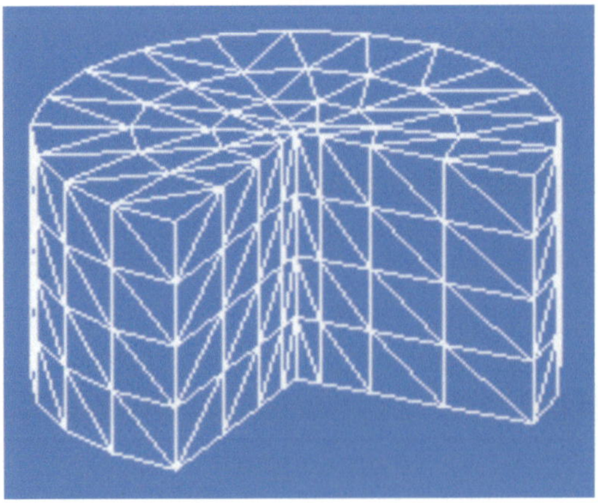

Figure 5. Discretization of the geometrical model.

each node. Thus, for example, the structural equation for a linear element, which always has two nodes, is given in the form [24]:

$$\begin{Bmatrix} \{\overline{\mathbf{F}}_i\} \\ \{\overline{\mathbf{F}}_j\} \end{Bmatrix} = \begin{bmatrix} [\overline{\mathbf{K}}_{ii}] & [\overline{\mathbf{K}}_{ij}] \\ [\overline{\mathbf{K}}_{ji}] & [\overline{\mathbf{K}}_{jj}] \end{bmatrix} \begin{Bmatrix} \overline{\mathbf{U}}_i \\ \overline{\mathbf{U}}_j \end{Bmatrix} \tag{8}$$

Each structure must be stable supported. Therefore, a part of the nodal displacements and rotations is known. They represent boundary conditions. In the finite-element method, the forces, which act on a structure, are always given in the global coordinate system and are introduced into the equation of the structure through the elements' nodes [24]. Numerical analysis represents the way of solving of equilibrium equations, or so-called structure equation [25]. Numerical analysis becomes very complex when it comes to solving nonlinear problems, because in solving equilibrium equations we have to take into account also the change in the geometry of the body in order to obtain the correct solution. Nonlinear models can only contain a few or an extremely large number of variables. Thus, instead of one solution, which is obtained from the linear problems, nonlinear problems are solved iteratively, since during computing the stiffness matrix and the shape of the deformation of the body are changing. The most frequently used iterative method for finding the roots in multidimensional spaces is a *Newton-Raphson method*. The convergence of this method is very effective for well-selected initial values.

2.3. Hybrid models

Hybrid models combine geometrically based and physically based techniques. In this method, the rough shape of the textile form is computed based on the geometrical model and physically based methods are then employed to refine the final shape of the textile form, which is computationally efficient [1].

The work by Rudomin [26] proposes to shorten the computation time needed in traditional physical techniques by using the geometrical approximation as a starting condition. Kunii and Gotoda [27] proposed a hybrid method for simulation of the fabric wrinkling. The fabric physical model in this method consists of spring connecting points, metric energy, and curvature energy. During the fabric simulation, the shape of the fabric was obtained by using a gradient descent method to find the energy minima. After that, singularity theory was used to characterize the resulting wrinkles. In the next approach proposed by Taillefer [2, 28], the hanging fabric's folds between two hanging points were characterized horizontal and vertical. The horizontal folds were modeled by using catenaries, whilst vertical fold were modeled by using the relaxation process, similar as suggested in the work by Wail [4]. In addition, also other hybrid models for simulation of fabric folds were proposed in works described in Ref. [2].

3. Textile forms' computer simulation

3.1. Case study 1: computer simulation of fabric and fused panel drape by using FEM

A number of modeling and simulation techniques have been used for representation of textile woven and knitted fabrics. Each of them has certain advantages, but also restrictions and limitations. Although finite element method is mainly applicable in mechanical, civil, and electrical engineering, it has been successfully used also in textile engineering for modeling of textile fabrics and complex multilayered textile forms.

3.1.1. Modeling of fabric and fused panel

Finite element method was used for modeling and simulating of a fabric and fused panel drape [29]. When modeling textile fabrics, we proceeded from the assumption that the fabric is a continuum with homogeneous orthotropic properties. Its structure is defined by the following rheological parameters: the modulus of elasticity in the warp and weft direction, the shear modulus in the warp and weft direction and the Poisson's number. The model of a fused panel is based on theoretical principles of laminate materials [30]. The fused panel is treated as a two-layer laminate; one lamina was the fabric and the other lamina was the fusible interlining. Fabrics and adhesive interlinings are characterized by local inhomogeneities and anisotropic properties. Therefore, we set up the assumption that interlining is a continuum with average homogeneous and orthotropic properties. Its structural features are described with the same rheological parameters as in the case of fabric.

Simulations of the fabric and fused panels drapes were carried out according to a measuring process using KES methodology for fabric and fused panel. The joint, which connects the fabric and the adhesive interlining, is formed by using the thermoplastic material, and thus forming a matrix of connections of the fused panel. The resulting joint typically is not uniform over the entire surface due to the thermoplastic layer in the form of points [31]. However, we have assumed that the joint was uniformly distributed across the entire surface of the model of the fused panel.

3.1.2. Geometrical model for simulation and numerical analysis of fabric and fused panel drape

The geometric model for numerical analysis related to draping of a fabrics and laminate was designed in the shape and size of the testing specimen using the measuring device Cusik Drape Tester. The test specimen with a diameter of 300 mm is centrally placed on a horizontal table/pedestal having a diameter of 180 mm. Thus, 60 mm of a specimen falls freely over the edge of a horizontal base due to its own weight. As a result, the folds in textile specimen are formed.

The geometric model is discretized with 240 finite elements. For this purpose, we have used thin 3D shell elements, type S9R5 [23], **Figure 6**. The part of the sample, which falls freely over the edge of the pedestal, is described by 120 shell elements. The remaining 120 shell elements describe the specimen positioned on the base. The pedestal for testing of the specimen is also modeled at the very edge of the base (for modeling the tangential rotational degree of freedom), **Figure 6**.

The specimen model was observed under the load of its own weight. Newton-Raphson's iterative method was used for solving the equations of a designed model.

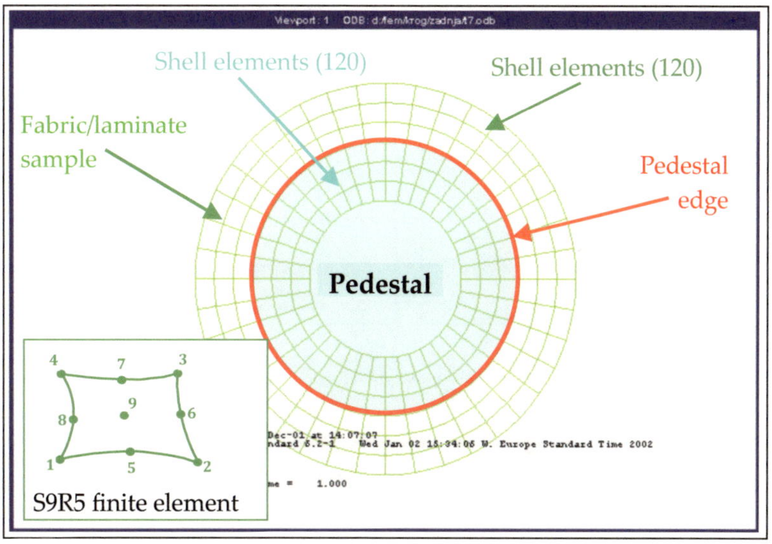

Figure 6. Discretized model for testing the draping of a fabric and fused panel.

3.1.3. Results and discussion of modeling and numerical simulations of fabric and fused panel drapes

Figure 7 represents the model for performing simulations of fabric and fused panel draping. The following parameters were analyzed: maximum and minimum amplitude of folds, maximum and minimum deflection, and the depth and number of folds.

The results of draping tests using a measuring device Cusik Drape Tester (five tests) and numerical simulations of a fabric (F-1), are shown in **Figure 8**. The results of draping tests for two fused panels consisting of the same fabric and two different fusible interlinings (F-1_L1 and F-1_L2) are shown in **Figures 9** and **10**.

The numerical analysis of draping of fabrics and fused panels was aimed at studying the impact of material properties of woven fabric and fused panel, as components of garments clothing, on their real behavior. Related approaches for modeling of material properties have been used in order to assure the comparability of all analyses. Here, the specimens were exposed to the gravitational force, which caused relatively large displacements.

Numerical computation of a problem related to draping of fabrics and fused panels was carried out using static analysis. Static analysis is more favorable than dynamic analysis in terms of computation time, while there were no significant differences between the obtained draping results.

The results of the experimentally obtained forms of draping of woven fabrics show the similarity when comparing with the draping results using numerical simulation with ABAQUS software, **Figure 8**. The figures indicate that the form of the draped fabric in experimental testing is never exactly the same (five tests). Therefore, it is also unrealistic to expect that the form of computer-simulated draped fabrics would be identical as in the real

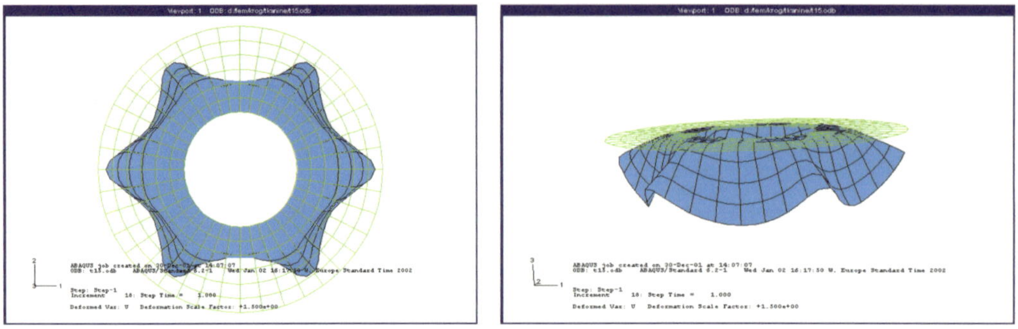

Figure 7. Model for simulation of a woven fabric and fused panel.

experiment. The form of a simulated fabric is symmetric due to the fact that the fabric is observed as an orthotropic material, **Figure 8a**. This cannot be expected by experimentally obtained forms of draped fabrics. Asymmetry in folds of tested fabrics is due to locally inhomogeneous structure of woven fabrics. The results of fabric draping show a good correlation between the experimental and calculated numerical values regarding the maximum and minimum deflection of folds, **Figure 8**.

The results of experimental testing and numerical simulation of draping of fused panels (F-1_L-1 and F-1_L-2) show particularly good match for the number and depth of folds, and the maximum amplitude, **Figures 9** and **10**. Comparison between the experimental and numerical results of draping of fused panels showed that the behavior of the simulated fused panels was more rigid (smaller number of folds, lower maximum and minimum deflection and maximum and minimum amplitudes, greater depth of folds), **Figures 9** and **10**. From detailed analysis, it was stated that the cause of such behavior lies in the approach of modeling the joint between the fabric and fused interlining. From the studies of bending it is apparent [32], that, if we have *n*-laminae, between which there is no connection, their bending stiffness is significantly lower than in the case, if we have *n*-laminae, fused by joints. The problem can be illustrated using a rectangular beam. Deflection of a beam *f* is inversely proportional to the moment of inertia of a cross-section of the beam. In the case of a rectangular beam, composed of *n*-laminae, the proportionality can be expressed in the following form:

$$f \infty \left(\frac{1}{n^{\infty}}\right) \tag{9}$$

where n is the number of laminae, α is the joint quality parameter, limited as follows: $1 \leq \alpha \leq 3$.

In case α equals 1, the laminae are not joined. If α equals 3, laminae are joined. The values of α are closer to 1 in fused panels with pointed deposit of glue. In fusible interlinings having a thermoplastic material applied in paste form, α is closer to 3. This was taken into account when modeling the joints of fused panels corresponding to the difference, which occurred in the observation and comparison of experimental and numerical results.

It can be concluded that draping represents a spatial problem. Therefore, for realistic modeling of draping of fused panels, it is necessary to carry out preliminary modeling of the joints with

http://dx.doi.org/10.5772/67738

Experimental draping test

Fabric code: F-1

Measured / calculated parameters

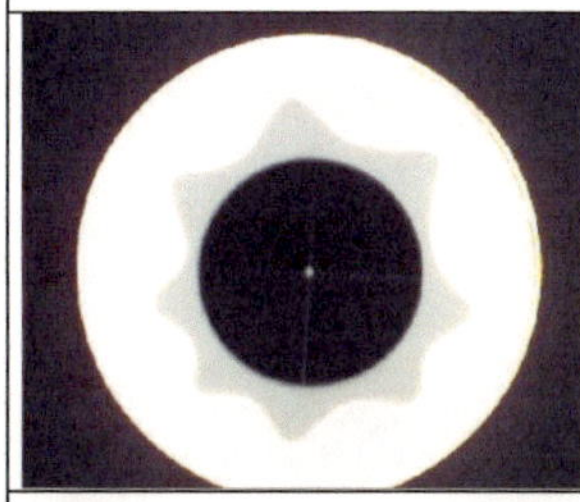

Measurement No.	1
Number of folds	8
Max. deflection / mm	59,24
Min . deflection / mm	36,13
Fold depth /mm	38,40
Max. amplitude / mm	137,9
Min. amplitude / mm	99,5

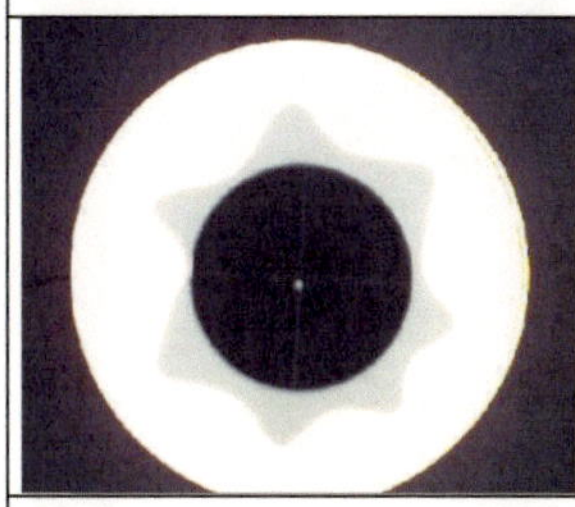

Measurement No.	2
Number of folds	7
Max. deflection / mm	59,85
Min . deflection / mm	35,73
Fold depth /mm	44,00
Max. amplitude / mm	138,2
Min. amplitude / mm	94,2

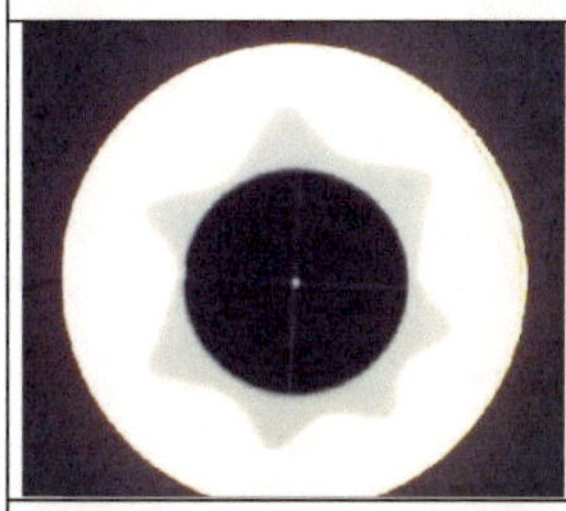

Measurement No.	3
Number of folds	7
Max. deflection / mm	59,70
Min . deflection / mm	33,90
Fold depth /mm	43,60
Max. amplitude / mm	139,5
Min. amplitude / mm	95,9

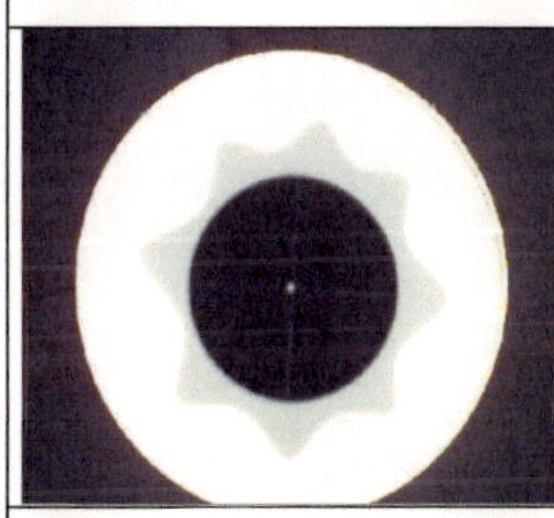

Measurement No.	4
Number of folds	8
Max. deflection / mm	59,70
Min . deflection / mm	37,79
Fold depth /mm	40,70
Max. amplitude / mm	136,6
Min. amplitude / mm	95,9

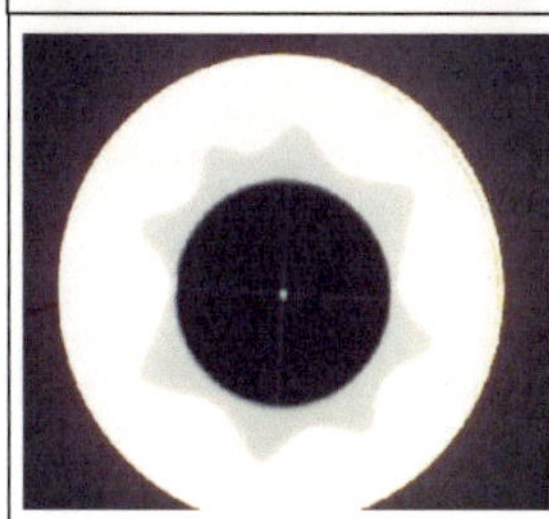

Measurement No.	5
Number of folds	8
Max. deflection / mm	59,70
Min . deflection / mm	38,04
Fold depth /mm	40,50
Max. amplitude / mm	136,4
Min. amplitude / mm	95,9

Draping simulation

Different views

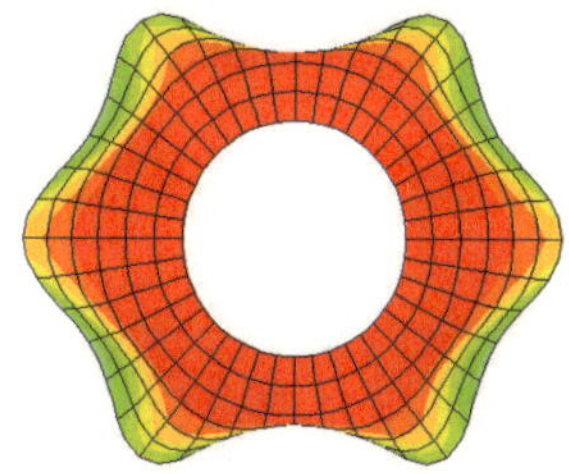

a

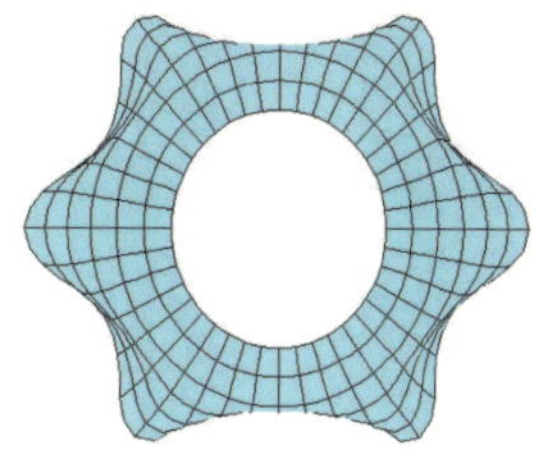

b

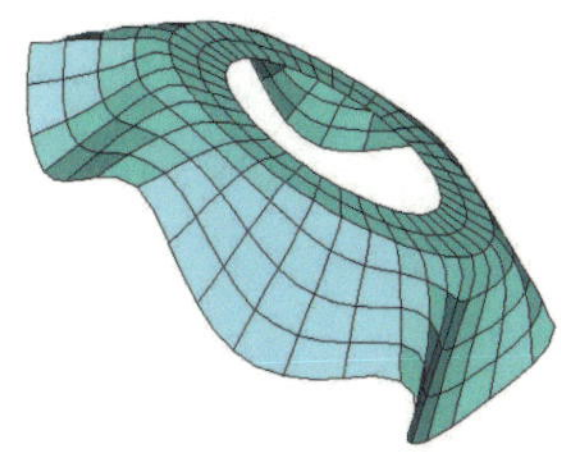

c

d

Calculated parameters

	Exper.	Simul.	Diff. (%)
Number of folds	7,6	6	1,6
Max. deflection / mm	59,64	59,7	0,06
Min . deflection / mm	36,32	36,4	0,08
Fold depth /mm	41,44	36,32	5,12
Max. amplitude / mm	137,72	149,25	11,53
Min. amplitude / mm	96,28	112,93	16,65

Figure 8. Results of experimental testing and numerical simulations of a fabric F-1.

Experimental draping test			Draping simulation
Fabric code: F-1_L-1	**Measured / calculated parameters**		**Different views**

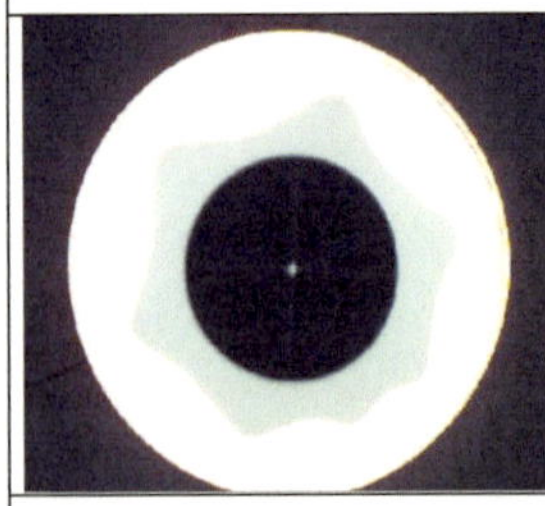

Measurement No.	1
Number of folds	7
Max. deflection / mm	56,31
Min . deflection / mm	27,93
Fold depth /mm	32,40
Max. amplitude / mm	143,1
Min. amplitude / mm	110,7

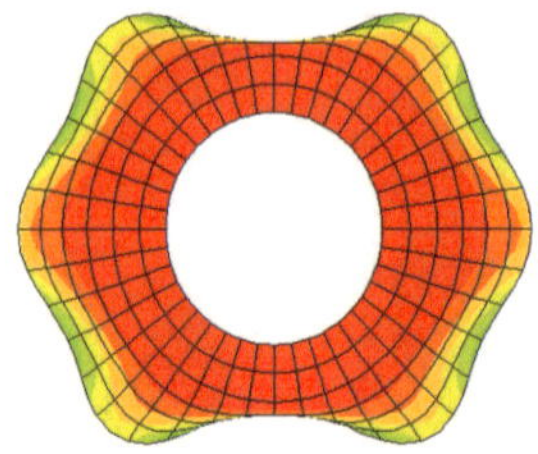

a

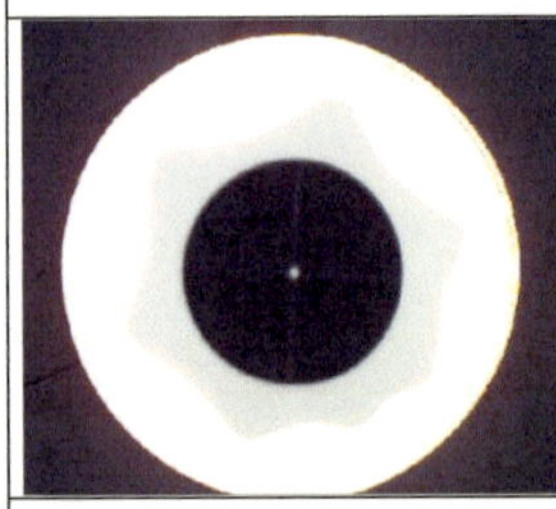

Measurement No.	2
Number of folds	7
Max. deflection / mm	56,60
Min . deflection / mm	29,40
Fold depth /mm	32,40
Max. amplitude / mm	142,3
Min. amplitude / mm	109,9

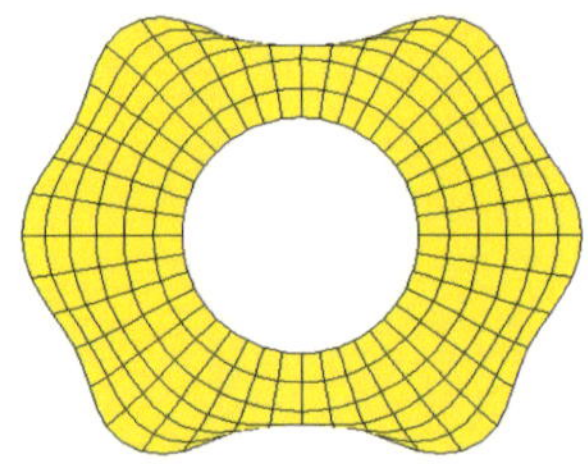

b

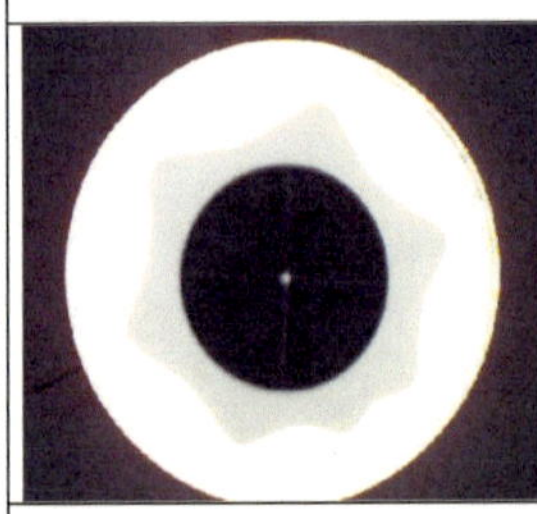

Measurement No.	3
Number of folds	7
Max. deflection / mm	57,76
Min . deflection / mm	28,86
Fold depth /mm	34,70
Max. amplitude / mm	142,6
Min. amplitude / mm	107,9

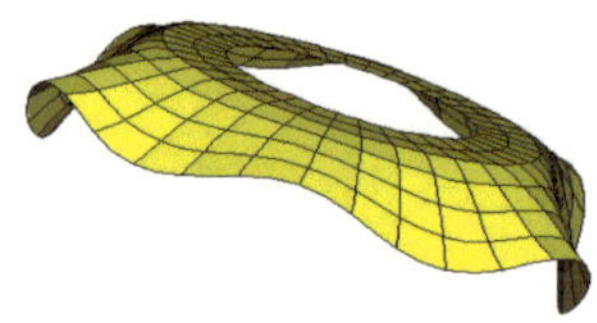

c

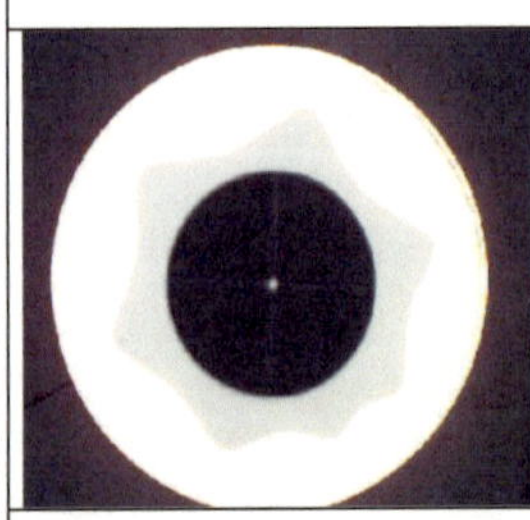

Measurement No.	4
Number of folds	7
Max. deflection / mm	57,45
Min . deflection / mm	29,22
Fold depth /mm	35,10
Max. amplitude / mm	142,4
Min. amplitude / mm	107,3

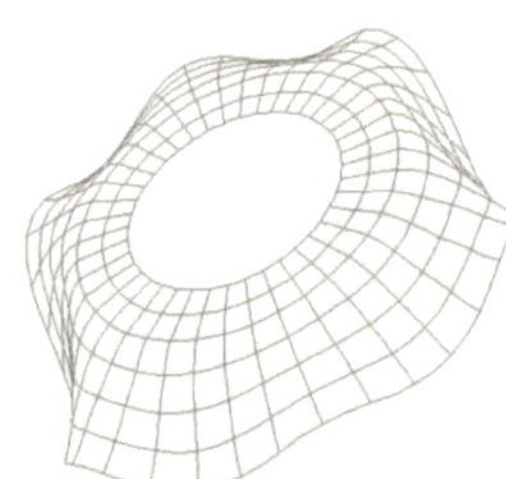

d

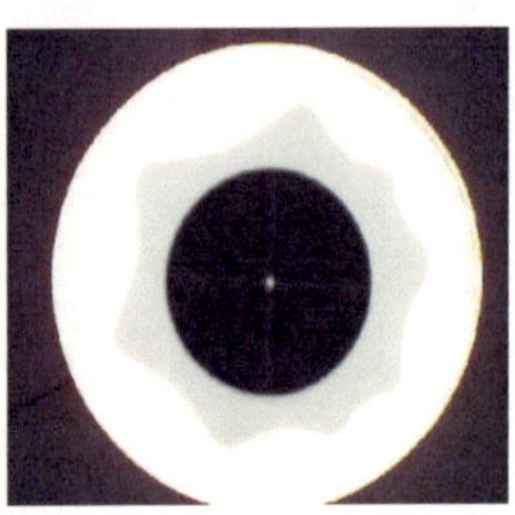

Measurement No.	5
Number of folds	8
Max. deflection / mm	56,77
Min . deflection / mm	31,60
Fold depth /mm	30,60
Max. amplitude / mm	141,0
Min. amplitude / mm	109,4

Calculated parameters

	Exper.	Simul.	Diff. (%)
Number of folds	7,2	6	16,67
Max. deflection / mm	56,98	45,33	20,45
Min . deflection / mm	29,40	23,63	19,63
Fold depth /mm	33,04	37,40	13,20
Max. amplitude / mm	142,28	139,5	1,95
Min. amplitude /	109,04	102,1	6,36

Figure 9. Results of experimental testing and numerical simulations of a fused panel F-1_L-1.

Experimental draping test | **Draping simulation**

Fabric code: F-1_L-2 | **Measured / calculated parameters** | **Different views**

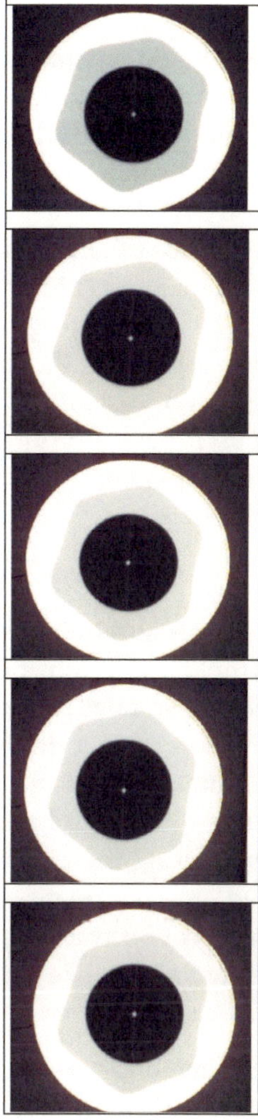

Measured / calculated parameters	
Measurement No.	1
Number of folds	6
Max. deflection / mm	51,72
Min . deflection / mm	26,15
Fold depth /mm	23,60
Max. amplitude / mm	144,0
Min. amplitude / mm	120,4
Measurement No.	2
Number of folds	6
Max. deflection / mm	51,60
Min . deflection / mm	27,55
Fold depth /mm	23,22
Max. amplitude / mm	143,3
Min. amplitude / mm	120,1
Measurement No.	3
Number of folds	6
Max. deflection / mm	51,90
Min . deflection / mm	26,96
Fold depth /mm	23,50
Max. amplitude / mm	143,6
Min. amplitude / mm	120,1
Measurement No.	4
Number of folds	6
Max. deflection / mm	52,01
Min . deflection / mm	26,76
Fold depth /mm	23,80
Max. amplitude / mm	143,7
Min. amplitude / mm	119,9
Measurement No.	5
Number of folds	5
Max. deflection / mm	51,78
Min . deflection / mm	26,76
Fold depth /mm	19,50
Max. amplitude / mm	143,7
Min. amplitude / mm	124,2

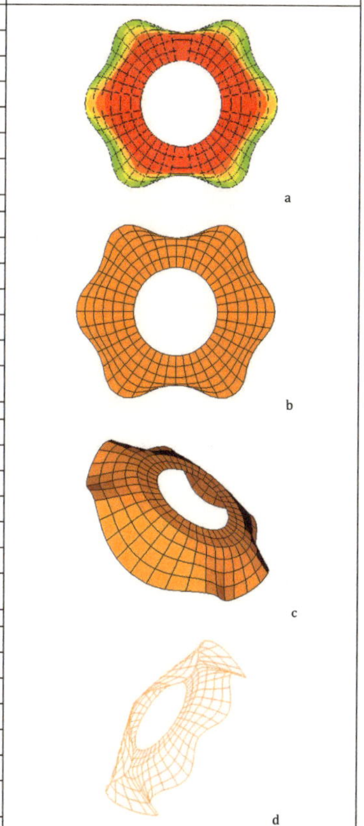

Calculated parameters	Exper.	Simul.	Diff. (%)
Number of folds	5,8	6	3,45
Max. deflection / mm	51,8	48,82	5,75
Min . deflection / mm	26,74	22,94	14,21
Fold depth /mm	22,72	24,3	6,95
Max. amplitude / mm	143,66	140,1	2,48
Min. amplitude / mm	120,94	115,8	4,25

Figure 10. Results of experimental testing and numerical simulations of a fused panel F-1_L-2.

respect to the function of friction. In our case, the friction depends on the normal force in the joint, as well as on relative displacement between the two layers. From experimental studies [31], it can be concluded that the rheological model functionally depends on the deformation state.

3.2. Case study 2: computer simulation of functional clothes for wheelchair users

3D scanning and computer simulation techniques were studied for development of individualized functional garments for wheelchair users from perspective of ergonomic comfort in a sitting posture, functional, and aesthetic requirements and needs regarding their health protection.

Some recent studies have shown that clothes for disabled users should not only be based on various design, fashion and comfort concepts, but should also consider particular medical problems [33–37]. The interviewing conducted in Slovenia among 58 adult respondents revealed that paraplegic wheelchair users are faced also with accompanying health problems because of their primary disease [35]. They are mostly faced with incontinence (66.7%), infection and inflammation of the urinary tract (50.0%), frequent colds (33.0%), while some of them also have pressure sores (14.6%), skin irritations and inflammations (12.5%). The hand pains (50.0%) and leg cramps (41.7%) are common health problems of paraplegics. It is well known that they are faced also with limited mobility of hands, atrophy of the leg muscles, poor blood circulation, and regulation of body temperature of lower extremities [34, 38, 39]. With the respect to the above facts, the paraplegic wheelchair users have difficulties in wearing regular garments due to their insufficient functionality and protection.

3.2.1. 3D scanning

Producers of 3D human body scanners usually offer software for visualization of the scanned (standing) 3D body model and automatic extraction of the anthropometrical dimensions based on standard ISO 8559 [43]. However, this software cannot represent scanned sitting body and extract anthropometrical body dimensions automatically. The research on a sitting posture's 3D body model, obtained by scanning with Vitus Smart XXL human body scanner and two general-purpose optical scanners (GOM Atos II 400 and the Artec™ Eva 3D hand scanner), showed that more appropriate digitized mesh can be achieved using the general purpose optical scanners [34, 40, 41], **Figure 11**. Digitizing was carried out on a rotation chair. The accurate sitting 3D body models were achieved after modeling and reconstruction procedures that are deeply described in a source [34]. In this research, the fully mobile persons were involved to avoid unnecessary burdening of paraplegics at this stage of the research.

The experiences gained from this study enabled us to include the immobile persons within the research. With respect to the poor body balance due to spine injury and modeling/reconstruction procedure of the scanned 3D body models, there was a need to develop a special chair for scanning, adjustable to the individuals' body dimensions, **Figure 12(a)**. Scanning of the paraplegic wheelchair users was performed by using the optical hand scanner Artec Eva 3D. The 3D body models were achieved after modeling and reconstruction procedures described in a source [34]. In addition, a comparative analysis of the scanned 3D bodies' virtual measurements and manual measurements was performed for fully mobile and immobile persons to find if the poor body balance of the immobile persons affects the accuracy of the 3D body models. During manual measurements, using a measuring tape, locations of the body dimensions, anthropometrical landmarks and standard procedure for the human body measuring were taken into account according to the standard ISO 8559 [42]. All dimensions of the limbs were measured on the left limbs. The virtual measurements of the scanned 3D body models were performed at the same locations as described for the manual measurements using the measuring tools of the OptiTex 3D system, **Figure 12(c)**. The statistical analysis of the virtual

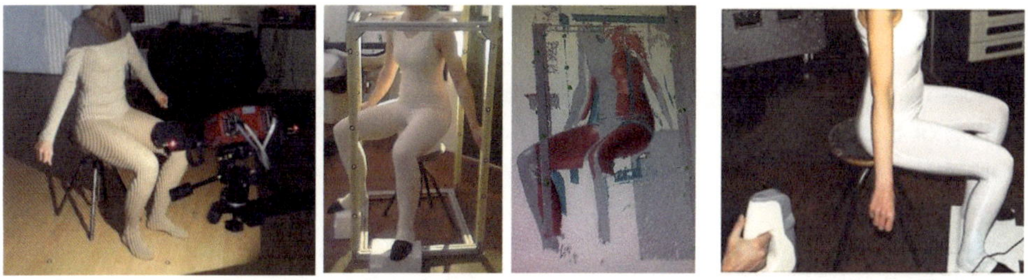

(a) GOM ATOS II 400 optical scanner (b) Artec Eva 3D hand scanner

Figure 11. Scanning of fully mobile persons in a sitting posture.

	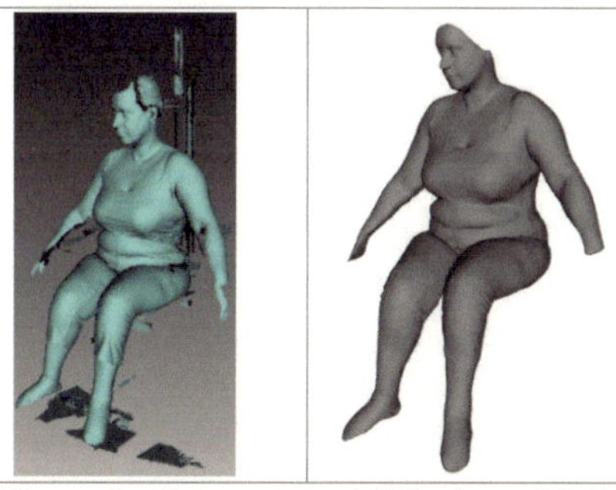	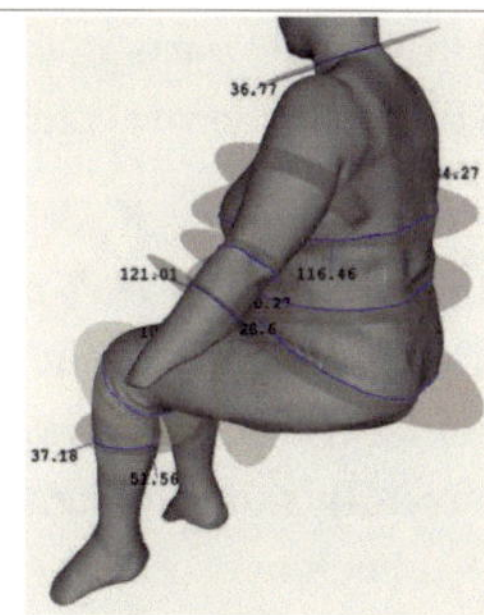
(a) Chair for scanning of IMP	(b) Scanned and reconstructed 3D body model of IMP	(c) Virtual measuring of 3D body dimensions

Figure 12. Scanning of the IMP by using a scanning chair and optical hand scanner Artec Eva 3D, and virtual measuring of the 3D body dimension [36].

and manual measurements indicated that the mobility of a person does not affect the accuracy of the virtual measurements and sitting posture 3D body models, respectively [36].

3.2.2. Development of functional garments for wheelchair user by using the computer simulation

In this part of the research, study regarding the virtual prototyping of functional garments was carried out on a sitting 3D body models by using the Optitex 3D program. Construction of the garments' pattern designs was based on the virtually measured 3D body models' dimensions.

In the study regarding the pants and blouse pattern designs for a sitting posture a reconstruction procedure of the basic patterns was performed in order to obtain well-fitted garments, which also meet demands of the wheelchair users due to additional health problems (pressure sores, obstruction of the blood flow, inflammation of the urinary tract, etc.) and aesthetic appearance [34]. In this research, a comparison between the real garments and virtual prototypes showed that development of functional garments for a sitting posture is extremely suitable when using scanned 3D body models and computer simulation techniques. In addition, experiments have proven a synergistic effect of the computer simulation techniques during the development process of the ergonomic garments and their great potential for use and radical changes in the production of custom-made garments for wheelchair users [36].

The 3D scanning and computer simulation approach was studied for design of functional garments for health protection of the wheelchair users [35, 37]. It was based on 58 in-depth interviews conducted with adult wheelchair users at the national level, as described at the beginning of this chapter. The study focused on development of functional pants, adapted to individuals who suffered from pressure sores, incontinence or sweating in the crotch area, between the thighs and under the buttocks. On the other hand, we concentrated on development of special protective garments, such as sitting bag and cape, in terms of human protection from external influences, i.e., cold, wind, humidity, which could cause to immobile persons problems with the temperature of lower extremities, the chronic urinary infections and frequent colds. The chronical moistening of the skin was found to be a major problem for potential skin irritations and inflammations or even wounds due to the incontinence or sweating. Therefore, by using the antimicrobial and antioxidative textile materials (AATM) [43] in specific parts in the pants (crotch area, between the thighs, contacts of the body with a wheelchair), the prevention against potential health problems can be achieved.

The development of well-fitted functional pants on the scanned 3D body model enabled us: (a) to simulate person's morphological shape and extract main features of the body shape and (b) to simulate and validate pants pattern design with integrated AATM in exact parts of the pants on the 3D human body, **Figure 13(a)**. The pants will act as a protection regarding the chronically skin moistening. In addition, the functional pants pattern design was developed for a wheelchair user with a pressure sore on the hips. The AATM was integrated in the exact part of the pants with help of 3D scanning of this person due to exact location of the wound and virtual simulation and validation of the pants pattern design on this 3D body model, **Figure 13(b)**. The pants will act in a curative manner regarding the pressure sore on hips. This study showed new steps toward the efficient approach to responsible development of functional garments not only for wheelchair users, but also for elderly and persons who are forced to a sitting posture during the day, and could not find appropriate clothes in regular stores. In addition, 3D scanning of the immobile persons with incontinence pads, diapers, or briefs is also challenging for development of well-fitting pants pattern designs for individuals by using the 3D virtual prototyping.

The garment's protective function can be achieved with the body heat balance in order to ensure the thermal comfort and physiological sense of safety. This can be obtained by appropriate textile materials properties, clothing design, and the design of the complete clothing system and its components. Virtual prototyping approach was used to develop the sitting bag and the cape pattern designs [35]. The development of the sitting bag was performed on scanned 3D body models of the wheelchair users, whilst for the cape on the scanned 3D body model with a wheelchair. The garments fitting was carried out due to measured mechanical properties of the used fabrics, which enabled us to develop correct form of the pattern pieces. The sitting bag was designed according to the trends of newer forms of the wheelchairs, which have narrower leg supports. Requests of interviewees related to the length of the sitting bag were also considered. Therefore, it covers only the lower extremities. The respondents' request that the cape should cover the backrest and wheels of a wheelchair has been also taken into account in the cape's design. The developed virtual prototypes of the special protective clothing are shown in **Figure 14**. In this figure, we can see that for development of the cape it was used the complex 3D model. The deformation of the cape occurred in location of the wheelchair handles and error in the fabric's collision with a sharp part of the 3D object, **Figure 14(a)**. We could not avoid it even at higher simulation resolutions. During simulations of the sitting bag, using the gravity of 0 ms^{-2} enabled us to develop a pattern design of suchlike dimensions that fits different body shapes, **Figure 14(b)**.

The study presented in this part of the chapter showed high usability, efficiency and benefits of 3D scanning, and virtual simulation techniques in the development process of custom-made functional garments and ready-made protective garments for wheelchair users. On the other hand, we are still facing with robustness at positioning of the 2D pattern pieces

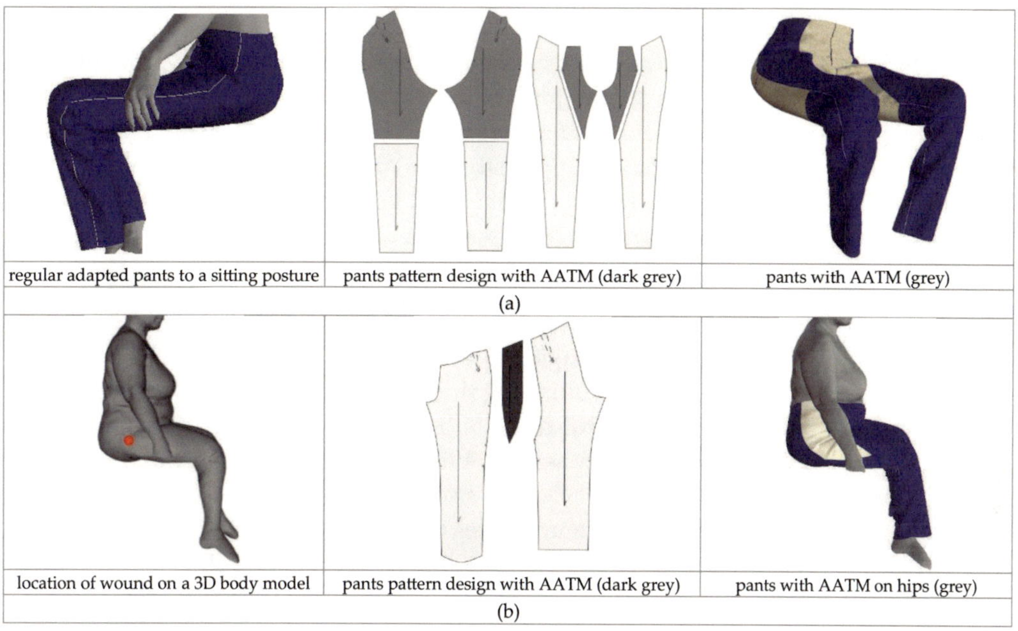

Figure 13. Development of functional pants pattern designs by using 3D scanning and virtual simulation techniques [37].

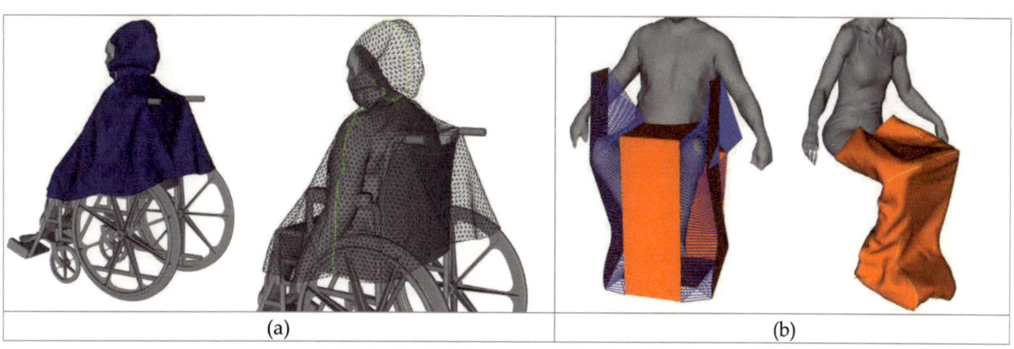

Figure 14. Virtual prototypes of special protective clothing for paraplegic wheelchair users [35].

around the sitting 3D body model due to limited possibilities of pattern pieces folding, which indicates the potential future challenge in the development of commercial 3D CAD programs for garments simulation on sitting body postures.

3.3. Case study 3: computer simulation of protective clothes for sport aircraft pilots

Since the protective equipment is necessary for different areas of human activity, it is essential to take an individual approach to the design of all protective elements (clothes, gloves, shoes, helmets, etc.). During the construction and design the protection and functionality of the protective clothes is of the utmost importance, where the designer and constructor have to have the necessary knowledge about the clothing elements, the usual body movements and additional elements of protection [44].

This study focuses on development of the special protective garment for sport aircraft pilots, or so-called anti-g suit. This is a special form of a flight suit, worn by sport aircraft pilots, who are exposed to high levels of acceleration forces. The pilot sits in a cramped airplane cabin in exact position. Therefore, we suppose that the suit should be developed according to body dimensions in this position. Namely, it is well-known that wearing comfort differs for variety of body shapes and dynamic body postures due to changes in body dimensions [45–48].

The present study is still at an early stage, therefore the importance of 3D body scanning and virtual simulation is shown through the development process of the suit pattern design. 3D body scanning was carried out using three scanning postures (SP), i.e., standard standing posture (SP1_StP), sitting posture (SP2_SiP) and driving-sitting posture (SP3_DSiP), **Figure 15**, by using the 3D human body scanner Vitus Smart XXL at the Textile Technology Faculty, University of Zagreb, Croatia. During scanning, especially for the SP3_DSiP, we were restricted by the volume of the scanning area (1 × 1 m). Therefore, we were not able to scan a person in every proper sitting posture. In addition, the scanned 3D mesh was highly deformed, particularly in areas of crotch, thighs, and calves. Therefore, the modeling and reconstruction of 3D body models was difficult and lengthy process. Based on the experience gained from the study, presented in Chapter 3.2, we can assume that it would be better to use in this research a general-purpose optical scanner, such as hand scanner Artec ™ Eva 3D.

In this study, 24 body dimensions were virtually measured according to the standard ISO 8559 [42] and three additional body dimensions that standard ISO 8559 does not specify (transverse hips girth in a sitting posture, front and back overall length in a standing/sitting posture) by using the software ScanWorks.

The cross sections of 3D body models at three measurement positions of body dimensions, i.e., chest girth, waist girth, and hips girth (sitting postures—transversal hips girth), are presented in **Figure 16**, as well as belonging dimensions in standard and dynamic body postures. In this figure, it can be seen that different cross sections and body dimensions were achieved for different body postures. The main reason for this are activated muscle groups in different body postures that should be considered when constructing the garment pattern

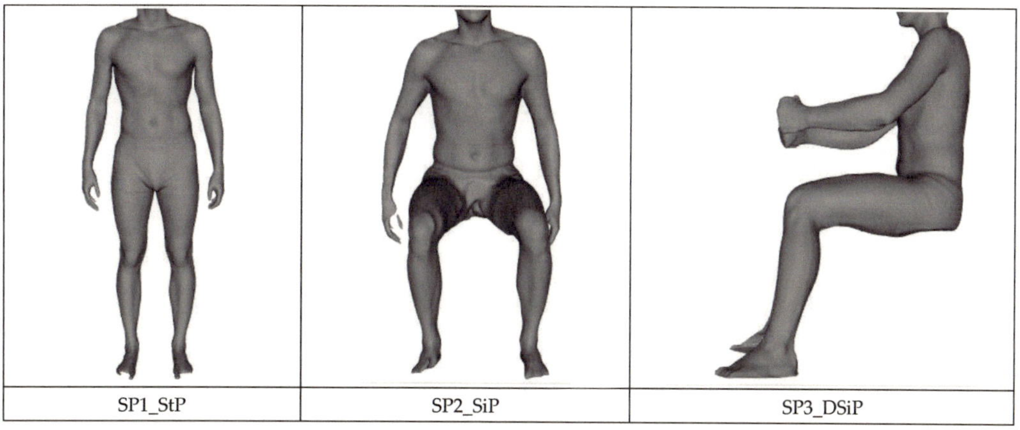

Figure 15. Scanned 3D body models in three different postures.

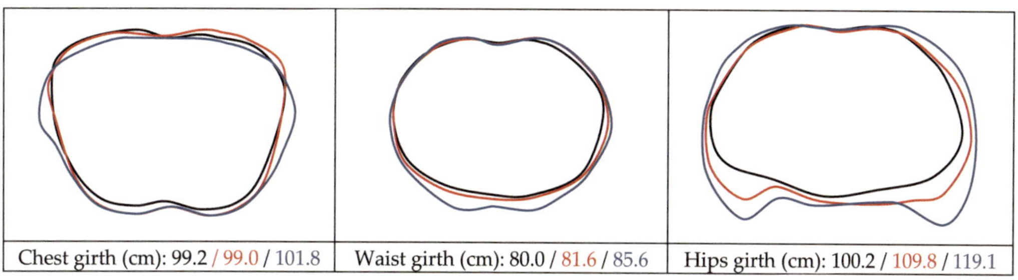

Figure 16. The cross-sections of the 3D body models and body dimensions.

design. The greatest chest, waist, and hips girths were obtained in a body posture SP3_DsiP. The greatest difference in hips girth was achieved between the standing and sitting body model in a driving posture, which was also expected. Therefore, construction of the basic suit pattern design was based on measured dimensions for a posture SP3_DsiP.

The virtual simulations of the suit for all body postures are shown in **Figure 17**. In this figure, a poor suit fit to the standing 3D body model can be seen, especially on the back and in the pants length. This result is understandable in terms of used body dimensions, measured in a sitting posture SP3_DSiP. For this posture, the greatest tension (red) was achieved in the area of armhole seams and over shoulders, which specifies that measure over shoulder should be increased. Even higher tension over shoulders can be seen on both sitting postures SP2_SiP and SP3_DSiP, which confirms the above indication. A more appropriate suit fit to the sitting 3D body model can be seen in a driving posture SP3_DSiP, with the exception of shoulders and hips positions, where the fit must be improved in continuation of the research. In our case, we need to construct the special protective suit, which requires very little freedom of movement.

Based on the above, we will, using the virtual prototyping, confirm the final pattern design of a suit, which will be upgraded with suitable elements into an anti-g suit.

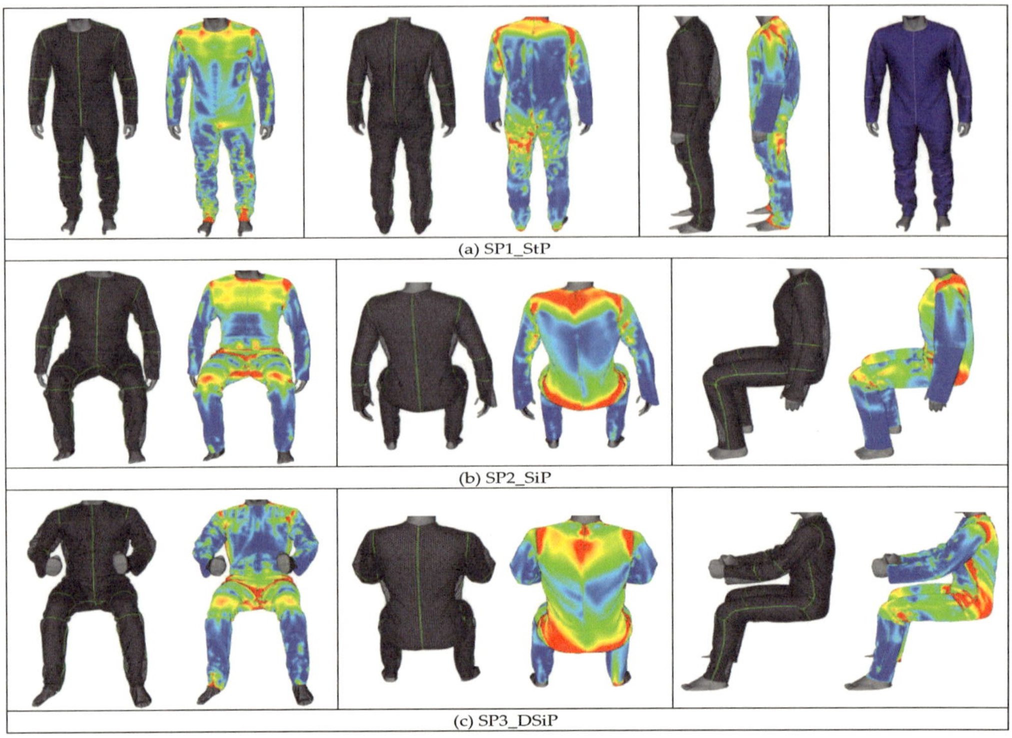

Figure 17. Virtual prototyping of the overall on 3D body model in different postures.

4. Conclusions and future challenges

Engineering approaches to textile forms' design for particular purposes, presented in this chapter, show benefits and limitations of 3D body scanning and computer simulation techniques and outline the future challenges.

The study regarding the fabric and laminate drape by using the FEM in Section 3.1 showed that draping represents a spatial problem. Therefore, for realistic modeling of draping of fused panels, it is necessary to carry out preliminary modeling of the joints with respect to the function of friction. In our case, friction depends on the normal force in the joint, as well as on relative displacement between the two layers. From experimental studies, it can be concluded that the rheological model functionally depends on the deformation state.

The case study in Section 3.2 indicated that 3D scanning and virtual simulation techniques are extremely accurate and appropriate in the development process of custom-made functional garments and ready-made protective clothing. However, there are still limitations in garments virtual simulations on the sitting 3D body models when using the commercial 3D CAD programs. A robust positioning of the 2D pattern pieces around the sitting 3D body model due to limited possibilities of pattern pieces folding and fabric's collision with a sharp parts of 3D objects, as in a case of a wheelchair's handle, is one of weaknesses. Therefore, future challenges in computer simulation techniques are certainly done in the development of commercial 3D CAD software for simulation of garments on a wide variety of nonstandard postures of 3D body models or 3D objects. One of the future challenges would certainly be to build a parametric sitting 3D body model, which would allow the development of garment patterns designs for a sitting population.

The present part of a case study in Section 3.3 showed that we are on the right way to develop the anti-g suit. We found out that in continuation of the study that there should be a general-purpose optical hand scanner, to digitize a person in proper sitting posture, which would enable the modeling of the accurate sitting 3D body model and the development of pattern design of this special protective clothing.

Author details

Andreja Rudolf[1]*, Slavica Bogović[2], Beti Rogina Car[2], Andrej Cupar[3], Zoran Stjepanovič[1] and Simona Jevšnik[4]

*Address all correspondence to: andreja.rudolf@um.si

1 Institute of Engineering Materials and Design, Faculty of Mechanical Engineering, University of Maribor, Maribor, Slovenia

2 Department of Clothing Technology, Faculty of Textile Technology, University of Zagreb, Zagreb, Croatia

3 Institute of Structures and Design, Faculty of Mechanical Engineering, University of Maribor, Maribor, Slovenia

4 Inlas, Slovenske Konjice, Slovenia

References

[1] Wong SK. Modeling and simulation techniques for garments. In: Hu J, editor. Computer Technology for Textiles and Apparel. 1st ed. Cambridge: Woodhead Publishing Ltd; 2011. pp. 173–200.

[2] Ng HN, Grimsdale RL. Computer graphics techniques for modeling cloth. IEEE Computer Graphics and Applications. 1996;**16**:28–41. DOI: 10.1109/38.536273

[3] Cloth Modeling and Simulation. In: Magnenat-Thalmann N, editor. Modeling and Simulating Bodies and Garments,1st ed. London: Springer-Verlag Ltd; 2010. pp. 71–138, DOI 10.1007/978-1-84996-263-6

[4] Weil J. The synthesis of cloth objects. ACM SIGGRAPH Computer Graphics. 1986;**20**:49–54. DOI: 10.1145/15886.15891

[5] Hinds BK, McCartney J. Interactive garment design. The Visual Computer. 1990;**6**:53–61. DOI:10.1007/BF01901066

[6] Ng HN, Grimsdale RL. GEOFF—A Geometrical, Editor for Fold Formation. In: Lecture Notes in Computer Science Vol. 1024: Image Analysis Applications and Computer Graphics, Chin R, Ip H, Naiman A, Pong TC, editors. Berlin: Springer-Verlag; 1995. pp. 124–131.

[7] Stumpp T, Spillmann J, Becker M, Teschner M. A Geometric Deformation Model for Stable Cloth Simulation. In: Faure F, Teschner M, editors. Proceedings of the Fifth Workshop on Virtual Reality Interactions and Physical Simulations, VRIPHYS 2008, Grenoble, France, 2008. Eurographics Association 2008, ISBN 978-3-905673-70-8 pp. 39–46

[8] Terzopoulos D, Platt J, Barr A, Fleischer K. Elastically deformable models. Computer Graphics (Proc. Siggraph '87). 1987;**21**:205–214. DOI: 10.1145/37401.37427

[9] Terzopoulos D, Fleischer K. Deformable models. In: Visual Computer. 1988;**4**:306–331. DOI: 10.1007/BF01908877

[10] Volino P, Magnenat–Thalmann N. Virtual clothing: Theory and Practice. 1st ed. Berlin: Springer-Verlag; 2000. DOI: 10.1007/978-3-642-57278-4.

[11] Breen DE, House DH, Wozny MJ. A particle-based model for simulating the draping behaviour of woven cloth. Textile Research Journal. 1994;**64**:663–685. DOI: 10.1177/004051759406401106

[12] Eberhardt B, Weber AG, Straßer W. A fast, flexible, particle-system model for cloth draping. IEEE Computer Graphics and Applications. 1996;**16**:52–59. DOI: 10.1109/38.536275

[13] Baraff D, Witkin A. Large steps in cloth simulation. In: Proceedings of SIGGRAPH 98, Computer Graphics Proceedings, Annual Conference Series: ACM, ACM Press/ACM SIGGRAPH. 1998. pp. 43–54.

[14] House DH, Breen DE, editors. Cloth Modeling and Animation. 1st ed. Massachusetts: AK Peters Natick; 2000. 360 p.

[15] Mozafary V, Payvandy P. Mass Spring parameters identification for knitted fabric simulation based on FAST testing and particle swarm optimization. Fibers and Polymers. 2016;**17**:1715–1725. DOI 10.1007/s12221-016-6567-8

[16] Provot X. Deformation constraints in a mass-spring model to describe rigid cloth behavior. In: Graphics Interface 95, May 17–19 1995; Quebec, Canada, 1995. pp. 147–154.

[17] Choi KJ, Ko HS. Stable but responsive cloth. ACM Transactions on Graphics (TOG) - Proceedings of ACM SIGGRAPH 2002. 2002;**21**:604–611. DOI: 10.1145/566654.566624

[18] Selle A, Su J, Irving G, Fedkiw R. Robust high-resolution cloth using paralelism, history-based collision, and accurate friction. IEEE Transactions on Visualization and Computer Graphics. 2009;**15**:339–350. DOI: 10.1109/TVCG.2008.79

[19] Hu J, Huang WQ, Yu KQ, Huang M, Li JB. Cloth simulation with a modified implicit method based on a simplified mass-spring model. Applied Mechanics and Materials. 2013;**373–375**:1920–1926. DOI: 10.4028/www.scientific.net/AMM.373-375.1920

[20] Eischen JW, Deng S, Clapp TG. Finite element modeling and control of flexible fabric parts. Computer graphics in textiles and apparel (IEEE Computer Graphics and Applications). IEEE Computer Society Press. 1996;**16**:71–80. DOI: 10.1109/38.536277

[21] Lin H, Clifford MJ, Long C, Lee K, Guo N. A finite element approach to the modelling of fabric mechanics and its application to virtual fabric design and testing. The Journal of the Textile Institute. 2012;**103**:1063–1076. DOI: 10.1080/00405000.2012.660755

[22] Chapra SC, Canale RP. Numerical Methods for Engineers. 2nd ed. New York: McGraw-Hill; 1988. 812 p.

[23] ABAQUS. Theory Manual. Version 6.2. Hibbitt, Karlsson & Sorensen, Inc. The United States, Plymouth, 2000.

[24] Prelog E. Finite Elements Method (in Slovene). University of Ljubljana, Faculty of Architecture, Ljubljana, 1975.

[25] ABAQUS. User Manual. Volume I, II, III, Version 6.2, Hibbitt, Karlsson & Sorensen, Inc. The United States, Plymouth, 2000.

[26] Rudomin IJ. Simulating cloth using a mixed geometry-physical method [doctoral thesis]. Department of Computer and Information Science, University of Pensilvania; 1990.

[27] Kunii TL, Gotoda H. Modeling and Animation of Garment Wrinkle Formation processes. In: Prof. Magnenat-Thalmann N, Thalmann D, editors. Computer Animation'90. Tokyo: Springer-Verlag; 1990. pp. 131–146. DOI: 10.1007/978-4-431-68296-7_10

[28] Taillefer F. Mixed modeling. In Compugraphics '91. 1991. pp. 467–478. http://www.worldcat.org/search?q=au%3ASanto%2C+Harold+P.&qt=hot_autho

[29] Jevšnik S. The analysis of drapability of shell fabric, interlining and fused panel as assembly parts of a garment [doctoral thesis]. Faculty of Mechanical Engineering, University of Maribor, Maribor; 2002.

[30] Hull D, Clyne TW, editors. An Introduction to Composite Materials. 1st ed. Cambridge: Cambridge University Press; 1981.

[31] Jevšnik S. The selection of fusible interlinings and a prediction of the properties of fused garment parts with knowledge system [master thesis]. Faculty of Mechanical Engineering, University of Maribor, Maribor, 1999.

[32] Beer FP, Johnston ER, Jr., editors. Mechanics of Material. 1st ed. New York: McGraw; 1981. 616p.

[33] Ng SF, Hui CL, Wong LF. Development of medical garments and apparel for the elderly and the disabled. Textile Progress. 2011;**43**:235–285. DOI: 10.1080/00405167.2011.573240

[34] Rudolf A, Cupar A, Kozar T, Stjepanovič Z. Study regarding the virtual prototyping of garments for paraplegics. Fibers and Polymers. 2015;**16**:1177–1192. DOI: 10.1007/s12221-015-1177-4

[35] Rudolf A, Drstvenšek I, Šauperl O, Brajlih T, Strnad M, Ermenc H. Research and development of functional garments for paraplegics: Final report on the performed project activities (in Slovene), Slovenian Ministry of Education, Science and Sport, University of Maribor, Faculty of Mechanical Engineering, 2015.

[36] Rudolf A, Görlichová L, Kirbiš J, Repnik J, Salobir A, Selimović I, Drstvenšek I. New technologies in the development of ergonomic garments for wheelchair users in a virtual environment. Industria Textila, 2017;**2** (paper in press).

[37] Rudolf A, Stjepanovič Z, Cupar A. Designing of functional garments for people with physical disabilities and postural disorders by using 3D scanning, CASP and computer simulation techniques, 2017 (paper in review)

[38] Chang WM, Zhao YX, Guo RP, Wang Q, Gu XD. Design and study of clothing structure for people with limb disabilities. Journal of Fiber Bioengineering and Informatics. 2009;**2**:61–66. DOI: 10.3993/jfbi06200910

[39] Šavrin R. Patient with chronic spinal cord lesion. In: Šavrin R (ed) Pozni zapleti pri bolnikih z okvaro hrbtenjače (in Slovene) (Late Complications of Patients with Spinal Cord Impairment). Ljubljana: University Rehabilitation Institute Republic of Slovenia-Soča. 2015. pp. 7–17.

[40] Rudolf A, Kozar T, Jevšnik S, Cupar A, Drstvenšek I, Stjepanović Z. Research on 3D body model in a sitting position obtained with different 3D scanners. In: Proceedings of The International Istanbul Textile Congress 2013, Istanbul, Turkey, May–June 2013, pp. 263–269

[41] Rudolf A, Cupar A, Kozar T, Jevšnik S, Stjepanovič Z. Development of a suitable 3D body model in a sitting position. In: Proceedings of 5th International Scientific-Professional Conference Textile Science and Economy (TNP 2013), Zrenjanin: Technical Faculty "Mihajlo Pupin", pp. 51–56.

[42] ISO 8559:1989 Garment construction and anthropometric surveys—body dimensions, 1989.

[43] Fras Zemljič L, Peršin Z, Šauperl O, Rudolf A, Kostić M. Medical textiles based on viscose rayon fabrics coated with chitosan-encapsulated iodine: Antibacterial and antioxidant properties, 2017 (paper in review)

[44] Bogović S, Hursa Šajatović A. Construction of protective clothing. In: Young Scientist in the Protective Textiles Research, University of Zagreb, Faculty of Textile Technology, FP7-Report, Zagreb. 2011. pp. 309–331.

[45] Shan Y, Huang G, Qian X. Research overview on apparel fit. In: Luo J, editor. Soft Computing in Information Communication Technology. AISC 161. Berlin, Heidelberg: Spring-Verlag; 2012. pp. 39–44. DOI: 10.1007/978-3-642-29452-5

[46] Gill S. Improving garment fit and function through ease quantification. Journal of Fashion Marketing and Management. 2011;**15**:228–241. DOI: 10.1108/13612021111132654

[47] Ng R, Cheung LF, Yu W. Dynamic ease allowance in arm raising of functional garments. Sen'i Gakkaishi. 2008;**64**:236–243. DOI: 10.2115/fiber.64.236

[48] Chen Y, Zeng X, Happiette M, Bruniaux P, Ng R, Yu W. A new method of ease allowance generation for personalization of garment design. International Journal of Clothing Science and Technology. 2008;**20**:161–173. DOI: 10.1108/09556220810865210

Chapter 5

Computer Simulation of Bioprocess

Jianqun Lin, Ling Gao, Huibin Lin, Yilin Ren,
Yutian Lin and Jianqiang Lin

Additional information is available at the end of the chapter

http://dx.doi.org/10.5772/67732

Abstract

Bioprocess optimization is important in order to make the bioproduction process more efficient and economic. The conventional optimization methods are costly and less efficient. On the other hand, modeling and computer simulation can reveal the mechanisms behind the phenomenon to some extent, to assist the deep analysis and efficient optimization of bioprocesses. In this chapter, modeling and computer simulation of microbial growth and metabolism kinetics, bioreactor dynamics, bioreactor feedback control will be made to show the application methods and the usefulness of modeling and computer simulation methods in optimization of the bioprocess technology.

Keywords: modeling, simulation, bioprocess, fermentation, bioreactor, control

1. Introduction

Bioindustry is important in utilization of reproducible resources, developments of environmental friendly production processes, and sustainable economy. In order to make the bioprocesses more efficient and economic, bioprocess optimization and automatic control are needed. The conventional optimization methods cost much labor, time, and money; on the other hand, modeling and computer simulation method can reveal the mechanisms behind the phenomenon to some extent, to assist the deep analysis and optimization of bioprocesses. The modeling and computer simulation method is much efficient and economic, and widely used in research and modern bioindustries.

Bioprocess efficiency depends on the cell capability, bioreactor performances, and the optimal control of the cultivation conditions. The metabolic network inside the cells involves thousands of enzymes, and the enzyme expression and activities are dynamically affected by the cultivation conditions. As a result, the cultivation condition affects the cell growth, metabolism, and product production in a sophisticated and nonlinear way. Control and maintain relatively optimal cultivation conditions through proper operation and control of the bioreactor are needed to improve the production efficiency of the bioprocess.

Bioprocess mathematical modeling involves the modeling of the dynamic changes of the metabolic rates and their distribution inside the cells with the changes of time and cultivation conditions, the modeling of the dynamic changes of the reaction rates and mass transfer rates as well as the cultivation conditions inside the bioreactor, and the modeling of the dynamics of the bioreactor control system etc., based on which optimizations of the bioreactor operation and control strategies can be made and the results can be predicted and evaluated by computer simulation. In this chapter, examples of modeling and computer simulation of microbial growth and metabolism kinetics, bioreactor dynamics, and the feedback control of the bioreactor are given to show the application methods and the usefulness of modeling and computer simulation methods in bioprocess technology.

2. Modeling of microbial cell growth and metabolism

2.1. Modeling of microbial cell growth

Cell growth is one of the most important variables to be investigated in bioprocess. The cell growth is usually described by the specific growth rate, μ, and the time course of cell concentration, X. The specific growth rate is defined by the increase in grams of cells (g) per gram dry cells (g) per hour (h), and can be modeled by Eq. (1)

$$\mu = \frac{1}{X} \cdot \frac{dX}{dt} \tag{1}$$

The specific growth rate is related with many process variables, like temperature (T), pH, dissolved oxygen (DO) concentration (C_L), substrate concentration (S), product concentration (P), X, and time (t). expressed by

$$\mu = f(T, pH, DO, S, P, X, t, \ldots) \tag{2}$$

In real applications, only the key process variable(s) are included in Eq. (2) for simplification. Monod equation [1] using the substrate concentration as the single independent variable is shown by Eq. (3), as T, pH, and in many cases C_L are controlled constant and can be neglected from the equation.

$$\mu = \frac{\mu_m \cdot S}{k_m + S} \tag{3}$$

where μ_m, is the maximum specific growth rate and k_m, is the substrate affinity coefficient.

The typical cell growth curve is of "S" type, which has a lag growth phase and cannot be properly modeled by Monod equation as discussed later. At the initial cultivation stage, the cells need some time to adapt to the new environmental conditions for induction of some new enzymes needed for cell metabolism, etc., and the specific growth rate is zero or at a low value resulting in the lag growth phase. One way to model the lag growth phase is to separate the newly inoculated cells as active cells, X, and inactive cells, Y, and the time for Y to turn into X conforms to Pearson distribution expressed by Eqs. (4)–(7) [2].

$$\frac{dX}{dt} = \mu(t) \cdot X \tag{4}$$

$$\mu(t) = \frac{\mu_m \cdot X}{X + Y} \tag{5}$$

$$Y = X_0 - X \tag{6}$$

$$x(t) = \int_{-a_1}^{t} c\left(1 + \frac{t}{a_1}\right)^{m_1} \left(1 - \frac{t}{a_2}\right)^{m_2} \exp\left(\mu t\right) dt \tag{7}$$

where a_1, a_2, m_1, and m_2 are the constants of the Pearson distribution. The other methods used to predict the lag growth phase simply defined the lag time in terms of cell growth, t_L [2, 3]. One way to deal with the lag growth phase is to relate it with the changes of μ defined by Eq. (8) [3].

$$\mu(S, t) = \frac{\mu_m \cdot S}{k_m + S} \cdot (1 - e^{-t/t_L}) \tag{8}$$

After the lag growth phase, the specific growth rate increases gradually and the cells go into the exponential growth phase, which is expressed by Eqs. (9) and (10)

$$\frac{dX}{dt} = \mu \cdot X \tag{9}$$

$$X = X_0 \cdot e^{\mu \cdot t} \tag{10}$$

where X_0 is the initial cell concentration. After the exponential growth phase, the specific growth rate decreases gradually to zero, because of nutrients limitation, accumulation of intracellular toxic intermediates, accumulation of inhibitors in the culture broth, etc., and the net cell growth tends to cease to enter into the stationary growth phase. In order to model the decreased cell growth rate and the stationary growth phase, the Logistic growth model was developed [4], in which μ decreases with the increase of cell concentration, X, and μ reaches zero when x reaches its maximum value, X_m, shown by Eq. (11)

$$\frac{dX}{dt} = \mu_m \cdot \left(1 - \frac{X}{X_m}\right) \cdot X \tag{11}$$

From above analysis, it can be seen that the specific growth rate will start from zero or a low value in the lag growth phase, increases gradually and reaches the maximum value in the exponential growth phase, and then decreases gradually in the declined growth phase, which makes the time course of the specific growth rate the "bell" type curve and the time course of cell concentration the typical "S" type curve (**Figure 1**), which cannot be well fitted by the

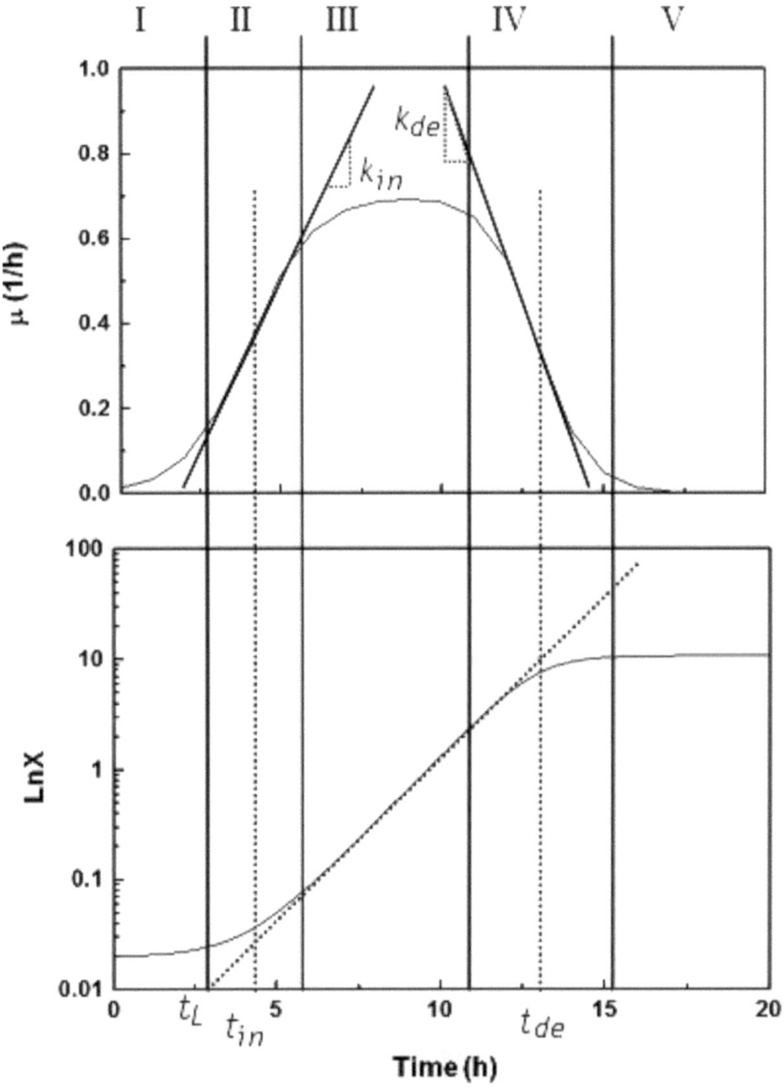

Figure 1. Graphically illustration of model parameters [5]. I is the lag growth phase; II is the increased growth phase; III is the exponential growth phase; IV is the decreased growth phase; V is the stationary growth phase. k_{in} is the maximum increasing rate of μ; k_{de} is the maximum decreasing rate of μ; t_{in} is the time point when $d\mu/dt$ equals k_{in}; t_{in} is the time point when $d\mu/dt$ equals k_{de}; and t_L is the lag time.

models discussed above. In order to simulate the "bell" type specific growth rate curve and the "S" type cell growth curve more accurately, the following model is developed shown by Eqs. (12) and (13) [5]

$$\mu(t) = \mu_m \cdot \frac{1}{1 + e^{-k_{in}(t - t_{in})}} \cdot \frac{1}{1 + e^{k_{de}(t - t_{de})}} \tag{12}$$

$$\frac{dX}{dt} = \mu(t) \cdot X \tag{13}$$

where k_{in} is the maximum increasing rate of μ; k_{de} is the maximum decreasing rate of μ; t_{in} is the time point when the increasing rate of μ equals k_{in}; t_{de} is the time point when the decreasing rate of μ equals k_{de}. All the parameters used in the model can be obtained graphically (**Figure 1**). One example of this model application is shown in **Figure 2**. In order to make wider application of above model, Eq. (12) can be combined with Monod model to develop Eqs. (12) and (13) into Eqs. (14) and (15)

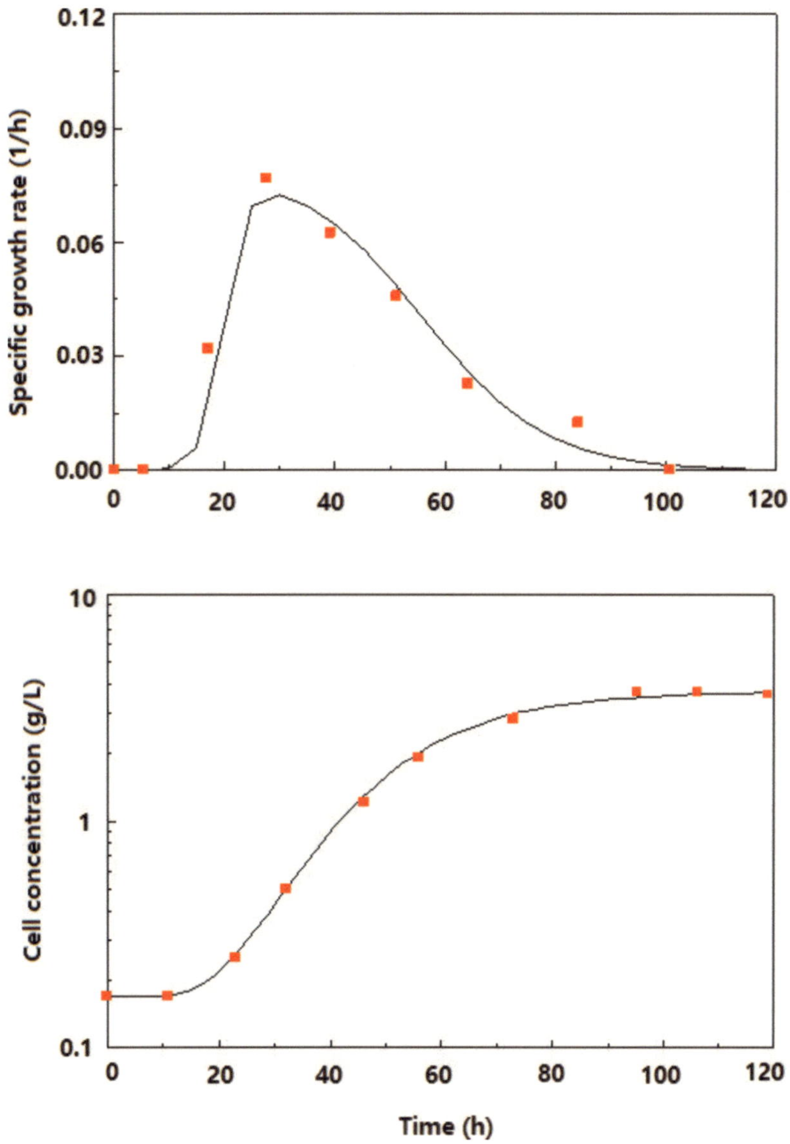

Figure 2. Simulation of cell growth of *Trichoderma reesei* [5].

$$\mu(S,t) = \frac{\mu_m \cdot S}{k_m + S} \cdot \frac{1}{1 + e^{-k_{in}(t-t_{in})}} \cdot \frac{1}{1 + e^{k_{de}(t-t_{de})}} \tag{14}$$

$$\frac{dX}{dt} = \mu(S,t) \cdot X \tag{15}$$

Even if Monod model has some limitations, it is still the widely used growth model in real applications for the major reasons of simplification and the single independent variable of substrate concentration, which is the key process variable to be investigated in many fermentation processes. In cases of high density fermentation, or substrate or product inhibition, modifications of Monod model are needed. Contois model shown by Eq. (16) is an example for high density fermentation, in which modeling the cell concentration is included in the denominator of the specific growth rate equation to show the limitation effect of high cell concentration on the growth, to make the specific growth rate to be reciprocal to the cell concentration ($\mu \propto X^{-1}$) at very low substrate concentration.

$$\mu = \frac{\mu_m \cdot S}{k_m \cdot X + S} \tag{16}$$

In some cases, the substrates which have inhibitory effect on cell growth, like ethanol or acetate, etc., are used. One example of the growth model under noncompetitive substrate inhibition with $K_I >> K_m$ is shown by Eq. (17)

$$\mu = \frac{\mu m \cdot S}{K_m + S + \frac{S^2}{KI}} \tag{17}$$

One example for modeling product inhibition, like ethanol or lactic acid fermentation, is shown by Eq. (18)

$$\mu = \frac{\mu m \cdot S}{(k_S + S)} \cdot \left(1 - \frac{P}{P_m}\right)^n \tag{18}$$

In case of dual substrates, the growth model in form of the sum or product of two Monod type terms is often used for the substitutable and nonsubstitutable substrates, respectively. For example, glucose and glycerol are substitutable substrates which can be modeled by Eq. (19), while glucose and oxygen are nonsubstitutable substrates which can be modeled by Eq. (20).

$$\mu = \mu m \cdot \left(\alpha_1 \cdot \frac{S_1}{K_{m1} + S_1} + \alpha_2 \cdot \frac{S_2}{K_{m2} + S_2}\right) \tag{19}$$

$$\mu = \mu m \cdot \frac{S_1}{K_{m1} + S_1} \cdot \frac{S_2}{K_{m2} + S_2} \tag{20}$$

Above growth models are relatively simple, which are unstructured and unsegregated models, and are useful for practical applications. Structured and segregated growth models, which involve the intracellular structure or the nonhomogeneity of the cells, respectively, are generally sophisticated and contain uneasily measurable model parameters, and are usually used for theoretical purposes.

2.2. Modeling of microbial substrate uptake and product production

In many cases, the ratio of cell mass produced per substrate utilized is a constant and defined as the cell yield from the substrate, $Y_{X/S}$, shown by Eq. (21)

$$Y_{X/S} = -\frac{\Delta X}{\Delta S} \tag{21}$$

The minus sign in Eq. (21) is to ensure $Y_{X/S}$ to be positive as ΔS is negative. From Eq. (21), it can be seen that substrate consumption is proportional to the cell growth, so that substrate consumption can be simply modeled by Eq. (22)

$$-\frac{dS}{dt} = \frac{1}{Y_{X/S}} \cdot \frac{dX}{dt} = \frac{\mu X}{Y_{X/S}} \tag{22}$$

Further, the total substrate consumed can be considered of two parts, with one part for real cell growth and the other part for life maintenance to develop Eq. (22) into Eq. (23)

$$-\frac{dS}{dt} = \frac{1}{Y_{X/S}} \cdot \frac{dX}{dt} = \frac{\mu X}{Y_{X/S}} = \left(\frac{\mu}{Y_G} + ms\right) \cdot X \tag{23}$$

where Y_G is the maximum cell yield when μ tends to μ_m; m_s the maintenance coefficient. From Eq. (23), Eq. (24) can be obtained showing the positive relationships between the specific growth rate, μ, and the cell yield, $Y_{X/S}$.

$$\frac{1}{Y_{X/S}} = \frac{ms}{\mu} + \frac{1}{Y_G} \tag{24}$$

From Eq. (24), it can be seen that in order to increase the cell yield, $Y_{X/S}$, a high value of μ should be maintained.

The specific substrate consumption rate is defined by the consumption in grams of substrate (g) per gram dry cells (g) per hour (h), and can be modeled by Eq. (25)

$$q_S = \frac{1}{X} \cdot \frac{-dS}{dt} \tag{25}$$

From Eqs. (23) and (25), Eq. (26) can be obtained

$$q_S = \frac{\mu}{Y_{X/S}} = \frac{\mu}{Y_G} + ms \tag{26}$$

Then, Eq. (22) or (23) can be expressed in a simple way by Eq. (27)

$$-\frac{dS}{dt} = q_S \cdot X \tag{27}$$

For the metabolism of facultative anaerobes grown in oxygen limited condition, the cell yield varies greatly depending on the degree of oxygen limitation. Catabolism of 1 mole of glucose can produce 36 (or 38) mole ATP under aerobic condition or produce 2 mole ATP under anaerobic condition. The ATP-based cell yield, Y_{ATP}, can be regarded a constant of 10 g dry-cell/mol ATP. So, the cell yield of $Y_{X/S}$ under anaerobic condition will only be 1/18 (or 1/19) of that under aerobic condition. The partition of the carbon source between aerobic pathway and anaerobic pathway in the catabolism is determined by oxygen supply or degree of oxygen limitation. Examples of cell growth under oxygen limited condition will be given in Sections 4.2 and 4.3.

In modeling of specific product production rate, Luedeking-Piret equation is most often used for its simplification and usefulness, which relates the specific product production rate to the growth related and nongrowth related parts by using α and β terms, respectively, as described by Eq. (28). The total product production is described by Eq. (29).

$$q_P = \alpha \cdot \mu + \beta \tag{28}$$

$$\frac{dP}{dt} = q_P \cdot X \tag{29}$$

3. Modeling of bioreactor with different operation methods

Continuous stirred tank reactor (CSTR) is the most popular type of bioreactor, which can be operated in batch, fed-batch, and continuous modes. For batch culture, no substrate is fed into the bioreactor except air for aeration or acid or base for pH control, and no culture broth is taken out of the bioreactor during the fermentation process. For modeling of a typical batch culture, the specific rates of cell growth (μ), substrate uptake (q_S), and product production (q_P) introduced in Section 2, and the mass balance equations of Eqs. (30)–(32) can be used.

$$\frac{dX}{dt} = \mu \cdot X \tag{30}$$

$$-\frac{dS}{dt} = q_S \cdot X \tag{31}$$

$$\frac{dP}{dt} = q_p \cdot X \tag{32}$$

For fed-batch culture, substrate is fed into the bioreactor but no culture broth is taken out during the fermentation process, so that the liquid volume is increasing. For modeling fed-batch culture, V is variant and the mass balance equations of Eqs. (33)–(36) can be used. The specific rates of μ, q_S, and q_P introduced in Section 2 can be used in the modeling.

$$\frac{d(VX)}{dt} = \mu VX \tag{33}$$

$$-\frac{d(VS)}{dt} = FS_f - \frac{1}{Y_{X/S}}\mu VX \tag{34}$$

$$\frac{d(VP)}{dt} = q_p \cdot VX \tag{35}$$

$$\frac{dV}{dt} = F \tag{36}$$

where F, the substrate feeding rate. Eqs. (33)–(35) can be transformed into Eqs. (37)–(39)

$$\frac{dX}{dt} = \mu X - \left(\frac{F}{V}\right)X \tag{37}$$

$$-\frac{dS}{dt} = \left(\frac{F}{V}\right)(S_f - S) - \frac{1}{Y_{X/S}}\mu X \tag{38}$$

$$\frac{dP}{dt} = q_p X - \left(\frac{F}{V}\right)P \tag{39}$$

In fed-batch culture, F can be continuous, for example, to be constant, linear increase, exponential increase with time, or uncontinuous, for example, operated in a repeated pulse-fed mode. Fed-batch culture has many advantages over batch culture. It has higher substrate conversion yield, extends production phase and can eliminate substrate inhibition or Crabtree effects, etc., and is widely used in industry.

Continuous culture is another kind of bioreactor operation method, with which method substrate is continuously fed into the bioreactor meanwhile the culture broth is continuously taken out of the bioreactor at the same rate so that the liquid volume remains unchanged. Continuous culture has the advantage of high production efficiency but the disadvantages of low substrate conversion yield, strain deterioration, and easy contamination, and is not often used in industry. As a result, examples of only batch and fed-batch cultures are investigated in next section.

4. Modeling and simulation of control of fermentation processes

4.1. Effects of early pulse aeration on ethanol fermentation

4.1.1. Mathematical modeling

Bioethanol is produced by anaerobic fermentation using *Saccharomyces cerevisiae,* which can grow anaerobically through fermentative pathway (glycolysis) catabolizing 1 mole of glucose and producing 2 moles of ethanol and 2 moles of ATP. *S. cerevisiae* can also grow aerobically through tricarboxylic acid (TCA) cycle catabolizing 1 mole of glucose producing 6 moles of

CO_2 and 38 moles of ATP. The cell yield from ATP, Y_{ATP}, is relatively constant, which is about 10 g dry-cell mass/mole ATP. *S. cerevisiae* will grow much faster aerobically than anaerobically for the reason to have more ATP used for cell growth.

Fermentation period, which can be roughly divided into growth phase and production phase, is one major factor affecting the production cost. Fermentation period will be shortened if the cell growth phase is shortened. By employing an aerobic condition during the cell growth phase to fasten the cell growth and an anaerobic condition during the ethanol production phase, the fermentation period should be shortened while the ethanol production remained. The growth phase aerobic pulse stimulated ethanol fermentation and the normal anaerobic ethanol fermentation operated in batch mode are investigated and compared by modeling and simulation [6].

The specific glucose consumption rate (q_S) subject to substrate and product inhibition effects is modeled by Eq. (40). In Eq. (41), Q is the on-off switch between anaerobic ($Q = 1$) and aerobic ($\overline{Q} = 1$) conditions ($\overline{Q}$ is not Q). Eq. (42) describes the ATP production from glucose under anaerobic or aerobic condition. The cell growth is based on the net ATP for cell synthesis shown by Eq. (43). Under aerobic condition, 6 moles of O_2 are needed for oxidizing 1 mole of glucose shown by Eq. (44). Ethanol is produced during the anaerobic production phase shown by Eq. (45).

$$q_S = \frac{q_{S.max} \times S}{k_S + S + S^2/k_{iS}} \times \left(1 - \frac{P}{P_{cri}}\right)^{\alpha} \tag{40}$$

$$Q = \begin{cases} 0 & \text{aerobic condition } (\overline{Q} = 1) \\ 1 & \text{anaerobic condition } (\overline{Q} = 0) \end{cases} \tag{41}$$

$$q_{ATP} = Q \times \frac{q_S}{M_{Gluc}} \times 2 + \bar{Q} \times \frac{q_S}{M_{Gluc}} \times 38 \tag{42}$$

$$\mu = \left(q_{ATP} - m_{S.ATP}\right) \times Y_{ATP} \tag{43}$$

$$q_{O2} = \overline{Q} \times q_S \times \frac{M_{O_2}}{M_{Gluc}} \times 6 \tag{44}$$

$$q_P = Q \times q_S \times \frac{M_{EtOH}}{M_{Gluc}} \times 2 \tag{45}$$

where S and P are the glucose and product (ethanol) concentrations, respectively; P_{cri} is the critical value of ethanol concentration for inhibition of glucose consumption; q_S and $q_{S.max}$ are the specific glucose consumption rate and its maximum value, respectively; k_S, ki_S, and α are the constants; q_{ATP}, q_P, q_{O2}, and μ are the specific rates of ATP and ethanol productions, oxygen consumption, and the specific growth rate; $m_{S.ATP}$ is the ATP consumption constant for cell maintenance; Y_{ATP} is the cell yield from ATP. The mass balance equations are shown by Eqs. (46)–(49)

$$\frac{dX}{dt} = \mu \times \left(1 - \frac{X}{X_{max}}\right) \times X \tag{46}$$

$$-\frac{dS}{dt} = q_S \times X \tag{47}$$

$$\frac{dP}{dt} = q_P \times X \tag{48}$$

$$\frac{d\text{OUR}}{dt} = q_{O2} \times X \tag{49}$$

where OUR is oxygen uptake rate.

4.1.2. Simulation results

Simulation was made using above mathematical model (**Figure 3**). The references for the parameter values used in the model or in calculation of the parameter values used in the model are shown in **Table 1**. In aerobic condition, $q_{S.\text{mas}}$ of 1 g/g/h and m_S of 0.1 mole/g/h, respectively, are used, which will be decreased and increased, respectively, compared with anaerobic condition.

The simulation results of the conventional anaerobic ethanol fermentation and the early growth phase aerobic pulse stimulated ethanol fermentation processes are shown in **Figure 3**. In simulation of the early growth phase aerobic pulse stimulated ethanol fermentation process, Q was set to zero ($\overline{Q} = 1$) for the first 3 h. The q_{ATP} and μ were abruptly decreased and the q_S and q_{EtOH} were abruptly increased with the shift of Q from 0 to 1 (**Figure 3B**). The results showed that early stage aerobic pulse stimulated ethanol fermentation and had the advantage in shortening the fermentation period for more than 10 h compared with the conventional anaerobic ethanol fermentation.

4.2. Fermentation with substrate feeding using DO stat control strategy

4.2.1. Mathematical modeling

In this section, glucose feeding control based on dissolved oxygen (DO) will be investigated by using a fed-batch fermentation process using *Escherichia coli*, which is often used as the host for recombinant protein production. This control strategy, which relates glucose concentration with DO changes [10, 11], is practical as DO sensor is widely used in fermentation technology. In the fermentation process, oxygen is continuously transferred into the liquid phase from the gas phase at a certain oxygen transfer rate (OTR) under aeration and agitation conditions; meanwhile, oxygen is continuously consumed by microbes at a certain oxygen uptake rate (OUR). After the cell reach high concentration, oxygen limitation occurs when OUR becomes larger than OTR so that DO decreases to nearly zero. On the other hand, *E. coli* catabolizes glucose aerobically through tricarboxylic acid (TCA) cycle, catabolizing one molecule of glucose into six molecules of CO_2 consuming six molecules of O_2. When glucose is depleted, O_2 consumption stops (OUR $= 0$) while OTR is positive so that DO rises suddenly. So, the sudden DO rise can be the indicator for glucose depletion and used as the signal for glucose feeding. After glucose feeding, glucose consumption and oxygen uptake resume and DO drops again. Then, the control system will monitor the next sudden DO rise for glucose feeding control, which strategy can maintain glucose concentration in low level and is called DO stat control strategy. This control strategy has been analyzed by modeling method [12].

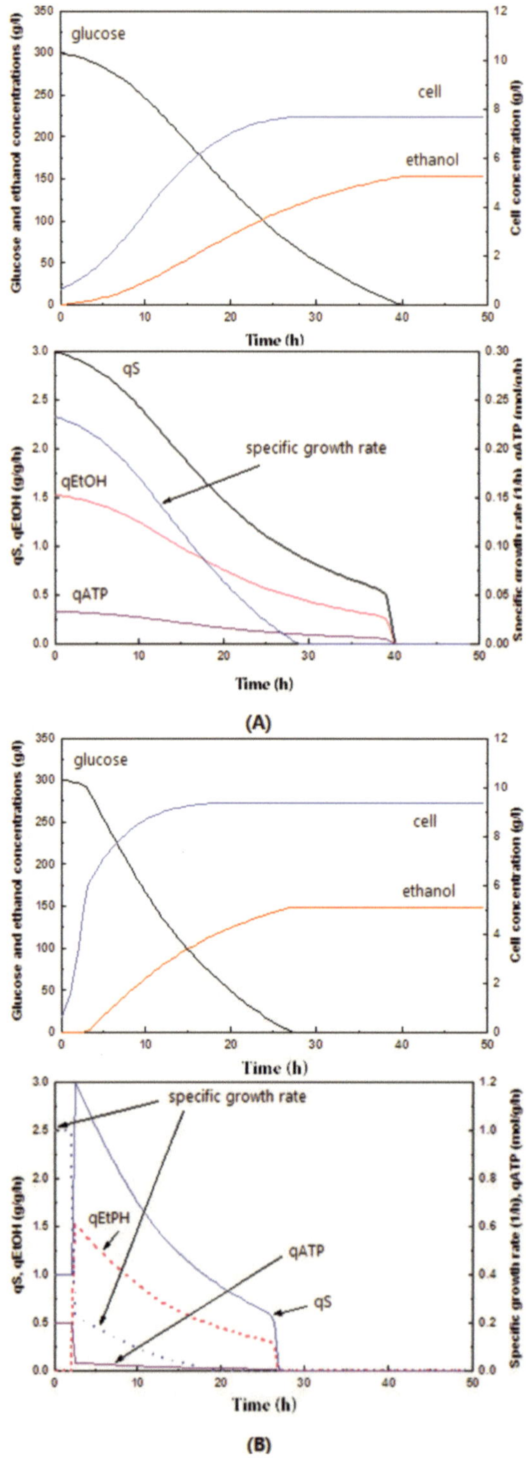

Figure 3. Simulation of ethanol fermentation. (A) Normal anaerobic fermentation. (B) Early 3 h aerobic pulse followed by anaerobic fermentation.

Parameter	Value	Reference
k_S	0.213 g/L	[7]
ki_S	386.64 g/L	[7]
P_{cri}	226 g/L	[7]
$\mu_{\max}$ (anaerobic)	0.45 L/h	[8]
$Y_{X/S}$ (anaerobic)	0.15 g/g	[8]
$q_{S.\text{mas}}$ (anaerobic)	3 g/g/h	$q_{S.\text{mas}} = \mu_{\max}/Y_{X/S}$
A	1.5	[8]
m_S	0.01 mole/g/h	[9]
$X_{\max}$ (anaerobic)	11 g/L	[7]
Y_{ATP}	10 g/mol	[9]

Table 1. Parameter values and references.

The specific growth rate is modeled by Logistic equation shown by Eq. (50). The specific glucose consumption rate is modeled to include two parts, one for the net growth and the other for the maintenance shown by Eq. (51). The mole specific oxygen consumption rate is six times of the specific glucose consumption rate as shown by Eq. (52). The specific product production rate is modeled by Luedeking-Piret [Eq. (53)]. OUR and OTR are shown by Eqs. (54) and (55), respectively.

$$\mu = \frac{\mu_m \cdot S}{k_m + S} \cdot \left(1 - \frac{X}{X_m}\right) \tag{50}$$

$$q_S = \frac{\mu}{Y_G} - m_S \tag{51}$$

$$q_{O_2} = q_S \cdot \frac{M_{O_2}}{M_{\text{Gluc}}} \times 6 \tag{52}$$

$$q_P = \alpha \cdot \mu + \beta \tag{53}$$

$$\text{OUR} = q_{O_2} \cdot X \tag{54}$$

$$\text{OTR} = k_L a \cdot (C^* - C_L) \tag{55}$$

where q_{O2} and q_P are the specific rates of O_2 consumption and product production, respectively; α, β, are the constants for Luedeking-Piret equation; k_{La}, is the volume oxygen transfer rate; C_L and C^* are the dissolved oxygen concentration and its saturated value, respectively; M_{O2} and M_{Gluc} are the molecular weights of O_2 and of glucose, respectively.

The mass balance equations for fed-batch culture can be made and transformed into Eqs. (56)–(60).

$$\frac{dX}{dt} = \mu X - \left(\frac{F}{V}\right) X \tag{56}$$

$$\frac{dS}{dt} = \left(\frac{F}{V}\right) \cdot (S_f - S) - q_S \cdot X \tag{57}$$

$$\frac{dP}{dt} = q_p \cdot X - \left(\frac{F}{V}\right) \cdot P \tag{58}$$

$$\frac{dC_L}{dt} = \text{OTR} - \text{OUR} - \left(\frac{F}{V}\right) \cdot C_L \tag{59}$$

$$\frac{dV}{dt} = F \tag{60}$$

where P is the product concentration; S_f is the substrate concentration in the feeding solution; V is the volume of the culture broth; F is the feeding rate.

4.2.2. Simulation results

In the simulation, glucose pulse feeding was made when DO increased over 10% in order to avoid noise interruptions. In each pulse feeding, a dosage equivalent to 20 g/L increase in glucose concentration was fed. The initial glucose was depleted at about 75 h and the product concentration was a little over 6 g/L at that time. By glucose pulse feeding, the product concentration was more than doubled (**Figure 4**). Glucose and DO concentrations go up and down in turn and fluctuate during the control period. By using this control strategy, glucose concentration can be maintained in an averaged low concentration, which is desired and helps to overcome the glucose effects and increase the product yields. In addition, the DO stat control strategy does not need the extra sensor and is easily applied.

4.3. Fermentation with DO feedforward-feedback control and substrate-feedback control

4.3.1. Mathematical modeling

DO control is important in fermentation process. The level of DO can affect the metabolic flux distribution and the product yield and production efficiency. As oxygen has low solubility in water, DO control is a hard task for fermentation process. Compared with feedback control, DO feedforward-feedback (FF-FB) control has the advantage in dealing with the time-varying characteristics resulted from the cell growth during the fermentation process. The oxygen consumption of the microbial cells is considered the disturbance to the control system and is estimated by using the mathematical model and compensated by the FF control action. The substrate is FB controlled by repeated pulse-fed of carbon source. The schematic diagram for the control system is shown in **Figure 5** [13].

The specific cell growth rate is modeled using double substrate Monod equation shown by Eq. (61). The equations for the specific glucose consumption rate, the specific oxygen consumption rate, OUR, and OTR are shown by Eqs. (62)–(65), which are the same as that of Section 4.2.1.

http://dx.doi.org/10.5772/67732

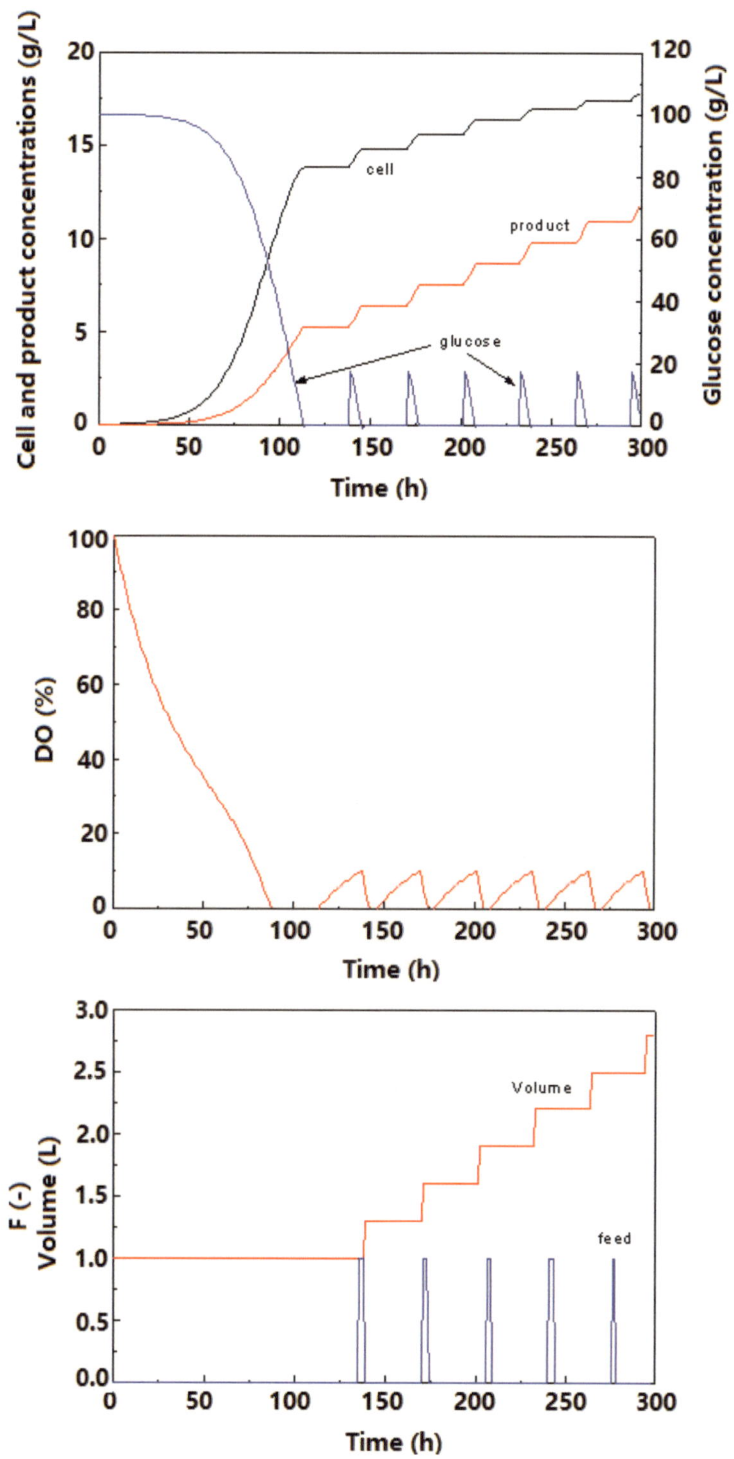

Figure 4. Computer simulation of process variables of DO stat fed-batch culture.

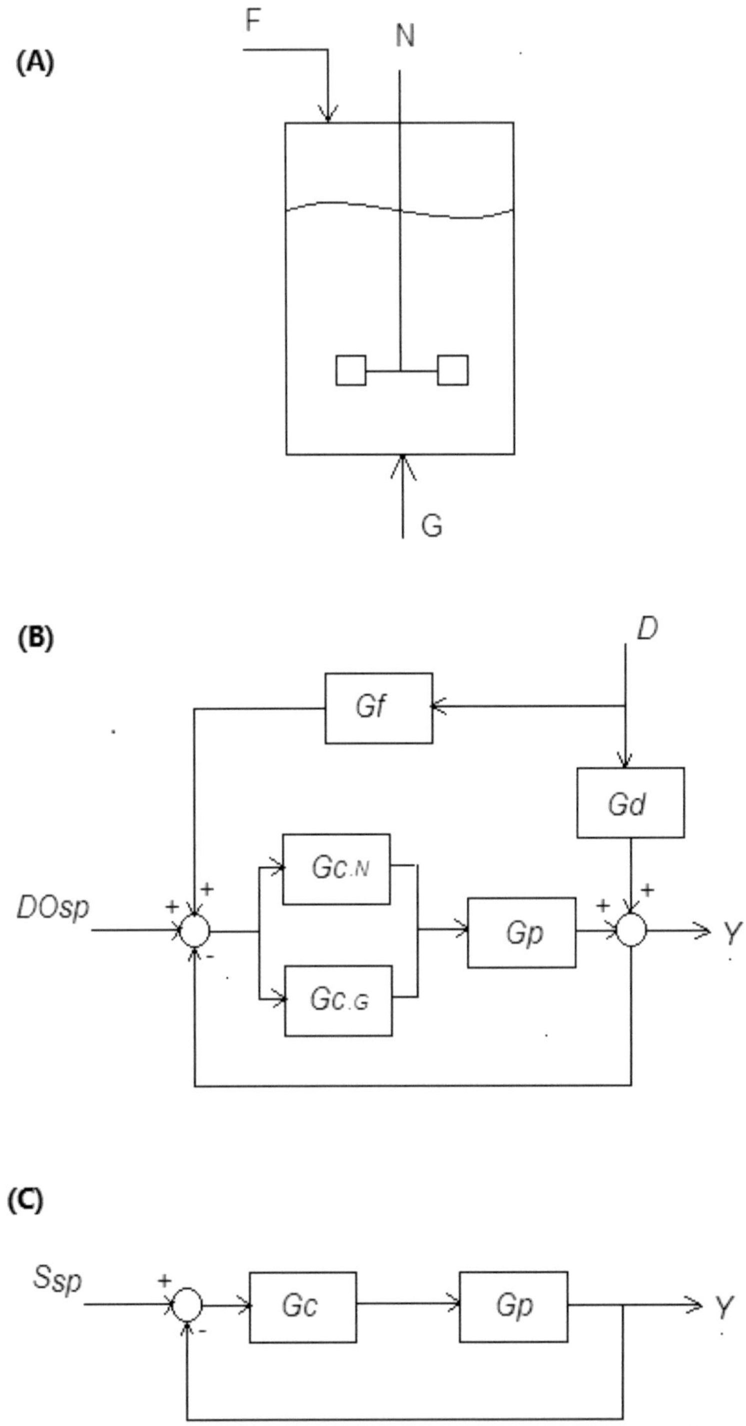

Figure 5. The schematic diagram of the bioreactor control system. (A) Bioreactor: F, substrate feeding rate; N, agitation speed; G, aeration rate. (B) DO FF-FB control. (C) Substrate FB control.

$$\mu = \frac{\mu_m \cdot S}{k_m + S} \cdot \frac{C_L}{k_{O_2} + C_L} \tag{61}$$

$$q_S = \frac{\mu}{Y_G} - m_S \tag{62}$$

$$q_{O_2} = q_S \cdot \frac{M_{O_2}}{M_{\text{Gluc}}} \times 6 \tag{63}$$

$$\text{OUR} = q_{O_2} \cdot X \tag{64}$$

$$\text{OTR} = k_L a \cdot (C_L{}^* - C_L) \tag{65}$$

The mass balance equations for the repeated fed-batch culture are described by Eqs. (66–69).

$$\frac{dX}{dt} = \mu \cdot X - \frac{F}{V} \cdot X \tag{66}$$

$$\frac{dS}{dt} = -q_S \cdot X + \frac{F}{V} \cdot (S_F - S) \tag{67}$$

$$\frac{dC_L}{dt} = \text{OTR} - \text{OUR} - \frac{F}{V} \cdot C_L \tag{68}$$

$$\frac{dV}{dt} = F \tag{69}$$

where S_F is the substrate concentration in the concentrated feeding solution. The substrate feeding solution is concentrated so that the volume change resulted from the substrate feeding can be neglected in Eqs. (66)–(68).

For FF control of DO, in order to compensate the DO disturbance resulted from the cell growth, OTR should be equal to OUR according to Eq. (68) if the dilution effect of the feeding is neglected so as to ensure C_L unchanged ($dC_L/dt = 0$) and remained at the set-point. As the oxygen transfer driving force, $\Delta C = (C_L{}^* - C_L)$, is relatively constant when C_L is maintained at the set-point, k_{La} should be controlled to meet Eq. (70) to compensate the time-varying OUR by the cell respiration according to Eqs. (65) and (68), and $dC_L/dt = 0$.

$$\frac{\text{OUR}}{(C_L^* - C_L)} = k_L a \tag{70}$$

The value of k_{La} is controlled by agitation speed (N) and aeration rate (G) shown by Eq. (71).

$$k_L a = k \cdot N^3 \cdot G^{0.5} \tag{71}$$

Between the two manipulated variables, N is more effective than G in controlling k_{La} [14]. Therefore, 70% of the control effort is assigned to N and 30% is assigned to G by using Eqs. (72) and (73), respectively, which are drawn from Eqs. (70) and (71).

$$N_{FF\times t} = \left(\frac{OUR}{(C_L^* - C_L)} \cdot \frac{1}{k \cdot G_{t-1}{}^{0.5}}\right)^{\frac{1}{3}} \cdot 70\% \tag{72}$$

$$G_{FF\times t} = \left(\frac{OUR}{(C_L{}^* - C_L)} \cdot \frac{1}{k \cdot N_{t-1}{}^{3}}\right)^{2} \cdot 30\% \tag{73}$$

where the subscripts *t* and *t−1* are the current and last time points, respectively. So, *N* and *G* control actions should be finished in several control rounds. Eqs. (72) and (73) are used in the FF control.

As model predictions may not be very accurate, FB control is used to eliminate the control error and ensure the control accuracy. In the case of FB control, the error between DO set-point and process variable is calculated by Eq. (74).

$$e = C_{L.sp} - C_L \tag{74}$$

where $C_{L.sp}$ is DO set-point. The proportional and integration (PI) control strategy is used for FB control by using Eqs. (75) and (76) for *N* and *G* control, respectively. Similarly, 70% of the control action is assigned to N_{FB} and 30% is assigned to G_{FB}.

$$N_{FB\cdot t} = \left(k_{P\cdot N} \cdot e + k_{I\cdot N} \int e\right) \cdot 70\% \tag{75}$$

$$G_{FB\cdot t} = \left(k_{P\cdot G} \cdot e + k_{I\cdot G} \int e\right) \cdot 30\% \tag{76}$$

Then, the total DO control actions of *N* and *G* are shown by Eqs. (77) and (78)

$$N_t = N_0 + N_{FF\cdot t} + N_{FB\cdot t} \tag{77}$$

$$G_t = G_0 + G_{FF\cdot t} + G_{FB\cdot t} \tag{78}$$

where N_0 and G_0 are the initial values of *N* and *G*, respectively.

4.3.2. Simulation results

In this system, DO is FF-FB controlled by agitation speed and aeration rate and the substrate concentration is FB controlled by repeated pulse-fed of certain amount of the concentrated feeding solution to make the substrate concentration reach 30 g/L when the substrate concentration is lower than the set-point of 5 g/L. In order to confirm the robustness of the control system under model prediction errors and noises, 5% randomized noises and 20% over estimate of the cell growth were added in the mathematical model predictions in FF control. Then, simulations were made with the above noises and prediction errors. The results indicated that even if the noises and relatively large model prediction errors existed, the control system still had good performance. The reason is that FB control finally compensated the inaccuracy of the FF control, as shown in **Figure 6** [13].

http://dx.doi.org/10.5772/67732

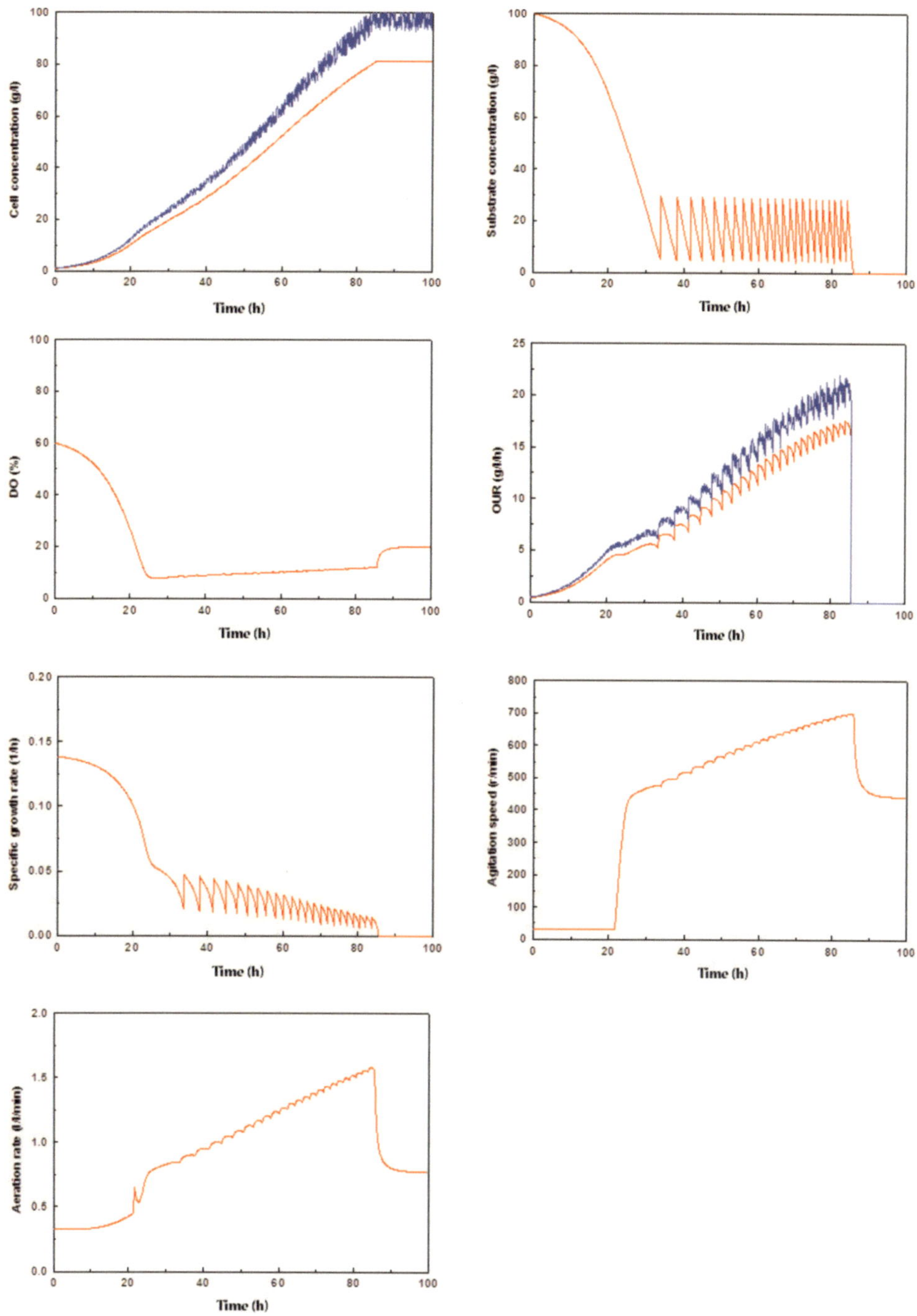

Figure 6. Simulation of DO FF-FB control and substrate FB control with prediction error and noise. The model predictions with 5% randomized noises and 20% over estimate of the cell growth in FF control.

5. Conclusion

Modeling and simulation are useful tools for understanding, analysis, and optimization of bioprocesses [14–17]. By using the modeling and computer simulation methods, the dynamics of cell growth and metabolism under different conditions and various fermenter operation modes can be evaluated and the information can be used for bioprocess optimization and bioreactor control.

Acknowledgements

This work was supported by grants from the Natural Science Foundation (Grant No. 31370138, 31570036), the National Basic Research Program (2010CB630902), the Natural Science Foundation (Grant No. 31400093, 31370084, 30800011), the Postdoctoral Science Foundation (Grant No. 2015M580585), and the State Key Laboratory of Microbial Technology Foundation (M2015-03) of China.

Author details

Jianqun Lin[1], Ling Gao[2], Huibin Lin[3], Yilin Ren[4], Yutian Lin[5] and Jianqiang Lin[1*]

*Address all correspondence to: jianqianglin@sdu.edu.cn

1 State Key Lab of Microbial Technology, School of Life Sciences, Shandong University, Jinan, China

2 Institute of Information Science and Engineering, School of Information Science and Engineering, Shandong Normal University, Jinan, China

3 Shandong Academy of Chinese Medicine, Jinan, China

4 School of Life Sciences, Tsinghua University, Beijing, China

5 College of Computer Sciences & Technology, University of Technology, Sydney, Australia

References

[1] Monod J. The growth of bacterial cultures. Annual Review of Microbiology. 1949;**3**:371

[2] Buchanan RE. Life phase in a bacterial culture. Journal of Infectious Diseases. 1918;**23** (1):109-125

[3] Moser, A. (1994) Bioprocess technology - kinetics and reactors. Translation (Chinese) Qu, Y., pp. 240-367. Hu Nan Science Press, China and Springer-Verlag, New York, USA

[4] Tsoularis A, Wallace J. Analysis of logistic growth models. Mathematical Biosciences. 2002;**179**(1):21-55

[5] Lin J, Lee SM, Lee HJ, Koo YM. Modeling of typical microbial cell growth in batch culture. Biotechnology and Bioprocess Engineering. 2000;**5**(5):382-385

[6] Jia X, Lin Y, Lin H, Gao L, Lin J, Lin J. Modeling and computer simulation of early pulse aeration effects on ethanol fermentation. WIT Transactions on Biomedicine and Health. 2014;**18**:576-582

[7] Liua CG, Linb YH, Bai FW. A kinetic growth model for *Saccharomyces cerevisiae* grown under redox potential-controlled very-high-gravity environment. Biochemical Engineering Journal. 2011;**56**:63-68

[8] Dantigny P. Modeling of the aerobic growth of *Saccharomyces cerevisiae* on mixtures of glucose and ethanol in continuous culture. Journal of Biotechnology. 1995;**4**:213-220

[9] Lin Y, Liu G, Lin H, Gao L, Lin J. Analysis of batch and repeated fedbatch productions of *Candida utilis* cell mass using mathematical modeling method. Electronic Journal of Biotechnology. 2013;**16**(4)

[10] Lee SY. High cell-density culture of *Escherichia coli*. Trends in Biotechnology. 1996;**14**:98-105

[11] Cutayar JM, Poillon D. High cell density culture of *E. coli* in a fed-batch system with dissolved oxygen as substrate feed indicator. Biotechnology Letters. 1989;**11**:155-160

[12] Gao L, Lin Y, Lin H, Jia X, Lin J, Lin J. Bioreactor substrate feeding control using DO stat control strategy: A modeling and computer simulation study. Applied Mechanics and Materials. 2014;**541-542**:1198-1202

[13] Gao L, Lin H. Simulation of model based feedforward and feedback control of dissolved oxygen (DO) of microbial repeated fed-batch culture. International Journal of Simulation: Systems, Science and Technology. 2016;**17**(14):4.1-4.6

[14] Salehmin MNI, Annuar MSM, Chisti Y. High cell density fed-batch fermentation for the production of a microbial lipase. Biochemical Engineering Journal. 2014;**85**:8-14

[15] Potvin G, Ahmad A, Zhang Z. Bioprocess engineering aspects of heterologous protein production in *Pichia pastoris*: A review. Biochemical Engineering Journal. 2012;**64**: 91-105

[16] Guo Q, Liu G, Dong N, Li Q, Lin J, Lin J. Model predictive control of glucose feeding for fed-batch *Candida utilis* biomass production. Research Journal of BioTechnology. 2013;**8**(7):3-7

[17] Lin J, Takagi M, Qu Y, Yoshida Y. Possible strategy for on-line monitoring and control of hybridoma cell culture. Biochemical Engineering Journal, 2002;**11**:205-209

Chapter 6

Developing a Hybrid Model and a Multi-Scale 3D Concept of Integrated Modelling High-Temperature Processes

Marcin Hojny

Additional information is available at the end of the chapter

http://dx.doi.org/10.5772/67735

Abstract

The chapter presents an idea of constructing a scientific workshop focused on high-temperature processes, based upon a concept of integrated modelling combining the advantages of computer and physical simulations. Examples of physical simulation results aiming at determining necessary material data and high-temperature characteristics for the needs of computer simulations are presented. They are complemented by an outline of numerical 3D models developed and results of test simulations of a 3D solver of the finite element method (FEM) and the smoothed particle hydrodynamics (SPH). This chapter is closed with a short summary, indicating trends in further research focused on a further development of the DEFFEM simulation package and research and measurement methods.

Keywords: extra-high temperature, finite element method (FEM), smoothed particle hydrodynamics (SPH), physical simulation, computer simulation, mushy zone

1. Introduction

In recent years, many companies have been working to develop a rolling process with the semi-solid core [1–6]. While thin strip casting combined with subsequent rolling is a simple, improved method of the conventional rolling process, rolling a strip, in which both the solid and liquid phases coexist, is a new process. Cold rolling following simple strand casting is a long process and it is not cost-effective because of energy reasons. For technological reasons, the process should be developed to simplify or eliminate some operations, which would drastically reduce the energy costs. This also involves beneficial environmental impact, due to the reduction of gas emissions. Casting processes followed immediately by rolling have various versions, which depend on the applying companies, and differ with details of industrial installations [7]. However, the need for controlled rolling of strands cast is pointed out.

Therefore, results of a computer simulation or a physical simulation of the process analysed will be useful to control the process parameters. This has inspired the author to take up intensive and time-consuming work related to the development of research methods and mathematical models, along with their numerical implementation [7]. The research and scientific work carried out since 2009 as part of two projects financed by Polish academic institutions resulted in the development of modelling concepts integrating physical and computer simulation areas, while providing full or partial exchange of information between those areas. The proposed concept utilizes capabilities of modern thermomechanical simulators of the Gleeble 3800 series in the modelling of steel deformation processes at extra-high temperatures, as well as in the modelling of integrated casting and rolling processes of flat strands with a solidifying core. The other necessary and unique component in the global scale is the original simulation package DEFFEM being developed for a few years, dedicated to two classes of issues, namely the processes of steel deformation modelling within a temperature range near the solidus line, and within a temperature range between the solidus and liquidus temperatures. The mentioned two classes of issues have been jointly classified as high-temperature processes. The whole modelling approach is complemented by the utilisation of modern testing and measurement instruments to verify the implemented solutions or to obtain additional information that cannot be obtained with traditional methods. This required adopting a number of simplifications and assumptions. Most important was systematic pursuit of the assumed goals and recent research in the context of planned work aiming at developing two unique numerical models: a full three-dimensional multi-scale model MCFE (Monte Carlo and finite elements) and a hybrid model combining the advantages of the finite element method (FEM) and the smoothed particle hydrodynamics (SPH). The author's research is therefore pioneering both in theory and practice. The general outline of the developed concept is presented in **Figure 1**. Coupling and exchange of information

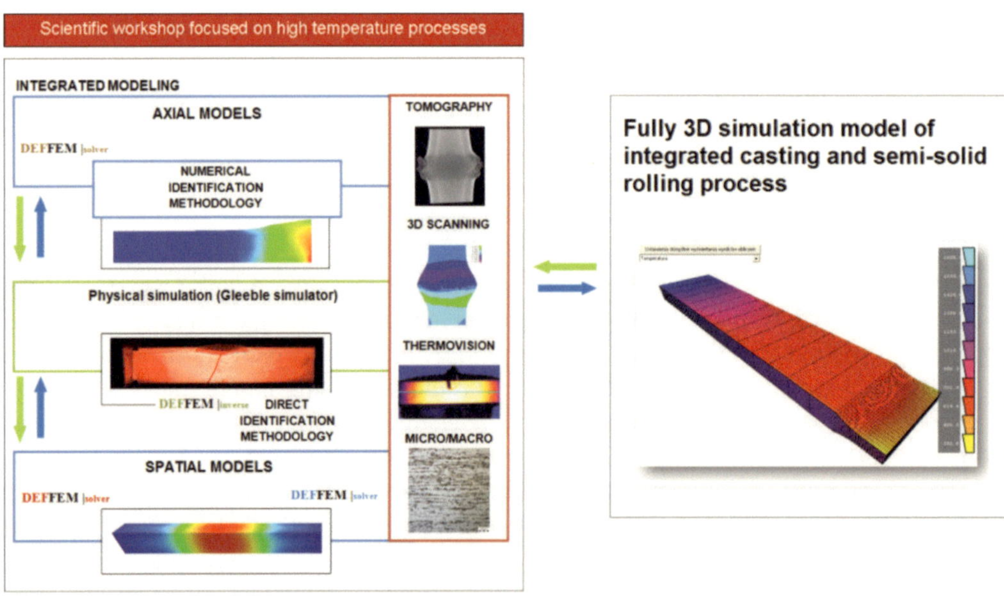

Figure 1. General outline of the concept of integrated modelling focused on high-temperature processes.

between the areas of physical and computer simulations allows, among others, the necessary data for the needs of numerical simulations (stress-strain curves, characteristics of changes of current intensity versus time, local temperature changes within the sample volume, etc.) to be identified. At the same time, the application of computer simulations using the dedicated simulation system DEFFEM allows the obtained physical simulation findings to be interpreted [7]. A few layers can be specified when analysing the general outline of the concept in **Figure 1**. The foundation constitutes axisymmetrical solutions, being a key to the developed NIM (numerical identification methodology) for determining mechanical properties of the steels tested, necessary for numerical analyses. Regardless of axisymmetrical solutions, the next layer constitutes 3D solutions, which become important in the context of designing the simulation system of integrated strip casting and rolling. Such approach is determined by the fact that the zone of solid and liquid phases mixing within the volume of the strand rolled often has a very irregular shape [7].

More details concerning the developed concept of integrated modelling or comprehensive physical tests can be found in the recapitulating monograph by Hojny [7].

2. The DEFFEM simulation system

The original simulation package DEFFEM is developed in accordance with the design philosophy **ONEDES** (**ONEDE**Cision**S**oftware) proposed by Hojny [8]. It is based on the assumption that a set of independent modules comprising the DEFFEM package is implemented numerically to enable a virtual test of resistance heating combined with deforming in a wide range of temperatures to be performed, in particular at extra-high temperatures near the solidus line, as well as in conditions of the solid and liquid phase coexistence, without the need for any commercial applications. In **Table 1** currently developed modules (solvers) are compared with the ones under development included in the DEFFEM package, along with their classification subject to the adopted numerical simulations (solver class) and the very possibilities for using the solver to simulate specific main features. The developed simulation

Module	Solver class	Main features
DEFFEM |solver_2D_TH v.1.0	2D thermal, finite element method	• Convection heat transfer • Transient heat flow
DEFFEM |solver_AX_TH v.1.0	Axially symmetric, thermal, finite element method	• Convection heat transfer • Transient heat flow • Resistance heating
DEF_SEMI_SOLID v. 5.0	Axially symmetric, thermo-mechanical, finite element method	• Compression tests • Integrated with magnetohydrodynamic module (MHD) ANSYS software
DEFFEM |solver_AX_TM v. 2.0		• Tension tests • Soft reduction simulation and rolling

Module	Solver class	Main features
		• Integrated with temperature field after resistance heating with DEFFEM I solver_AX_TH
DEFFEM I solver_3D_TH v.1.0	3D thermal, finite element method	• Convection heat transfer • Transient heat flow • Resistance heating
DEFFEM I solver_3D_TM v.1.0	3D thermomechanical, finite element method	• Compression tests • Solidification
DEFFEM I solver_3D_MCFE Beta version	3D multi-scale thermomechanical, Monte Carlo + finite element method	• Compression tests • Solidification
DEFFEM I solver_3D_FLUID v. 1.0	3D fluid, meshless method	• Viscosity • Porous structure • Solidification
DEFFEM I solver_3D_HYBRID Beta version	3D fluid, meshless method +finite element method	• Solidification
Supporting module	Main features	
DEFFEM I pre&post	Full pre- and post-processor for all solvers	
DEFFEM I inverse	Stand-alone inverse module	

Table 1. Component modules of the DEFFEM simulation package.

package also provides tools oriented at the full identification of the selected parameters of numerical models on the basis of data coming directly from physical simulations (**DEFFEM I inverse** module). In parallel with the design of such an advanced simulation tool, the development of visualisation tools and the analysis of findings are being implemented. Advanced numerical algorithms have been developed for plotting the isolines of scalar fields, visualising vector fields or enabling stereoscopic data to be visualised (module **DEFFEM I pre&post**).

3. High-temperature testing methodology

The testing methodology is illustrated with the currently newly tested steel 11SMn30. According to the adopted concept of integrated modelling, physical simulations are performed with a thermomechanical Gleeble 3800 simulator. **Figure 2A** presents a view of the simulation system before starting the physical simulation. During the tests, cylindrical samples (**Figure 2B/C**) and hexahedral samples (**Figure 2D**) with various dimensions were used, along with copper grips with a long zone of contact with the sample (**Figure 2B**).

http://dx.doi.org/10.5772/67735

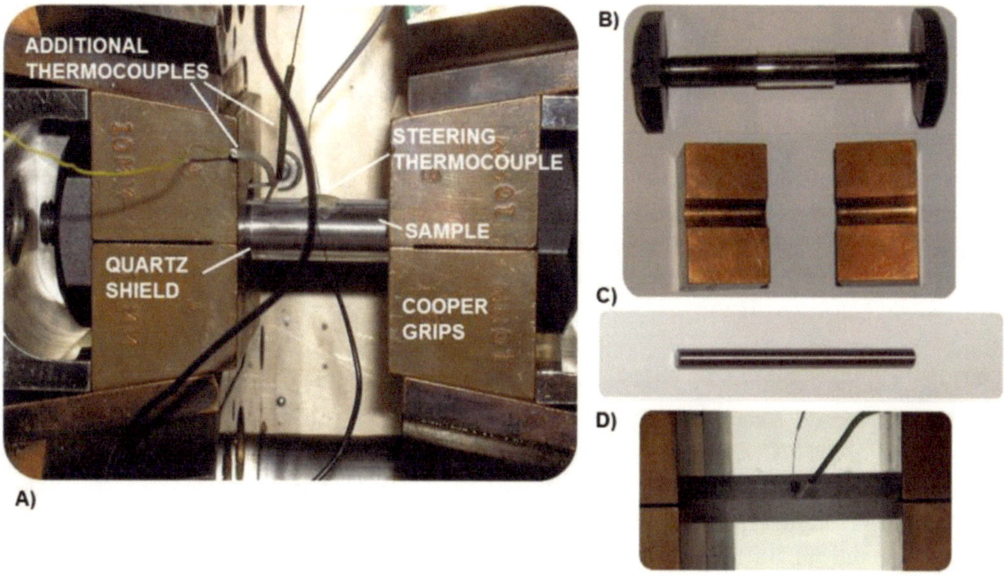

Figure 2. The view of the Gleeble simulator system (A), a cylindrical sample and 'cold' grips (B), a sample for testing the nil strength temperature (NST)(C), and the view of the installed hexahedral sample in the Gleeble simulator system (D).

For the execution of the remelting process, additionally a cylindrical quartz shield was applied to prevent potential leakages of liquid steel into the simulator. To carry out numerical simulations, it was necessary to define material properties characterising the specific steel grade. To determine the necessary thermophysical data, a commercial program JMatPro was used. This program determines the requested dependences (resistivity, thermal conductivity and specific heat) on temperature based on the chemical composition. In order to transfer the simulation results into the industrial conditions, a number of ideas and parameters were introduced to characterise mechanical properties of steel in the semi-solid state. As the 'semi-solid state' we refer hereinafter to the material state able to withstand loads (where within a cohesive solid phase skeleton also the liquid phase coexists). The basic high-temperature characteristics include:

1. Nil strength temperature (NST), at which the material strength determined during steel heating drops to zero. This temperature is determined after applying a very small tensile force, which for the tests carried out with the Gleeble 3800 simulator is about 80 N.

2. Strength recovery temperature (SRT), at which the material regains its strength (>0.05 kg/mm^2 $= 0.4909$ MPa). It is determined during cooling after previous heating of steel to the liquid state.

3. Nil ductility temperature (NDT), at which ductility determined by reduction of area drops to zero. This temperature is determined during steel heating.

4. Ductility recovery temperature (DRT), at which the reduction of area achieves the value of ≥5%. The temperature DRT is determined during cooling from a temperature over NDT.

5. The determination of changes of stress versus strain on the basis of tensile tests for the selected temperature range and the tool stroke rate.

The tests were carried out on plain samples Ø6 × 82 mm and two-sided threaded samples Ø10 mm × 125 mm. On the basis of computation results based on chemical composition, carried out with the JMatPro program, the calculated liquidus T_l and solidus T_s temperatures were 1518 and 1439°C, respectively. When determining the temperature NST, initially two tests are made. If the difference between the obtained values NST is >20°C, then the third test should be performed. The average value is the temperature NST. In this study, the temperature NST was arbitrary assumed as the mean value for seven samples. The samples for the determination of the nil strength temperature NST first were heated at a rate of 20°C/s to a temperature of 1350°C, and next at a rate of 1°C/s to the temperature of failure. The determined temperature NST for steel 11SMn30 was 1410 ±15°C. The next stage of tests of steel 11SMn30 included determining the nil ductility temperature NDT. The samples for the determination of the nil ductility temperature NDT first were heated at a rate of 20°C/s to a temperature of 1300°C, and next at a rate of 1°C/s to the deformation temperature, using additional 5 s holding at a constant temperature before the deformation process. The samples were tensioned at a rate of 20 mm/s. In steel 11SMn30, the loss of reduction of area was recorded after exceeding the temperature of 1425°C; therefore, it was the temperature NDT. The ductility recovery temperature DRT was determined by heating samples to a temperature of 1300°C at a rate of 20°C/s, and next at a rate of 1°C/s to a temperature of 1425°C. After 5 s of temperature equalisation, the samples were cooled to the deformation temperature, which was between 1370 and 1420°C. The cooling rate was 1°C/s. The deformation was preceded by 5 s holding at a set deformation temperature. The samples were tensioned to failure at a rate of 20 mm/s. The temperature DRT value is determined when 5% of reduction of area is recovered. In steel 11SMn30, the reduction of area of 5% was recorded (when cooled) at a deformation temperature of 1400°C, therefore it is the temperature DRT. The temperature range between NST and DRT is considered the brittle temperature range [7]. For the steel tested the brittle temperature range (BRT) is about 25°C (at a tensioning rate 20 mm/s). The strength recovery temperature SRT was determined by heating samples to a temperature of 1350°C at a rate of 20°C/s, and next at a rate of 1°C/s to a temperature of 1460°C (with zonal sample remelting). After 30 s of holding, the samples were cooled to the deformation temperature, which was between 1400 and 1460°C. The cooling rate was 10°C/s. The deformation was preceded by 5 s holding at a set deformation temperature. The samples were tensioned to failure at a rate of 20 mm/s. The temperature SRT value was determined when a stress of about 0.49 MPa had been recovered. For the conducted tests for steel 11SMn30, it corresponded to the temperature of about 1455°C. At determining the stress value, a correction was applied, namely 60 N was deducted from the maximum force value. This correction was related to overcoming the mechanical system resistance to motion. The knowledge of characteristic temperatures also allows us to determine the steel susceptibility to fracture, which is characterised by the following fracture resistance indicator R_f:

$$R_f = \frac{\mathrm{NST} - \mathrm{NDT}}{\mathrm{NDT}} \tag{1}$$

When the condition NST – NDT < 20C is met, it is assumed that no fracture occurs in steels. As the assumed extreme bottom temperature NST for the steel 11SMn30 tested was 1395°C, the above condition was not met. It indicates that the cast strand shell can break during its formation within the mould, and within the secondary cooling zone. Therefore, we can suppose that this steel is characterised by a high susceptibility to fracture. From the perspective of numerical simulations, the issue of developing a function describing changes in stress versus strain, strain rate and the test nominal temperature becomes very important. The relationships of changes in stress versus strain were determined on the basis of tensile tests. In the experiment, a cylindrical sample was heated to a temperature of 1380°C at a rate of 20°C/s and next at a rate of 1°C/s to 1460°C. The last stage was cooling at a rate of 10°C/s to the deformation temperature. The samples were deformed within the temperature range of 1200–1460°C at three various tool stroke rates of 1, 20 and 100 mm/s.

Figures 3 and **4** present the stress-strain curves obtained directly from the experiment for two various tool stroke rates. The issues of determining the mentioned relationships are complex due to the fact that the temperature field within the sample volume is highly heterogeneous.

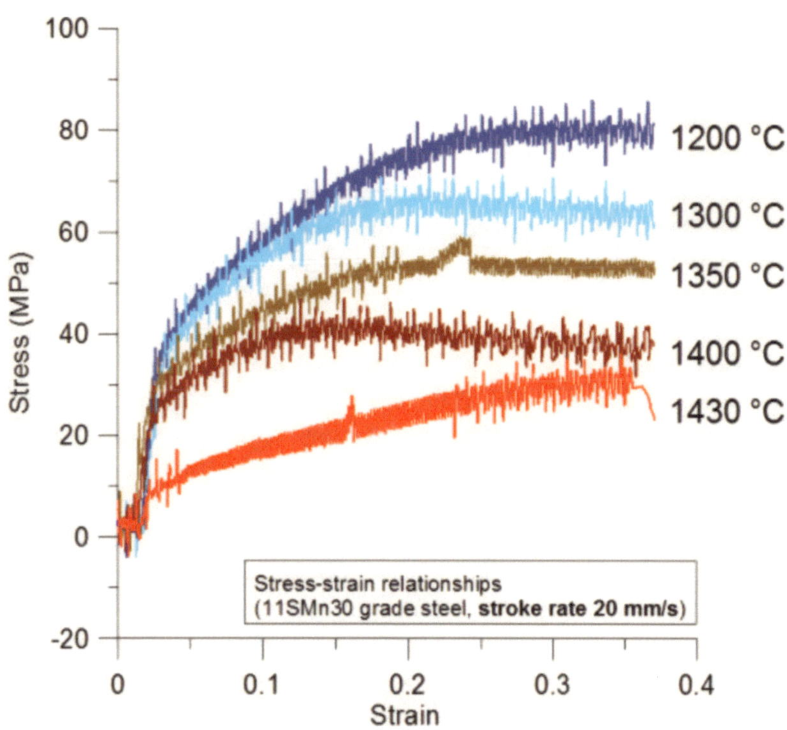

Figure 3. Stress-strain relationships for 11SMn30 grade steel (stroke rate 20 mm/s).

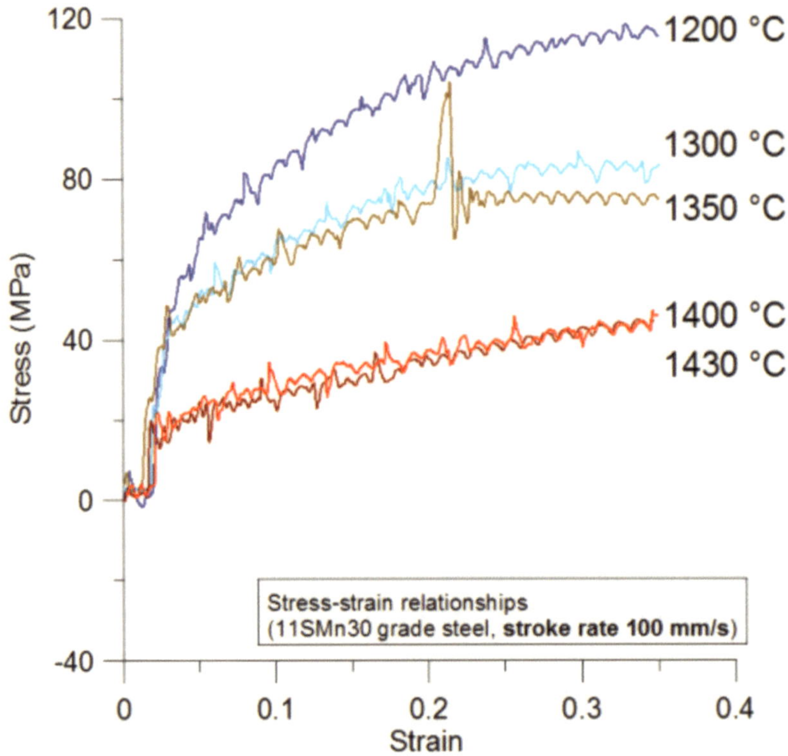

Figure 4. Stress-strain relationships for 11SMn30 grade steel (stroke rate 100 mm/s).

At temperatures a high, even small local temperature variations cause rapid local changes in the stress values. The originally applied NIM methodology supported with inverse calculations, and its later modifications, used axially symmetrical solutions [7]. Comprehensive experimental research carried out as part of the project showed substantial discrepancies between the measured values (e.g. force, temperature) for identically repeated tests. In addition, the developed methodology of a 3D analysis of the sample remelting zone using a modern computer tomograph NANOTOM 180N showed a very high asymmetry of the remelting zones obtained [7], which also proved a high asymmetry of the temperature field within the sample volume. Therefore, the obtained results and the conducted analyses suggested a question whether the use of the NIM methodology—very time consuming and complex in terms of computing—was reasonable. Another relevant aspect was the quality of the developed functions describing changes in stress versus strain, strain rate and temperature. The conducted variant calculations in the first approach using inverse computing and next a new functional model of resistance heating (presented hereinafter) to determine the temperature field after the resistance heating process have led to completely different graphs of stress-strain changes. The mentioned discrepancies, among others, arose from differences in the distribution of the computed temperature field between the two methods, sometimes reaching a few Celsius degrees just in the zone of deformation, and the limitations themselves that arose from the application of axially symmetrical models. In the light of the above inconveniences, a new methodology DIM (direct identification methodology) was developed. This methodology is presented in detail in the monograph [7]. The DIM utilises data directly recorded by the Gleeble 3800 simulator and the capabilities of the DEFFEM simulation package (**DEFFEM | inverse** module). The new methodology has a great advantage of being fast and flexible in determining function $\sigma_p = f(\varepsilon, \dot{\varepsilon}, T)$ parameters, while maintaining a good compatibility of force parameters between the actual and virtual processes.

In addition, as part of the developed methodology for determining high-temperature characteristics, also macro- and micro-structural tests were performed for each steel tested [7]. Examples of micro-structure of the tested steel 11SMn30 (sample core) deformed at the nominal temperatures of 1350 and 1410°C are presented in **Figure 5**. The analysis of microstructure shows that in the deformation zone acicular ferrite prevails, because of a high deformation temperature and a relatively high cooling rate. The other components of micro-structure are bainite and probably martensite.

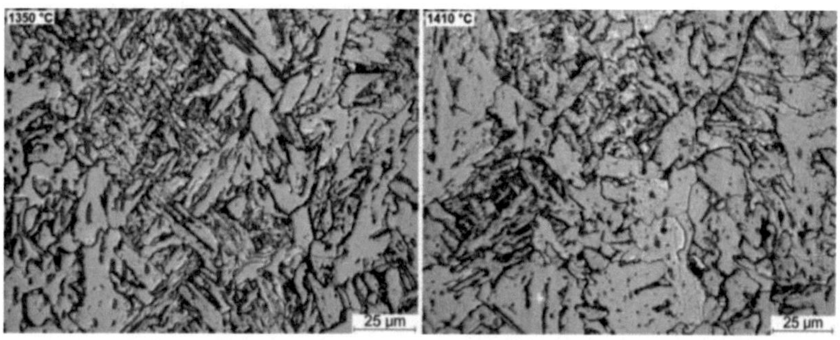

Figure 5. Micro-structure of the core of a sample deformed at a nominal temperature of 1350 and 1410°C (stroke rate 20 mm/s, magnification 400×).

4. Spatial mathematical models

This section presents main assumptions of the implemented 3D models within the DEFFEM package. As mentioned before, two alternative model approaches are developed. The first model approach is the multi-scale model MCFE, which enables heating-remelting, and next deforming in conditions of simultaneous solidification to be simulated. The proposed solution consists of three sub-models: a macro model based on the finite element method providing information about macroscopic behaviour of the medium deformed, a micro-model of the grain-growth process, melting and solidification based upon the Monte Carlo. The last third model is a model that couples the macro- and micro-solutions and facilitates exchange of information between them. The other alternatively developed model approach is a hybrid FESPH model of melting/solidification simulation combining the finite element method (FE) with the smoothed particle hydrodynamics (SPH).

4.1. Multi-scale model

The macro-solution of the mechanical model is based upon the application of a rigid-plastic model for a physical continuum. As showed by tests under conditions of hot deformation, the share of elastic strain in the strain tensor components is small [9, 10]. Applying the law of conservation of energy for a certain isolated system, which in the case concerned is the volume of the metal deformed, one can find that the total work performed in the system in a time unit is equal to the energy that this system gains in the same time. The energy balance for the zone deformed, referred to a time unit may be expressed by the relationship:

$$J = \int_V (\sigma_i \dot{\varepsilon}_i + \lambda \dot{\varepsilon}_{\text{vol}}) dV \tag{2}$$

where σ_i is the effective stress, $\dot{\varepsilon}_i$ is the effective strain rate, $\dot{\varepsilon}_{\text{vol}}$ is the volumetric strain rate and λ is the Lagrange multiplier. Discretisation of the functional (2) is performed in a typical finite element manner using hexahedral elements. The solution in the form of temperature field for the macro-model was searched by solving the Fourier equation, which in the general form can be written as follows:

$$\nabla^T (\lambda \nabla T) + \left(Q - c_p \rho \frac{\partial T}{\partial \tau} \right) = 0 \tag{3}$$

where T is the absolute temperature, λ is the thermal conductivity coefficient, Q is the heat generation rate for volume unit, c_p is the specific heat, ρ is the density and τ is the time.

The thermomechanical solution was directly adapted to the boundary conditions reflecting the Gleeble 3800 thermomechanical simulator system [7]. It allows an easy and fast verification of the obtained simulation results on the basis of experimental data. In classic rigid-plastic solutions, also the term responsible for the power generated as a result of friction on the metal-tool contact should be included in the power functional (2) [9]. Samples in the Gleeble simulator system are fixed in a rigid manner; therefore, the fraction term (coefficient of friction, $\mu = 0$) was not taken into account in the presented model. The resistance heating method is applied for heating of samples in the simulator system. As part of the project, a solution was developed in which a function associating change in the current intensity characteristics over the time, and resistivity versus temperature, was developed. The heat source efficiency Q in the model discussed is a function of resistance R, which in turn depends on temperature T and function A which represents intensify of heating:

$$Q = f\left(A(\tau) I^2(\tau) R(T) \right) \tag{4}$$

It corresponds to resistance changing in the actual model, and the internal heat source efficiency changes together with the resistance. When modelling the Joule heat generation, it was assumed that its equivalent in the numerical model will be the voluminal heat source with its power related to the resistance and the square of electric current I during simulation time τ.

The characteristics of the current intensity change as a function of heating time can be directly recorded during physical tests with the Gleeble 3800 simulator.

The Monte Carlo method was applied to simulate grain growth, melting and solidification. The main idea of the Monte Carlo technique is to divide a solution domain of the material into three-dimensional lattices of cells, where cells have clearly defined interaction rules between each other. Monte Carlo simulations have probabilistic character and base on minimalise system energy. The equation used for grain growth simulations only considers grain boundary energy. The total energy of the system is the total grain boundary energy, which is calculated as the sum of all links between neighbouring cells with dissimilar states multiplied by the link energy as

$$E = J_{gbe} \sum_{<i,j>} (1 - \delta_{ij}) \tag{5}$$

where J_{gbe} is the grain boundary energy, i is each cell ranging from 1 to the total numbers of cells, j is the neighbor of site i ranging from 1 to the number of neighbours of i and δ is the Kronecker delta. The kinetics of grain growth is simulated by the selection of a cell and an attempt to change its state and identifier (the number that identifies affiliation to a specific grain) into the state of the neighbouring grain cell. Cells inside a grain, which do not have neighbours belonging to another grain, cannot change their state. When a grain boundary cell attempts to change its state, it selects randomly a state from one of its neighbouring grains. The change energy accompanying this state swap is calculated using Eq. (5) and is accepted with the probability P:

$$P = \begin{cases} e^{-\frac{\Delta E}{kT}} & \Delta E > 0 \\ 1 & \Delta E \leq 0 \end{cases} \tag{6}$$

where kT is the parameter and in the context here and is the simulation temperature. The attempted change in cell state is always successful when $\Delta E \leq 0$. When $\Delta E > 0$, change in cell state is predicted in proportion to the probability P using the Metropolis algorithm [11]. If a randomly generated number R_n from 0 to 1 is less than P, the cell's state is changed into a new one. Otherwise, the cell's state does not change. The very specificity of the heating/remelting process analysed in the Gleeble 3800 simulator system is very similar to the issues related to the welding process and the utilisation of the Monte Carlo method to analyse those processes [11]. **Figure 6** presents macro-structures of samples for two extreme cooling rates (maximum and minimum) and for the rate being their average. Here, we can distinguish four zones: remelting zone (RZ), transition zone (TZ), heat impact zone (HIZ) and grip impact zone (GIZ). The analysis of macro-structures obtained by the experiment and the numerical simulations indicates a large diversification of grain size in individual zones. This arises primarily from various cooling rates achieved locally in individual zones.

The solidification process (without deformation) may be modelled using both the Monte Carlo model and model based on Rappaz-Gandin solutions [7]. The concept of modelling the sample solidification process with its simultaneous deformation required developing an innovative

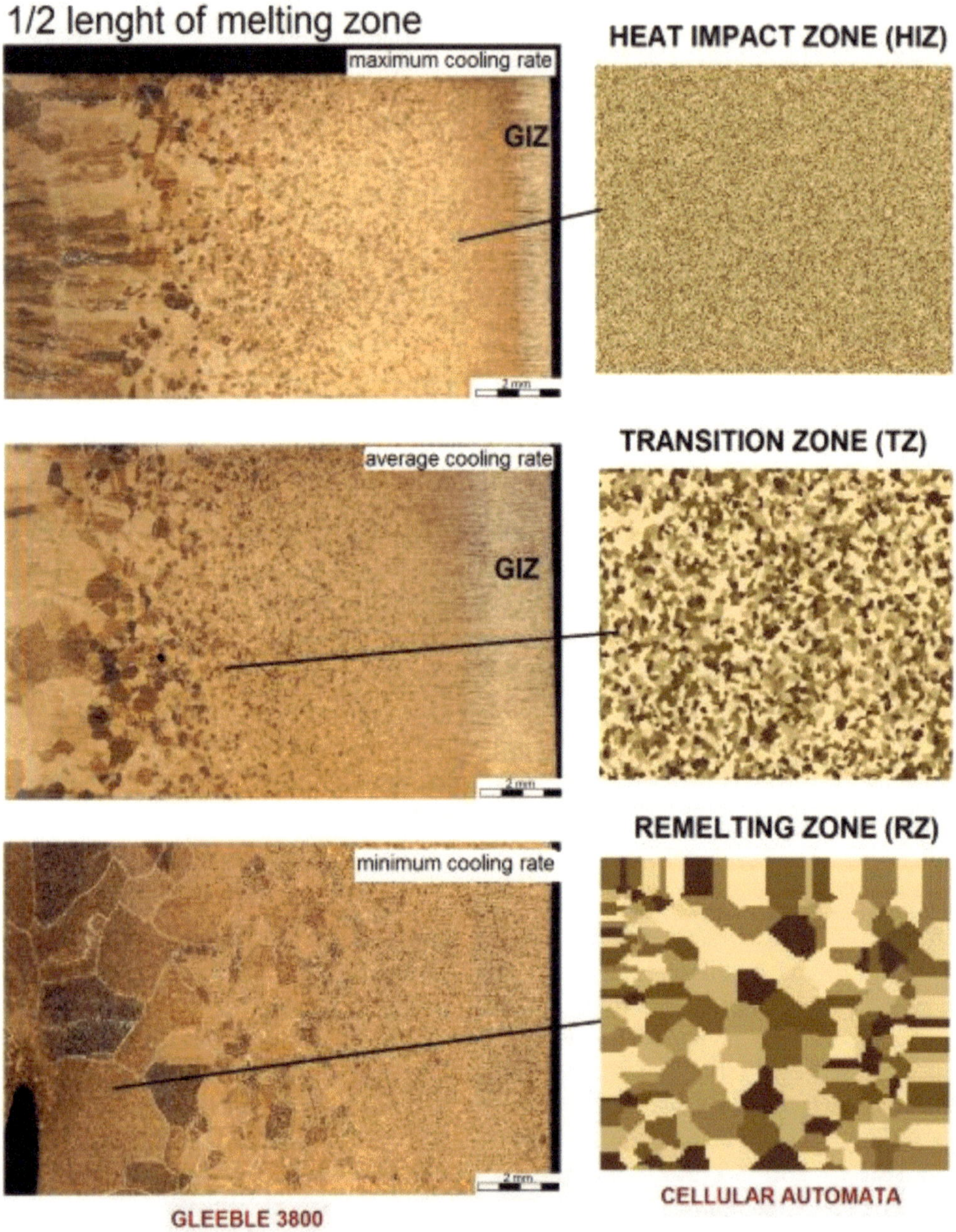

Figure 6. Macro-structure of samples cooled at various rates (physical simulation, computer simulation).

approach to the coupling of the macro-model with the micro-model. The developed MCFE model is based on the assumption that the cells directly correspond to the finite element integration points. As a result, the grain growth, melting and solidification is modelled by the

MC model and deformation process is modelled by the finite element model. A diagram of the macro-(FE) and micro-(MC) model coupling and the information flow is presented in **Figure 7**. Coupling between FE model and MC model is realised by the special Fortran subroutine

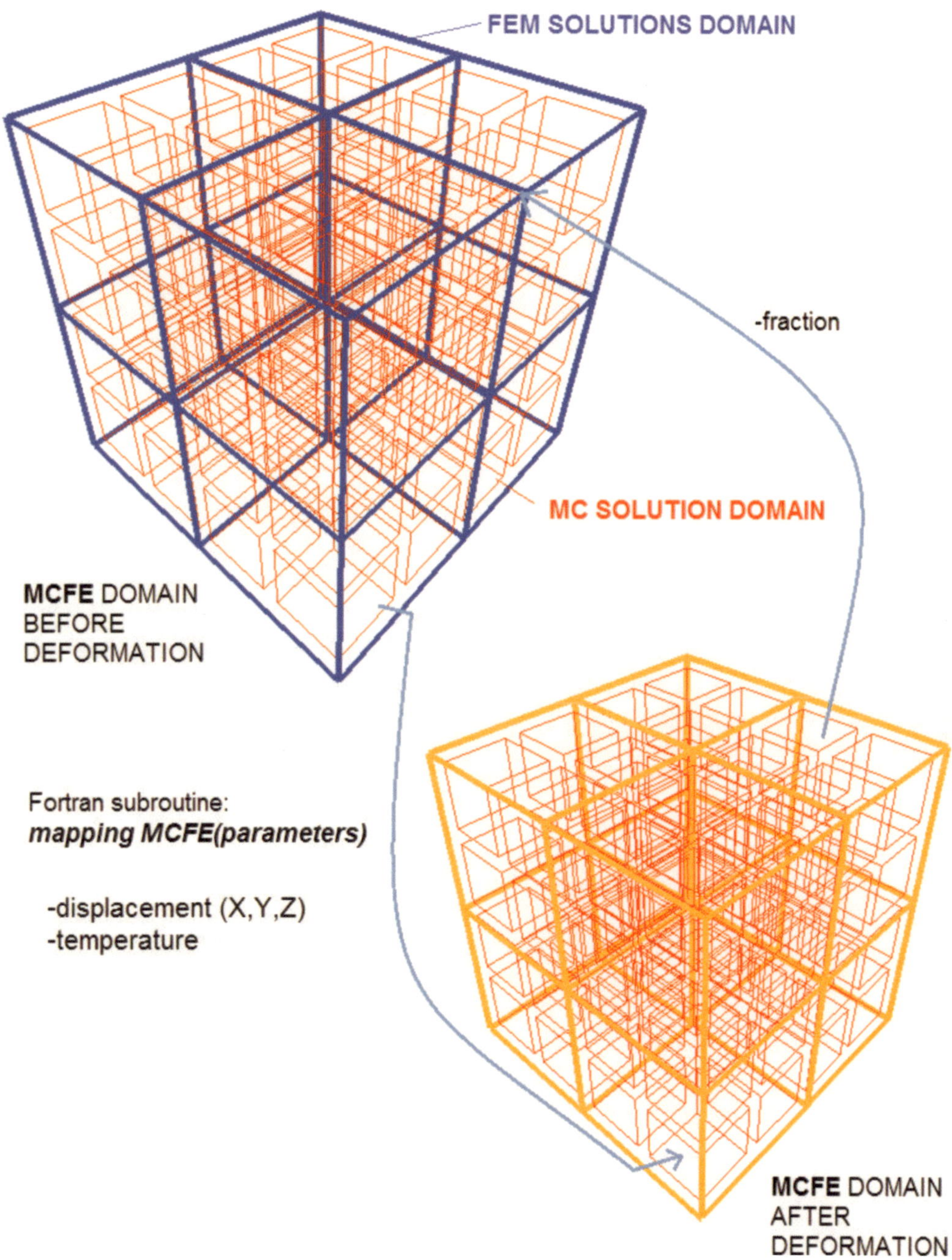

Figure 7. Diagram of the macro (FEM) model and micro (MC) model coupling and the information flow.

mappingMCFE(parameters). In each solution step, information from macro-model regarding positions of integration points and calculated temperatures is send to the micro model. The feedback for the macro-model may be the estimated share of liquid and solid phases which is used to modify the flow stress value for the specified integration point during the next solution step. The whole procedure is performed in a loop to the end of simulation.

4.2. Hybrid model

The hybrid model of the solidification process consists of two solution domains and a special coupling model. The solution of the thermal model based on the finite element method (FEM) is the first solution domain. As part of the first domain, the process of controlled heating/remelting is performed, and next the sample is controlled cooled in the Gleeble 3800 simulator system. The simulation of the solidification process and the liquid steel flow within the solid phase skeleton is performed by the second solution domain based on the smoothed particle hydrodynamics. The governing equations of fluids in the SPH method are based on the Navier-Stokes equations in the Lagrangian form. The main equations are given by [12, 13]

$$\frac{d\rho}{d\tau} = -\rho\nabla \cdot v \tag{7}$$

$$\rho\frac{dv}{d\tau} = -\nabla p + \nabla \cdot \theta + \rho F \tag{8}$$

where τ is the time, v is the velocity, p is the pressure, F is the external force and θ is a second-order tensor containing τ_{ij} stresses. Equation (7) is the continuity equation, which describes the evolution of the fluid density over time, and Eq. (8) is the momentum equation, which describes the acceleration of the fluid medium. By employing the SPH interpolation given by

$$\langle \nabla f(r_i) \rangle \approx \sum_{j=1}^{N} \frac{m_j}{\rho_j} f_j \nabla_i W(r_i - r_j, h) \tag{9}$$

to Eq. (7), the SPH representation of the continuity equation can be written as follow [12, 13]:

$$\frac{d\rho_i}{d\tau} = \sum_{j=1}^{N} m_j(v_i - v_j) \cdot \nabla_i W_{ij} \tag{10}$$

where m_j and ρ_j are the mass and the density for particle j, respectively, W is the smoothing kernel, index j corresponds to any neighbouring particle of particle i, f_j is the value of f for particle j, N is the total number of particles and h is the smoothing length that defines the radius of influence around the current particle i.

The momentum equation can be rewritten in the SPH formalism as

$$\frac{dv_i}{d\tau} = -\sum_{j=1}^{N} m_j \left(\frac{p_j}{\rho_j^2} + \frac{p_i}{\rho_i^2} + \Pi_{ij} \right) \cdot \nabla_i W_{ij} + F \tag{11}$$

The viscous force used in this implementation is the viscosity term which was introduced by Monaghan [12] denoted by Π_{ij}. Equation (11) shows that the change of the motion of a particle is due to the pressure field, the viscosity and the body forces acting on the fluid. An equation of state is required to calculate the pressure in Eq. (11). The equation of state used in the presented model is a quasi-compressible form, which is calculated using the density calculation from Eq. (10) and is given by [12]

$$p = \beta \left[\left(\frac{\rho}{\rho_{\text{ref}}} \right)^{\gamma} - 1 \right] \tag{12}$$

where ρ_{ref} is the reference density, c is the speed of sound, β is the magnitude of pressure, $\gamma=7$ for liquid steel. The dynamic particle was selected as a definition of boundary conditions [14].

The model of heat conduction is based on the enthalpy method which is given by [15, 16]

$$\frac{dH}{d\tau} = \frac{1}{\rho} \nabla (\lambda \nabla T) \tag{13}$$

where H is the enthalpy, λ is the thermal conductivity and T is the temperature. The SPH formulation of Eq. (13) is approximated using the SPH which is given by [15]

$$\frac{dH_i}{d\tau} = \sum_j \frac{m_j}{\rho_i \rho_j} \frac{4\lambda_i \lambda_j}{(\lambda_i + \lambda_j)} (T_i - T_j) \frac{(r_i - r_j) \cdot \nabla_i W_{ij}}{(r_i - r_j)^2 + \eta^2} \tag{14}$$

where η is a small parameter to prevent singularity when $(r_i - r_j)$ goes to zero. This equation guarantees that the heat flux is automatically continuous across the different material interfaces, such as between the liquid and solid metals. This also allows multiple phases with different conductivities to be accurately simulated [15]. The model coupling the both domains (FE+SPH) is based upon a solution of coupling by fixing particles to the FE nodes.

5. Computer simulations: example results

This section presents examples of results of numerical simulations performed with the DEFFEM package developed. The first simulation range included the process of heating and deforming within temperature ranges close to the solidus line (without the liquid phase). The obtained findings were verified on the basis of the developed methodology of deformation zone measurement using 3D scanning technology with blue light [7]. The second stage of work included simulations concerning fluid mechanics. The obtained findings were verified on the basis of well-known laws of physics.

5.1. Test simulations of the DEFFEM|solver_3D_TM

The numerical simulations and experiments were carried out with two types of hexahedral samples with a cross-section 10 × 10 mm and lengths of 100 mm (sample type B) and 125 mm (sample type C) made of steel S355 [7, 17]. The experiments and numerical computations were conducted on the basis of the research methodology presented in study [7]. In the simulation, a sample was heated to a temperature of 1400°C at a rate of 20°C/s, and next to a temperature of 1450°C at a rate of 1°C/s. **Figures 8–11** present the temperature distribution for the selected heating stages for both sample types. Referring to the observed temperatures at the sample surface and the maximum temperatures achieved in the sample core, one may observe an increasing temperature gradient on its cross-section as the heating time passes. For a sample type B, after 10 s this difference was 4.4°C, after 70 s growing up to 33.9°C. For the variant with a sample type C (longer), these differences were slightly bigger and were 4.7 and 35.2°C, respectively.

In order to verify the obtained results of the heating simulation in the experiments, a thermo-vision camera was used to record the profile of the temperature change along the sample heating zone (**Figure 12**).The obtained results of the experiment and simulation are characterised by a parabolic course, and the correct compatibility between the experimental and calculated values. The average relative error calculated for 13 checkpoints was 14.5%. At the last stage, the deformation process was performed, assuming the stroke of 5 mm and the stroke rate of 1 mm, following sample cooling at a rate of 10°C/s to the nominal deformation temperature. The deformation experiments were performed for a temperature scope 1200–1400°C. **Figure 13** presents the total Z displacement distribution and the general characteristics of boundary conditions identified in the Gleeble simulator system and adapted to the numerical solution [7]. Three main zones can be distinguished for both sample types. The first zone (sample fixed) defines the grip contact area that does not move during the physical simulation

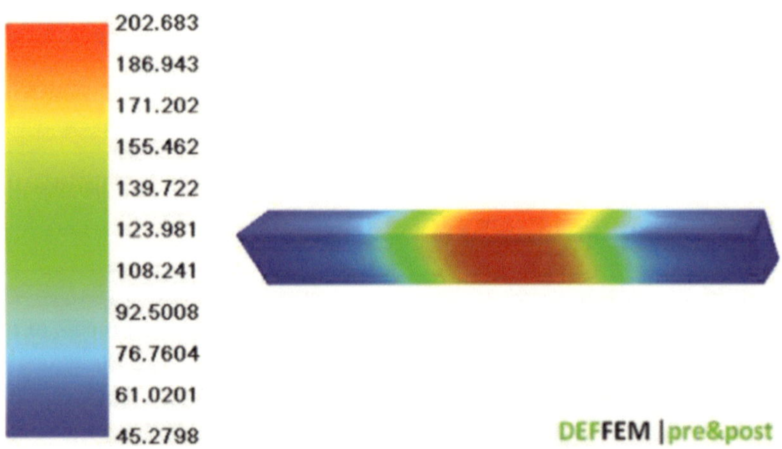

Figure 8. Temperature distribution after 10 s of heating (sample type B, surface temperature 198.286°C).

http://dx.doi.org/10.5772/67735

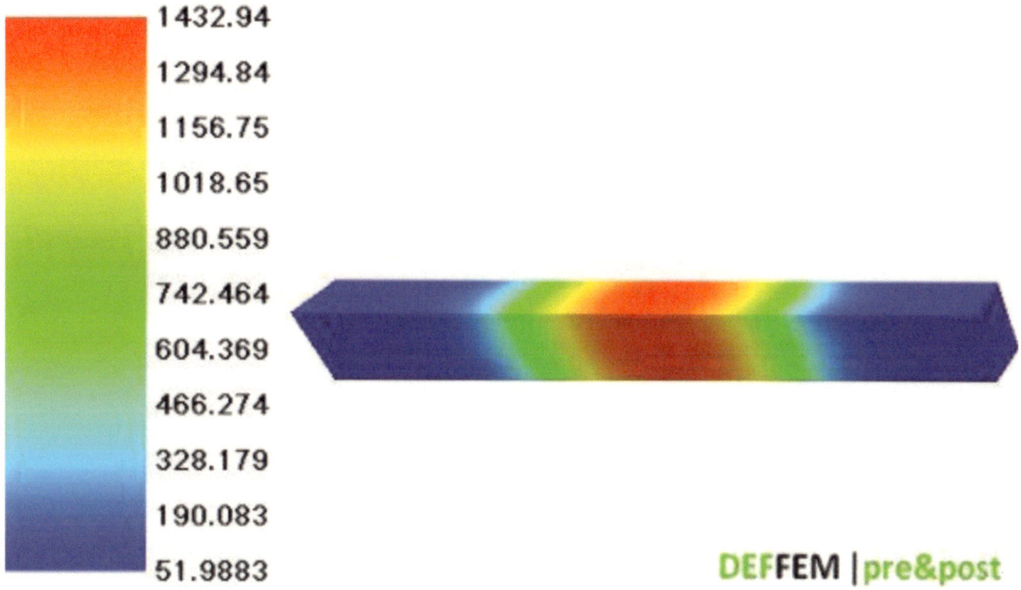

Figure 9. Temperature distribution after 70 s of heating (sample type B, surface temperature 1.399.13°C).

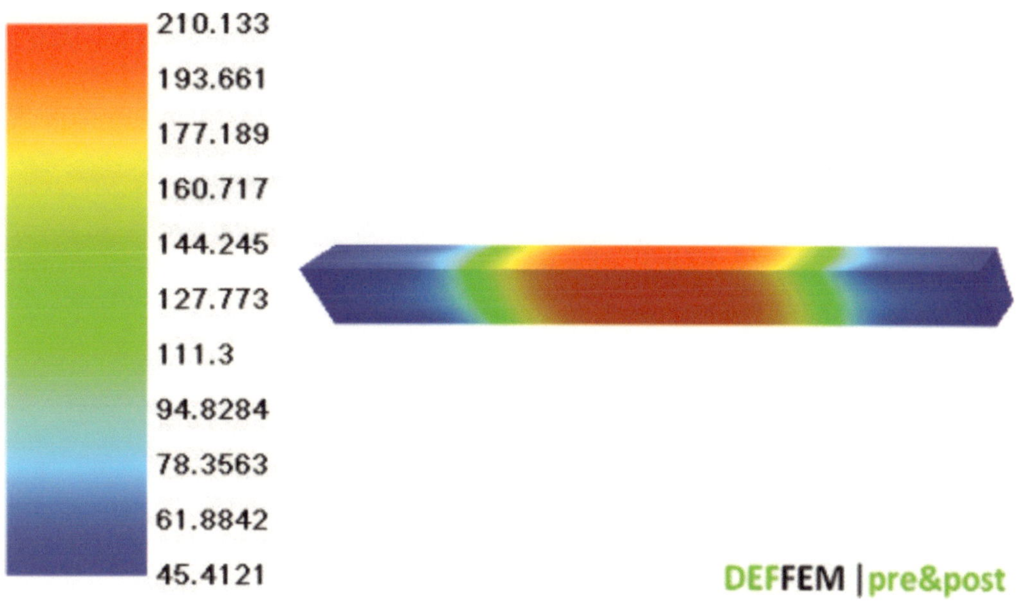

Figure 10. Temperature distribution after 10 s of heating (sample type C, surface temperature 205.405°C).

and the second zone (sample movement) is the grip contact zone that moves by a set stroke. The central zone is a free zone with the highest strain accumulation, which for a sample type B is 39.5 mm long.

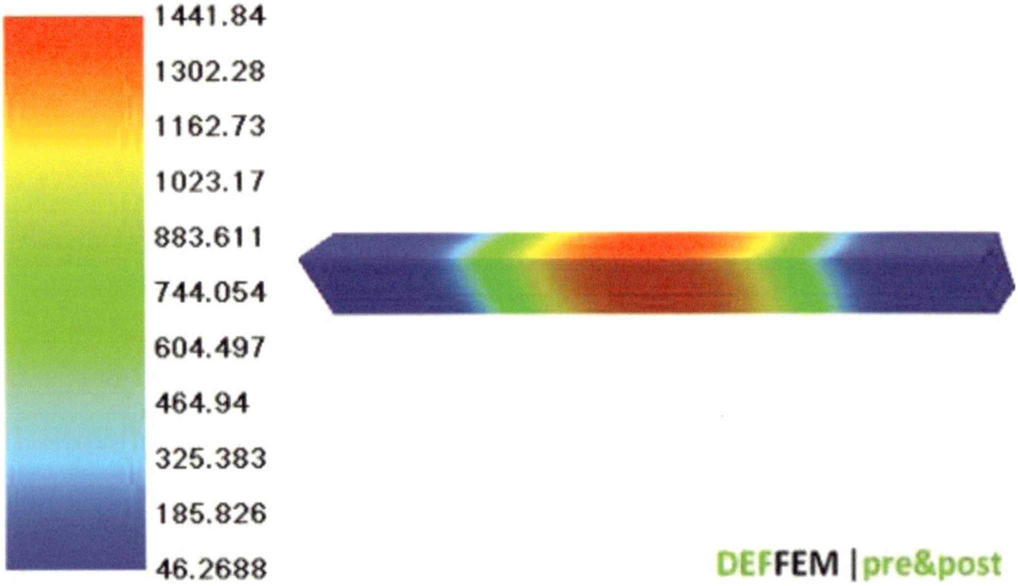

Figure 11. Temperature distribution after 70 s of heating (sample type C, surface temperature 1.406.63°C).

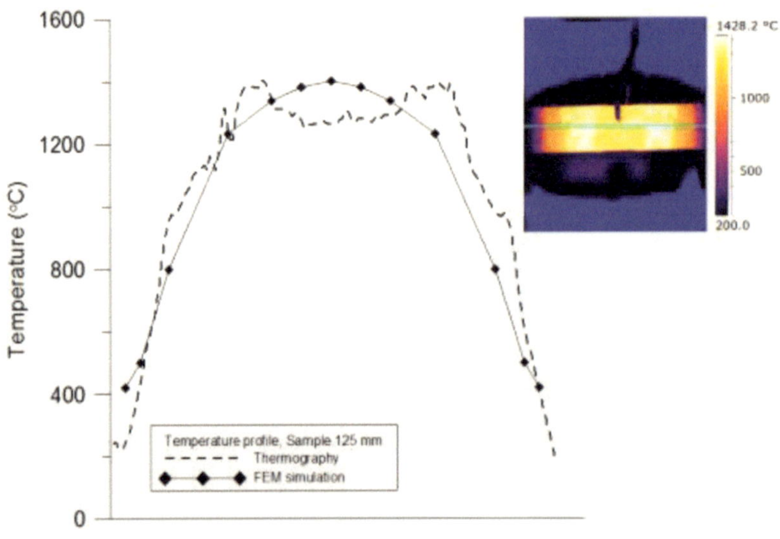

Figure 12. The temperature profile along the heating zone calculated and determined by the experiment (test nominal temperature 1400°C, sample type C).

Figures 14 and **15** present the strain distribution (ε_z component) for the strain variant at two nominal temperatures 1200 and 1400°C. Strain cumulates mainly in the central deformation zone, reaching slightly higher values for the deformation test performed at a temperature of 1400°C.

http://dx.doi.org/10.5772/67735

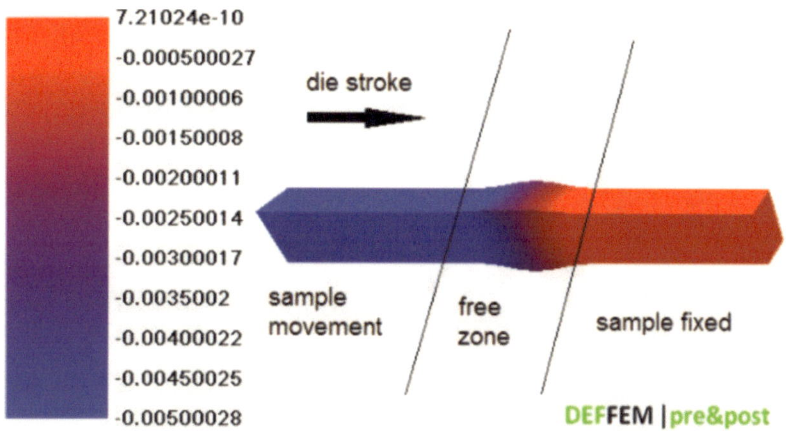

Figure 13. Total Z displacement distribution (sample type B, test nominal temperature 1400°C).

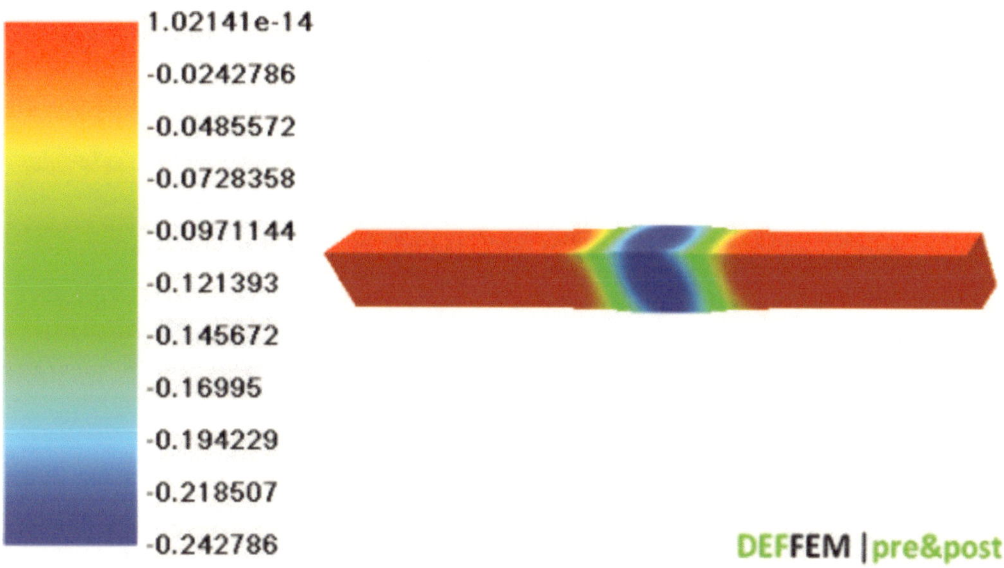

Figure 14. Strain distribution, ε_z component (sample type C, test nominal temperature 1200°C).

Analysing the shape and size of the strain zones resulting from the simulation (**Figures 14** and **15**) and experiment (**Figure 16**), one may observe that they feature a very high geometrical similarity. To verify the obtained findings, the developed measurement methodology with blue light scanning was applied [7]. **Figure 17** presents a map of deviations between the obtained numerical calculation meshes after the deformation process at a temperature of 1200 and 1400°C. The sample deformed at 1200°C was selected as the standard in the mapping procedure. The analysis of the obtained results indicates an increase in the cross-section of the sample deformed at 1400°C, and a slight decrease in the strain zone length compared to the sample deformed at 1200°C.

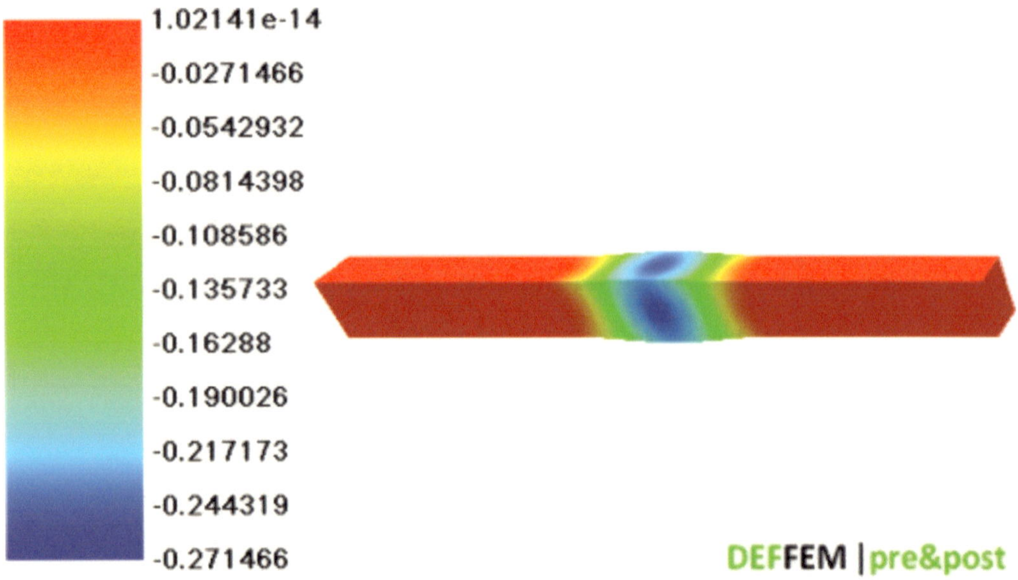

Figure 15. Strain distribution, ε_z component (sample type C, test nominal temperature 1400°C).

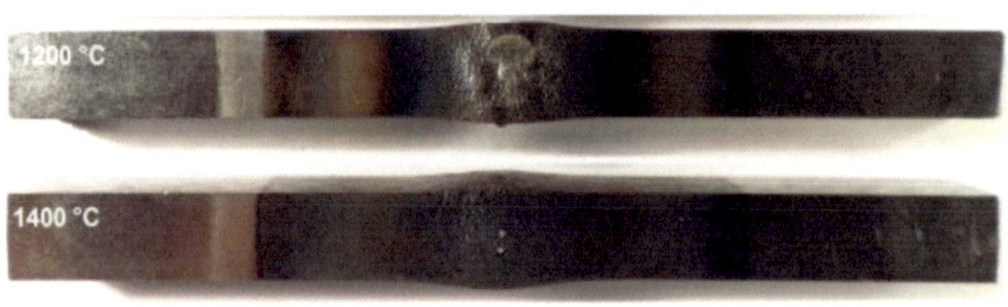

Figure 16. Pictures of samples after deforming at 1200 and 1400°C (sample type C).

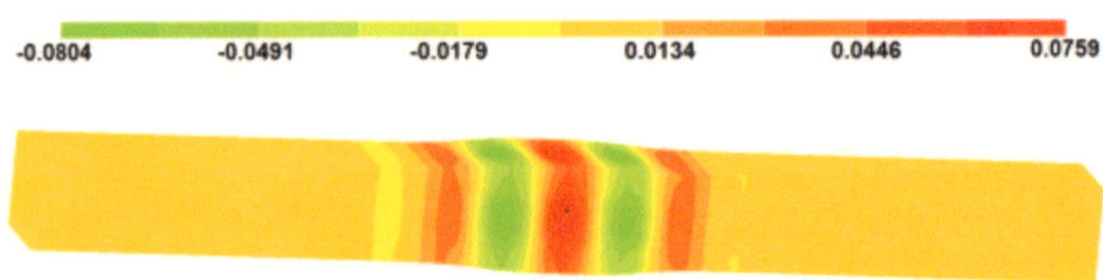

Figure 17. The deviation map between two finite element meshes for two deformation temperatures (sample type C).

An analogous methodology was applied to compare the obtained shape of the deformation zone from the computer simulation to the experimental shape (**Figures 18–25**). An analysis of the obtained deviation maps indicates that the local difference of 1 mm was not exceeded in any case. The maximum absolute value was 0.99 mm for a sample type B deformed at a temperature of 1400°C and the minimum absolute value of 0.4583 mm for a sample type B deformed at 1350°C.

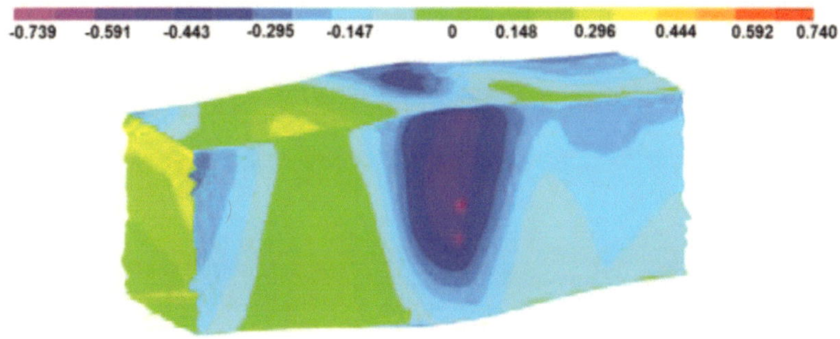

Figure 18. The deviation map between the finite element mesh and the mesh obtained from the 3D scanner (sample type C, 1200°C).

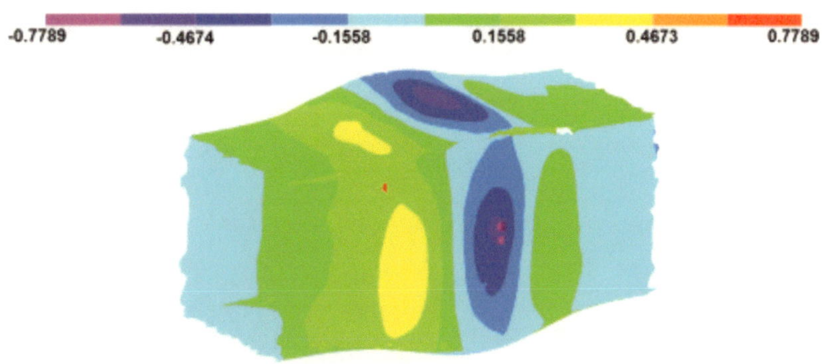

Figure 19. The deviation map between the finite element mesh and the mesh obtained from the 3D scanner (sample type B, 1200°C).

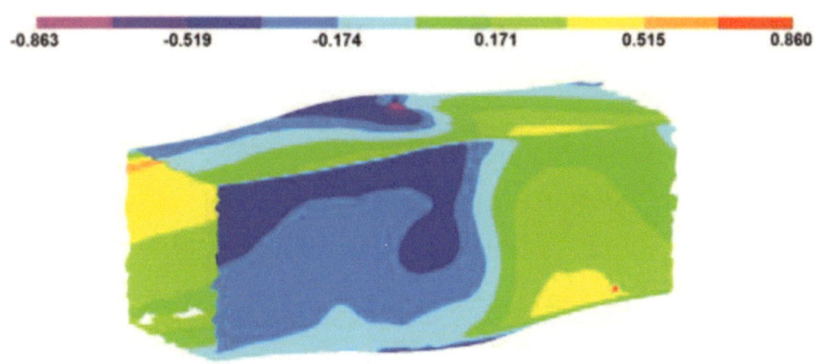

Figure 20. The deviation map between the finite element mesh and the mesh obtained from the 3D scanner (sample type C, 1300°C).

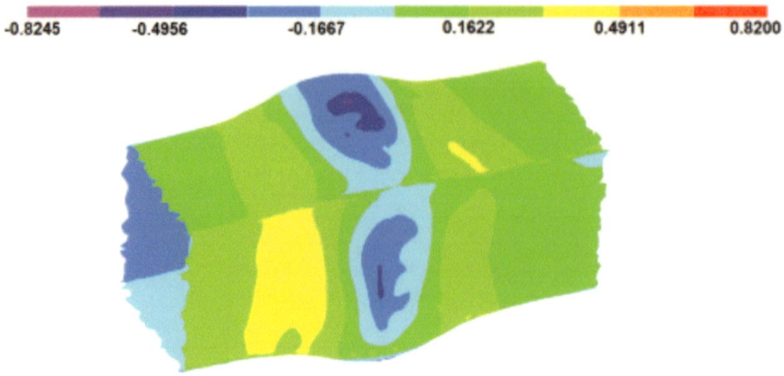

Figure 21. The deviation map between the finite element mesh and the mesh obtained from the 3D scanner (sample type B, 1300°C).

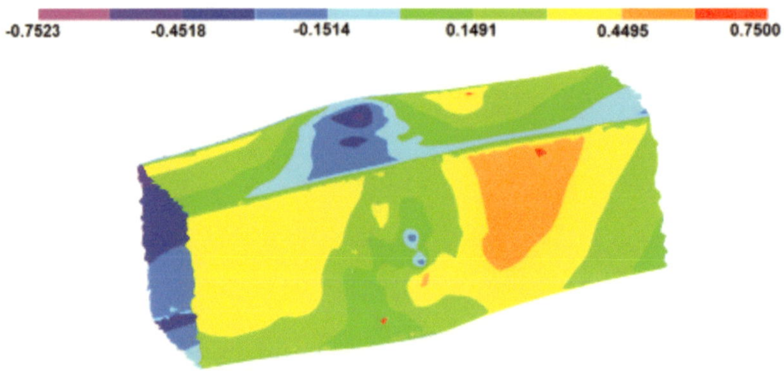

Figure 22. The deviation map between the finite element mesh and the mesh obtained from the 3D scanner (sample type C, 1350°C).

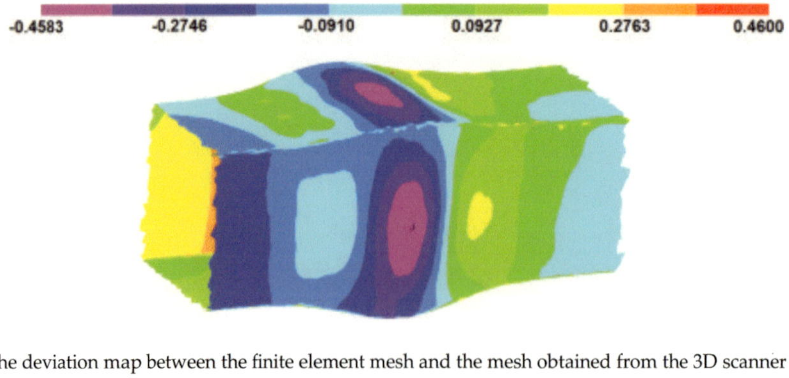

Figure 23. The deviation map between the finite element mesh and the mesh obtained from the 3D scanner (sample type B, 1350°C).

http://dx.doi.org/10.5772/67735

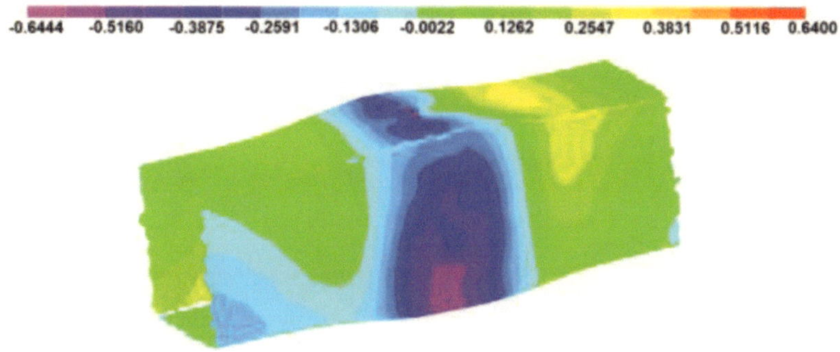

Figure 24. The deviation map between the finite element mesh and the mesh obtained from the 3D scanner (sample type C, 1400°C).

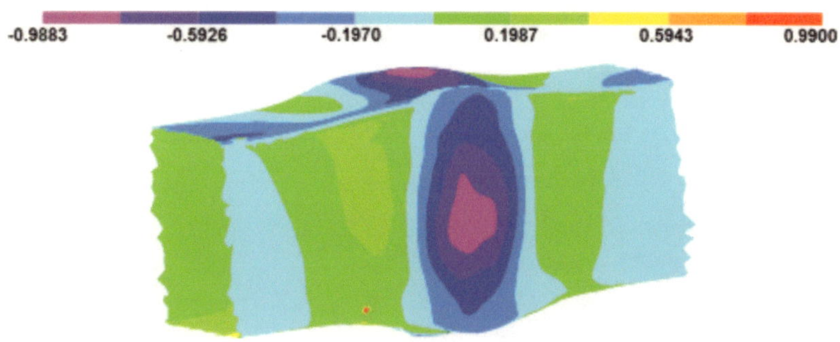

Figure 25. The deviation map between the finite element mesh and the mesh obtained from the 3D scanner (sample type B, 1400°C).

5.2. Test simulations of the DEFFEM | solver_3D_FLUID

Two simulations were carried out as part of the test simulations of the fluid mechanics solver. The first case of free particles fall was carried out in order to check the Runge-Kutta integration scheme used in the implementation. The second one is oriented for a structure impact simulation based on dynamic particles. The main feedback from this case is: can the dynamic particles handle this kind of boundary condition. The schemes of initial geometries of these problems are presented in **Figures 26** and **27**. Solution domain consists of 7351 (free fall case)/29,791 (barrier case) moving particles and 29,402 (free fall case)/34,443 (barrier case) dynamic particles represents boundary condition as a box given from particle to particle (width = 1.0 m, height = 1.0 m and length = 1.0 m). The initial drop height for free fall case was set 0.3 m. Other parameters adopted as: initial smoothing length= 0.024 m, speed of sound 30 m/s, α is equal to 0.5 and simulation time: 2.0 s.

Figure 28 presents the velocity field for a simulation time of 0.2 s, where the solution domain (fluid) did not interact with the substrate defined by dynamic particles representing the boundary condition. The mean particle velocity is around a given value 2 m/s. The current velocity perfectly corresponds to what is expected by the analytical solution (~1.96 m/s). On

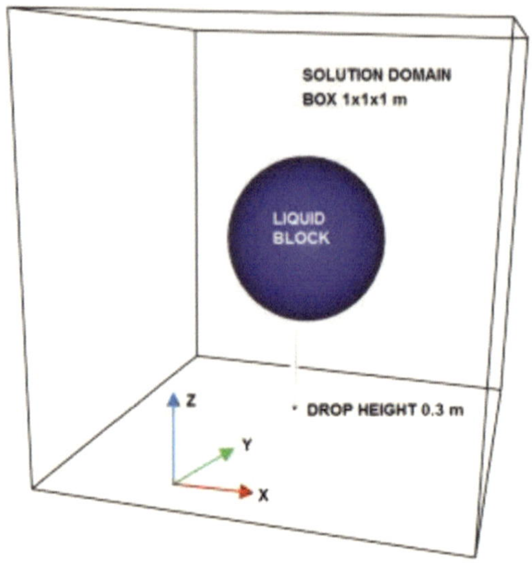

Figure 26. Solution domains for the 'free fall' test simulation.

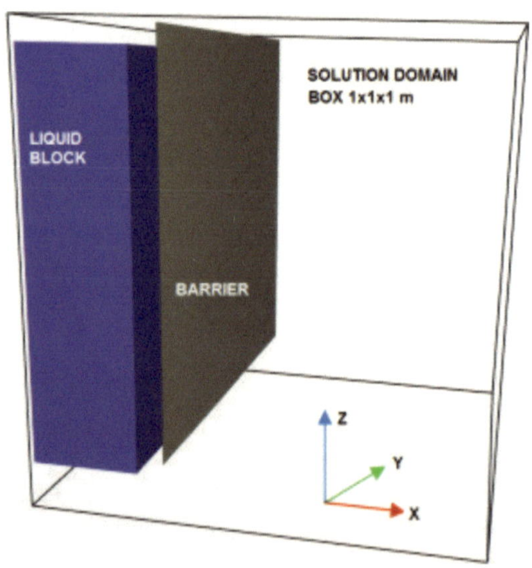

Figure 27. Solution domains for the 'barrier' test simulation.

the other hand, **Figure 29** presents the velocity field for a simulation time of 1.96 s, where the velocity field has already stabilised.

Analytical solutions and numerical solutions of a particle fall in respect to z position correspond excellent to what is expected by the analytical solution. Starting z position of particle ID:1 = 0.44 m, calculated z position of particle ID:1 = 0.24372551083597468 m after 0.2 s. Analytical solution z position of particle ID:1= 0.243718462 m after 0.2 s. This result indicates

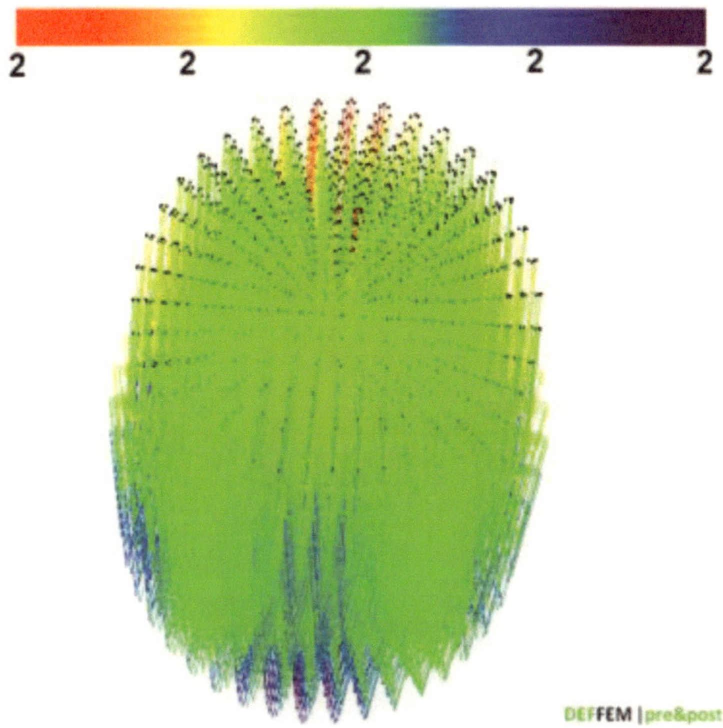

Figure 28. Vector velocity field (simulation time 0.20004155454510358 s).

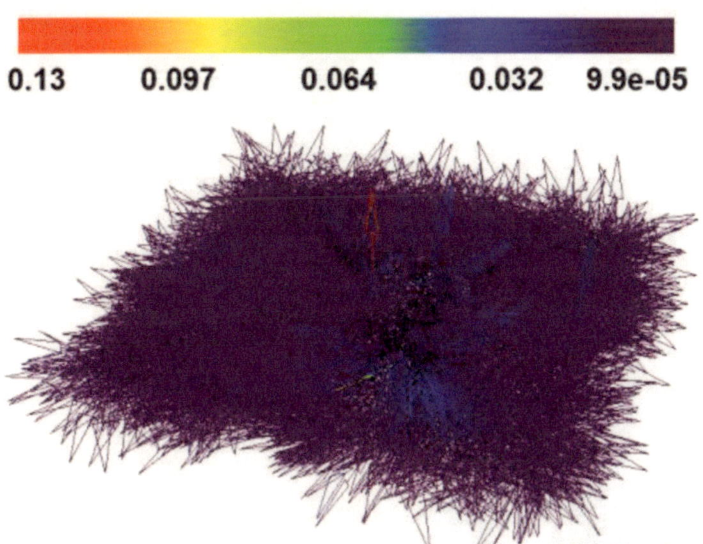

Figure 29. Vector velocity field (simulation time 1.9600608766537435 s).

that the Runge-Kutta integration scheme used in the implementation works correctly. **Figures 30–35** present the selected stages of the free flow simulation taking account of the fluid-structure interaction. The analysis of the obtained results indicates that the implemented

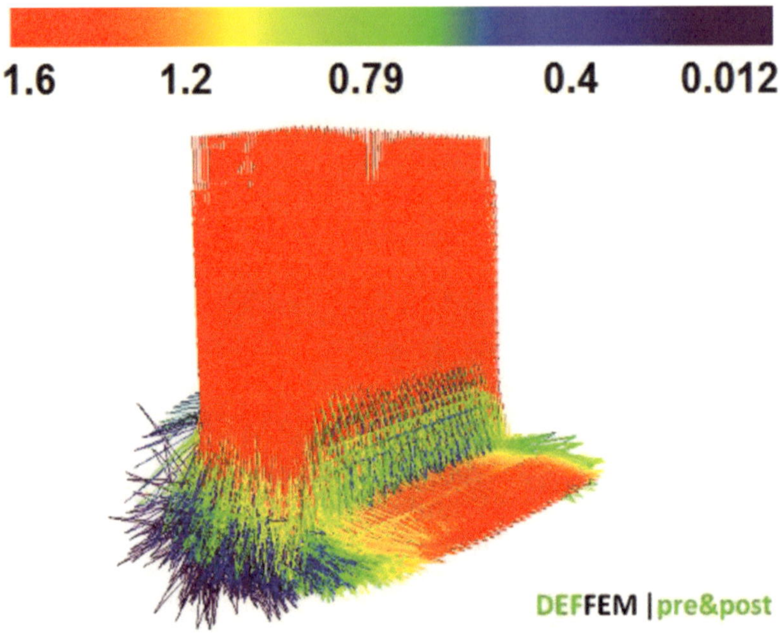

Figure 30. Vector velocity field (simulation time 0.16001791210049551 s).

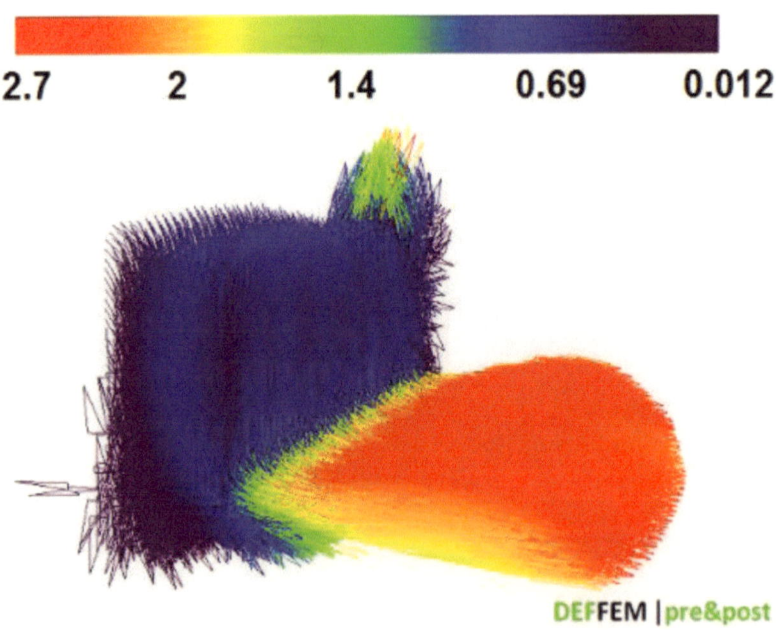

Figure 31. Vector velocity field (simulation time 0.36004176147624667 s).

http://dx.doi.org/10.5772/67735

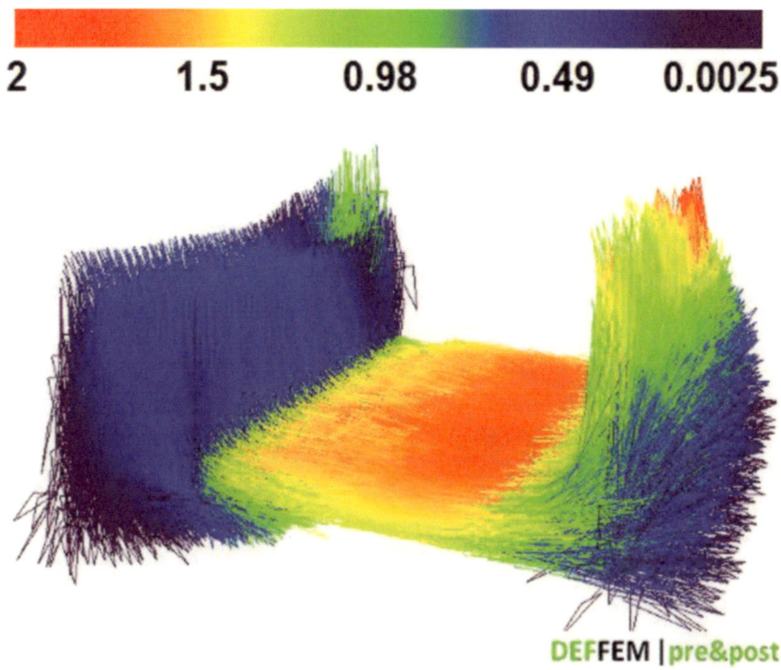

Figure 32. Vector velocity field (simulation time 0.56007371089547675 s).

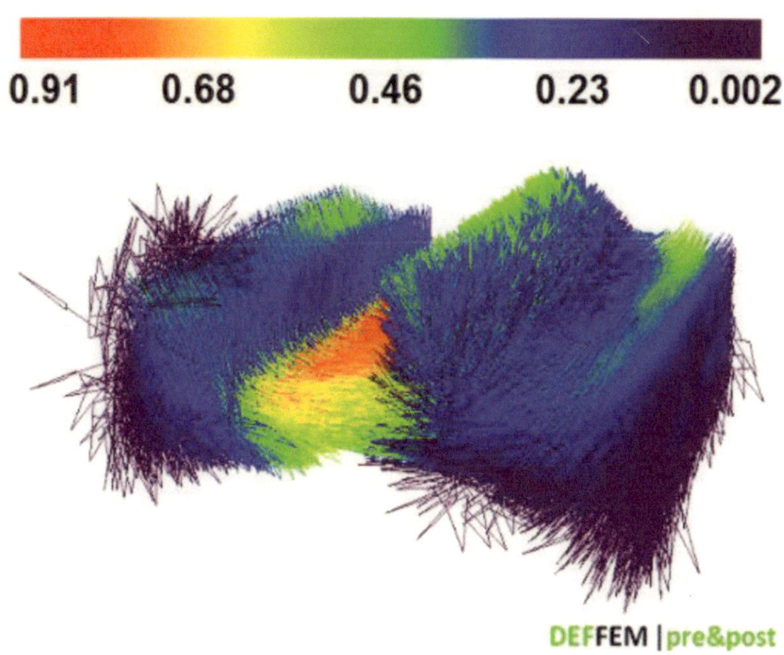

Figure 33. Vector velocity field (simulation time 0.96000801664997626 s).

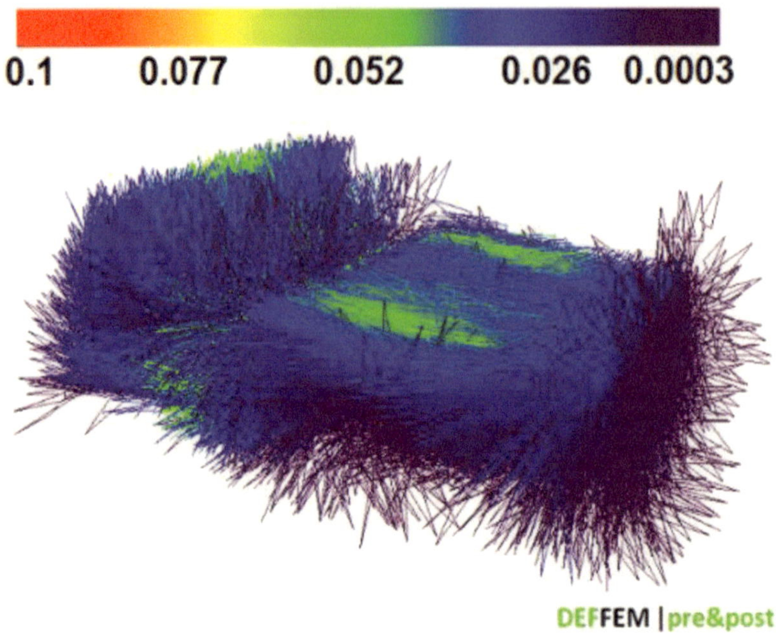

Figure 34. Vector velocity field (simulation time 1.5600837463861228 s).

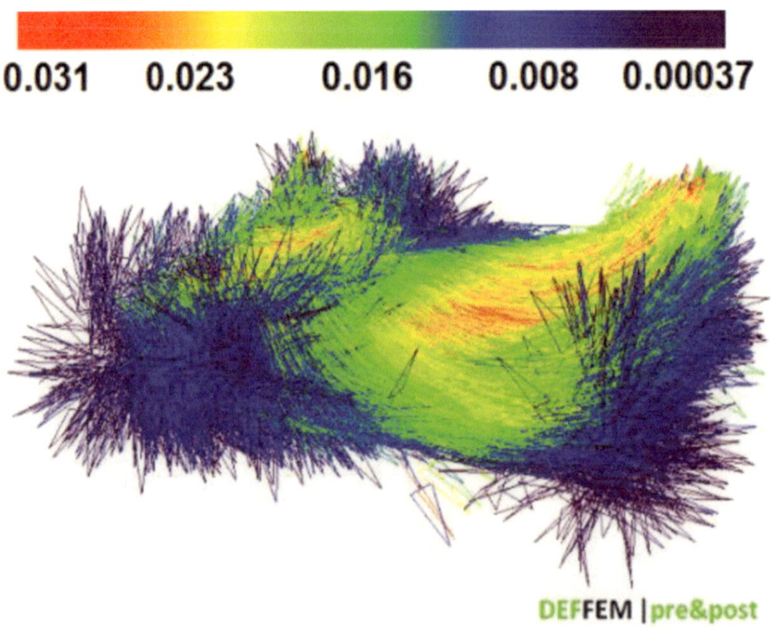

Figure 35. Vector velocity field (simulation time 2.0000482073234136 s).

interaction model is correct. We can observe a greater speed when the fluid passes through the barrier defined by dynamic particles. The velocity is increased as a high repulsion force is created by the boundary defined by dynamic particles (**Figure 31**). In the subsequent steps of the simulation, the fluid in the computing domain slowly equalises and the velocity field slowly stabilises (**Figures 34** and **35**). However, more tests for various variants are required for further detailed verification.

6. Summary

This chapter presents a multi-scale model MCFE (Monte Carlo and finite element) and a hybrid model FESPH combining the advantages of the finite element method (FEM) and the smoothed particle hydrodynamics (SPH). The developed models and methods constitute the basis of the scientific workshop focused on high-temperature processes. A great advantage of a solution like this is the full openness of source codes of the simulation system designed, which will be the basis for developing further new and innovative solutions. The conducted test simulations concerning continuum mechanics (the FEM solution) and fluid mechanics (the SPH solution) indicate the correctness of the implemented mathematical models in the context of determining temperature fields, strains or velocity fields. The DEFFEM package was successfully applied in practical projects accomplished with industrial partners as a design aiding tool. The present tests in collaboration with an industrial plant from the aviation and casting industry will allow us to perform additional industrial tests and to evaluate the suitability of the software in the computer-aided design.

Acknowledgements

The research has been supported by the Polish National Science Centre (2012–2017), decision number: DEC-2011/03/D/ST8/04041.

Author details

Marcin Hojny

Address all correspondence to: mhojny@metal.agh.edu.pl

AGH University of Science and Technology, Kraków, Poland

References

[1] Bald W et al. (2000) Innovative technologies for strip production. Steel Times Int. 24: 16–19.

[2] Cook R, Grocock PG, Thomas PM et al. (1995) Development of the twin-roll casting process. J Mater Proc Technol. 55:76–84.

[3] Fan P, Zhou S, Liang X et al. (1997) Thin strip casting of high speed steels. J Mater Proc Technol 63:792–796.

[4] Park CM, Kim W, Park GJ. (2003) Thermal analysis of the roll in the strip casting process. Mech Res Commun. 30:297–310.

[5] Seo PK, Park K, Kang C. (2004) Semi-solid die casting process with three steps die system. J Mater Proc Technol. 154:442–449.

[6] Watari H, Davey K, Rasgado MT, et al. (2004) Semi-solid manufacturing process of magnesium alloys by twin-roll casting. J Mater Proc Technol. 156:1662–1667.

[7] Hojny M (2017) Modeling of steel deformation in the semi-solid state. Advanced Structured Materials, vol. 78, Springer Switzerland.

[8] Hojny M. (2014) Projektowanie dedykowanych systemów symulacji odkształcania stali w stanie półciekłym. Wzorek, Krakow, Poland.

[9] Pietrzyk M. (1992) Metody numeryczne w przeróbce plastycznej metali. AGH, Krakow.

[10] Glowacki M. (1998) Termomechaniczno-mikrostrukturalny model walcowania w wykrojach kształtowych. AGH, Krakow, Poland.

[11] Yang Z, Sista S et al. (2000) Three dimensional Monte Carlo simulation of grain growth during GTA welding of titanium. Acta Mater. 48:4813–4825.

[12] Monaghan JJ. (1992) Smoothed particle hydrodynamics. Annu Rev Astron Astrophys. 30:543–574.

[13] Monaghan JJ. (1994) Simulating free surface flows with SPH. J Comput Phys. 110: 399–406.

[14] Crespo AAJC et al. (2007) Boundary Conditions Generated by Dynamic Particles in SPH Methods. Cmc—Tech Science Press USA 5:173–184.

[15] Cleary PW, Monaghan JJ. (1999) Conduction modelling using smoothed particle hydrodynamics. J Comput Phys. 148:227–264.

[16] Faqih RA, Naa CF. (2013) Three-dimensional smoothed particle hydrodynamics simulation for liquid metal solidification process. Mater. Proc. ISCS.

[17] Hojny M, Glowacki M. (2011) Modeling of strain-stress relationship for carbon steel deformed at temperature exceeding hot rolling range. J Eng Mater Technol, 133:021008-1–021008-7.

Chapter 7

Computer-Aided Physical Simulation of the Soft-Reduction and Rolling Process

Marcin Hojny

Additional information is available at the end of the chapter

http://dx.doi.org/10.5772/intechopen.68606

Abstract

The chapter presents experimental problems related to research aiming at obtaining data necessary to formulate a physical model of deformation of steel containing a zone consisting of a mixture of the solid and the liquid phases. This issue is strictly related to the application of the soft-reduction process in integrated strip casting and rolling. The original part of the developed methodology is the experiment computer aid performed with the proprietary simulation package DEFFEM. In order to solve problems related to the deformation of materials with a semi-solid core or at extra-high temperatures, comprehensive tests were applied, which covered both physical modelling with a Gleeble 3800 thermo-mechanical simulator and mathematical modelling. Examples of research findings presented in this chapter show that the developed methodology is correct in the context of experiment computer aid and show the need to develop software in order to implement full 3D models.

Keywords: mushy zone, finite elements method, extra-high temperature, resistance heating, tomography

1. Introduction

In recent years, a strong trend towards the development of integrated metallurgical processes can be observed. In these processes, the strand is cast to shape and dimensions near the final product and combined with product rolling [1–7]. Processes of integrated strip casting and rolling, which feature less material processing, and a direct connection of the casting process and strand rolling, can be used as an example. Here, problems related to the steel ductility and the formation of an appropriate product microstructure are very relevant. During an integrated process, contrary to classic hot forming processes, the strand is not cooled to a temperature at which austenite disintegrates [1–7]. Therefore, the original structure of the input material to the rolling process is the as-cast structure, which causes serious difficulties during the production cycle. The increasing access to modern Gleeble series physical simulators allows us to use the knowledge obtained during experiment with tests of designing processes of strip integrated casting and rolling [8, 9]. A Gleeble 3800 simulator enables the so-called physical simulation of a specific process to be carried out. The objective of a simulation like this is to use a small sample, which is made of the same material that is used in the production process. Changes of stress, strains and temperatures, the material is subjected to in the actual production process, are reconstructed in the mentioned sample, which most often is cylindrical [10]. On the basis of the performed physical simulation cycle (variants for various cooling rates, stroke rates, etc.), process maps are developed, and then these maps help to estimate the optimal parameters of the process line equipment. Special diagrams are then constructed, where areas with a limited ductility are marked. Knowing such areas thoroughly allows the process parameters to be adjusted so as to avoid potential strand cracking. Despite huge capabilities of thermo-mechanical simulators as regards a simulation combining a physical simulation of solidification with a simultaneous plastic deformation set during, as well as immediately after the total solidification, each steel grade requires separate comprehensive tests. Therefore, a computer simulation is recommended. The main problem with computer simulations involves lack of constitutive equations, which allow the plastic behaviour of the steel tested to be determined. We need to emphasize that testing mechanical and physical properties, as well as the sample deformation itself at such high temperatures is only possible to a limited extent, with a strictly specified test methodology [10]. Therefore, the goal of this study is to develop a methodology to enable a multi-stage simulation combining the steel deformation process in the semi-solid state and in the solid state, as well as to evaluate its suitability for the future research and development work.

2. Physical simulation

The experimental tests were conducted with a Gleeble 3800 thermo-mechanical simulator. The basic tests were conducted with cylindrical samples made of steel S355, with a length of 125 mm and a diameter of 10mm, using two types of copper grips, so-called "hot" and "cold" ones. The selection of an appropriate grip type determines the attainable size of the free zone of the sample deformed [10]. For "cold" grips, the free zone is about 30mm, whereas for "hot" grips, it is about 67mm. In addition, the type of the applied grips substantially influences the attainable width of the remelting zone, which increases as the nominal test temperature increases, and the obtained temperature gradient along the heating zone and on the sample cross-section [10]. During the tests, the temperature was recorded as indicated by thermocouples: TC1 (near the place of the sample-grip contact), TC2 (at a distance of 7.5mm from the heating zone centre), TC4 (the centre of the heating zone, control thermocouple) and TC3 (temperature measurement within the sample core) (**Figure 1**).

Changes in force versus tool movement, and changes in electrical current versus time were additional values measured during the experiments. From the perspective of methodology development one should take into account the temperatures that are characteristic to the

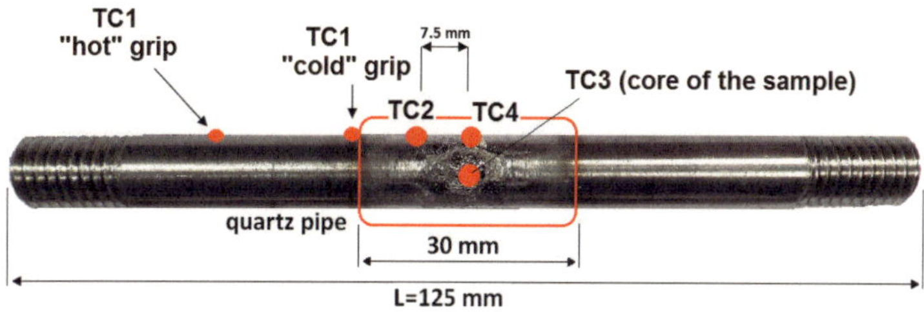

Figure 1. A cylindrical sample used during experiments with the thermocouple location.

specific tested material [10]. The liquidus T_l and solidus T_s temperatures, the nil strength temperature (NST), the nil ductility temperature (NDT) and the ductility recovery temperature (DRT) are the most important. The determined characteristic temperatures allow a thermal map of the process (TMP) to be developed. This map allows us, among others, to determine the temperature ranges in which the liquid phase appears or disappears, or the temperature above which the mechanical properties of the medium analysed degrade. For steel S355 the liquidus T_l and solidus T_s temperatures were 1513 and 1465°C, respectively. The knowledge of characteristic temperatures allows us also to determine the steel susceptibility to fracture, which is characterised by the following fracture resistance indicator R_f:

$$R_f = \frac{\mathrm{NST} - \mathrm{NDT}}{\mathrm{NDT}} \tag{1}$$

Under the procedure of continuous casting physical simulation [10], it is assumed that the steel tested is not susceptible to cracking when the difference between the temperature NST and NDT is less than just 20°C. Referring to the characteristic temperatures NST and NDT of the steel S355 tested, which are 1448 and 1420°C respectively, it can be observed that this condition is not met. It indicates that the steel tested is susceptible to cracking during the production cycle. More details concerning the determination of temperature characteristics of steel S355 can be found in publications [8–10]. The execution of experiments at temperatures reaching the solidus temperature range required a strictly planned and controlled experiment course. **Figure 2** presents the view of a sample at three selected stages of physical simulation, where remelting within the liquidus and solidus temperature range was performed. At the first stage (left) one may observe the explicit remelting zone (a mixture of the solid and liquid phases) being formed. At the second and third stages (middle and right), when the deformation started, an adverse effect of liquid steel blow-out occurred within the remelting phase. In order to eliminate this problem the orientation of the injection nozzles situated perpendicularly to the sample was changed to an

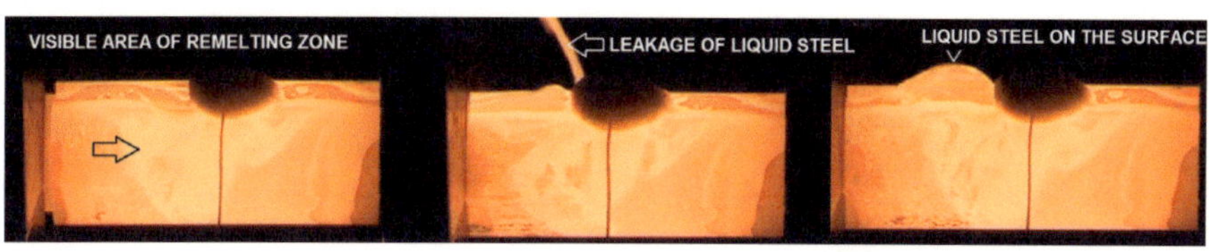

Figure 2. The view of the sample at the selected physical simulation stages (S355 grade steel).

angle of about 45°. This change stabilized the injection, by reducing the blowing of the liquid steel out of the sample.

The problem of an uncontrolled leakage was also observed for deformation within the mixed phase using relatively low tool stroke rates between 1 and 20 mm/s. Using a tool stroke rate of around 100 mm/s allowed us to fully accomplish the assumed experiment plan [10]. Therefore, one may conclude that the obtained pilot simulation results open and indicate new research areas directed towards high stroke rate testing. In a part of the primary tests, in order to reduce the risk of liquid steel leakage into the simulator, a quartz shield was applied with a length of about 30 mm, and a gap of 2–3 mm along the shield in order to enable thermocouples to be installed (**Figure 1**). Another problem encountered during the tests was the occurrence of rapid strength changes. One of the basic relationships determining the plastic behaviour of metal at a very high temperature is the dependence of the yield stress on temperature, strain rate and the strain. The plastic deformation at higher temperatures is subject to a number of further restrictions. The material changes its density during cooling, and at a certain temperature range it shows a limited formability or complete lack of ductility. The occurring large inhomogeneity of deformation, and the fact that even small temperature changes in these conditions cause rapid changes in the yield stress, lead to diverging results. **Figure 3** presents examples of results of maximum forces achieved during two identical compression tests at the selected nominal temperatures of deformation. On the other hand, **Figure 4** presents examples of results of maximum values of tensile stress for two identical tests at the selected nominal temperatures of deformation. The presented results concern tests conducted with steel C45 (carbon content 0.45%). For temperature measurements also slight temperature measurement differences were observed, reaching a few degrees [10]. Therefore, as mentioned before, the sample deformation itself at such high temperatures is only possible to a limited extent, with a strictly specified test methodology.

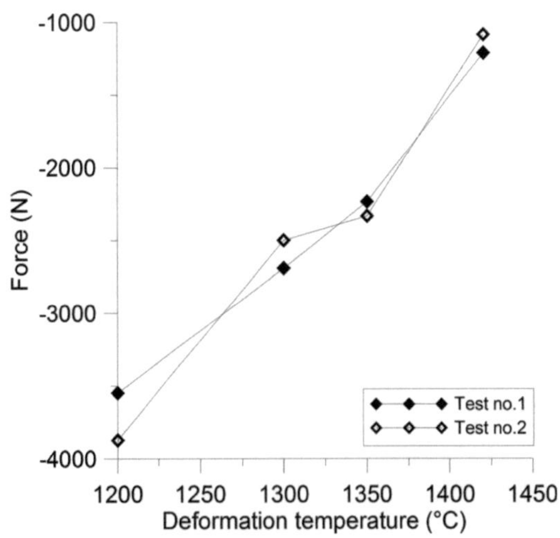

Figure 3. The maximum values of forces achieved during compression tests for the selected nominal temperatures of deformation.

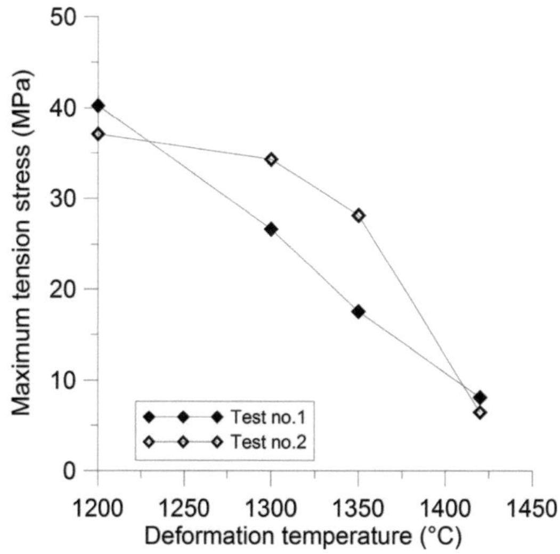

Figure 4. The maximum values of tensile stress achieved during tests for the selected nominal temperatures of deformation.

The adopted test methodology included:

- developing and conducting a physical simulation cycle,
- developing a numerical model of resistance heating in the Gleeble 3800 simulator system,
- developing a new methodology of direct determination of the strain-stress relationship on the basis of data obtained from physical simulations,
- test simulations with the DEFFEM package and experimental verification of the developed methodology. The tests were combined with a cycle of micro and macrostructural tests.

As part of the starting physical simulation, three experiments were carried out. The fundamental difference between these experiments was in the execution of deformation in various phases of the process. In the first test, the sample was deformed in the remelting phase. The experiment schedule consisted of heating the sample to a temperature of 1400°C at a heating rate of 20°C/s, in the next stage, the heating rate was reduced to 1°C/s until the temperature of 1485°C was reached. The third stage was holding at a temperature of 1485°C for 30 s in order to stabilize the temperature within the sample volume. The last stage was the deformation in the remelting phase (stroke = 1.2 mm and stroke rate = 0.04 mm/s). The first three stages of the second test were analogous to the first test. The last stage was the execution of the deformation process (stroke = 1.5 mm and stroke rate = 0.25 mm/s) in the solidification stage, starting when the sample has cooled down. The third test was a combination of the first and the second ones. The deformation was executed in the remelting phase (stroke = 1.2 mm and stroke rate = 0.04 mm/s), and next in the solidification stage (stroke = 1.5 mm and stroke rate = 0.25 mm/s). **Figures 5–7** present macrostructures of samples for individual tests. Their nature differs depending on the applied tool variant. After the process of sample etching, the occurrence of a columnar zone was found in the

Figure 5. Macrostructure of samples deformed in the remelting phase ("hot" and "cold" grips).

Figure 6. Macrostructure of samples deformed in the solidification phase ("hot" and "cold" grips).

remelting zone. The crystals were growing in the heat discharge direction (**Figures 5–7**). When analysing macrostructures made in the sample longitudinal section, the formation of porous areas of various intensities can be observed (**Figures 5–7**). Here, the variant of selected experimental tools is very important. For the variant with "hot" grips and deformation in the remelting phase (**Figure 5**), the formation of a large shrink hole was observed. Application of deformation

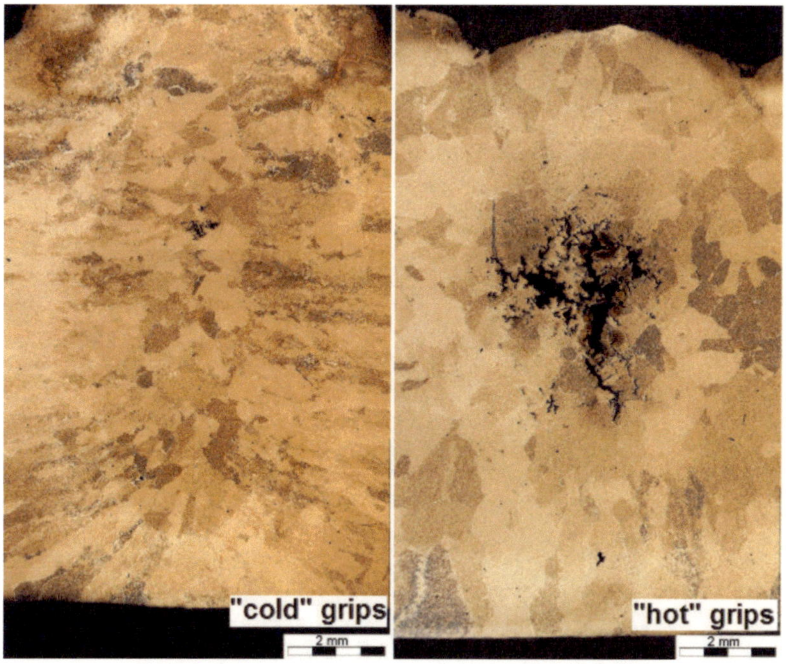

Figure 7. Macrostructure of samples deformed in the remelting and solidification phase ("hot" and "cold" grips).

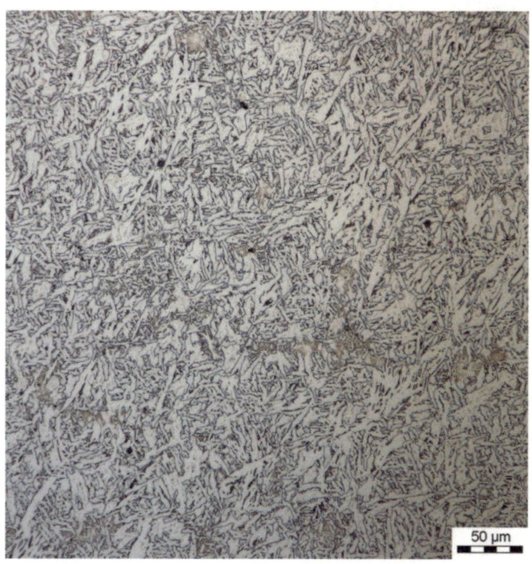

Figure 8. Microstructure of samples deformed in the solidification phase (core, "hot" grips).

in the solidification phase partially eliminated this effect (**Figure 6**). However, analyses of the macrostructure for the "hot" grip variant still showed small areas of central porosity (**Figures 6** and **7**). It may indicate that the applied strain value is insufficient.

Figures 8–11 present examples of microstructures of the selected two areas of the sample, i.e. the sample core and a place located next to the sample tip (near the place of thermocouple installation) for both tool variants. Analysing the sample centre microstructure (**Figures 8** and **10**), we can detail white (slightly needle-shaped) ferrite and/or bainite. The former austenite is mainly martensite formed after cooling to the ambient temperature, and it is more dominating for the simulation variant carried out with cold grips (**Figure 10**). Martensite is light brown

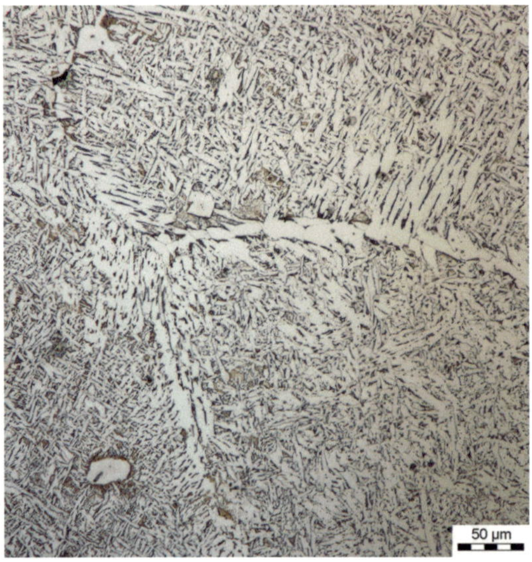

Figure 9. Microstructure of samples deformed in the solidification phase (tip, "hot" grips).

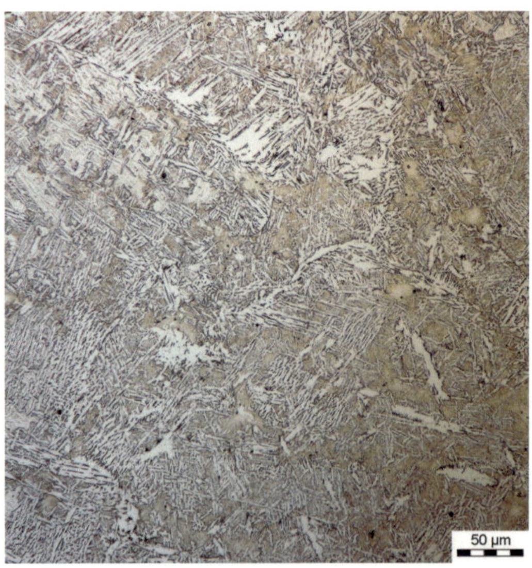

Figure 10. Microstructure of samples deformed in the solidification phase (core, "cold" grips).

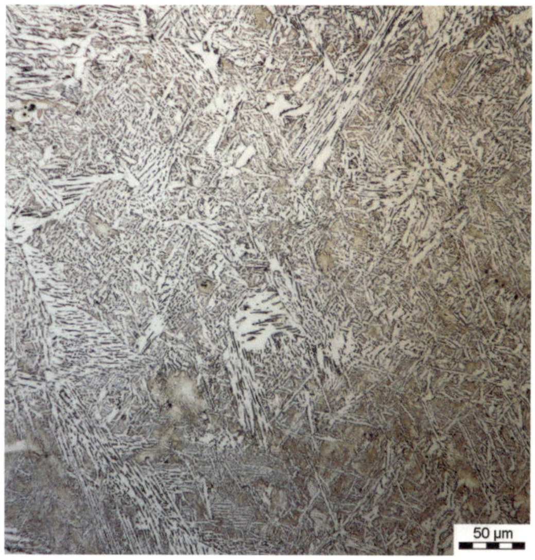

Figure 11. Microstructure of samples deformed in the solidification phase (tip, "cold" grips).

in the presented microstructures. The analysis of the microstructure of the surface zones (**Figures 9** and **11**) shows a slightly different nature of the share of individual phases. The obtained differences arise mainly from the cooling rate, which is two times lower for the samples heated in hot grips, and from the difference in the cooling rates between the individual zones of the sample deformed.

The conducted first cycle of physical simulations allowed us to plan and carry out a pilot simulation of the integrated strip casting and rolling process. In the performed simulation, the deformation process was conducted in crystallization phase and finally rough-rolling simulation was made. The main goal of deformation in the crtstallization stage was to ensure the filling of the full volume of the remelted sample as well as to eliminate shrinkage effects. The second cycle of physical simulations included tests aiming at providing data to the computer-aided methodology of determination of the strain-stress relationship, necessary to build the model of changes in stress versus strain, strain rate and temperature for the needs of numerical simulations. The results of computer-aided physical simulations are presented hereinafter.

3. Computer aid of experiment

As part of the computer-aided experiment the proprietary simulation package DEFFEM [10] according to the ONEDES (ONEDEcisionSoftware) was used. More information on the simulation system designed, details of the implemented mathematical models, or definitions of boundary conditions may be found in book [10] or in the author's second chapeter in the current book.

3.1. Modelling the resistance heating

The process of numerical modelling a high-temperature experiment performed with a Gleeble 3800 thermo-mechanical simulator can be broken down into two main stages. At the first stage the process of sample resistance heating and melting is performed according to a set programme. This stage is very important from the perspective of the specificity of the process analysed, where even small temperature changes may locally cause rapid changes in mechanical properties. As accurate estimation of the temperature distribution within the sample volume as possible will significantly determine the quality of the obtained findings, including the determined strain-stress relationships, which ultimately will strongly influence the process force parameters of the deformation process itself (stage 2). In the first modelling approach, a commercial simulation system ANSYS was used, and the obtained final temperature field was then read in by the DEFFEM solver as the initial condition for the deformation process performed [11]. Resistance heating was modelled with an additional magnetohydrodynamical (MHD) module. This additional program extension concerns the effect of electromagnetic field and the electrically conducting medium. The module enables the conductor behaviour influenced by a constant and variable electromagnetic field to be analysed. In this study, the method in which the current density is the result of the solution of the electrical potential equation and Ohm's law was used. The electrical field is described by equation:

$$\vec{E} = -\nabla \varnothing \tag{2}$$

where $\varnothing$ is the electric potential.

The current density is calculated from Ohm's law.

$$\vec{j} = \sigma \vec{E} \tag{3}$$

where σ is the specific conductance.

For a medium with a high conductivity, the principle of electric charge conservation is met additionally.

$$\nabla \cdot \vec{j} = 0 \tag{4}$$

The ANSYS program solver solves equations of continuity, moment, energy and electric potential iteratively in a loop. The energy equation contains an additional energy source, Joule's heat.

$$Q = \frac{1}{\sigma} \vec{j} \cdot \vec{j} \tag{5}$$

where Q is the Joule's heat; j is the current density vector.

A number of simulations were performed, where various heating schedules were used and their impact on the obtained final temperature field was analysed. In the model tests alternatively both types of grips were used. It was found that the grips had a substantial impact on the attainable heating rate to the nominal deformation temperature. **Figure 12** presents the temperature changes measured by a numerical sensor placed on the sample surface (1/2 of the heating zone length). Heating simulations for both variants of tools were performed with a constant current intensity of 2000 A, assuming the heating time of 66 s. The obtained difference of the maximum calculated temperatures for both tool variants was 123°C. Regardless of the adopted temperature schedule, grip type or the grade of the steel tested, the distribution of generated voluminal sources is parabolic (**Figure 13**).

Regardless of the applied grips the temperature gradient was observed both on the cross-section and on the longitudinal section of the sample (**Figure 14**). For a sample heated with a

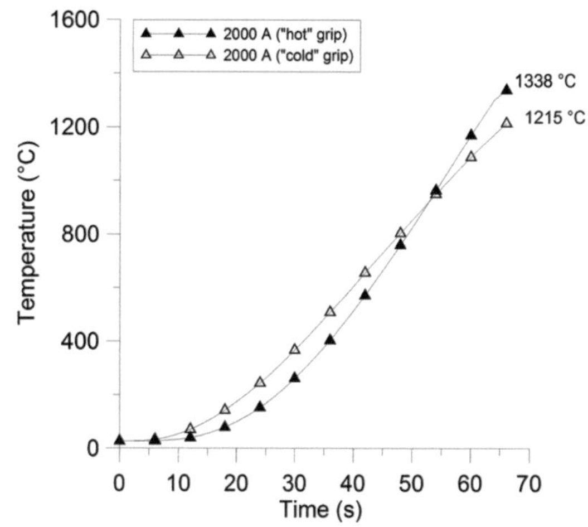

Figure 12. Change in the surface temperature of a sample heated with two types of grips (current intensity 2000 A).

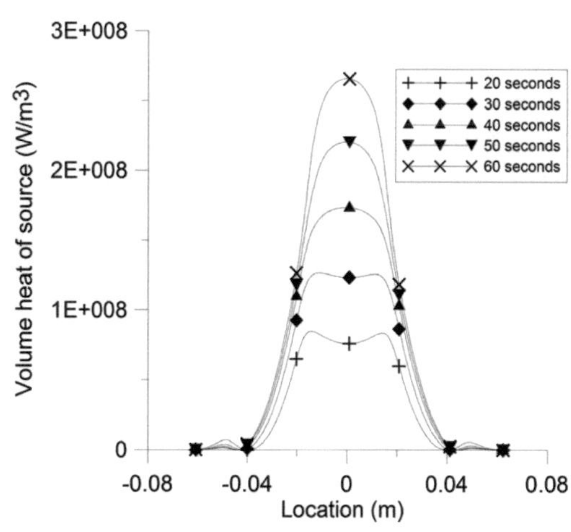

Figure 13. The distribution of voluminal heat sources in the sample Z axis for the selected resistance heating stages ("hot" grips).

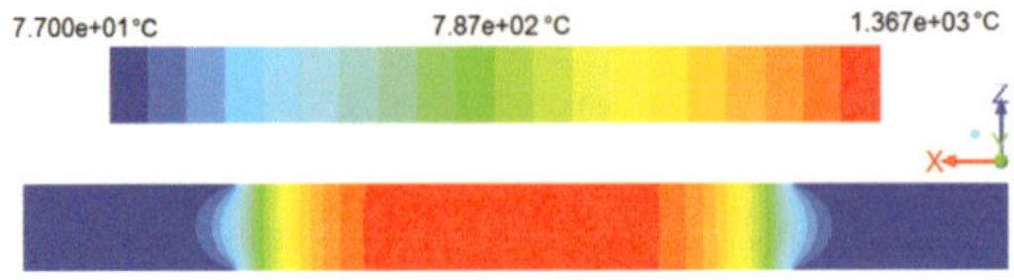

Figure 14. Temperature distribution on the sample section after 66 s of heating ("hot" grips, current intensity 2000 A).

2000 A current for 66 s using "hot" grips, the achieved sample surface temperature was 1338°C, while the core temperature was 1367°C. The temperature difference between the sample core and the surface (nominal temperature) was therefore 29°C. The current intensity characteristics is a relevant control parameter in the numerical model, which is decisive to the attainable nominal temperature of the test (possibility for remelting). For instance, a change in the current intensity from 2000 to 1000 A caused a decrease in the amount of heat generated within the system, which translated into the attainable maximum temperature of 366°C for the sample core (**Figure 15**).

In the second model approach the ADINA commercial system was used, in which the temperature field solution was based upon the classic solution of Fourier's equation combined with inverse calculations [12, 13]. Assuming a constant current intensity, and on the basis of temperatures measured during the experiments, the values of voluminal heat sources were selected so as to obtain compatibility of results with experimental findings. Alternatively a constant value of voluminal heat sources was assumed (constant for a single simulation time interval, estimated previously with commercial simulation systems, e.g. **Figure 15**), and next the current intensity was determined. The adopted model assumptions not only allowed results featuring the correct compatibility with the experimental findings to be obtained, but also lead to an ambiguity of the solution. Examples of results using the foregoing approaches can be found in papers [12–15]. Regardless of the adopted model approach the calculations were very time consuming and painstaking. This moment has inspired the author and has resulted in the ONEDES term (ONEDEcisionSoftware) as an approach philosophy for designing dedicated original simulation systems [9, 10]. Intensive support of the Polish National Science Centre as part of research projects and huge amounts of time sacrificed by the author for the implementation of the developed solutions allowed a globally unique tool dedicated for aiding high-temperature processes to be developed. The effect of the design-implementation work was the development of a resistance heating model in the Gleeble 3800 simulator system (ONEDES approach) and the experimental verification methodology. When modelling the Joule heat generation, it was assumed that its equivalent in the numerical model would be a voluminal heat source (function A) with its power proportional to the resistance R and the square of electric current I:

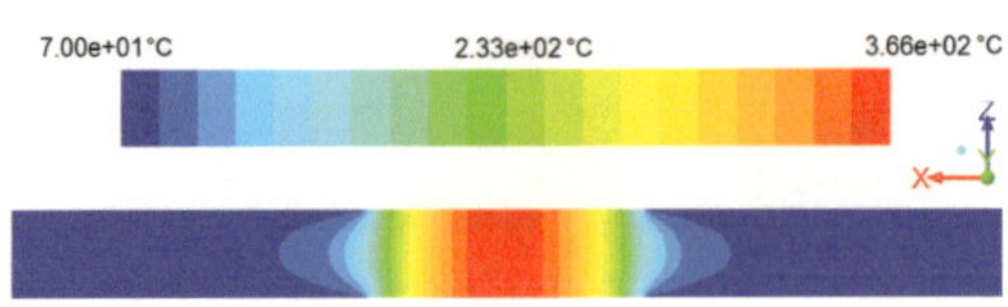

Figure 15. The temperature distribution on the sample section after 66 s of heating ("cold" grips, current intensity 1000 A).

$$Q = f\left(A(\tau)\left[I^2(\tau)R(T)\right]\right) \tag{6}$$

The relationship of the current intensity change as a function of heating time are directly recorded during physical tests with Gleeble 3800 thermo-mechanical simulator. **Figure 16** presents examples of results in the form of temperature change versus time measured (thermocouples TC1, TC4, see **Figure 1**) and calculated (numerical sensors) during physical and computer simulations of sample heating to a temperature of 1485°C (steel S355).

The heating process was performed with two heating rates: to the temperature of 1450°C at a rate of 20°C/s, and next at a rate of 1°C/s to the nominal temperature of 1485°C. On the other hand, **Figure 17** presents temperature changes versus time measured and calculated during physical and computer simulations of sample heating to the temperature of 1200°C (steel S355) at a constant rate of 5°C/s.

The obtained graphs feature a very good compatibility between the calculated and experimentally determined temperatures. The estimated relative error oscillated within 2–3%. **Figures 18** and **19** present the temperature distribution on the longitudinal section of the sample and the symmetry with respect to the Z axis, after 3 s of heating, and after heating to the test nominal temperature of 1485°C, respectively. The simulations were conducted with "hot" grips. Analysing **Figure 18** one can observe an intensive temperature gradient near the place of tool-sample contact. The temperature gradient on the sample section at this simulation stage features a practically uniform temperature distribution of around 60°C, achieving its maximum value of 48°C after heating to a temperature of 1485°C.

The application of the simulation variant using "cold" grips leads to slightly different results (**Figure 20**). The attainable width of the remelting zone becomes shorter. In addition, one can observe that the obtained gradient on the sample section of 37°C is smaller than for the variant with "hot" grips (**Figure 19**).

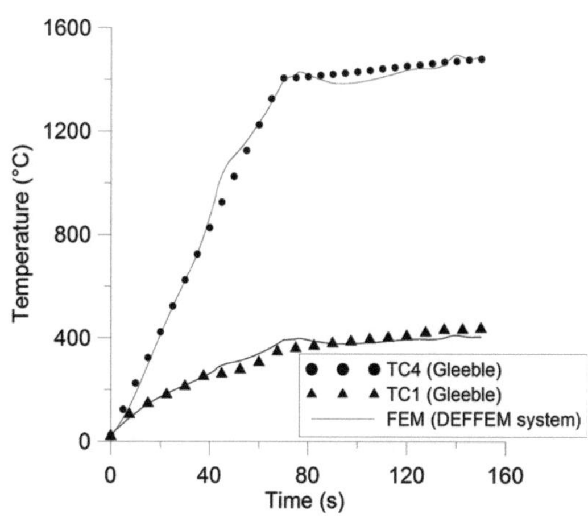

Figure 16. Temperature changes versus time obtained as a result of the experiment and computer simulation (thermocouples TC4 and TC1, "hot" grips).

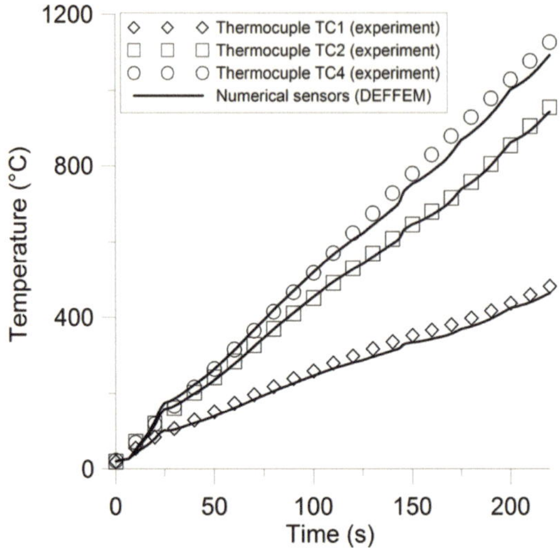

Figure 17. Temperature changes versus time obtained as a result of the experiment and computer simulation (thermocouples TC4, TC2 and TC1, "cold" grips, heating rate 5°C/s).

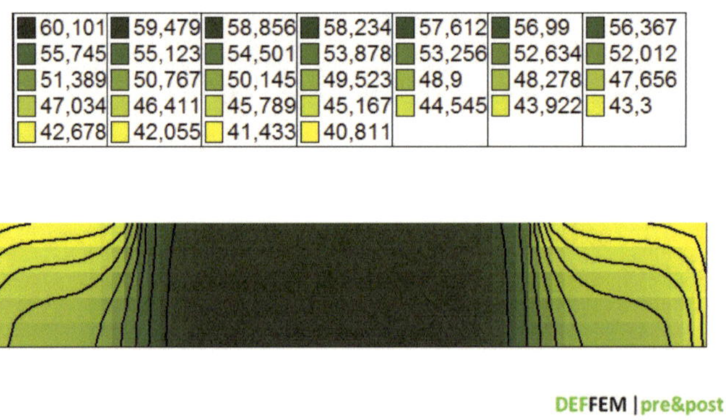

Figure 18. Temperature distribution on the sample section after 3s of heating ("hot" grips).

The obtained results of computer simulations of the resistance heating process feature a considerable compatibility with the results obtained by physical simulations (for both tool variants). In the implemented numerical solution, couplings of the electrical field and the temperature field were not included directly. The heat that is generated within the sample volume as a result of the electrical current flow is modelled by an internal voluminal heat source. By applaying this approach, the influence of the changing electrical properties of the solution domain (sample volume) on the electrical charge density and local voluminal heat source power could not be analysed. It is difficult to state that taking the thermo-electrical impact into account would constitute significant progress and would allow more precise results to be obtained. More details can be found in publication [10].

http://dx.doi.org/10.5772/intechopen.68606

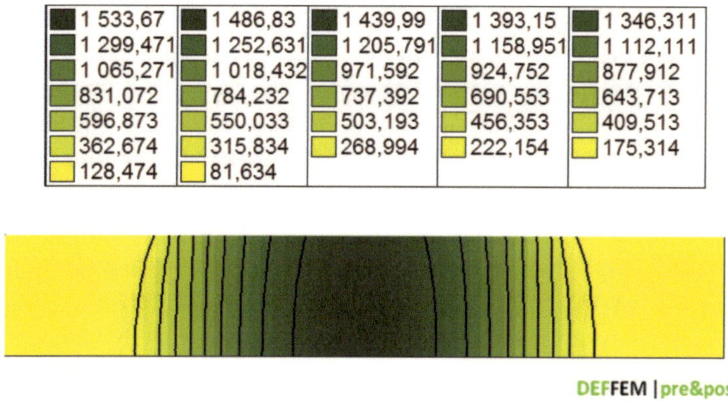

Figure 19. Temperature distribution on the sample section after heating to the nominal temperature of 1485°C ("hot" grips).

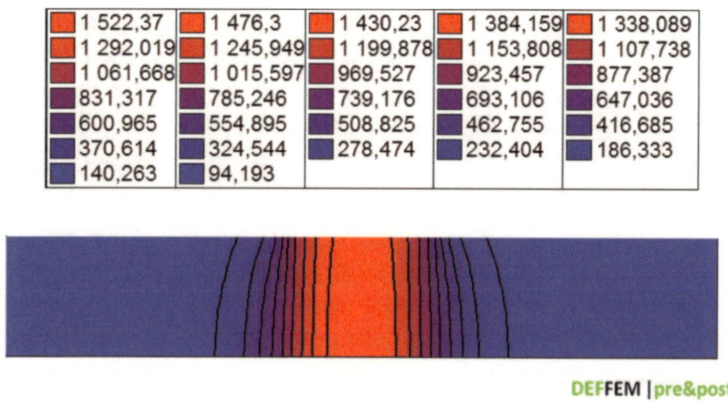

Figure 20. Temperature distribution on the sample section after heating to the nominal temperature of 1485°C ("cold" grips).

3.2. The methodology of direct determination of mechanical properties (S355 grade steel)

The problem of determining characteristics describing changes in stress versus strain, strain rate and temperature is a very complex issue. As showed by research presented herein, the repeatability of test as regards anticipating changes in temperature or force parameters may significantly differ between two identical tests (see **Figures 3** and **4**). In the context of determining mechanical properties, the accuracy of determination of the temperature field becomes therefore particularly significant. It is caused by the fact that even small local temperature variations may cause rapid changes in mechanical properties. One of methods applied by the author was the use of a methodology [Numerical Identification Methodology (NIM)] based upon the inverse solution and a methodology of modelling with a model concept based upon axially symmetrical models [10]. As part of the current project (3D model development), it has been found that this approach is ineffective in terms of computing, as well as of the quality of the obtained curves. Depending on the adopted solution of the model resistance heating process in the aspect of the temperature field determination (inverse calculations, temperature field from the commercial program, or the function description presented herein), it leads to slightly different temperature values within the deformation zone. Bearing in mind that mechanical properties rapidly change as a result of small temperature fluctuations, the obtained stress-strain curves are considerably different (their nature). In the context of verification of the yield stress function model, the obtained results of the process force parameters or the deformation zone shape itself showed a convergence with the experimental data. Thus a question comes: which approach in the context of modelling of mechanical properties at such high temperatures is the optimum solution? It was one of the factors that inspired the author to take up implementing and development work in the context of formulating a full multi-scale 3D model of high-temperature effects. Therefore, as part of project work, the Direct Identification Methodology (DIM) to determine the mentioned dependences directly was developed. The DIM utilizes the capabilities of the Gleeble 3800 simulator as regards experimental research, and the original DEFFEM simulation system for identification of model parameters [10]. The proposed research methodology consists of the following stages: In the first stage samples are prepared for tests, along with the installation of measurement thermocouples, and copper grips and the experiment programme are selected [10]. The second stage includes physical tensile tests on the basis of the assumed physical simulation schedule. The experiment programme included heating to a temperature of 1400°C at a rate of 20°C/s, and next to a temperature of 1480°C at a rate of 1°C/s. Finally, cooling to the nominal deformation temperature was made at a rate of 10°C/s, and after holding for 10s at the set temperature the deformation process (tension test) was made with stroke 0.5–2mm and a tool stroke rate of 1 and 20mm/s. In the third stage, the preliminary simulations in order to estimate the length of the deformable zone are performed. On the basis of the preliminary test results, as well as the analysis of the temperature fields, the length L_0 of the effective working zone can be estimated at 20mm. Within this zone, the strain rate and the stress are supposed as uniaxial. The nominal strain ε_{nom} and the nominal strain rate $\dot{\varepsilon}_{nom}$ are defined as follows:

$$\varepsilon_{nom} = \frac{\Delta L}{L_0} \tag{7}$$

where ΔL is the grip stroke (the elongation of the effective working zone at time τ) and L_0 effective working zone.

$$\dot{\varepsilon}_{nom} = \frac{stroke\_rate}{L_0} \tag{8}$$

The nominal stress is calculated with the following relationship:

$$\sigma_{nom}^{exp} = \frac{F}{S_0} \tag{9}$$

where F is the tensile force measured by the Gleeble 3800 simulator and S_0 is the original cross-sectional area of the sample. In the fourth stage, the yield stress function form is selected. In the presented solution, the function form describing the dependence of the nominal stress on the nominal strain is the function in the following form [10]:

$$\sigma_{nom}^{exp} = \frac{{\varepsilon_{nom}}^{n}}{\alpha} \text{ASINH}\left[\left(\frac{\dot{\varepsilon}_{nom}}{A}\right)^{m} exp\left(\frac{mQ}{RT_{nom}}\right)\right] \tag{10}$$

The last parameter that should be defined in function (10) is the value of the nominal temperature T_{nom}. In this study, the nominal temperature was defined as the sample surface temperature:

$$T_{nom} = T_{surf}^{exp} \tag{11}$$

In the last stage of the proposed methodology, the objective function for the purpose of identification of the searched parameter vector $x = (\alpha, n, A, m, Q)$ of the function (10) is defined [16]:

$$\varphi(x) = \frac{1}{N_t}\frac{1}{N_{pr}}\sum_{i=1}^{N_t}\sum_{j=1}^{N_{pr}}\left[\frac{\sigma_{nom,\,ij}^{calc}(x) - \sigma_{nom,\,ij}^{exp}}{\sigma_{nom,\,ij}^{exp}}\right]^2 \tag{12}$$

where N_t, N_{pr} are the number of tensile tests and measurement points, respectively. σ_{nom}^{calc}, σ_{nom}^{exp} are the nominal stress from calculations and experiments, respectively.

The searched parameter vector x can be identified by minimization of the objective function (12). Gradient-free optimisation was used to minimize the objective function (12). The identified parameters of vector x, based on the DIM, are presented in **Table 1**.

The calculated and deducted nominal stress-strain curves are shown in **Figures 21–26**. All measurement points obtained from the experiment are included in the graphs, in order to present the scatter of the experimental data. Before using them in the optimisation procedures, such data were previously subjected to a smoothing procedure. A reasonable agreement can be observed between the calculated and the directly predicted nominal stress-strain curves. The mean relative errors was within range 0.9–8.6%.

3.3. Computer simulations: examples

The tension simulations were conducted while attempting to reflect the conditions of the conducted experiments as accurately as possible (see point 2 in Direct Identification Methodology). The first simulation variant covered deformation in the solidification phase for the nominal test temperature of 1450°C, tool stroke rates of 1 and 20mm/s, and elongation of 2 mm. The basic aim of the simulation was to evaluate the suitability of the developed function

α [MPa^{-1}]	n	A [s^{-1}]	m	Q [J/mol]
5.4623641E − 02	0.2089816	1.65E+17	0.1855337	511111.2

Table 1. Identified parameters by the Direct Identification Methodology (DIM).

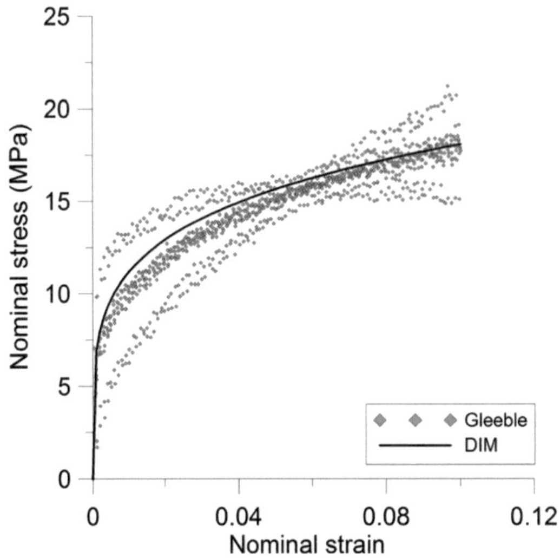

Figure 21. Comparison between measured (points) and calculated (line) stress-strain curve at the nominal temperatures of 1300°C and the nominal strain rate 0.05 s^{-1}.

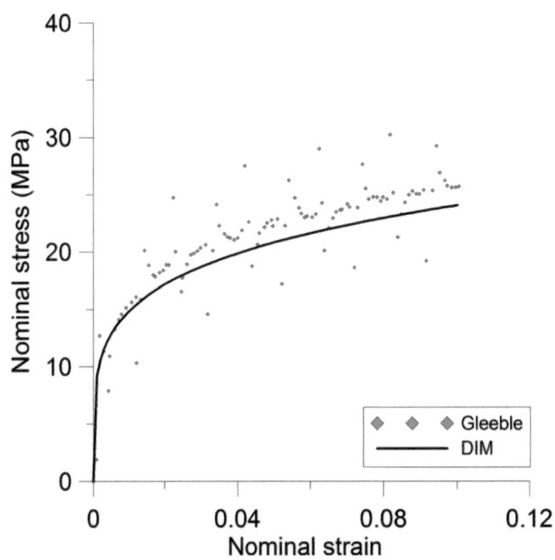

Figure 22. Comparison between measured (points) and calculated (line) stress-strain curve at the nominal temperatures of 1300°C and the nominal strain rate 1 s^{-1}.

describing changes in stress versus strain for the defined temperature range. **Figure 27** presents the initial temperature field for the nominal deformation test performed at a temperature of 1450°C using "hot" grips. The temperature difference between the sample surface and core was 33°C.

Figure 28 presents the ultimate temperature distribution and the strain intensity after the tensioning process at a tool stroke rate of 1mm/s and a grip stroke of 2mm. Visualisations

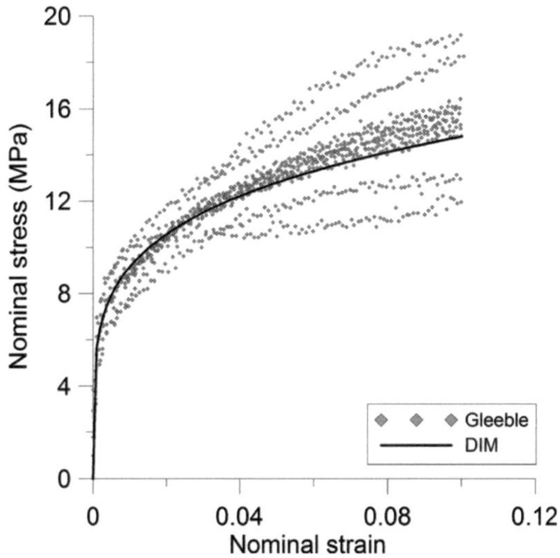

Figure 23. Comparison between measured (points) and calculated (line) stress–strain curve at the nominal temperatures of 1350°C and the nominal strain rate 0.05 s^{-1}.

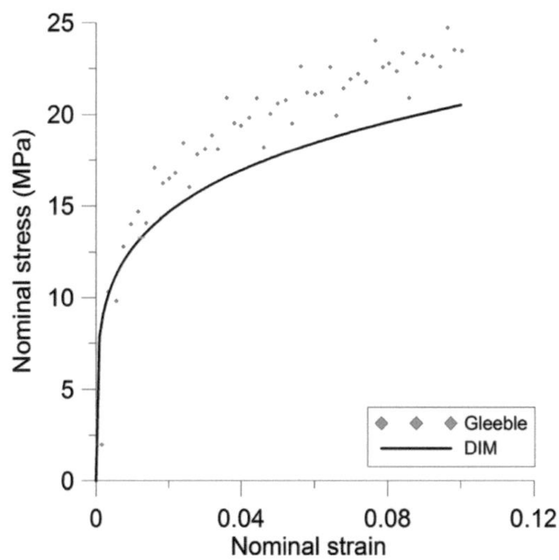

Figure 24. Comparison between measured (points) and calculated (line) stress-strain curve at the nominal temperatures of 1350°C and the nominal strain rate 1 s^{-1}.

were made along the sample maintaining the symmetry with respect to the *Z* axis. When analysing the temperature field after the resistance heating process (**Figure 27**), which at the same time is the initial condition for the mechanical solution, and the temperature field after the tensioning process (**Figure 28**), one may observe a slight reduction of the maximum temperature from 1483 to 1482°C. For the analysed temperature range even such small temperature changes within the deformation zone can cause rapid changes in the plastic and

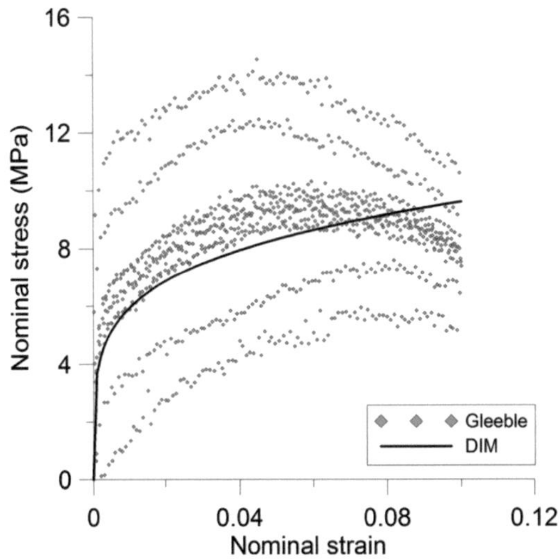

Figure 25. Comparison between measured (points) and calculated (line) stress-strain curve at the nominal temperatures of 1450°C and the nominal strain rate 0.05 s^{-1}.

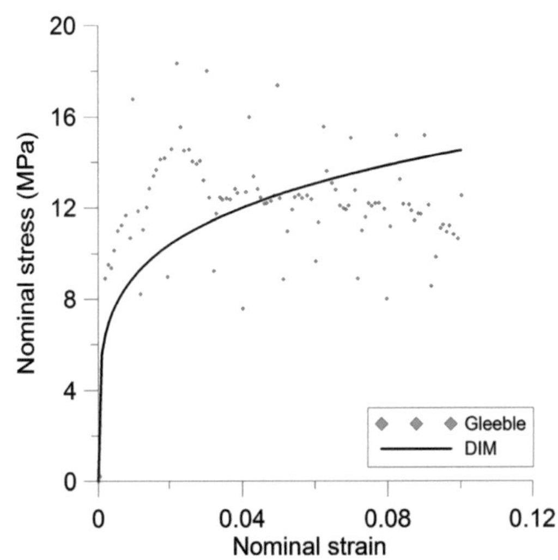

Figure 26. Comparison between measured (points) and calculated (line) stress-strain curve at the nominal temperatures of 1450°C and the nominal strain rate 1 s^{-1}.

mechanical properties. When analysing the obtained results one may observe a concentration of the maximum strain intensity values in the middle sample part.

In **Figures 29** and **30**, the comparison between measured and calculated loads at a nominal temperature of 1450°C and two stroke rates of 1 and 20mm/s is presented. The presented courses of loads changes feature a fairly large discrepancy between the measured and calculated loads. The obtained simulation results point that the application of the developed Direct Identification Methodology to determine parameters of the function describing changes leads

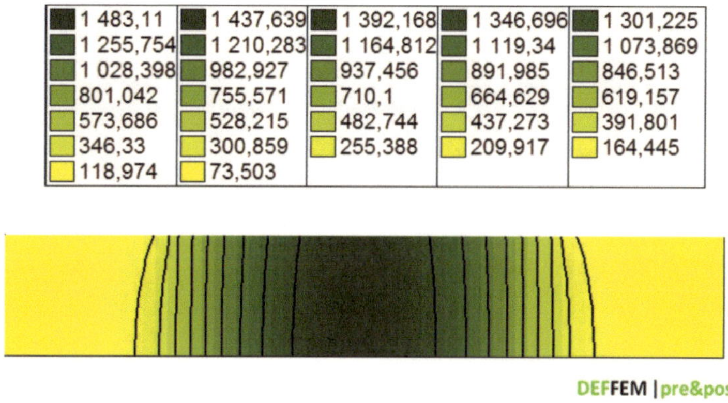

Figure 27. Temperature distribution on the sample section after heating and cooling to the nominal temperature of 1450°C ("hot" grips).

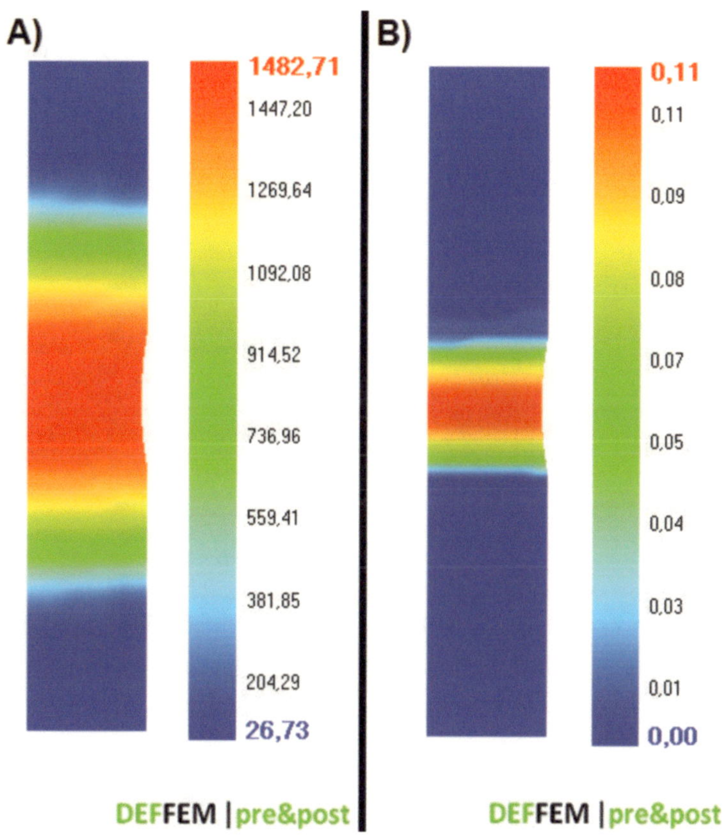

Figure 28. Distribution of (a) temperature (b) strain intensity on the cross-section of a sample deformed at the nominal temperatureof 1450°C ("hot" grips, stroke rate 1 mm/s, stroke 2 mm).

to the final results. The average error value is at a level of 8.1% for the deformation variant at a temperature of 1450°C (stroke rate 1 mm/s) and 19.1% for the test at a temperature of 1450°C (stroke rate 20 mm/s). However, the obtained results indicate a certain non-uniformity of the

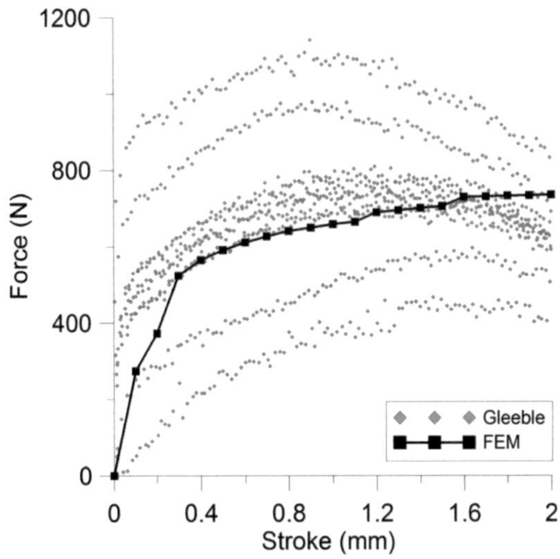

Figure 29. The comparison between measured and calculated loads at a nominal temperature of 1450°C and stroke rate of 1 mm/s.

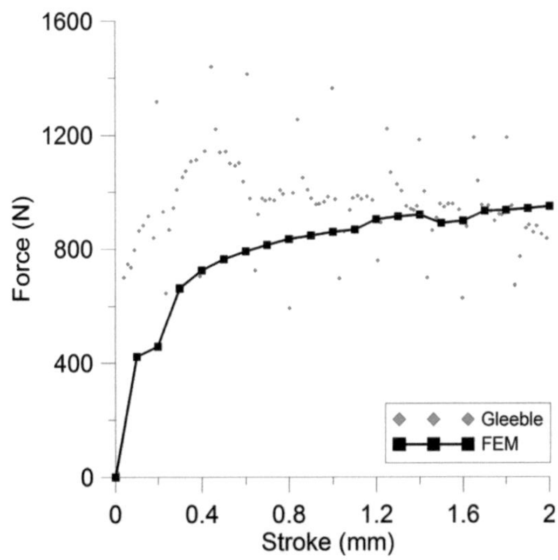

Figure 30. The comparison between measured and calculated loads at a nominal temperature of 1450°C and stroke rate of 20 mm/s.

deformation zone itself, as well as rapid changes in the plastic and mechanical properties along with a temperature change.

In the second variant, a pilot simulation of the integrated strip casting and rolling process was performed where the deformation was performed in two primary phases: crystallization followed by the rough-rolling simulation. Conducting a multi-stage simulation required intensive implementation work and a partial reorganization of numerical codes in order to ensure transfer of strain and stress states, and the temperature field for the needs of the next stage simulation. The pilot physical and computer simulation included heating to a temperature of 1450°C at a rate of 20°C/s, and next to a temperature of 1485°C at a rate of 1°C/s in order to remelt the sample. The deformation process (compression) in the crystallisation phase was performed at a stroke rate of 0.25mm/s, a stroke of 1.5mm at a nominal temperature of 1460°C. Next, the sample was cooled at an average cooling rate of 50°C/s to the nominal rolling temperature of 1000°C. In the rolling process the sample was deformed (compressed) at a stroke rate of 1.25mm/s and a stroke of 4.0mm. The obtained results of the pilot numerical simulations were verified by comparison of the calculated and experimentally determined maximum force values at the individual stages, which are presented in **Table 2**.

At both stages the values of maximum forces calculated numerically were higher than the ones determined experimentally. The calculated relative error reached the maximum value of 13.77% for the stage of deformation at the crystallisation phase. Bear in mind that calculations within the DIM were performed for the adopted nominal test temperature equal to the surface temperature, and remember that the sample core temperature was higher by 33°C. Therefore, further research is necessary to determine the nominal temperature, e.g. adopting the core temperature as the nominal temperature, which effectively will allow the differences between the process force parameters to be reduced. The other essential fact influencing the obtained discrepancies in results of physical and computer simulations is lack of temperature field symmetry within the sample volume. From the perspective of the essence of the axially symmetrical numerical model and the computing accuracy, the temperature field in each section plane in ideal conditions should be the same or very similar. **Figure 31** presents a picture from a NANOTOM N190 tomograph showing the formed porous zone. The visible porous zone formed starting from the sample core, propagating towards the sample surface (place of installation of the control thermocouple TC4, see **Figure 1**). It is the place where the sample surrounded by a quartz shield has a 2–3mm gap enabling thermocouples to be installed. The other areas are thermally insulated, and the said gap is the main source of disturbances in the heat exchange between the sample and its environment (simulator inside). Therefore, one may conclude that the elimination of the quartz shield combined with the precise control of the process (manual control) will allow lack of the temperature field symmetry to be eliminated. As a result, the obtained results of numerical simulations should feature a higher accuracy.

	Solidification stage [N]	**Rolling stage [N]**
Physical simulation	617	7144
Computer simulation	702	7737
Relative error	13.77%	8.30%

Table 2. Comparison of the maximum forces determined experimentally and numerically at the individual stages.

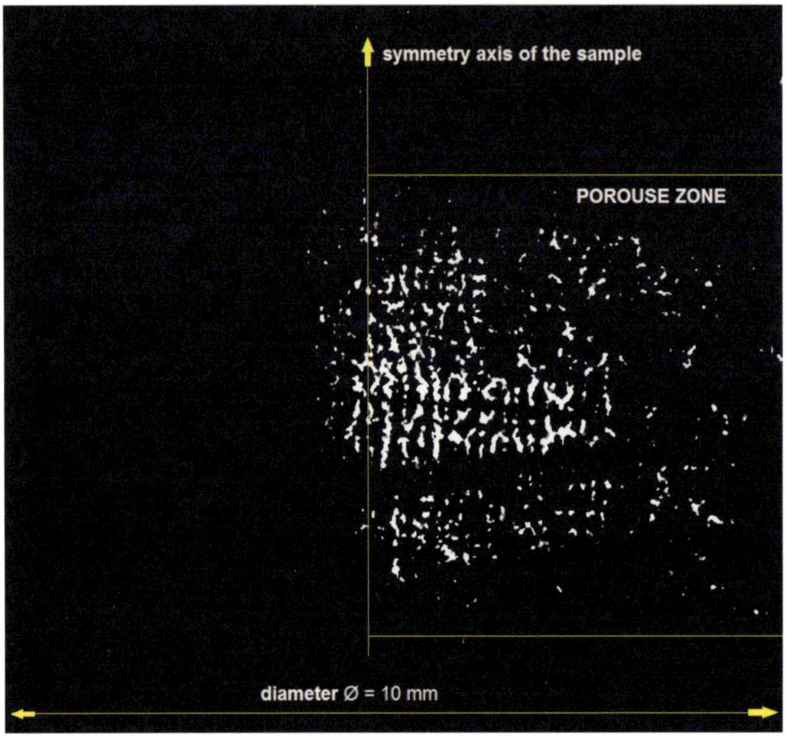

Figure 31. A longitudinal section with a visible formed porous zone ("hot" grips, cylindrical sample heating zone centre).

4. Conclusions

The primary aim presented in this chapter is to show experimental and modelling problems related to research aiming at obtaining data necessary to develop a physical model of steel deformation in the semi-solid state. The computer aid to the experiment, using the process computer simulation, is an inherent part of the presented methodology. It is difficult to imagine experimental research of steel deformed during the final solidification phase without this simulation. This issue is strictly related to the signalled problems related to the application of the soft-reduction process. The formulated resistance heating model in the simulator system and the computer-aided methodology of direct determination of mechanical properties of the steel tested allowed the preliminary concept of multi-stage modelling (integrated casting and rolling process) to be developed with the DEFFEM package. The obtained results in the form of force parameters feature a correct compatibility, albeit constraints resulting from the application of axially symmetrical models indicate new trends in the development of models and methods. In order to fully describe the behaviour of the semi-solid steel during its deformation in the integrated casting and rolling process the constructed mathematical model must be fully three-dimensional. The necessity of application of spacial models arises from the fact of existence of zones in high temperatures: the solid and semi-solid zone, many's the time having a complex geometrical shape. Such models should be applied to the issue concerned regardless of the fact that traditional strip rolling processes in the hot metal forming conditions can be modelled in the flat strain condition.

Acknowledgements

The research has been supported by the Polish National Science Centre (2012–2017), Decision number: DEC-2011/03/D/ST8/04041

Author details

Marcin Hojny

Address all correspondence to: mhojny@metal.agh.edu.pl

AGH University of Science and Technology, Kraków, Poland

References

[1] Project report. (AGH Krakow-IMZ Gliwice); Number: B0–1124, 2010 (not published)

[2] Bald W, et al. Innovative technologies for strip production. Steel Times International. 2000;**24**:16–19

[3] Cook R, Grocock PG, Thomas PM et al. Development of the twin-roll casting process. Journal of Materials Processing Technology. 1995;**55**:76–84

[4] Fan P, Zhou S, Liang X et al. Thin strip casting of high speed steels. Journal of Materials Processing Technology. 1997;**63**:792–796

[5] Park CM, Kim WS, Park GJ. Thermal analysis of the roll in the strip casting process. Mechanics Research Communications. 2003;**30**:297–310

[6] Seo PK, Park KJ, Kang CG. Semi-solid die casting process with three steps die system. Journal of Materials Processing Technology. 2004;**154**:442–449

[7] Watari H, Davey K, Rasgado MT et al. Semi-solid manufacturing process of magnesium alloys by twin-roll casting. Journal of Materials Processing Technology. 2004;**156**:1662–1667

[8] Głowacki M, Hojny M, Kuziak R. Komputerowo wspomagane badania właściwości mechanicznych stali w stanie półciekłym. Kraków: Wyd. AGH; 2012

[9] Hojny M. Projektowanie dedykowanych systemów symulacji odkształcania stali w stanie półciekłym. Krakow, Poland: Wzorek; 2014

[10] Hojny M. Modeling of steel deformation in the semi-solid state. In: Advanced Structured Materials. Vol. 78. Springer, Switzerland; 2017

[11] Hojny M, Siwek A. Computer and physical modeling of resistance heating in the Gleeble 3800 simulator. Proc. KomPlasTech conference, 17–20 stycznia, 2016, Wisła, Poland, pp. 66–67

[12] Hojny M, Glowacki M. Computer modelling of deformation of steel samples with mushy zone. Steel Research International. 2008;**79**:868–874

[13] Hojny M, Glowacki M. The physical and computer modelling of plastic deformation of low carbon steel in semi-solid state. Journal of Engineering Materials and Technology. 2009;**131**:041003-1-041003-7

[14] Hojny M, Glowacki M. Modeling of strain-stress relationship for carbon steel deformed at temperature exceeding hot rolling range. Journal of Engineering Materials and Technology. 2011;**133**:021008-1-021008-7

[15] Hojny M, Głowacki M, Malinowski Z. Computer aided methodology of strain-stress curve construction for steels deformed at extra high temperature. High Temperature Materials and Processes. 2009;**28**(4):245-252. ISSN 0334–6455

[16] Szyndler D. Problem odwrotny w zastosowaniu do identyfikacji parametrów procesu plastycznej przeróbki metali. PhD. thesis. Krakow; 2001

Chapter 8

Surrogate Modelling with Sequential Design for Expensive Simulation Applications

Joachim van der Herten, Tom Van Steenkiste,
Ivo Couckuyt and Tom Dhaene

Additional information is available at the end of the chapter

http://dx.doi.org/10.5772/67739

Abstract

The computational demands of virtual experiments for modern product development processes can get out of control due to fine resolution and detail incorporation in simulation packages. These demands for appropriate approximation strategies and reliable selection of evaluations to keep the amount of required evaluations were limited, without compromising on quality and requirements specified upfront. Surrogate models provide an appealing data-driven strategy to accomplish these goals for applications including design space exploration, optimization, visualization or sensitivity analysis. Extended with sequential design, satisfactory solutions can be identified quickly, greatly motivating the adoption of this technology into the design process.

Keywords: surrogate modelling, sequential design, optimization, sensitivity analysis, active learning

1. Introduction

Amongst the countless research domains and the fields of research revolutionized by the merits of computer simulation, the field of engineering is a prime example as it continues to benefit greatly from the introduction of computer simulations. During product design, engineers encounter several complex input/output systems, which need to be designed and optimized. Traditionally, several prototypes were required to assure quality criteria that were met or to obtain optimal solutions for design choices and to evaluate the behaviour of products and components under varying conditions. Typically, a single prototype is not sufficient, and lessons learnt are used to improve the design, back at the drawing table. Therefore, the development process used involves building several prototypes in order to gain more confidence in the solutions. A direct consequence of this approach is that the development process is both slow and not cost effective.

The introduction of computer simulations caused revolution: by bundling implementations of material, mechanical and physical properties into a software package, simulating the desired aspects of a system and performing the tests and experiments virtually; the number of required prototypes can be drastically reduced to only a few at the very end of the design process. These prototypes can be regarded purely as a validation of the simulations. The simulation itself can be interpreted as a *model* and serves as an abstract layer between the engineer and the real world. Performing a virtual experiment is faster and is very inexpensive. A direct consequence was an acceleration of development and system design, contributing to a shorter time-to-market and a more effective process in general. In addition, it was also possible to perform more virtual experiments, providing a way to achieve better products and design optimality.

However, as simulation software became more precise and gained accuracy over the years, its computational cost grew tremendously. In fact, the growth of computational cost was so fast it has beaten the growth in computational power resulting in very lengthy simulations on state-of-the-art machines and high performance computing environments, mainly due to the never ending drive for finer time scales, more detail and general algorithmic complexity. For instance, a computational fluid dynamics (CFD) simulation of a cooling system can take several days to complete [1], or a simulation of a single crash test was reported to take up to 36 hours to complete [2]. This introduces a new problem: large-scale parameter sweeping and direct use of this type of *computationally expensive* simulations for evaluation intensive tasks such as optimization and sensitivity analysis are impractical and should be avoided.

To counter this enormous growth in computational cost however, an additional layer of abstraction between the complex system in the real world and the engineer was proposed, more specifically between the simulation and the engineer. Rather than interacting directly with the simulator, a cheaper approximation is constructed. Roughly three approaches to obtain this approximation exist:

- **Model driven** (known as model order reduction) takes a top-down approach by applying mathematic techniques to derive approximations directly from the original simulator. This, however, exploits information about the application domain and is therefore problem specific.
- **Data driven** assumes absolutely nothing is known about the inner workings of the simulator. It is assumed to be a *black-box* and information about the response is collected from evaluations. From these data, an approximation is derived. Because this approach is very general, it is not bound to a specific domain.
- **Hybrid** is the overlap zone between both model driven and data driven. Attempts to incorporate domain-specific knowledge into a data-driven process to obtain better traceability and reach accuracy with less evaluations.

http://dx.doi.org/10.5772/67739

In this chapter, the focus is on a data-driven approach: the response of a simulator as a function of its inputs is mimicked by *surrogate models* (metamodels, emulators or response surface models are often encountered as synonyms). These cheap-to-evaluate mathematical expressions can be evaluated efficiently and can replace the simulator. A more extensive overview of usage scenarios and a formal description of surrogate modelling are given in Section 2. Before the surrogate model can be used, it must first be constructed and trained during the surrogate modelling process on a number of well-chosen evaluations (*samples*) to be evaluated by the simulator in order to satisfy the requirements specified upfront. The problem of selecting an appropriate set of samples is further explored in Section 3. Section 4 briefly introduces an integrated platform for surrogate modelling with sequential design. Finally, these techniques are demonstrated on three use-cases in Section 5.

2. Surrogate modelling

The introduction of this chapter highlighted the global idea of approximation and the benefits of introducing an additional layer of abstraction when simulations are expensive. Now, the data-driven approach (surrogate modelling) is discussed more in depth, both from a usability point of view and a more formal description of the technique.

2.1. Goals and usage scenarios

The most direct implementation of surrogate modelling is training a globally accurate model over the entire design space. This approximation can then replace the expensive simulation evaluations for a variety of engineering tasks such as design space exploration, parameterization of simulations or visualization.

A different use-case of surrogate models is sensitivity analysis of the complex system. Especially when many input parameters are present, it is very difficult to achieve global accuracy due to the exponential growth of the input space (known as the *curse of dimensionality*). Fortunately, not all input parameters contribute equally to the output variability, in fact some might not have any impact at all [3]. The surrogate models can be used directly for evaluation-based sensitivity analysis methods such as Sobol indices [4], Interaction indices [5] or gradient-based methods. For some kernel-based modelling methods, analytical computation of sensitivity measures is possibly resulting in faster and more reliable estimation schemes, even before global accuracy is achieved [6].

Another task at which surrogates excel is the optimization of expensive objective functions. This discipline is often referred to as surrogate-based optimization (SBO). A globally accurate surrogate model can be built and optimized using traditional optimization methods such as gradient descent, or metaheuristics such as particle swarm optimization [7]. Although this approach is correct and works faster than simulating each call of the objective function, it is not necessarily the most efficient methodology: when seeking a minimum, less samples can be devoted to the regions that are clearly shown to be the opposite. This results in specific methodologies, which explore the search space for optima and exploit the available knowledge to refine optima. This is a difficult trade-off and will be discussed in detail in Section 3.2.

All tasks described so far were forward tasks, mapping samples from a design space to the output or objective space. It is also possible to do the opposite: this is referred to as inverse surrogate modelling. This can be interpreted as identifying the areas of the design space corresponding to a certain desired or feasible output range. Typical approaches involve training a (forward) surrogate model first, then optimizing the model using an error function between the output and the desired output as objective function. This optimization is often preferred to be a robust optimization to account for the error of the forward surrogate model [8]. Specific sampling schemes to identify these regions directly were also proposed [9]. Finally, it is also possible to translate the inverse problem into a forward problem involving discretizing the output (feasible/infeasible point) and learning the class boundaries.

Because the concept of surrogate modelling is both flexible as well as generic, allowing several modifications tailored for the task at hand, it has been applied in wide range of fields including metallurgy, economics, operations research, robotics, electronics, physics, automotive, biology, geology, etc.

2.2. Formalism

Formally, the surrogate modelling process can be described as follows. Given an expensive function f and a collection of data samples with corresponding evaluations represented by D, we seek to find an approximation function $\tilde{f}$:

$$\begin{aligned} &\arg\max_{t \in T} \arg\min_{\theta \in \Theta} -\Lambda\left(\kappa,\ \tilde{f}_{t,\vartheta}, D\right) \\ &\text{subject to } \Lambda\left(\kappa,\ \tilde{f}_{t,\vartheta}, D\right) \leq \tau. \end{aligned} \tag{1}$$

It is clear that the selection of the approximation function is a complex interaction of several aspects, more specifically: κ represents an error function such as the popular root-mean-square error (RMSE), τ the target value for the quality as expressed by the error function, all under the operation of the model quality estimator Λ. The quality estimator drives the optimization of both the model type t out of the set of available model types T and its hyperparameters θ. Typical examples of surrogate model types are Artificial Neural Networks (ANNs), Support Vector Machines (SVMs), Radial Basis Functions (RBFs), rational and polynomial models, Kriging and Gaussian Process (GP) models. Examples of hyperparameter optimization include tuning kernel parameters or regularization constants or identifying the optimal order of a polynomial or the most appropriate architecture for a neural network.

The choice of Λ is therefore crucial to obtain a satisfying surrogate model at the end of the process as it is the metric driving the search for θ. This aspect is often overlooked at first, requiring several iterations of the process to obtain satisfactory results. Consulting the users of the surrogate model and defining what is expected from the model and what is not, is a good starting point. These requirements can then be formally translated into a good quality estimator. Unfortunately, defining Λ does not end with casting user requirements. Often, hyperparameters have a direct impact on the model complexity or penalization thereof, thus tuning them is tricky due to the bias-variance trade-off [10].

For instance, a straightforward approach is minimizing the error between the surrogate model response and the true responses for the samples used to train the surrogate. This is often referred to as *training error* or *sample error* and pushes the hyperparameter optimization to favour complex models interpolating the data points perfectly. Although this solution might be considered satisfactory at first sight, in reality this rarely provides a good model as the optimization problems do not consider model quality at other, unobserved samples in the design space. This approach inevitably leads to very unreliable responses when these unobserved samples are to be predicted, hence the model is said to be *overfitting* or to have poor *generalization performance*. Popular quality estimators accounting for generalization performance include crossvalidation and validation sets.

3. Experimental design

A typical requirement for the surrogate model is to be *accurate*, hence the objective of the modelling process is the ability to obtain accuracy with only a small number of (expensive) simulator evaluations. A different kind of requirement is optimizing the response of the simulator. This requires fast discovery of promising regions and fast exploitation thereof to identify the (global) optimum. Hence, a different strategy for selecting the samples is required as the accuracy of the surrogate in non-optimal is of lesser importance. A refined set of model requirements and the goal of the process are required, as they greatly affect the choice of samples to be evaluated. The choice of samples is referred to as the experimental design.

3.1. One-shot design

The traditional approaches to generate an experimental design are the *one-shot* designs. Prior to any evaluation, all samples are selected in a space-filling manner: at this point, no further information is available due to the black-box assumption on the simulator itself (as part of the data-driven approach). Therefore, the information density should be approximately equal over the entire design space and the samples are to be distributed uniformly. To this end, several approaches related to *Design of Experiments* (DoEs) have been developed. However, only the space-filling aspect has an impact within in the context of computer experiments, as other criteria such as blocking and replication lose their relevance [11]. This led to the transition and extension of these existing statistical methods to computer experiments [11, 12]. Widely applied are the factorial designs (grid-based) [13] and optimal (maximin) Latin Hypercube designs (LHDs) [14]. Both are illustrated in **Figures 1** and **2**, respectively, for a two-dimensional input space and 16 samples. An LHD avoids collapsing points should the input space be projected into a lower dimensional space. Other approaches include maximin and minimax designs, Box and Behken [15], central composite designs [16] and (quasi-)Monte Carlo methods [17–19].

Despite their widespread usage, these standard approaches to generate experimental designs come with a number of disadvantages. First and foremost: the most qualitative designs (with the best space-filling properties) can be extremely complex to generate (especially for problems with a high-dimensional input space) due to their geometric properties. For instance, gener-

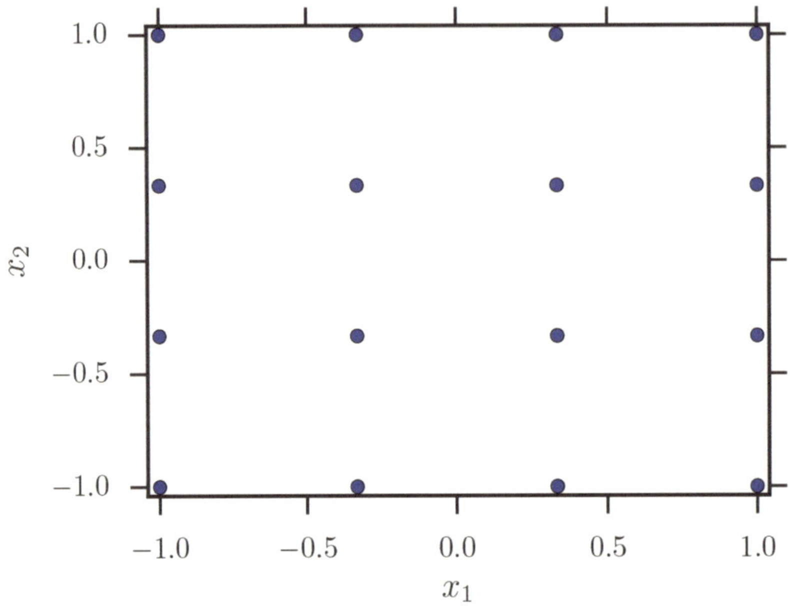

Figure 1. Two-dimensional factorial design with four levels per dimension.

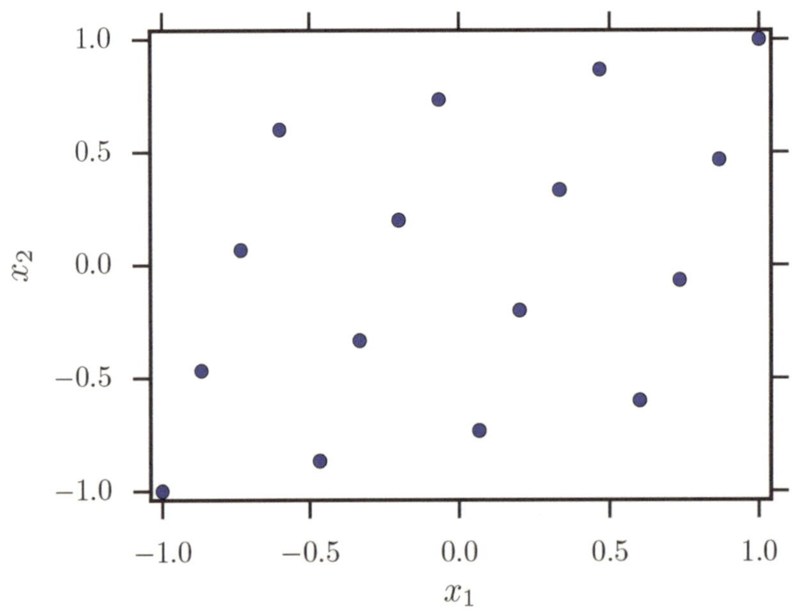

Figure 2. Two-dimensional optimal maximin Latin Hybercube design of size 16.

ating an LHD with optimal maximin distance is very time-consuming process. In fact, the generation of an optimal LHD is almost a field of its own, with several different methods for faster and reliable generation [14, 20]. Fortunately, once a design is generated, it can be reused.

For some other design methodologies, it is not possible to generate them for an arbitrary size. Given the expensive nature of each evaluation, this can result in an unacceptable growth of required simulation time. Factorial designs for instance always have size k^d with level k and dimension d, making them infeasible choises for problems with many input parameters.

Another disadvantage of one-shot methodologies is the arbitrary choice of size of the design. The choice should depend entirely on the nature of the problem (i.e. larger design spaces with more complex behaviour require more evaluations). However, this information is unavailable at the time the design is generated. Hence, one-shot approaches risk selecting too few data points resulting in an underfitted model, or selecting too much data points causing loss of time and computational resources.

3.2. Sequential experimental design

As a solution, sequential design was adopted [21]. This methodology starts from a very small one-shot design to initiate the process. After evaluation of these samples a model is built, and a loop is initiated which is only exited when either one of the specified stopping criteria is met. Within the loop, an *adaptive sampling* algorithm is run to select additional data points for evaluation which are used to update the model. **Figure 3** displays this process graphically.

This approach has a number of advantages. First of all, constraints on the surrogate modelling process can be explicitly imposed through the stopping criteria. Typical criteria include how well the model satisfied the model requirements, a maximum number of allowed evaluations, or a maximum runtime. Second, the *adaptive sampling* method can be designed to select new data points specifically in terms of the requirements. Sampling to obtain a globally accurate model will differ from sampling to discover class boundaries or sampling to obtain optima. These choices can also be guided by all information available about the input-output behaviour: when n samples have been selected, a history of intermediate models and all simulator responses is avail-

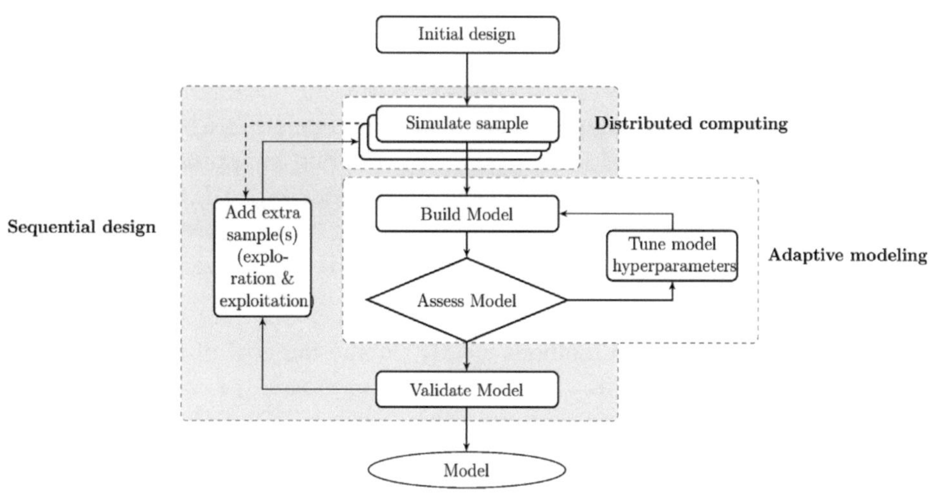

Figure 3. Surrogate modelling with sequential design.

able to guide the selection of new samples. Because of the information available, this selection no longer has to be purely based on a black-box approach, and information can be exploited.

Roughly, all methods for adaptive sampling are based on any of the following criteria (discussed more in detail below):

- Distance to neighbouring points (space-filling designs)
- Identification of optima
- Model uncertainty
- Non-linearity of the response
- Feasibility of the candidate point w.r.t. constraints

Depending on the goal and model requirements, a strategy can be designed involving a complex combination of these criteria. Fundamentally, each approach will involve two competing objectives:

1. **Exploration**: sampling regions of the design space where proportionally only little information has been acquired.
2. **Exploitation**: sampling promising (w.r.t to the goal) regions of the design space.

It is clear, however, that a good strategy strikes a balance between these goals as both are required to obtain satisfactory results.

Exploration-based algorithms are typically less involved with the goal of the process. They are crucial to assure that no relevant parts of the response surface are completely missed. Roughly the space-filling and model uncertainty criteria focus mostly on exploration. Space-filling sequential experimental design usually involves distance to neighbouring points, e.g. the maximin/minimax criteria, potentially complemented with projective properties [22]. Model uncertainty is either explicitly available, or must be derived somehow. Bayesian model types represent the former type of models, e.g. the prediction variance of Kriging and Gaussian Process models, which can be applied directly for maximum variance sampling [23, 24] or maximum entropy designs [25]. For these kinds of models, a better way is expressing the uncertainty on the model hyperparameters resulting in approaches to reduce this uncertainty and hence, enhancing the overall model confidence [26]. Model uncertainty can also be derived by training several models and comparing their responses. Areas with most disagreements are then marked for additional samples. This can be a very effective approach in combination with ensemble modelling.

On the other hand, exploitation methods clearly pursue the goal of the process. In case a global accurate model is required, a very effective approach is raising the information density in regions with non-linear response behaviour (e.g. LOLA-Voronoi [27], FLOLA-Voronoi [28]). The latter approach does not even require intermediate models as it operates on local linear interpolations. For optimization purposes, specific adaptive sampling methodologies can be applied, depending on the specific tasks. For single-objective optimization examples of such sampling methods include CORS [29] and Bayesian optimization acquisition functions such as Expected Improvement [30] (combined with Kriging models this corresponds to the well-known Efficient Global Optimization approach [31]), the Knowledge Gradient [32] and Predictive Entropy Search [33]. Many of these methods for optimization can also be used in combination with a method, which learns about the feasibility of input regions of the design space: during the iterative process an additional model learns the feasibility from the samples (as reflected by the simulation thereof). This information is then used during the selection of new samples with specific criteria such as the Probability of Feasibility (PoF) [34].

Surrogate-based optimization has also been extended to problems with two or more (potentially conflicting) objectives. The goal of this type of multi-objective optimization is the identification of a Pareto front of solutions, which presents the trade-off between these objectives. Existing approaches include hypervolume-based methods such as the Hypervolume Probability of Improvement (HvPoI) [35, 36], the Hypervolume Expected Improvement [37] or multi-objective Predictive Entropy Search [38].

4. SUMO Toolbox

Designed as a research platform for sequential sampling and adaptive modelling using MATLAB, the SUMO Toolbox [39, 40] has grown into a mature design tool for surrogate modelling, offering a large variety of algorithms for approximation of simulators with continuous and discrete output. The software design is fully object oriented allowing high-extensibility of its capabilities. By default, the platform follows the integrated modelling flow with sequential design but can also be configured to approximate data sets, use a one-shot design, etc.

The design goals of the SUMO Toolbox support approximation of expensive computer simulations of complex black-box systems with several design parameters by cheap-to-evaluate models, both in a regression and a classification context. To obtain these goals, the SUMO Toolbox offers sequential sampling and adaptive modelling in a highly configurable environment, which is easy to extend due to the microkernel design. Distributed computing support for evaluations of data points is also available, as well as multi-threading to support the usage of multi-core architectures for regression modelling and classification. Many different plugins are available for each of the different sub-problems, including many of the algorithms and methods mentioned in this chapter.

The behaviour of each software component is configurable through a central XML file, and components can easily be added, removed or replaced by custom implementations. The SUMO Toolbox is free for academic use and is available for download at http://sumo.intec.ugent.be. It can be installed on any platform supported by MATLAB. In addition, a link can be found to the available documentation and tutorials to install and configure the toolbox including some of its more advanced features.

5. Illustrations

To illustrate the flexibility of the surrogate modelling framework with sequential design, some example cases are considered. The SUMO Toolbox was used for each case.

5.1. Low-noise amplifier

This test case consists of a real world problem from electronics. A low-noise amplifier (LNA), a simple radio frequency circuit, is the typical first stage of a receiver, providing the gain to suppress noise of subsequent stages. The performance of an LNA can be determined by means of computer simulations where the underlying physical behaviour is taken into account. For this experiment, we chose to model the input noise-current, in function of two (normalized) parameters: the inductance and the MOSFET width. The response to the inputs for this test case is smooth with a steep ridge in the middle. This type of strong non-linear behaviour is difficult to approximate.

The model type for this problem is an ANN, trained with Levenberg-Marquard backpropagation with Bayesian regularization (300 epochs). The network topology and initial weights are optimized by a genetic algorithm, with a maximum of two layers. The process initiates by combining a 10-point LHD with a two-level factorial design (the corner points). As adaptive sampling methodology, the FLOLA-Voronoi algorithm was chosen to select a single-point iteration. Once the steep ridge has been discovered, the information density in this area will be increased. As model quality estimator, crossvalidation was used, with the root relative square error (RRSE) function:

$$\mathrm{RRSE}(x, \tilde{x}) = \sqrt{\frac{\sum_{i=1}^{n} (x_i - \tilde{x}_i)^2}{\sum_{i=1}^{n} (x_i - \overline{x})^2}}. \tag{2}$$

The stopping criterion was set to an RRSE score below 0.05. This was achieved after evaluating a total of 51 samples. A plot of the model is shown in **Figure 4**. Additionally, the distribution of the samples in the two-dimensional input space is shown in **Figure 5**. The focus on the ridge can be clearly observed. In comparison, repeating the experiment in a one-shot setting with an LHD of 51 points and keeping all other settings results in an RRSE score of only 0.11. This is mostly caused by an inadequate detection of the non-linearity (only a few samples are near the non-linearity), whereas a lot of samples are on the smoothly varying surfaces.

5.2. Optimization: gas cyclone

The next illustration is more involved and is a joint modelling process aiming both at design optimality as well as feasibility. The goal is to optimize the seven-dimensional geometry of a gas cyclone. These components are widely used in air pollution control, gas-solid separation for aerosol sampling and industrial applications aiming to catch large particles such as vacuum cleaners. An illustration is given in **Figure 6**. In cyclone separators, a strongly swirling turbulent flow is used to separate phases with different densities. A tangential inlet generates a complex swirling motion of the gas stream, which forces particles toward the outer

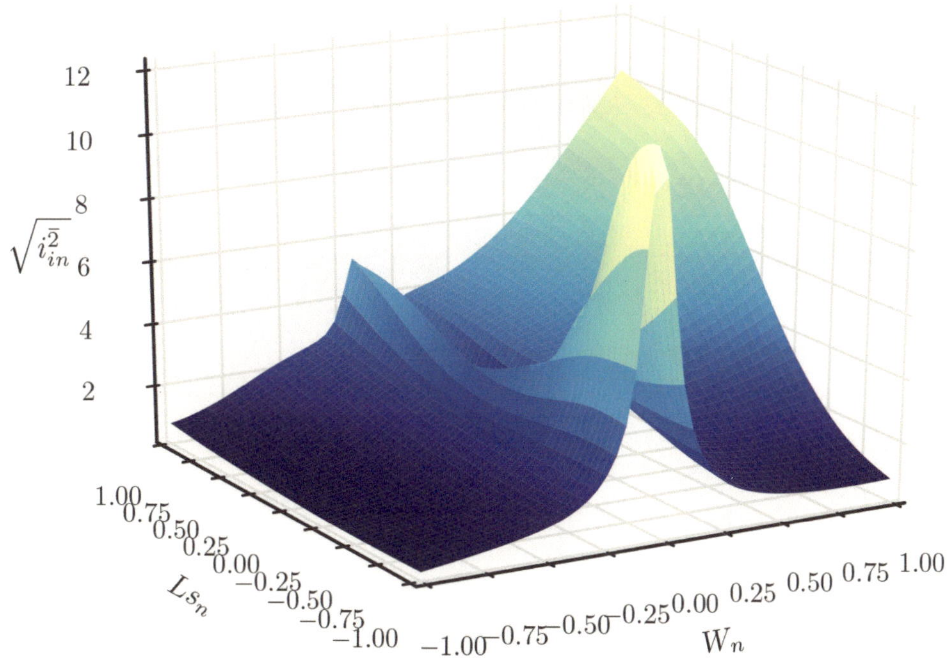

Figure 4. LNA: final surrogate model for the LNA illustration. The sharp peak is clearly present.

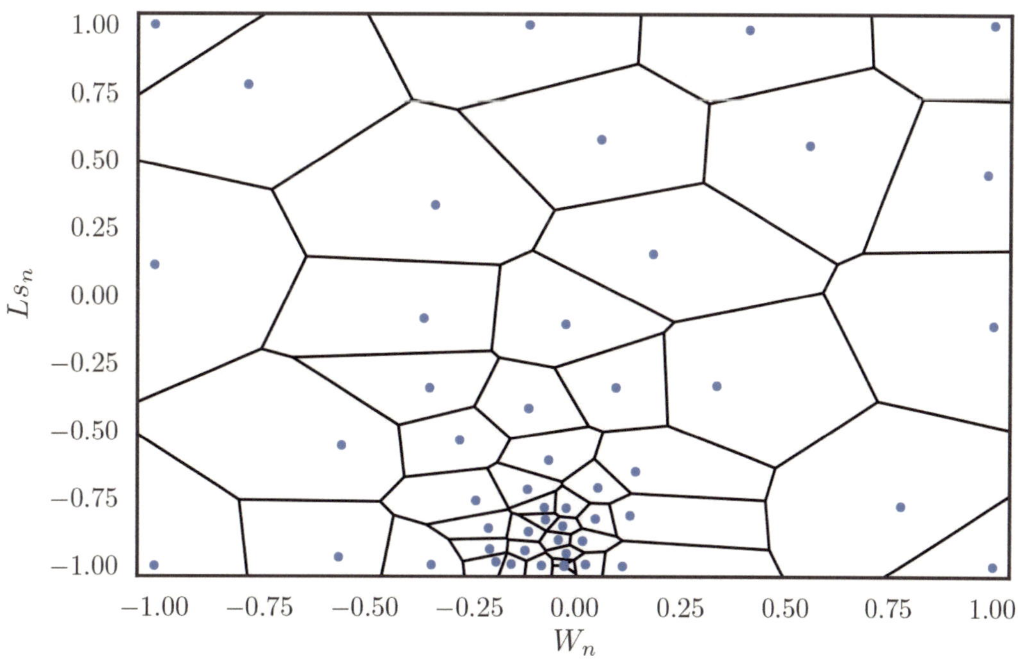

Figure 5. LNA: sample distribution as constructed sequentially by the FLOLA-Voronoi adaptive sampling algorithm.

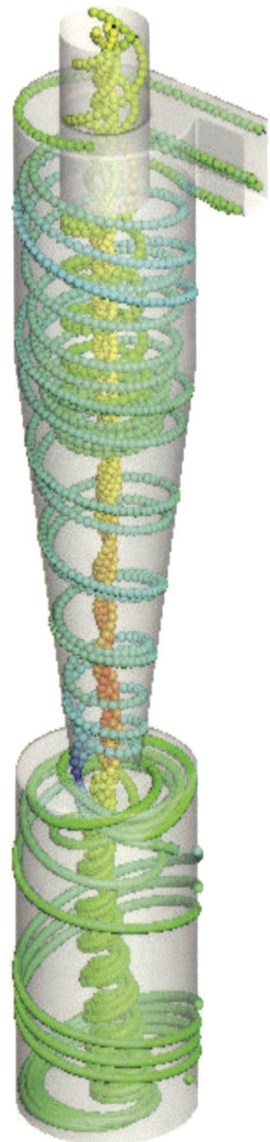

Figure 6. Cyclone: illustration of a gas cyclone.

wall where they spiral in the downward direction. Eventually, the particles are collected in the dustbin (or flow out through a dipleg) located at the bottom of the conical section of the cyclone body. The cleaned gas leaves through the exit pipe at the top. The cyclone geometry [41] is described by seven geometrical parameters: the inlet height a, width b, the vortex finder diameter D_x, and length S, cylinder height h, cyclone total height H_t and cone-tip diameter B_c. Modifying these parameters has an impact on the performance and behaviour of the gas cyclone itself.

Design optimality for the gas cyclone, however, is not represented by a unique and optimal number. In fact, it is represented by two different aspects: the pressure loss (expressed by the Euler number) and the cut-off diameter, which is expressed by the Stokes number. Both aspects represent a trade-off, and the proper scaling to sum both into a single objective is unknown. Hence, the correct way to proceed is to identify a set of Pareto optimal solutions representing the trade-off inherent to this problem, rather than a single solution. Presented with this trade-off, the designer has to make the final decision on what the optimal design should be. The shape of the Pareto front is informative and of great value for the designer (w.r.t. robustness of the solution for example). For the optimization, the two outputs of a simulation corresponding to these objectives are approximated with the built-in Kriging models [22].

In addition, geometry optimization usually involves constraints as some configurations are not feasible, or result in gas cyclones, which do not work according to specifications. In addition to the Euler and Stokes objectives, the simulation of a sample also emits four binary values indicating if their corresponding constraint was satisfied or not (denoted as c_1, c_2, c_3 and c_4). As each evaluation is computationally demanding, this additional knowledge should be included in order to maximize the probability of selecting feasible solutions. Each of the constraint outputs will therefore be approximated by a probabilistic SVM. For selecting new samples, both the Pareto optimality and the feasibility need to be considered. To this end, the HvPoI and PoF criteria are used, respectively. The PoF score is not computed explicitly (as it would be for a Gaussian Process) but interpreted as the SVM probability for the class representing feasible samples. This results in the following joint criterion:

$$\alpha(x) = \mathrm{HvPoI}(x) \prod_{\{c_1,c_2,c_3,c_4\}} \mathrm{PoF}_c(x) \tag{3}$$

For each iteration of the sequential design, this criterion is optimized resulting in a new sample maximizing the probability of a more feasible and more optimal solution. To start, an LHD is constructed in seven dimensions. The kernel bandwidth and regularization constant hyperparameters for the SVMs are optimized with the DIRECT optimization algorithm [42], using crossvalidation with the popular F_1-score of the positive class as error function. The hyperparameters for the Kriging models are optimized with maximum-likelihood estimation. The sampling criterion is first optimized randomly with a dense set of random points, then the best solution serves as a starting point for applying gradient descent locally to refine the solution. The stopping criterion was set to a maximum of 120 evaluated data points.

Figure 7 shows the scores for all evaluated samples on both objectives. The bullets and squares represent the samples forming the Pareto front. The black-box constraints were learned as the optimization was proceeding, hence many evaluated samples do not satisfy the constraints (as this was unknown at that time): 8% of the evaluated samples however satisfy the constraints. Fortunately, four of them are Pareto optimal and represent valid optimal configurations. The exact optimal Pareto front was unknown upfront: in order to provide a comparison and verify the integrity of the identified solutions the traditional NSGA-II [43] multi-objective optimization algorithm was applied directly on the CFD simulations for a total of 10,000 evaluations. Clearly, the Pareto optimal solutions found by the surrogate-based approach form a similar

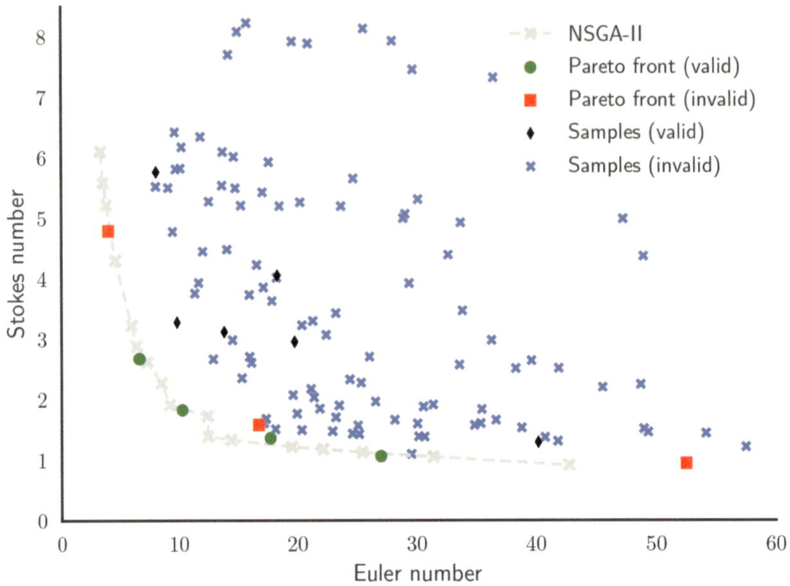

Figure 7. Cyclone: Pareto front obtained after 120 evaluations for the gas cyclone optimization. The plot also distinguishes between feasible and infeasible points and shows the Pareto front obtained by NSGA-II after an extensive 10,000 evaluations.

front. Our approach was able to identify these solutions with significantly fewer evaluations and hence significantly faster. Therefore, the identified Pareto front is a very good approximation given the budget constraint of 120 evaluations.

5.3. Satellite braking system

Finally, we demonstrate the use of surrogate models for performing analysis into the relevance of input parameters. A simulation of a braking system of the Aalto-1 student satellite [44, 45] was modelled with sequential design. The brake consists of a small mass m attached to a tether, which is extended at a constant speed v_{feed}. The satellite is spinning around with an angular velocity ω_{sat}, which is also the angular velocity of the mass at the beginning of the deployment. As the distance of the tip of the tether to the satellite increases, the angular velocity of the tip, ω_{tip}, decreases. This results in a displacement angle γ of the tether from its initial balance position. This causes a tangential force negative to the rotational direction of the satellite, causing it to spin around slower. The same tangential force accelerates the tip, which results in a decrease of the angle, until the tether has extended sufficiently again to further decrease the rotation of the satellite. **Figure 8** illustrates the setup graphically.

Although the displacement angle effectively causes the braking effect, it must remain within an acceptable range to prevent a range of undesired effects and issues. To this end, a simulation for γ was developed with five input parameters (the time after deployment time, initial angular velocity of the satellite, the mass of the tip, the deployment speed of the tether and

http://dx.doi.org/10.5772/67739

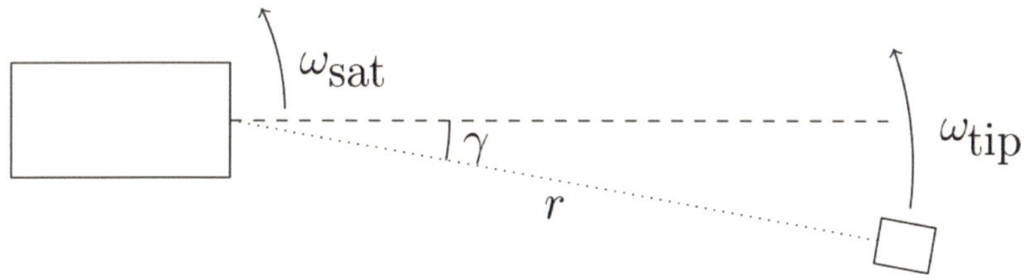

Figure 8. Satellite: illustration of the breaking system.

the width of the satellite). Using surrogate models, the aim is to find the parameters, which influence the displacement angle the most.

To approach this problem, the process starts from a LHD of 20 points. Iteratively, a space-filling sequential design selects 10 additional samples for evaluation on the simulator. The space-filling approach incorporates both the maximin distance and projective properties as described in Ref. [46]. The model type selected is a GP with the Matérn 3/2 covariance function with Automated Relevance Determination (ARD). When 300 samples were evaluated, the process was terminated and the analytical approach presented in Ref. [6] was used to compute the first-order Sobol indices, as well as the total Sobol indices (first-order indices augmented with all indices of higher order interactions containing this parameter) [4]. Both indices are plotted in **Figure 9**.

From the results, it can be clearly observed that the mass of the tip has no impact at all on the displacement angle. It can therefore be disregarded from any further design decisions. All other parameters do have some impact, as expected. The deployment speed clearly has the

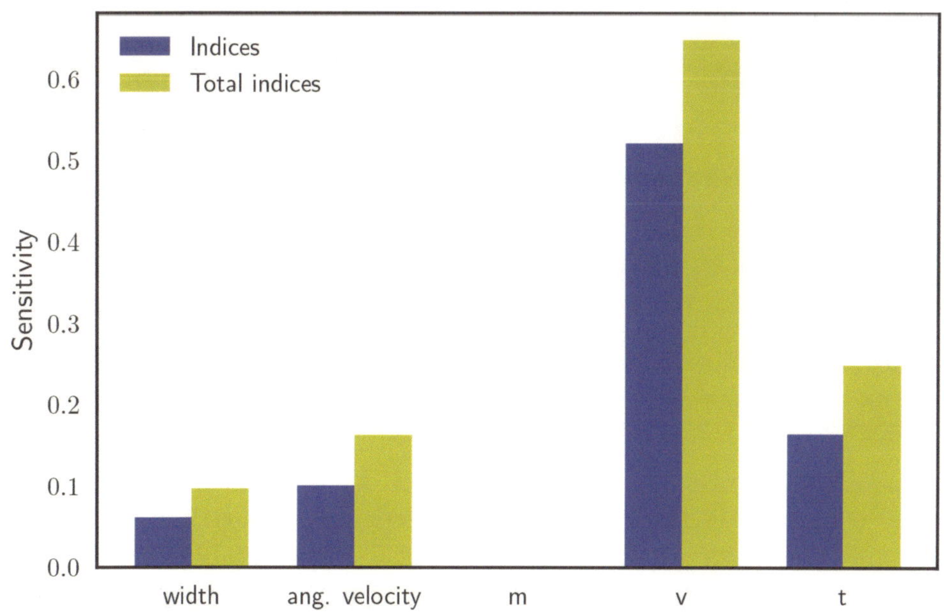

Figure 9. Satellite: Sobol indices for the final GP model.

highest impact. This is intuitive, as faster deployment results in more significant differences between the angular velocities of the satellite and the tip.

6. Conclusion

The benefits of surrogate modelling techniques have proven to be successful to work with expensive simulations and expensive objectives in general. Within this flexible methodology, and complemented with intelligent sequential sampling (sequential design) several tasks ranging from design space exploration, sensitivity analysis to (multi-objective) optimization with constraints can be accomplished efficiently with only a small number of evaluations. This greatly enhances the capabilities to virtually design complex systems, reducing the time and costs of product development cycles resulting in a shorter time-to-market. The strengths and possibilities were demonstrated on a few real world examples from different domains.

Acknowledgements

Ivo Couckuyt is a post-doctoral research fellow of FWO-Vlaanderen. The authors would like to thank NXP Semiconductors and Jeroen Croon in particular for providing the LNA simulator code.

Author details

Joachim van der Herten*, Tom Van Steenkiste, Ivo Couckuyt and Tom Dhaene

*Address all correspondence to: joachimvanderherten@intec.ugent.be

Department of Information Technology, IDLab, Ghent University - imec, Ghent, Belgium

References

[1] Goethals K, Couckuyt I, Dhaene T, Janssens A. Sensitivity of night cooling performance to room/system design: surrogate models based on CFD. Building and Environment. 2012;**58**:23-36. DOI: 10.1016/j.buildenv.2012.06.015

[2] Simpson TW, Booker AJ, Ghosh D, Giunta AA, Koch PN, Yang R-J. Approximation methods in multidisciplinary analysis and optimization: a panel discussion. Structural and Multidisciplinary Optimization. 2004;**27**(5):302-313. DOI: 10.1007/s00158-004-0389-9

[3] Saltelli A. Sensitivity analysis for importance assessment. Risk Analysis. 2002;**22**(3):579-590. DOI: 10.1111/0272-4332.00040

[4] Sobol IM. Global sensitivity indices for nonlinear mathematical models and their Monte Carlo estimates. Mathematics and computers in simulation. 2001;**55**(1-3):271-280. DOI: 10.1016/S0378-4754(00)00270-6

[5] Keiichi I, Couckuyt I, Poles S, Dhaene T. Variance-based interaction index measuring heteroscedasticity. Computer Physics Communications. 2016;**203**:152-161. DOI: 10.1016/j.cpc.2016.02.032

[6] Van Steenkiste T, van der Herten J, Couckuyt I, Dhaene T. Sensitivity Analysis of Expensive Black-box Systems Using Metamodeling. In: Roeder TMK, Frazier PI, Szechtman R, Zhou E, Huschka T, Chick SE, editors. Proceedings of the 2016 Winter Simulation Conference; 11-14 December 2016; Washington, D.C., USA; 2016. Institute of Electrical and Electronics Engineers, Inc. DOI: 10.1109/WSC.2016.7822123

[7] Kennedy J, Eberhart R. Particle swarm optimization. In: Proceedings of the IEEE International Conference on Neural Networks; 27 November–1 December 1995; IEEE; Piscataway, New Jersey, USA. 1995. DOI: 10.1109/ICNN.1995.488968

[8] Dellino G, Kleijnen JPC, Meloni C. Robust simulation-optimization using metamodels. In: Rossetti MD, Hill RR, Johansson B, Dunkin A, Ingalls RG, editors. Proceedings of the Winter Simulation Conference; 13-16 December 2016; Austin, TX, USA: IEEE; 2009. p. 540-550. DOI: 10.1109/WSC.2009.5429720

[9] Couckuyt I, Aernouts J, Deschrijver D, De Turck F, Dhaene T. Identification of quasi-optimal regions in the design space using surrogate modeling. Engineering with Computers. 2013;**29**(2):127-138. DOI: 10.1007/s00366-011-0249-3

[10] Vapnik V. The Nature of Statistical Learning Theory. 2nd ed. New York: Springer-Verlag; 2000. 334 p. DOI: 10.1007/978-1-4757-3264-1

[11] Sacks J, Welch WJ, Mitchell TJ, Wynn HP. Design and analysis of computer experiments. Statistical Science. 1989;**4**(4):409-423.

[12] Kleijnen, JPC. Design and Analysis of Simulation Experiments. 2nd ed. Springer International Publishing; New York City, USA. 2015. 337 p. DOI: 10.1007/978-3-319-180 87-8

[13] Montgomery, DC. Design and Analysis of Experiments. 8th ed. John Wiley & Sons; Hoboken, New Jersey, USA. 2008. 752 p. DOI: 10.1002/qre.458

[14] Van Dam ER, Husslage B, Den Hertog D, Melissen H. Maximin Latin hypercube designs in two dimensions. Operations Research. 2007;**55**(1):158-169. DOI: 10.1287/opre. 1060.0317

[15] Box GEP, Behnken D. Some new three level designs for the study of quantitative variables. Technometrics. 1960;**2**:455-475. DOI: 10.1080/00401706.1960.10489912

[16] Raymond HM, Montgomery DC, Anderson-Cook CM. Response Surface Methodology: Process and Product Optimization Using Designed Experiments. 4th ed. John Wiley & Sons; Hoboken, New Jersey, USA. 2016. 856 p.

[17] Hendrickx W, Dhaene T. Sequential design and rational metamodelling. In: Kuh ME, Steiger NM, Armstrong FB, Joines JA, editors. Proceedings of the Winter Simulation Conference; 4 December 2005; Orlando, FL, USA: IEEE; 2005. pp. 290-298. DOI: 10.1109/WSC.2005.1574263

[18] Jin R, Chen W, Sujianto A. An efficient algorithm for constructing optimal design of computer experiments. Journal of Statistical Planning and Inference. 2005;**134**(1):268-287. DOI: 10.1016/j.jspi.2004.02.014

[19] Niederreiter, H. Random Number Generation and Quasi-Monte Carlo Methods. 1st ed. Society for Industrial and Applied Mathematics; Philadelphia, Pennsylvania, United States. 1992. 241 p. DOI: 10.1137/1.9781611970081

[20] Viana FAC, Gerhard V, Vladimir B. An algorithm for fast optimal Latin hypercube design of experiments. International Journal for Numerical Methods in Engineering. 2010;**82**(2):135-156. DOI: 10.1002/nme.2750

[21] Gorissen D. Grid-enabled adaptive surrogate modeling for computer aided engineering [dissertation]. Ghent, Belgium: Ghent University. Faculty of Engineering; 2010. 384 p. Available from: https://biblio.ugent.be/publication/1163941/file/4335278.pdf

[22] Couckuyt I, Dhaene T, Demeester P. ooDACE Toolbox: a flexible object-oriented Kriging implementation. Journal of Machine Learning Research. 2014;**15**:3183-3186.

[23] Kleijnen JPC, van Beers WCM. Application-driven sequential designs for simulation experiments: kriging metamodelling. Journal of the Operational Research Society. 2004;**55**(8):876-883. DOI: 10.1057/palgrave.jors.2601747

[24] Sasena, MJ. Flexibility and efficiency enhancements for constrained global design optimization with kriging approximations [dissertation]. 2002.

[25] Farhang-Mehr A, Azarm S. Bayesian meta-modelling of engineering design simulations: a sequential approach with adaptation to irregularities in the response behaviour. International Journal for Numerical Methods in Engineering. 2005;**62**(15):2104-2126. DOI: 10.1002/nme.1261

[26] Garnett R, Osborne M, Hennig P. Active learning of linear embeddings for Gaussian processes. In: Zhang ML, Tian J, editors. Proceedings of the 30th Conference on Uncertainty in Artificial Intelligence; 23-27 July 2014; Quebec, Canada: AUAI Press; 2014. p. 230-239.

[27] Crombecq K, Gorissen D, Deschrijver D, Dhaene T. A novel hybrid sequential design strategy for global surrogate modeling of computer experiments. SIAM Journal on Scientific Computing. 2011;**33**(4):1948-1974. DOI: 10.1137/090761811

[28] van der Herten J, Couckuyt I, Deschrijver D, Dhaene T. A fuzzy hybrid sequential design strategy for global surrogate modeling of high-dimensional computer experiments. SIAM Journal on Scientific Computing. 2015;**37**(2):A1020–A1039. DOI: 10.1137/140962437

[29] Regis, RG, Shoemaker CA. Constrained global optimization of expensive black box functions using radial basis functions. Journal of Global Optimization. 2005;**31**(1):153-171. DOI: 10.1007/s10898-004-0570-0

[30] Močkus, J. Marchuk, G.I. On Bayesian methods for seeking the extremum. In: Optimization Techniques IFIP Technical Conference; Springer; Novosibirsk, Berlin, Heidelberg. 1975. p. 400-404.

[31] Jones DR, Schonlau M, Welch WJ. Efficient global optimization of expensive black-box functions. Journal of Global Optimization. 1998;**13**(4):455-492. DOI: 10.1023/A:1008306431147

[32] Scott W, Frazier PI, Powell W. The correlated knowledge gradient for simulation optimization of continuous parameters using Gaussian process regression. SIAM Journal on Optimization. 2011;**21**(3):996-1026. DOI: 10.1137/100801275

[33] Hernández-Lobato JM, Hoffman MW, Ghahramani Z. Predictive entropy search for efficient global optimization of black-box functions. In: Ghahramani Z, Welling M, Cortes C, Lawrence ND, Weinberger KQ, editors. Advances in Neural Information Processing Systems 27; 8-13 December 2014; Montreal, Canada: Curran Associates, Inc.; 2014. p. 918-926.

[34] Gardner J, Kusner M, Weinberger KQ, Cunningham J, Xu, Z. Bayesian optimization with inequality constraints. In: Jebara T, Xing EP, editors. Proceedings of the 31st International Conference on Machine Learning (ICML-14); 21-26 June 2014; Beijing, China: JMLR.org; 2014. pp. 937-945.

[35] Emmerich M, Beume N, Naujoks, B. Coello Coello C.A., Hernández Aguirre A., Zitzler E. An EMO algorithm using the hypervolume measure as selection criterion. In: International Conference on Evolutionary Multi-Criterion Optimization; 9-11 March 2005; Guanajuato, Mexico: Springer Berlin Heidelberg; 2005. p. 62-76.

[36] Couckuyt I, Deschrijver D, Dhaene T. Fast calculation of multiobjective probability of improvement and expected improvement criteria for Pareto optimization. Journal of Global Optimization. 2013;**60**(3):575-594. DOI: 10.1007/s10898-013-0118-2

[37] Emmerich M, Hingston P, Deutz AH, Klinkenberg JW. Hypervolume-based expected improvement: monotonicity properties and exact computation. In: IEEE Congress on Evolutionary Computation (CEC); 5-8 June 2011; New Orleans, LA, USA: IEEE; 2011. p. 2147-2154. DOI: 10.1109/CEC.2011.5949880

[38] Hernández-Lobato D, Hernández-Lobato JM, Shah A, Adams RP. Predictive Entropy Search for Multi-objective Bayesian Optimization. In: Balcan MF, Weinberger, KQ, editors. Proceedings of the 33rd International Conference on Machine Learning (ICML-16); 19-24 June 2016; Manhattan, New York: JMLR.org; 2016. p. 1492-1501.

[39] Gorissen D, Crombecq K, Couckuyt I, Demeester P, Dhaene T. A surrogate modeling and adaptive sampling toolbox for computer based design. Journal of Machine Learning Research. 2010;**11**:2051-2055.

[40] van der Herten J, Couckuyt I, Deschrijver D, Dhaene T. Adaptive classification under computational budget constraints using sequential data gathering. Advances in Engineering Software. 2016;**99**:137-146. DOI: 10.1016/j.advengsoft.2016.05.016

[41] Elsayed K. Optimization of the cyclone separator geometry for minimum pressure drop using Co-Kriging. Powder Technology. 2015;**269**:409-424. DOI: 10.1016/j.powtec.2015.09.003

[42] Jones DR, Perttunen CD, Stuckman BE. Lipschitzian optimization without the Lipschitz constant. Journal of Optimization Theory and Applications. 1993;**79**(1):157-181.

[43] Deb K, Pratap A, Agarwal S, Meyarivan T. A fast and elitist multiobjective genetic algorithm: NSGA-II. IEEE Transactions on Evolutionary Computation. 2002;**6**(2):182-197. DOI: 10.1109/4235.996017

[44] Kestilä A, Tikka T, Peitso P, Rantanen J, Näsilä A, Nordling K, Saari H, Vainio R, Janhunen P, Praks J, Hallikainen M. Aalto-1 nanosatellite–technical description and mission objectives. Geoscientific Instrumentation, Methods and Data Systems. 2013;**2**(1):121-130. DOI: 10.5194/gi-2-121-2013

[45] Khurshid O, Tikka T, Praks J, Hallikainen M. Accommodating the plasma brake experiment on-board the Aalto-1 satellite. Proceedings of the Estonian Academy of Sciences. 2014;**63**(2S):258-266. DOI: 10.3176/proc.2014.2S.07

[46] Crombecq K, Laermans E, Dhaene T. Efficient space-filling and non-collapsing sequential design strategies for simulation-based modeling. European Journal of Operational Research. 2011;**214**(3):683-696. DOI: 10.1016/j.ejor.2011.05.032

Chapter 9

Computer Simulation of High-Frequency Electromagnetic Fields

Andrey D. Grigoriev

Additional information is available at the end of the chapter

http://dx.doi.org/10.5772/67497

Abstract

High-frequency and microwave electromagnetic fields are used in billions of various devices and systems. Design of these systems is impossible without detailed analysis of their electromagnetic field. Most of microwave systems are very complex, so analytical solution of the field equations for them is impossible. Therefore, it is necessary to use numerical methods of field simulation. Unfortunately, such complex devices as, for example, modern smartphones cannot be accurately analysed by existing commercial codes. The chapter contains a short review of modern numerical methods for Maxwell's equations solution. Among them, a vector finite element method is the most suitable for simulation of complex devices with hundreds of details of various forms and materials, but electrically not too large. The method is implemented in the computer code radio frequency simulator (RFS). The code has friendly user interface, an advanced mesh generator, efficient solver and post-processor. It solves eigenmode problems, driven waveguide problems, antenna problems, electromagnetic-compatibility problems and others in frequency domain.

Keywords: electromagnetics, numerical methods, computer simulation, microwaves, cellular phones

1. Introduction

High-frequency electromagnetic fields are used now in telecommunications and radar systems, astrophysics, plasma heating and diagnostics, biology, medicine, technology and many other applications. Special electromagnetic systems excite and guide these fields with given time and space distribution. A designer or a researcher of such systems ought to know in detail their electromagnetic field characteristics. This goal can be achieved or by experimental study, often too long in time and expensive, or by computer simulation. The last choice becomes more and more preferable with fast progress of computational electrodynamics and computer efficiency.

All macroscopic electromagnetic phenomena are governed by Maxwell's equations. Unfortunately, these remarkable equations have so many solutions, that choice of the one satisfying given initial and boundary conditions (BC) often becomes very difficult problem. A number of commercial computer codes based on numerical solution of Maxwell's equations are available at this time. These codes make possible high-frequency electromagnetic field simulation.

Researches have not yet created a universal code, efficiently simulating electromagnetic field excited by an arbitrary technical or nature source in an arbitrary medium. Some codes are more suitable for solving one kind of problems and other codes—another kind. Hence, developing new, more universal and efficient computer codes is an actual task. On the other side, a designer of electromagnetic devices and systems has to choose most efficient computer code for solving his/her particular problem. He/she can do right choice only if he/she understands the basics of a numerical method used in the given code.

The goal of the presented chapter is to formulate electromagnetic problems and to describe in short prevailing numerical methods of its solving. As an example, the chapter also gives more detailed description of the radio frequency simulator (RFS) computer code, developed in collaboration of Saint-Petersburg State Electrotechnical University and LG Russian R&D Centre. Some results obtained by means of this code demonstrate its accuracy and efficiency.

The author hopes that this chapter would be useful for researchers and designers of modern telecommunication devices and systems.

2. Basic equations

Maxwell's equations are the basic ones, describing macroscopic electromagnetic fields in an arbitrary medium. In modern notation, these equations have the form

$$\nabla \times \mathbf{H} = \frac{\partial \mathbf{D}}{\partial t} + \mathbf{J} \tag{1}$$

$$\nabla \times \mathbf{E} = -\frac{\partial \mathbf{B}}{\partial t} \tag{2}$$

$$\nabla \cdot \mathbf{D} = \rho \tag{3}$$

$$\nabla \cdot \mathbf{B} = 0 \tag{4}$$

In these formulas, $\mathbf{J}, \rho$ are the electric current and electric charge densities (field sources), $\mathbf{E}, \mathbf{H}$ are the electric and magnetic field intensities (or simply electric and magnetic fields), $\mathbf{D}, \mathbf{B}$ are the electric and magnetic flux densities, ∇ is Hamilton's differential operator and $\times$ is the sign of vector and scalar products.

The constitutive relations couple flux densities and field intensities:

http://dx.doi.org/10.5772/67497

$$\mathbf{D} = \varepsilon\mathbf{E} = \varepsilon_0\varepsilon_r\mathbf{E} \tag{5}$$

$$\mathbf{B} = \mu\mathbf{H} = \mu_0\mu_r\mathbf{H} \tag{6}$$

Here, ε, μ are the absolute permittivity and permeability, $\varepsilon_0 = 10^7/(4\pi c^2)$, $\mu_0 = 4\pi \cdot 10^{-7}$ are the dielectric and magnetic constants (we use the SI units in this chapter) and ε_r, μ_r are the relative permittivity and permeability, which can be scalars or tensors, depending on medium properties. Equations (1), (2), (5) and (6) form a system of 12 scalar differential equations of the first order with 12 unknowns—components of $\mathbf{E}, \mathbf{H}, \mathbf{D}, \mathbf{B}$ vectors, which are functions of space coordinates and time. To solve this system, one needs to define initial and boundary conditions. These conditions together with the equations form an electrodynamics problem (EMP).

Initial conditions define electric and magnetic field intensities in the computational region at the initial moment of time.

The most frequently used boundary conditions (BC) are as follows:

- On the surface separating two dielectrics:

$$\mathbf{n}\times(\mathbf{E}_2 - \mathbf{E}_1) = 0; \quad \mathbf{n}\times(\mathbf{H}_2 - \mathbf{H}_1) = \mathbf{J}_s \tag{7}$$

  where $\mathbf{n}$ is the unit normal to the surface directed from the first medium to the second and $\mathbf{J}_s$ is the surface electric current density.

- On the surface of perfect electric conductor (PEC):

$$\mathbf{n}\times\mathbf{E} = 0 \tag{8}$$

- Similarly, on the surface of perfect magnetic conductor (PMC)

$$\mathbf{n}\times\mathbf{H} = 0 \tag{9}$$

- Approximate Leontovich boundary condition holds on the impedance surface:

$$\mathbf{e}_n\times(\mathbf{e}_n\times\dot{\mathbf{E}}) - j\frac{Z_s}{k_0\eta_0\mu_r}\mathbf{e}_n\times(\nabla\times\dot{\mathbf{E}}) = 0 \tag{10}$$

  where Z_s is the surface impedance. For metals, $Z_s = (1+j)\sqrt{\omega\mu/(2\sigma)}$.

- We define radiation (adsorption) condition on the surface throw where radiation propagates without reflections. Higdon [1] proposed general absorption boundary conditions (ABCs) theory of arbitrary order of approximation. For a wave, propagating under arbitrary angle φ to the border $x =$ Const, the first-order Higton's ABC are

$$\left(\frac{\partial}{\partial x} + \frac{\cos\varphi}{u}\frac{\partial}{\partial t} + \xi\right)\mathbf{E}_\tau = 0 \tag{11}$$

where ξ is constant, providing solution stability and u is the phase velocity of the wave. Higher order ABC can be constructed by multiplying several first-order operators (11).

Another expression for ABC can be derived from the wave equation. For the wave propagating along the normal $\mathbf{e}_n$ to the border, we get

$$(\nabla\times\dot{\mathbf{E}})_\tau + jk_0\sqrt{\varepsilon_r\mu_r}\,\mathbf{e}_{n\times}\times\dot{\mathbf{E}} = 0 \tag{12}$$

There are two types of EMPs: an inner problem, when the solution is defined in a closed space region with certain boundary conditions on its border, and an outer problem presuming existence of the solution in the unbounded space excluding some regions with prescribed conditions on their boundaries. We ought also to define field sources in the computational region and initial conditions—electrical and magnetic fields at some moment of time. The proper initial and boundary conditions guarantee existence and uniqueness of the solution [2, 3].

Equations (1)–(4) presume arbitrary time dependence of sources and fields. But very often field dependence on time expresses by the harmonic law: $a = a_m\cos(\omega t + \varphi)$, where a is any component of the field, $\omega = 2\pi f$ is the angular frequency, f is frequency and φ is the initial angle. In this case, we can simplify Maxwell's equations, using notation

$$\mathbf{E}(\mathbf{r},t) = \mathrm{Re}\left[\dot{\mathbf{E}}(\mathbf{r})e^{j\omega t}\right], \tag{13}$$

where $\dot{\mathbf{E}}(\mathbf{r}) = E_x e^{j\varphi_x}\mathbf{e}_x + E_y e^{j\varphi_y}\mathbf{e}_y + E_z e^{j\varphi_z}\mathbf{e}_z$ is the complex electric field amplitude (phasor). Magnetic field $\mathbf{H}$ is presented similarly. Using these notations, we can write Maxwell's equations for phasors:

$$\nabla\times\dot{\mathbf{H}} = j\omega\dot{\varepsilon}\dot{\mathbf{E}} + \dot{\mathbf{J}} \tag{14}$$

$$\nabla\times\dot{\mathbf{E}} = -j\omega\dot{\mu}\dot{\mathbf{H}} \tag{15}$$

$$\nabla\cdot(\dot{\varepsilon}\dot{\mathbf{E}}) = \dot{\rho} \tag{16}$$

$$\nabla\cdot(\dot{\mu}\dot{\mathbf{H}}) = 0 \tag{17}$$

Here, $\dot{\varepsilon} = \varepsilon_0\dot{\varepsilon}_r$, $\dot{\mu} = \mu_0\dot{\mu}_r$ are the complex absolute permittivity and permeability and $\dot{\varepsilon}_r = (\varepsilon'_r + j\varepsilon''_r)$, $\dot{\mu}_r = (\mu'_r + j\mu''_r)$ are the relative complex permittivity and permeability. The equation systems (14)–(17) are simpler than the original one because it does not contain time as independent variable and has only six unknown functions.

3. Basis stages of electromagnetic problem solution

Solution of a given electromagnetic problem can be divided on several subsequent steps (stages):

1. Problem formulation—defining the goal of the computation, necessary input and output data, admissible inaccuracy of the results.

2. Analytical treatment—formulating of equations, initial and boundary conditions, geometrical description of the computational region and filling medium properties. The choice of the numerical solution method, transforming equations to the form, most suitable for the chosen method, a-priory analysis of equations and their solutions properties.

3. Problem discretization—transfer from continuous functions to discrete ones and from functional equations to the system of linear algebraic equations (SLAE), in the certain sense approaching the initial problem.

4. Algebraic solution—choosing the most efficient numerical method and solving the SLAE with the prescribed accuracy.

5. Post-processing—calculation of fields, characteristics and parameters of the electromagnetic system and visualization of the results.

Each stage of the solution adds its own contribution to the total solution error. The first step adds the so-called *inherent error* arising due to inaccuracy of input data. This error cannot be eliminated on the next stages of solution. The second stage adds *mathematical model error* caused by imperfect adequateness of the model to the real physical process. Problem discretization adds the so-called *numerical method error*, the value of which depends on the quality of the discretization process. At last, *computational error* arises on stages 4 and 5 due to finite accuracy of numbers presentation in a computer and finite number of operations. With progress in the computational mathematics and computer, the main error sources move from the uncontrolled first stages to the fourth and fifth stages, where we can often predict the error value a-priory.

4. Numerical methods classification

The solution of real-life electromagnetic problem is a very complicated task. There are no universal methods, capable to solve efficiently an arbitrary problem. Hence, a number of numerical methods were elaborated, each of them is the most efficient for its particular range of problems. The numerical methods divide on two large groups.

The first group solves problems involving Maxwell's equation (1)–(4), containing time as an independent variable. This group makes possible to find the solution in time domain (TD) with arbitrary time dependence of fields. This group of methods is the most suitable for solving non-linear problems. If the problem is linear, Fourier transform can be used to find frequency spectrum of the solution.

The most popular method of this group is the *Finite Difference Time Domain* (FDTD) method, proposed by Yee [4, 5]. Another method, successfully used in time domain, is the *Finite Integration Technique* (FIT), firstly proposed by Weiland [6]. The *Transmission Line Matrix* (TLM) method, proposed by Johns and Beurle [7], also works efficiently in time domain. Its detailed description can be found in [8]. These methods were implemented in a number of computer codes, such as SPEAG SEMCAD™ (FDTD), CST Studio Suite™ (FIT, TLM) and many others.

The second group deals with Eqs. (14)–(17) for field phasors, supposing harmonic time dependence of fields. This group provides solution in Frequency (or Spectral) Domain (FD). The *finite element method* (FEM) is one of the most efficient representatives of this group. The first application of this method to the solution of mechanical problems refers to the year 1943 [9]. The book [10] contains detailed description of the method, which is rather universal and accurate. The *Method of Moments* (MoMs) and its varieties are also frequently used in FD. In contrast with FEM, MoM uses integral form of basic equations, where electric current density distribution on conducting surfaces excited by external sources is unknown. The book [11] reflects modern state of the MoM. Mentioned methods were implemented in codes ANSIS HFSS™ (FEM), Altair FEKO™ (MoM, FEM) and other commercial computer codes. Of course, there exist many other numerical methods and various implementations.

Most of modern methods allow implementation both in TD and in FD.

Because it is impossible to give detailed representation of all numerical methods in a limited space, we give here more detailed information about the FEM method, which was implemented in the computer code radio frequency simulator (RFS) [12].

5. Finite element method for electromagnetics

5.1. Main features of the method

The finite element method belongs to the variational methods of solving partial differential equation (PDE). It presumes formulating a functional, which is stationary (has minimum or maximum value) on the equation solution. In order to find functional extremum, the computational region is partitioned on a number of subregions (*finite elements*). After that, we approximate an unknown function in each finite element (FE) by superposition of basis functions. Basis functions have to be simple and form a linearly independent system. Applying Ritz method or Galerkin algorithm, we fulfil discretization of the problem, that is, transition from the partial difference equation to the system of linear algebraic equations (SLAE). Numerical solution of the SLAE gives unknown coefficients of basic functions, which are used to restore electromagnetic field. At last, needed components of electromagnetic field and system parameters are calculated.

5.2. Mesh generation

Partitioning of the computational region (mesh generation) is the first stage of problem solution by FEM. It supposes dividing the computation region on a set of subregions—finite elements. FEs must densely fill the region and be nearly conformal to its border. In contrast to FDTD or FIT methods, a FEM mesh can be irregular and contain FEs of different forms. Tetrahedron FEs are used most commonly, because they allow dense packing and quite correctly approximate curvilinear borders. However, mesh generation for regions with complex forms filled with different materials is a very complex task.

http://dx.doi.org/10.5772/67497

Delaunay tessellation is a common way of mesh building. It includes several stages. Firstly, a surface triangle mesh is generated. Then, a volume mesh based on the surface mesh and covering the whole computational region is being built. The method can build a rather good mesh without self-intersections. Some commercial codes, such as SYMMETRIX MeshSym™, can be used to generate mesh by this procedure.

Unfortunately, this method cannot be applied to tessellation of complex geometrical models consisting of hundreds of parts made from various materials. Usually, an electromagnetic simulation code imports such models from various CAD systems (see, e.g. **Figure 1**). As a rule, imported models contain a number of errors caused by insufficient attention of a designer or arising in the process of graphic formats transforms. As a result, mesh generator fails to build the mesh.

On the other side, CAD models are often excessively detailed. They contain peculiarities, not influenced on electromagnetic field. **Figure 2** shows an example of such extra detailed CAD model. The application of standard mesh generator to such a model can result in excess mesh size. Correction and simplification of the model manually needs several working days of the qualified engineer.

An advanced method of mesh generation was developed and implemented in the RFS simulation code. The algorithm begins from assigning materials and attributes to the model parts. Most important objects, such as ports, printed circuit board (PCB) and antennas, are labelled as 'electrically important'. This is the only stage of the algorithm, which is made manually. This stage can be omitted for simple models. Then the code builds surface meshes for each detail of the system. The third stage presumes elimination of individual meshes interceptions and building united surface mesh. Electrically important, metal parts and parts with higher permittivity have priority in this process. At last, a global volume mesh is generated [13]. The user

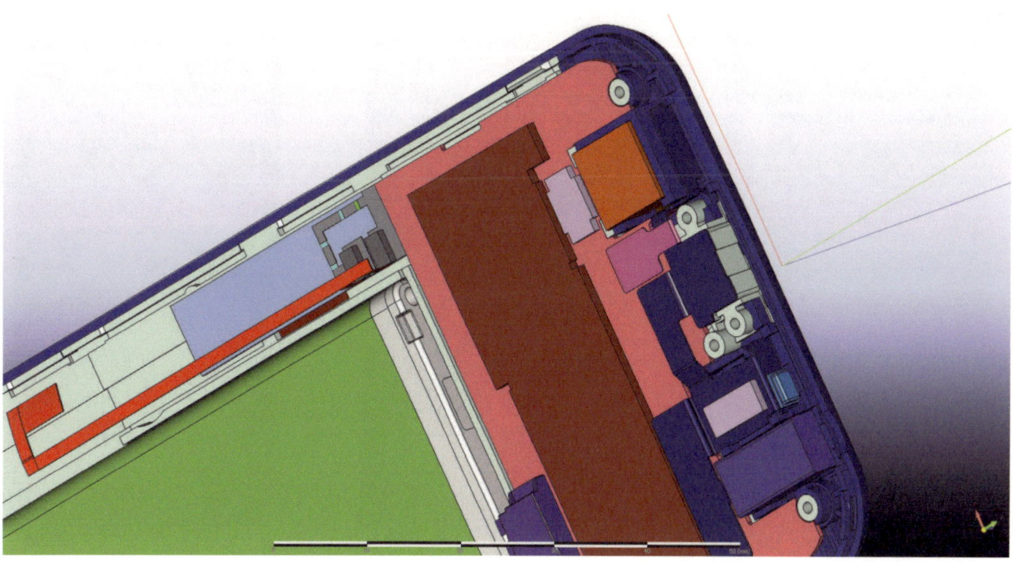

Figure 1. A part of the handset CAD model.

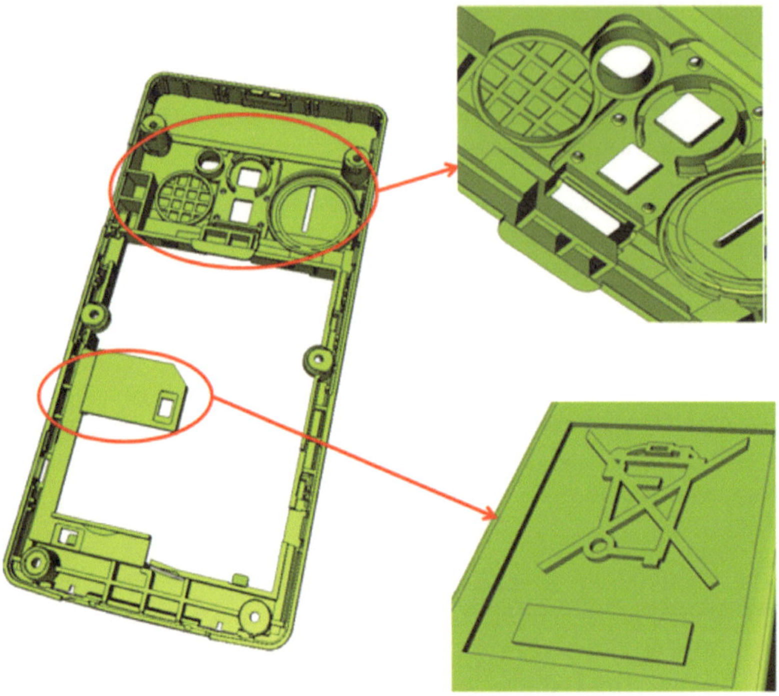

Figure 2. A part of the CAD model with excessive details.

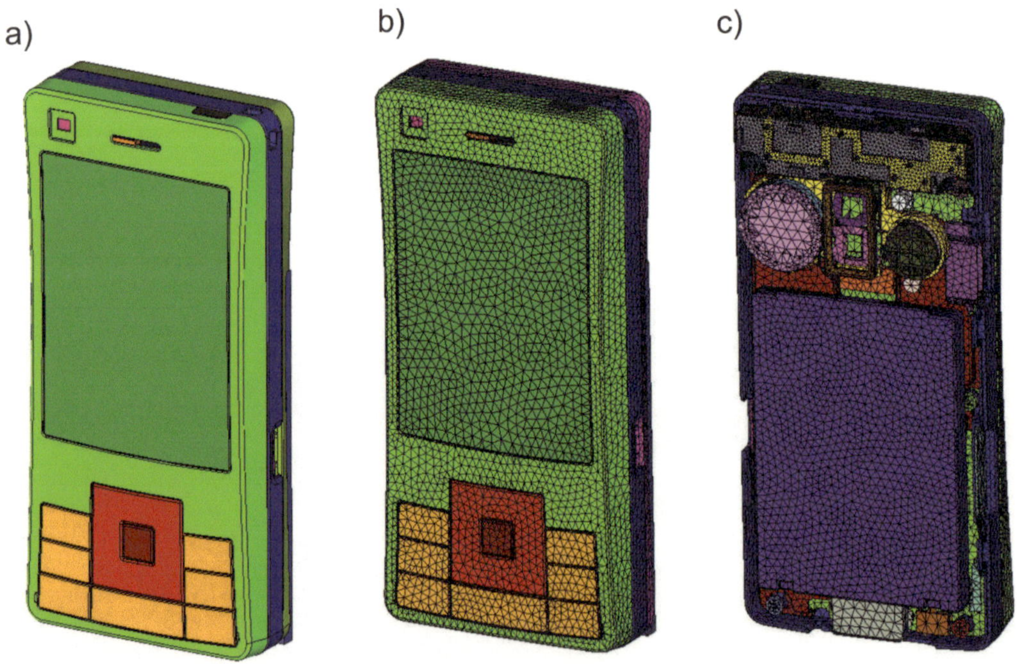

Figure 3. CAD model of the handset (a), united surface mesh (b) and volume mesh (c).

http://dx.doi.org/10.5772/67497

can control mesh quality (maximum to minimum ratio of tetrahedron's dimensions and other mesh parameters).

We proved this algorithm on more than 190 models of mobile handsets and showed its 100% reliability. Generated meshes contained more than 1.5 billion tetrahedrons. **Figure 3** shows a CAD model of the handset (a), surface mesh (b) and volume mesh (c), built by the described algorithm.

5.3. Basic equation

Consider a region V, delimited by a surface S, where electromagnetic field has to be calculated. We suppose that the region V is filled by linear medium. Applying curl operator to Eq. (15) and substituting into result Eq. (14), we get PDE of the second order

$$\nabla\times(\dot{\mu}_r^{-1}\nabla\times\dot{\mathbf{E}})+j\sigma\eta_0 k\dot{\mathbf{E}}-\dot{\varepsilon}_r k^2\dot{\mathbf{E}}=-jk\eta_0\dot{\mathbf{J}}^{imp}, \tag{18}$$

where $\dot{\mathbf{J}}^{imp}$ is the imposed current density, $k=\omega/c$ is wave number, $c=(\varepsilon_0\mu_0)^{-1/2}$ is the light velocity in free space, σ is medium conductivity and $\eta_0=\sqrt{\mu_0/\varepsilon_0}=120\pi$ ohm is the intrinsic impedance of free space. After solving this equation, we can find magnetic field by means of Eq. (15):

$$\dot{\mathbf{H}}=\frac{j}{k\eta_0\dot{\mu}_r}\nabla\times\dot{\mathbf{E}}. \tag{19}$$

To solve Eq. (16), we divide the computation region on finite elements and approximate the field in each FE by superposition of basis functions. It is natural to approximate vector unknown function in Eq. (16) by a set of vector basis functions. We name such variant of FEM as *vector finite element method (VFEM).*

Nedelec [14] proposed a set of vector basis functions for triangle and tetrahedral FE. These functions are associated with tetrahedron edges and have the form

$$\mathbf{w}_m=\zeta_{m1}\nabla\zeta_{m2}-\zeta_{m2}\nabla\zeta_{m1}, \tag{20}$$

where ζ_{mn} is the barycentric function of the vertex (node) node n of the edge m $(m=1,\ldots,6,\ n=1,2)$. The barycentric functions are polynomials of the first order. For a given Descartes coordinate system

$$\zeta_p=a_p+b_p x+c_p y+d_p z, \tag{21}$$

where p is vertex number. As a tetrahedron has six edges, Nedelec's basis consists of six functions. **Figure 4** shows the numbering scheme for nodes and edges, needed for the correct use of Nedelec's functions.

Coefficients in Eq. (17) can be found from the equation

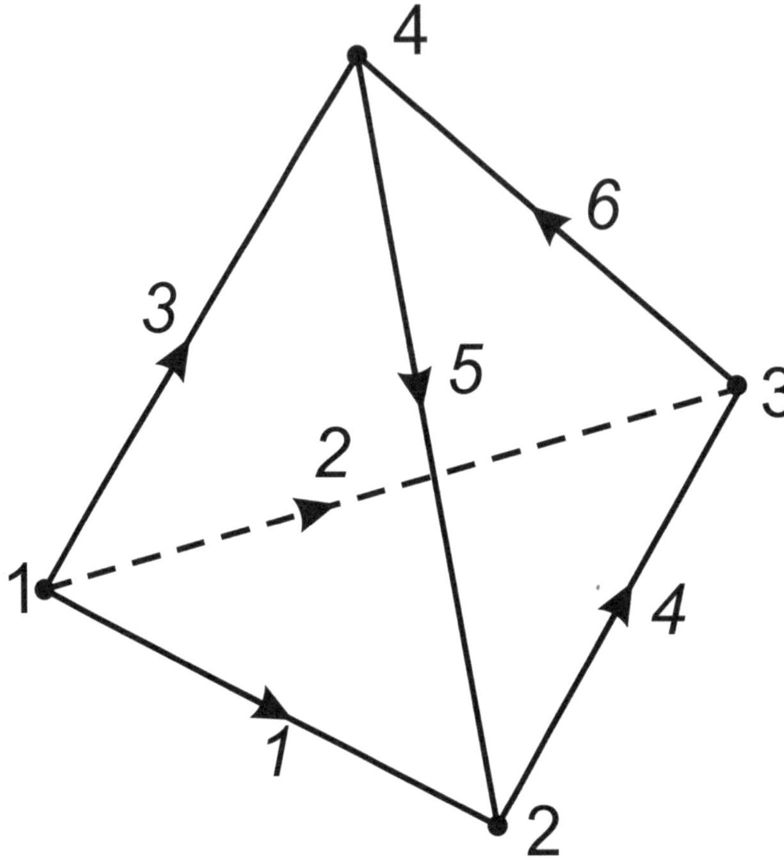

Figure 4. Numbering order of a tetrahedron's vertices and edges.

$$\begin{bmatrix} b_1 & c_1 & d_1 & a_1 \\ b_2 & c_2 & d_2 & a_2 \\ b_3 & c_3 & d_3 & a_3 \\ b_4 & c_4 & d_4 & a_4 \end{bmatrix} = \begin{bmatrix} x_1 & x_2 & x_3 & x_4 \\ y_1 & y_2 & y_3 & y_4 \\ z_1 & z_2 & z_3 & z_4 \\ 1 & 1 & 1 & 1 \end{bmatrix}^{-1}. \tag{22}$$

where $x_p, y_p, z_p,\ p = 1...4$ are the coordinates of the p-th tetrahedron's node.

Nedelec's basis functions have the following properties:

1. Dimension of these functions is L^{-1}.

2. They have zero divergence and their curl is constant inside the FE. This property provides the absence of spurious solutions of the problem.

3. Projection of the function $\mathbf{w}_m$ on the edge m is constant, and its projection on the other edges is equal to zero. Hence, these functions provide continuity of tangential electric field on the border between neighbouring tetrahedrons.

4. Circulation of function $\mathbf{w}_m$ along its edge is equal to unity.

Full first-order polynomial set for electric field approximation contains 12 functions (3 E-vector projections, each needs four functions). However, Nedelec's set contains only six basis functions. Hence, it does not form full first-order polynomial system. The order of approximation by these functions is lower than one. Finite elements with these functions are called FE of order 1/2 or CT/LN (constant tangential/linear normal) according to the behaviour of these functions along edges and in normal direction to them.

Striving for increasing approximation accuracy led to creating another set of basis functions with higher order of approximation. A set of 20 functions (12 associated with edges and eight with faces) forms FE of order 1.5 or LN/QN (linear tangential/quadratic normal) [15, 16]. There exist basis functions of order 2.5 and higher, but they are rarely used.

With the aim of simplicity, we consider further only Nedelec's basis functions. So, electric field intensity in q-th tetrahedron is approximated as

$$\dot{\mathbf{E}}^q(\mathbf{r}) = \sum_{n=1}^{6} \dot{x}_n^q \mathbf{w}_n^q(\mathbf{r}), \quad q = 1, \ldots, N_q, \tag{23}$$

where N_q is the total number of tetrahedrons.

Coefficients $\dot{x}_m^q$ have the sense of voltage on edge (with reverse sign). Really, taking integral along an edge

$$V_m^q = -\int_{L_q} \dot{\mathbf{E}}^q \cdot d\mathbf{l}_m = -\sum_{n=1}^{6} \dot{x}_n^q \mathbf{w}_n^q d\mathbf{l}_m = -\dot{x}_m^q, \tag{24}$$

due to the fourth property of basis functions.

Let us consider q-th tetrahedron. According to Galerkin's method, we multiply Eq. (16) by basis function $\mathbf{w}_m^q$, belonging to this tetrahedron and integrate the product over the tetrahedron volume V_q. As a result, we obtain the so-called week form of Eq. (16):

$$\int_{V_q} [\nabla \times (\dot{\mu}_r^{-1} \nabla \times \mathbf{E}^q)] \cdot \mathbf{w}_m^q dV + j\eta_0 k \int_{V_q} \sigma \mathbf{E}^q \cdot \mathbf{w}_m^q dV - k^2 \int_{V_q} \dot{\varepsilon}_r \mathbf{E}^q \cdot \mathbf{w}_m^q dV = -jk\eta_0 \int_{V_q} \mathbf{J}^{imp} \cdot \mathbf{w}_m^q dV.$$

Transformation of the first term of this equation and subsequent substitution into result approximation (19) gives a system of linear algebraic equations:

$$\sum_{n=1}^{6} \dot{x}_n^q \Big[\int_{V_q} (\dot{\mu}_r^{-1} \nabla \times \mathbf{w}_n^q) \cdot (\nabla \times \mathbf{w}_m^q) dV + jk \int_{V_q} \eta_0 \sigma \mathbf{w}_n^q \cdot \mathbf{w}_m^q dV - k^2 \int_{V_q} \dot{\varepsilon}_r \mathbf{w}_n^q \cdot \mathbf{w}_m^q dV\Big]$$
$$= -\oint_{S_q} [(\dot{\mu}_r^{-1} \nabla \times \dot{\mathbf{E}}^q) \times \mathbf{w}_m^q] d\mathbf{S} - jk \int_{V_q} \eta_0 \dot{\mathbf{J}}^{imp} \cdot \mathbf{w}_m^q dV, \quad m = 1, 2, \ldots, 6; \quad q = 1, 2, \ldots, N_q, \tag{25}$$

where N_q is the total number of FE in the computation region.

The system of Eq. (25) can be written in matrix form:

$$\overline{\mathbf{Q}}^q \mathbf{X}^q \equiv (\overline{\mathbf{T}}^q + jk\overline{\mathbf{U}}^q - k^2\overline{\mathbf{R}}^q)\overline{\mathbf{X}}^q = -\overline{\mathbf{S}}^q - jk\overline{\mathbf{B}}^q, \tag{26}$$

where $\mathbf{Q}^q, \overline{\mathbf{T}}^q, \overline{\mathbf{U}}^q, \overline{\mathbf{R}}^q$ are square matrices having dimension 6 × 6, $\overline{\mathbf{S}}^q, \overline{\mathbf{B}}^q$ are column vectors having six components, dependent on the given boundary conditions and implicit current density in the q-th finite element. Depending on BC, $\mathbf{S}^q$ can sometimes be a square 6 × 6 matrix.

Equation (26) is called the *local matrix equation,* and matrix $\mathbf{Q}^q$ is the local matrix of q-th FE. Such matrices should be built for every FE in the computational region.

Components of matrices $\overline{\mathbf{T}}^q, \overline{\mathbf{U}}^q, \overline{\mathbf{R}}^q$ and vectors $\overline{\mathbf{S}}^q, \overline{\mathbf{B}}^q$ are defined by the expressions

$$t_{mn} = \dot{\mu}_r^{-1} \int_V (\nabla \times \mathbf{w}_m) \cdot (\nabla \times \mathbf{w}_n) dV; \tag{27}$$

$$u_{mn} = \eta_0 \sigma \int_V \mathbf{w}_m \cdot \mathbf{w}_n dV; \tag{28}$$

$$r_{mn} = \dot{\varepsilon}_r \int_V \mathbf{w}_n \cdot \mathbf{w}_m dV; \tag{29}$$

$$s_m = \dot{\mu}_r^{-1} \oint_S [(\nabla \times \dot{\mathbf{E}}) \times \mathbf{w}_m] d\mathbf{S}; \tag{30}$$

$$b_m = \eta_0 \int_V \dot{\mathbf{J}}^{imp} \cdot \mathbf{w}_m dV. \tag{31}$$

Medium in these expressions is supposed to be homogeneous inside the FE. Index 'q' denoted FE number is omitted. We can see that in order to calculate elements (27)–(31), it is sufficient to calculate two integrals:

$$f_{mn} = \int_V (\nabla \times \mathbf{w}_n) \cdot (\nabla \times \mathbf{w}_m) dV \text{ and } h_{mn} = \int_V (\mathbf{w}_n \cdot \mathbf{w}_m) dV. \tag{32}$$

We use the next algorithm for the calculation of matrices and vectors elements:

For each tetrahedron

- Coefficients of the barycentric functions are calculated by means of Eq. (22).
- Auxiliary values are calculated:

$$\mathbf{v}_{ij} = \nabla \zeta_i \times \nabla \zeta_j = (c_i d_j - c_j d_i)\widehat{\mathbf{x}} + (d_i b_j - d_j b_i)\widehat{\mathbf{y}} + (b_i c_j - b_j c_i)\widehat{\mathbf{z}}; \tag{33}$$

$$\varphi_{ij} = \nabla \zeta_i \cdot \nabla \zeta_j = b_i b_j + c_i c_j + d_i d_j. \tag{34}$$

It can be easily shown that $\nabla \times \mathbf{w}_m = 2\mathbf{v}_{m1,m2}$.

http://dx.doi.org/10.5772/67497

- We introduce matrix $\overline{\mathbf{G}}$ with components

$$g_{ij} = V^{-1}\int_V \zeta_i \zeta_j dV. \tag{35}$$

Using integration formula for three-dimensional (3D) simplex, we can prove that

$$\overline{\mathbf{G}} = \frac{1}{20}\begin{vmatrix} 2 & 1 & 1 & 1 \\ 1 & 2 & 1 & 1 \\ 1 & 1 & 2 & 1 \\ 1 & 1 & 1 & 2 \end{vmatrix}. \tag{36}$$

- Integrals (32) are calculated:

$$f_{mn} = 4V(\mathbf{V}_{m1,m2} \cdot \mathbf{V}_{n1,n2})dV; \tag{37}$$

$$h_{mn} = V(\varphi_{m2,n2}g_{m1,n1} - \varphi_{m2,n1}g_{m1,n2} - \varphi_{m1,n2}g_{m2,n1} + \varphi_{m1,n1}g_{m2,n2}), \quad m, n = 1, \ldots, 6. \tag{38}$$

In these expressions, V is the volume of the tetrahedron.

Construction of the global matrix (assembling) for all tetrahedrons is a rather complex task, because many nodes, edges and faces are common for neighbour FEs (see **Figure 5**, which shows two neighbour tetrahedrons, separated for reader's convenience). They have three common vertices and three common edges. Hence, the united matrix for two FEs has only 9 dimensions instead of 12.

The code RFS uses the next algorithm for building the global matrix:

1. Calculate a local matrix for the tetrahedron number one (q = 1). Give its edges global numbers from 1 to $N_c = 6$.
2. Choose the tetrahedron with q = 2

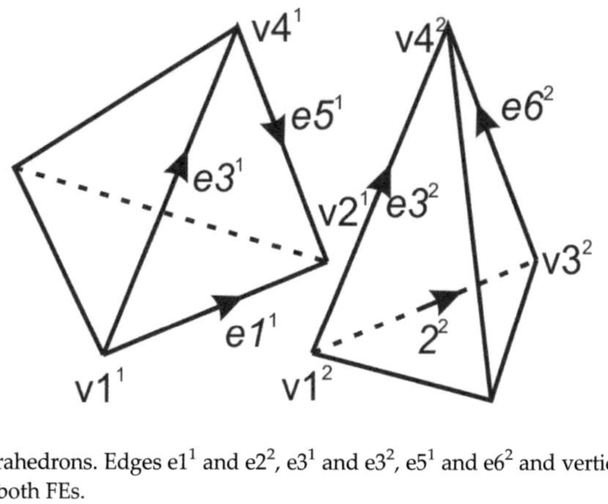

Figure 5. Two neighbour tetrahedrons. Edges $e1^1$ and $e2^2$, $e3^1$ and $e3^2$, $e5^1$ and $e6^2$ and vertices $v1^1$ and $v1^2$, $v2^1$ and $v3^2$, $v4^1$ and $v4^2$ are common for both FEs.

a. Choose the edge of this tetrahedron with $m = 1$. Check whether this edge coincides with any edge of the previous tetrahedron. If it does, calculate its matrix elements and add them to corresponding matrix elements of the previous tetrahedron. In the other case, give the edge global number $N_c + 1$ and fill a corresponding element of the global matrix. Set $N_c = N_c + 1$.

b. Do this procedure for all edges of the tetrahedron.

3. Repeat point 2 for every tetrahedron in the region testing whether a given edge of the tetrahedron coincides with any edge, previously included in analysis.

Similar assembling procedure is valid for basis functions of higher order.

As a result, we get a global matrix of the problem, a global vector of the right side of Eq. (26) and a global vector of unknowns. Dimension of the global matrix is equal to the total number of coefficients (degrees of freedom) in formulas (23).

5.4. Numerical approximation of boundary conditions

- **Border between two dielectrics**. A finite element mesh is built so that every tetrahedron lies inside one of the media. Hence, the common face of two neighbour tetrahedrons lies on the separation surface or approximate it in the case of curvilinear border. Due to basis function properties, tangential electric field of both tetrahedrons is equal on the face edges, consequently electric fields are equal on the whole face area. As a result, BCs (7) for electric field are satisfied automatically. As for magnetic field intensity, its continuity on the border between media with different permeabilities is not guaranteed.

- **Electrical wall**. According to Eq. (8), tangential electric field on PEC surface is equal to zero. Hence, three coefficients of Eq. (25) belonging to edges, lying on the surface, are equal to zero. Corresponding rows and columns of local matrix of the given tetrahedron have to be eliminated.

- **Magnetic wall**. According to Eq. (9), surface tangential magnetic field on the PMC is equal to zero. We can see from Eqs. (27)–(31) that only term s_m has to be changed:

$$s_m = jk_0\eta_0\int_S (\mathbf{H}\times\mathbf{w}_m)\mathbf{e}_n = 0. \tag{39}$$

  This expression is equal to zero as the mixed product under the integral has two vectors $(\mathbf{H}, \mathbf{e}_n)$ with the same direction. Therefore, PMC BC does not change local matrix.

- **Absorption boundary conditions.** Formula for matrix elements s_{mn} can be derived from Eq. (11):

$$s_{mn} = jk_0\sqrt{\mu_r/\varepsilon_r}\int_S (\mathbf{e}_n\times\mathbf{w}_m)\cdot(\mathbf{e}_n\times\mathbf{w}_n)dS. \tag{40}$$

  Expressions for the higher order ABC can be found in [10].

http://dx.doi.org/10.5772/67497

- **Impedance surface.** Impedance surface has finite surface conductivity σ_s. Such surface is a good approximation of the metal surface in microwave frequency band. Using Leontovich BC (10), we can derive expression

$$s_{mn} = -jk_0\eta_0\sigma_s\int_S \mathbf{w}_m \cdot \mathbf{w}_n dS. \tag{41}$$

  These values must be added to the corresponding elements of the local matrix. Of course, they are nonzero only for functions associated with edges lying on the impedance surface.

- **Excitation sources.** Electromagnetic field in the system excites by electric current or by electric or magnetic fields, defined on a part of the system border. In the first case, we use Eq. (26) to calculate right-hand vector elements. In the second case, we define the so-called ports—surfaces on which nonzero excitation field exists. Frequently, we define port as cross section of the regular transmission line (TL). Such ports are called *wave ports*. If TL cross section has simple form (rectangular, circular, etc.), we can define field on the port analytically. Otherwise, we have to solve two-dimensional (2D) boundary problem.

  Together with wave ports, lumped ports (LPs) are often used. These ports are defined by current I and intrinsic admittance Z_i. LPs are used when excitation source dimensions are very low compared to the whole-system dimensions or wavelength. Geometrical model of LP is a segment of a straight line (linear LP) or a rectangle (planar LP). Linear and planar LPs are implemented in the RFS code. Arbitrary number of tetrahedron's edges or (and) faces can cover such LPs. We suppose that surface current density and electric field distributions on the PL are homogeneous. Values of right-hand vector for a planar LP are calculated by Eq. (31), where $\dot{\mathbf{J}}^{imp} = I/w$, I is port current and w is port width. Implemented model of the LP excludes limitations imposed on the mesh generator by other models.

- **Lumped elements.** Embedding of lumped elements (LEs) into 3D field model enlarges the capability of the code, as an LE excludes the necessity of generating very fine mesh inside such parts as resistors, capacitors and inductors. In the RFS code, linear and planar LEs are implemented [17].

  The presence of LEs modifies the global matrix by adding to diagonal matrix elements terms

$$q'_{mm} = -jk_0\eta_0 Yl, \tag{42}$$

  where Y is the admittance of the LE, l is its length. The RFS code implements models of a resistor, capacitor and inductor, and their parallel connection. The number of LEs in the model is unlimited.

5.5. Fast-frequency sweep

The finite element method in frequency domain solves the problem at one specific frequency. Calculation of the system frequency response (e.g. S-matrix) needs solving the problem many times (often several hundreds or even thousands). This procedure takes much computation time.

Considerable economy of computational resources can be achieved by implementing the so-called fast-frequency sweep (FFS). The algorithm of FFS is based on model-order reduction (MOR) technique. According to the MOR, we seek solution in one frequency point and then expand left and right sides of Eq. (21) in frequency power series. Terms with the same power are equated and full solution as a function of frequency is restored. The RFS code implements one of such algorithms—*well conditioned asymptotic wave form evaluation* (WCAWE) [18]. This method was adapted to the RFS procedures, particularly for LE models, and showed high efficiency, making possible to calculate system fields and parameters in three-octave frequency band using full solution only in one frequency point. Hence, computation time for wideband systems decreases by tens and hundreds times without losing accuracy.

6. The RFS code description

The RFS code is designated to solve complex 3D electromagnetic problems, especially mobile handsets modelling. It contains graphic user interface for creating and editing geometric objects or for import CAD models. Geometric primitives, besides boxes, cylinders, spheres, pyramids and cones, include coaxial and strip lines and wizards for creating human head and hand models (phantoms), spiral antennas and other objects. All Boolean operations, such as extrusion, skinning and others, are also implemented. The code includes a rich material library.

Two types of meshing are available: exact automatic meshing based on Delaunay tessellation and hand meshing with automatic geometry corrections. We recommend the last one for meshing complex models, imported from CAD codes, for example, for full models of a handset. Two types of basis functions can be used: low order (CT/LN) and high order (LT/QN). The last is used as default, but for complex models with many small details, we recommend low-order basis.

The code solves several types of problems: driven solution in one frequency point, driven solution in frequency band with given frequency step (solution in each point or FFS), eigenmode, EMS and EMI problems. The code can perform parametric solution when one or several geometric or (and) material parameters changes in a given order. The results can be represented as functions of these parameters.

Post-processing includes the calculation of S-, Y- and Z-parameters, field distribution in a volume, on a surface or along a line, the calculation of cavities intrinsic impedance, specific absorption rate (SAR) and EMC/EMI parameters. Results are represented in one-dimensional (1D), 2D and 3D graphs, tables and can be exported in a file.

7. Computation results

Firstly, we validated the code by solving problems having analytical solution. One of such problems is an eigenvalue problem for cylindrical cavity. A cylindrical cavity has curvilinear surface, so calculation can demonstrate the quality of surface approximation by a tetrahedron mesh. The analysed cavity had radius 10 mm and height 15 mm. Cavity walls were supposed to be perfectly conducting. Eight eigen frequencies and eigen fields were calculated using high-order basis functions (LT/QN).

http://dx.doi.org/10.5772/67497

Computation results together with analytical data are shown in **Table 1**. The table also contains relative calculation error δ. Azimuthal inhomogeneous modes are twice degenerated. Numerical errors remove this degeneration, so two eigen frequencies for each mode are given. Degenerated modes differ by their field, turned by 90° in azimuth direction and computation results confirm this phenomenon. Difference between degenerated eigen frequencies is no more than hundreds of per cent.

Mode	Analytical eigen frequency (EF), GHz	Mesh size					
		6768		15,026		26,580	
		EF, GHz	δ, %	EF, GHz	δ, %	EF, GHz	δ, %
TM_{010}	11.474	11.502	0.235	11.4905	0.135	11.4848	0.085
TE_{111}	13.302	13.317	0.11	13.3132	0.084	13.3104	0.063
		13.319	0.135	13.3139	0.089	13.311	0.067
TM_{011}	15.216	15.232	0.098	15.2287	0.077	15.2241	0.052
TE_{211}	17.670	17.696	0.147	17.6853	0.086	17.6802	0.058
		17.705	0.198	17.6877	0.102	17.6811	0.063
TM_{110}	18.284	18.3246	0.222	18.3081	0.131	18.299	0.082
		18.3287	0.244	18.3102	0.143	18.291	0.083

Table 1. Comparison of analytical and computational eigen frequencies for a cylindrical cavity.

The table demonstrates that eigen frequency calculation error decreases with mesh refinement and not exceeds 0.1% on the last mesh.

Another example, an electric dipole, consisted of two perfectly conducting cylinders, connected to the linear-lumped source (**Figure 6**). To solve this outer problem, we ought to constrain

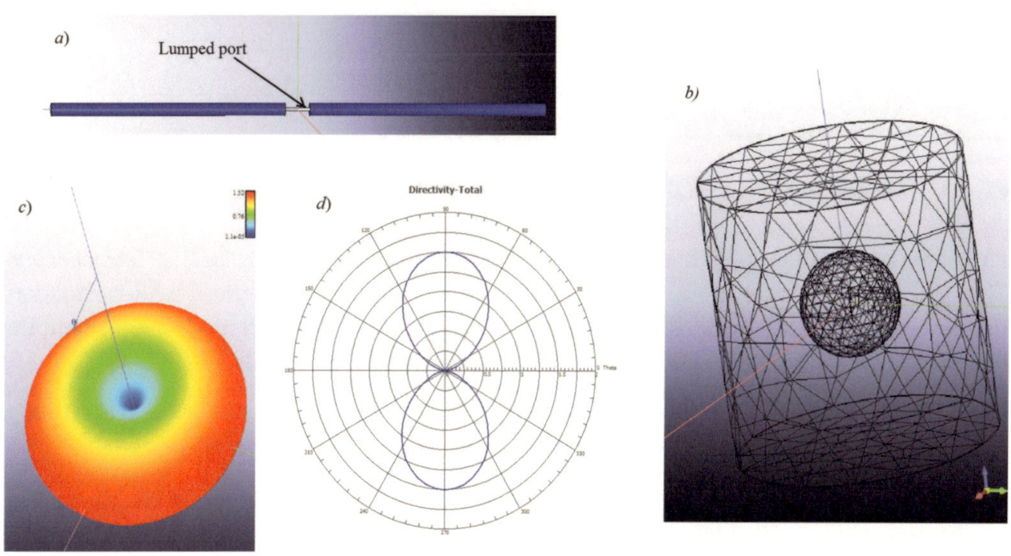

Figure 6. A dipole model: *a*, dipole structure; *b*, mesh; *c*, 3D directivity chart; *d*, 2D directivity chart in the plane $\varphi = 0$.

computational region by the so-called air box with ABC on its surface. The code automatically determines air box size so that the minimal distance between the dipole and the air box is not less than $\lambda/4$, where λ is wavelength in free space.

Cylinders have diameter 0.5 mm and length 9.5 mm. Together with a lumped port of 1-mm length, the total dipole length is 20 mm. Excitation frequency was chosen to be 1.5 GHz, so the ratio $l/\lambda = 0.1$. Such a dipole can be considered as elemental (**Figure 6*a***). Its directivity is described by the formula $D(\theta, \varphi) = 1.5sin^2\theta$.

Figure 6*b* shows mesh used in simulation. The sphere inside cylinder contains refined local mesh, surrounding the dipole. The total number of tetrahedrons is 64553. The 3D directivity chart is shown in **Figure 6*c***, and 2D directivity chart in plain $\varphi = 0$ in **Figure 6*d***. Calculated dipole directivity is 1.506 with relative error of 0.4 %. This error can be caused by the finite diameter of cylinders.

Figure 7a shows handset together with human head and hand phantoms. The handset has PIFA-type antenna. Reflection coefficient of this antenna in the presence of the phantoms was calculated by RFS code and code SEMCAD [19], based on FDTD method.

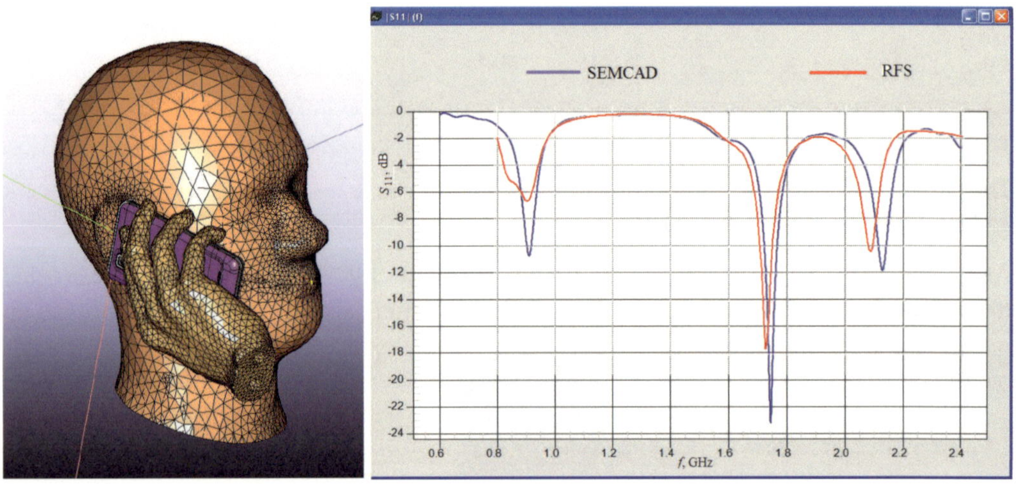

Figure 7. A handset with human head and hand phantoms: *a*, model; *b*, reflection coefficient chart.

Finite element mesh built by the RFS code in the phantom contains only 200,000 tetrahedrons. The total mesh size was about 450,000 tetrahedrons. Efficient algorithm of SAR calculation, implemented in the RFS code, provides using such comparatively small mesh size without the loss of accuracy. SEMCAD hexagonal mesh had about 1.5 billion of cells.

Figure 7b shows the module of reflection coefficient versus frequency for FRS and SEMCAD. As can be seen, both codes give similar results, especially for resonant frequencies.

We also calculated maximum SAR level in a brain tissue, averaged on 1 g of the tissue. The results are shown in **Table 2**. As can be seen, both codes give similar results, but SEMCAD solution time was nearly five times greater than RFS.

http://dx.doi.org/10.5772/67497

Frequency, MHz	SAR, W/kg	
	RFS	SEMCAD
900	1.08	1.06
2000	1.18	0.99

Table 2. SAR, averaged over 1 g of brain tissue

8. Conclusion

The problem of high-frequency electromagnetic field simulation is formulated. A short survey of numerical methods for solving high-frequency electromagnetic problems is presented. It was shown that one of the most efficient methods for solving inner EMP and outer EMP with moderate electrical size is the vector finite element method in frequency domain. The algorithm of this method, including mesh generation, building of the global matrix, boundary conditions approximation, SLAE solving and FFS technique was described. Some peculiarities of lumped ports and elements implementation into the RFS computer code were also depicted. Simulation results for a simple systems having analytical solution, as well as for complex problems, such as handset antenna analysis near human head show high accuracy and efficiency of the code. The code can be used for the solution of antenna problems, waveguide problems, PCB analysis and microwave resonator problems.

Acknowledgements

The author expresses his deep gratitude for valuable help provided by R.V. Salimov and R.I. Tikhonov from the Russian R&D Centre LG Electronics Inc.

Author details

Andrey D. Grigoriev

Address all correspondence to: adgrigoriev@eltech.ru

Saint-Petersburg State Electrotechnical University 'LETI', Saint-Petersburg, Russia

References

[1] Higdon R.L. Numerical absorbing boundary conditions for wave equation. Math. Comp. 1987;**49**:65–90.

[2] Stratton J.A. Electromagnetic Theory. 1st ed. New York and London: McGraw-Hill Book Company; 1941. 648 p.

[3] Jackson J.D. Classical Electrodynamics. 3rd ed. New York: John Wiley & Sons, Inc.; 1999. 815 p.

[4] Yee K.S. Numerical solution of initial boundary value problems involving Maxwell's equations in isotropic media. IEEE Trans. Antennas Propag. 1966;**14**(5):302–307.

[5] Taflov A., Hagness S.C. Computational Electrodynamics: The Finite-Difference Time-Domain Method. 3rd ed. New York: Artech House; 2006. 1006 p.

[6] Weiland T. A discretization method for the solution of Maxwell's equations for sis-component fields. Electron. Commun. 1977;**31**(3):401–410.

[7] Johns P.B., Beurle R.L. Numerical solution of 2-dimensional scattering problems using a transmission-line matrix. Proc. IIE. 1971;**118**(9):1203–1208.

[8] Christpoulos C. The Transmission-Line modelling Method. Oxford: Morgan and Claypool; 2006. 124 p.

[9] Courant R.L. Variational methods for solution of problems of equilibrium and vibration. Bull. Am. Math. Soc. 1943;**5**(1):1–23.

[10] Jin J. The Finite Element Method in Electromagnetic. 2nd ed. New York: John Wiley & Sons, Inc.; 2002. 752 p.

[11] Gibson W.C. The Method of Moments in Electromagnetics. Boca Raton, FL: Taylor & Francis Group; 2008. 272 p.

[12] Grigoriev A.D., Salimov R.V., Tikhonov R.I. Cellular handsets antenna modelling by finite element method. J. Commun. Technol. Electron. 2012;**53**(3):261–270.

[13] Grigoryev A.D., Salimov R.V., Tikhonov R.I. Efficient Analysis of Full Mobile Hanset CAD Models with Automatic Correction Geometric Errors. In: 26th Annual Review of Progress in Applied Computational Electromagnetics; April 26–29; Tampere, Finland. Tampere: Tampere University of Technology; 2010. pp. 416–420.

[14] Nedelec J.C. Mixed finite elements in R3. Numer. Meth. 1980;**35**:315–341. doi:10.1007/BF01396415.

[15] Webb J.P. Hierarchical vector basis functions of arbitrary order for triangular and tetrahedral finite elements. IEEE Trans. Antennas Propag. 1999;**47**(8):1244–1253.

[16] Andersen L.S., Volakis J.L. Hierarchical tangential vector finite elements for tetrahedra. IEEE Microw. Guided Wave Lett. 1998;**8**(3):127–129.

[17] Grigoryev A.D., Salimov R.V., Tikhonov R.I. Multiple-cell lumped element and port models foe the vector finite element method. Electromagnetics. 2008;**25**(6):18–26.

[18] Slone R.D., Lee R., Lee J.-F. Well-conditioned asymptotic wave form evaluation for finite elements. IEEE Trans. Antennas Propag. 2003; **51**(9):2442–2447.

[19] SPEAG. SEMCAD X, intuitive, powerful, DC to light [Internet]. 2014. Retrieved from http://www.speag.com/

Chapter 10

Modeling and Simulation of Task Allocation with Colored Petri Nets

Mildreth Alcaraz-Mejia,
Raul Campos-Rodriguez and
Marco Caballero-Gutierrez

Additional information is available at the end of the chapter

http://dx.doi.org/10.5772/67950

Abstract

The task allocation problem is a key element in the solution of several applications from different engineering fields. With the explosion of the amount of information produced by the today Internet-connected solutions, scheduling techniques for the allocation of tasks relying on grids, clusters of computers, or in the cloud computing, is at the core of efficient solutions. The task allocation is an important problem within some branch of the computer sciences and operations research, where it is usually modeled as an optimization of a combinatorial problem with the inconvenience of a state explosion problem. This chapter proposes the modeling of the task allocation problem by the use of Colored Petri nets. The proposed methodology allows the construction of compact models for task scheduling problems. Moreover, a simulation process is possible within the constructed model, which allows the study of some performance aspects of the task allocation problem before any implementation stage.

Keywords: colored Petri nets, task allocation problem, modeling and simulation, distributed computing

1. Introduction

The services provided by Internet-based modern applications require the execution of massively parallel processes in order to produce time-effective information for different requirements. The processing of these "Big Data" is very computing, demanding in almost all of the cases. Thus, vast server farms installed over the world are ready to process the requests from different users. The digital data available in the web are huge and diverse, therefore complex, and in a continuous growth rate.

Nowadays, most of the queries on Internet are produced from smartphones and personal computers. However, the data traffic on web is expected to grow in an exponential rate, as the technology related to the Internet of Things (IoT) allows the connection of other devices from the houses, smart warehouses, automated driving cars, machinery from the agriculture, UAV's for goods delivering, or smart cities, to mention a few. In order to cope with the challenges related to a massive number of connected devices, new ways of computing emerged. Most of them are based on parallel and distributed computing, such as clusters, grids, and cloud computing paradigms.

At the core of these paradigms are the tasks scheduling and resources allocation problems. Adaptations of theory, methods, algorithms, tools, and others are arising in order to cope with the increasing number of cores per processor, as well as with the interconnected and heterogeneous computers, considering that, in many cases, those computing architectures are connected through the Internet. The tasks scheduling and resources allocation were well studied in the context of architectures with a relatively small number of processors. One of the fundamental concerns deals with designing algorithms for an efficiently allocation of the tasks among all the available processes and resources.

The answer to this question may lead to a hard work, since, in the worst case, it involves an exponential number of possible solutions [1]. Thus, a simulation process, for scenarios with a big number of computing elements, or cores, as in cloud and grid computing, is a valuable tool. In this context, the modeling and simulation are disciplines widely used to obtain feedback and statistics information, to improve associated applications and algorithms. Through experimentation in simulators, a fast prototyping process allows performance evaluation and parameter tuning for different workload conditions. To perform an efficient simulation process, a suitable modeling method is required. The Petri nets (PN's) and its extension, such as colored PN (CPN), have been considered as an efficient modeling technique for concurrent and distributed systems.

The simulation and implementation stages of scheduling and resource allocation problems in distributed systems have been successfully addressed [2–9]. Moreover, variants of PN's are used for modeling and simulation of other distributed concepts related to cloud services and computing [9–16], as well as in the field of the diagnosis of discrete event systems [17–19], reconfiguration [20–24], fuzzy inference [25] or identification [26].

This work proposes the modeling of the task allocation problem by the use of a methodology based on CPN's. It also shows how to simulate these models in order to obtain relevant information for the design process. To illustrate the techniques, this work considers a tree structure and supposes that the set of tasks and the set of processes are fixed and defined before the task allocation is performed as in Ref. [27]. The proposed CPN modeling method represents the behavior of a set of processors, or working threads, that traverse a tree structure from the root to a single leaf in order to acquire a task. The processes decide what route to take at each node of the tree structure, by using a decision function. Then, it routes the tree backwards updating some global variables that serves as inter-process communication mechanism.

The proposed method allows obtaining a CPN, which is a compact representation of the problem, and at the same time, it allows simulating its behavior and obtaining performance

http://dx.doi.org/10.5772/67950

graphics. The colored tokens represent the processes, tasks, and other variables of interest in the problem. A decision function is attached to some transitions of the CPN model. This function influences the behavior of the process or thread. Due to the graphical nature of the CPN, in addition to the mathematical fundamentals, this methodology provides a great framework to simulate and analyze the task allocation problem, avoiding the state space explosion, and thus, having a compact representation of a complex behavior. The flexibility of the modeling framework allows simulating different scenarios, using different decision functions, as well as varying the number of initial processes or threads. Additionally, the Petri Net model can be easily extended to simulate a wider number of tasks.

The rest of this chapter includes a background of the task allocation and several techniques that have been used for addressing this problem. The modeling framework based on colored Petri nets is next presented and the modeling methodology is detailed. This methodology highlights the main aspects of the task allocation problem, such as the concepts of task and process, as well as the balancing policies and how to capture them by CPN blocks. The simulation of the obtained CPN models is then presented and discussed. Some performance charts are provided. The charts allow the study of key aspects of task allocation problem such as the effective work done by a processor, the task contention, the effects of different balancing policies, to mention a few. With this information, the scientists and engineers are able to study different aspects of the problem prior any implementation stage in a particular field of interest.

2. Task allocation problem

Task allocation problem has been addressed for several purposes and using different techniques. Analytic solutions are in some cases prohibitive since they require the analysis of an exponential number of possible solutions. Thus, some designs use probabilistic approaches to produce good solutions in a reasonable time. Jevtić et al. [28] present a distributed bee's algorithm for static task allocation inspired on the behavior of a colony of bees and based on the optimization of a cost function. They also show results using the Arena simulator. Delle Fave et al. [29] introduced a decentralized optimization for static task assignment based on a constrained utility function, firstly evaluated by simulations. Johnson et al. [30] state a distributed multi-agent algorithm for static multi-task allocation as an optimization problem based on mixed-integer programming. They also provide some results of Monte Carlo simulation. Zhao-Pin et al. [31] introduced a distributed and static task allocation algorithm for multi-agents that learn how to determine by themselves what tasks should realize and how to form coalitions for cooperation, via their proposed profit-sharing learning mechanism. Macarthur et al. [32] introduced a dynamic and distributed algorithm for multi-agent task allocation problems, based on fast-max-sum algorithm combined with a branch-and-bound technique, in order to reduce the execution time in the allocation of task to its respective agent. Alistarh et al. [27, 33] present a decentralized task allocation, static and dynamic, based on to-do trees, where decisions on every inner node are based on a probability function.

One of these most used techniques, due to its simplicity of implementation, is based on a rooted tree structure that the process traverses in order to acquire a task [7, 8]. The tree structure allows to the working processes for executing a non-deterministic behavior, which is quite suitable for real environments. Typically, in these tree structures, every reference to a task is allocated on the leaves. Thus, every internal vertex allows to a working process taking a decision based on a function over the number of tasks in every leaf of the subtrees from each child of the current vertex. Hence, the decision function, which could be a simple deterministic algorithm, or a sophisticated statistical or stochastic procedure, is a key element for which a process traverses through the tree structure, in this kind of task allocation techniques.

Figure 1 shows a binary tree that represents a scheduling problem where eight tasks have to be attended. The height of the tree is $H = \log_2(8) = 3$, where the level of $v_{2,2}$ is 2, the vertex $v_{1,0}$ is said to be parent, or ancestor, of $v_{2,0}$ and $v_{2,1}$, and the latter two are said to be children, or descendant, of $v_{1,0}$. The vertex $v_{0,0}$ is the root, and every vertex is internal except for all of the level 3, i.e., $v_{3,x}$ with $x \in [0, 7]$, which are known as leafs of the tree. The tree formed by the vertexes $v_{2,1}$, $v_{3,2}$, $v_{3,3}$ and the corresponding edges that connects them, is a subtree with $v_{2,1}$ as a root.

From the graph theory point of view, a DT is an acyclic graph in which a unique path connects every node to others, represented in a top-to-bottom fashion, where the root, i.e., initial node, is plotted at the top of the tree. The DT is a binary decision tree (BDT) if at every node is considered at most two possible decisions, as shown in **Figure 1**. For more information on trees see Ref. [34].

2.1. Task scheduling with DT

By using a tree structure like the one depicted in **Figure 1**, the task allocation algorithm is relatively simple. Each working process shares the tree structure and iterates in an infinite loop, trying to acquire a new task to execute, which is located at the leafs of the tree. Each working process starts at the root node of the tree and decides whether to go to the left or the right child node. The process knows an approximation of the total pending tasks at the left and right subtrees at every step. For example, in **Figure 1**, each working thread knows that at the beginning of the scheduling process, at the root node, that there exist four pending tasks at the

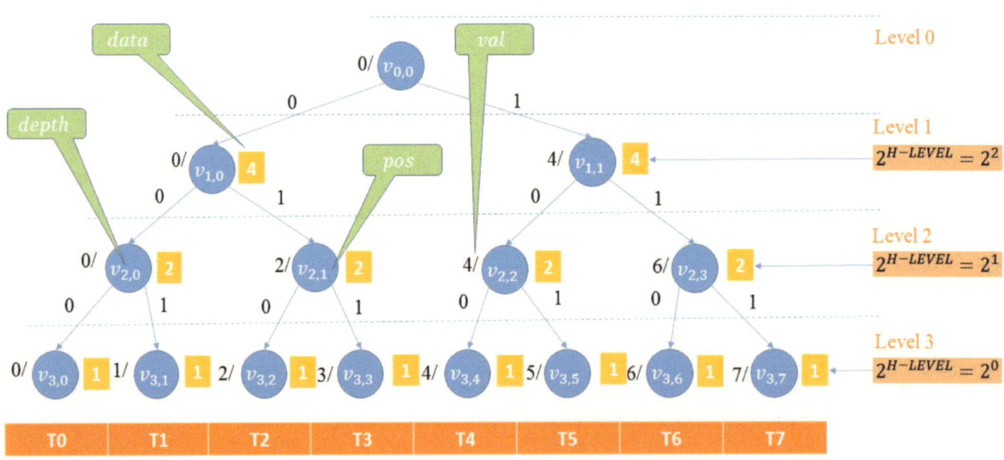

Figure 1. A direct rooted full binary tree.

left subtree and four pending tasks at the right one. Then, at every stage, the processes decide to traverse to the left or right in an asynchronous fashion. The total number of pending tasks is backward updated from the lower nodes to the uppers as the tasks are successfully executed by the threads. Notice that, the number of pending tasks at the left or right subtree is an approximation since this number may be not updated yet.

Since the processes are asynchronous among them, it is possible that they arrive to the leaf nodes that may occur at different rates. Every time that a process reaches a leaf, it asks for the execution of the task. If such a task is free, then the process blocks this task, executes the activity, and marks the task as executed. Then, it goes back to the root node to seek for a new task to execute, while the information of the remaining tasks is backward updated from the leaf to the root node. It is possible that when a process reaches a leaf node, the corresponding task was already executed by another process. In this case, the process goes back to the root node, and this miss is counted to measure the effectiveness of the algorithms.

$$r < \frac{x}{x+y} \tag{1}$$

In Eq. (1), it represented a decision rule that a working process may execute at every level of the BDT. Let x be the total number of pending tasks in the left subtree and y be the total number of pending tasks in the right subtree, while r is a random number. Thus, the probability to go to the left subtree in a flip coin is given by r. As greater the ratio, it is greater the probability to go to the left child of the current node. One of the main objectives of this work is to measure the effectiveness of a decision rule as Eq. (1) by means of a simulation process.

3. Colored Petri nets

PN's are a modeling framework that combines a graphical visualization with a mathematical model [35]. The CPN's are one of the extensions to PN's [9, 17, 35–42], which allow the construction of compact representations of big models. In this section, basic notions of CPN are presented.

The main characteristic that differentiates CPN from other type of nets resides in the token definition. In a CPN, the tokens can stand for complex data besides of a single value, such as an integer, a real, Boolean or strings. This characteristic allows for the representation of elaborated data types, similar to those used by high-level programming languages. This ability exploits the multi-set cardinality to construct compact models that otherwise are in the power set of the colored tokens. The formal definition of a CPN is as follows [35].

Definition 1. A Colored Petri Net (CPN) is a tuple

$\mathcal{N} = \langle P, T, Pre, Post, B, F, Cp, Ct \rangle$ where its elements are described as:

- P is a finite set of places of $\mathcal{N}$, with $m = |P|$,
- T is a finite set of transitions of $\mathcal{N}$, such that $T \cap P = \varnothing$, with $n = |T|$,

- B is finite set of color classes,
- F is a set of conditions,
- $C_p : P \to B$ is the color domain mapping,
- $C_t : T \to F$ is a conditional color mapping, and
- $Pre, Post \in S^{|P| \times |T|}$ are matrices representing the input and output incidence matrices of $\mathcal{N}$, such that $Pre[p, t] : C_t(t) \to Bag(C_p(p))$ and $Post[p, t] : C_t(t) \to Bag(C_p(p))$ are mappings for every pair $(p, t) \in P \times T$; where $Bag(S) = \cup\, b(s_i)$ for all $s_i \in S$, such that $b(s_i) = \sum s_i \in S$.

The incidence matrix is $C = Post - Pre$. The mapping given by $Pre[p, t] : C_t(t) \to Bag(C_p(p))$, defines for each conditional color mapping f of t (*i.e.* $\forall f_i \in C_t(t)$), the token bag to be removed from p, in the occurrence of t, under color condition f. In the same way, $Post[p, t](f)$ specifies the token bag to be added to p, in the occurrence of t, under color condition f.

Definition 2. A marking M of a CPN $\mathcal{N}$ is a vector of size $m = |P|$, such that $M(p) \in Bag(C_p(p))$ for every $p \in P$. The vector M_0 denotes the initial marking of the net $\mathcal{N}$ and the pair $(\mathcal{N}, M_0)$ is known as a CPN System.

Definition 3. A transition in a CPN System $(\mathcal{N}, M_0)$ is said to be enabled for a color condition f in a marking M iff $M \geq Pre[\blacksquare, t](f)$, denoted as $M \overset{t,f}{\to}$.

Definition 4. The marking evolution w.r.t a color condition f is given by $M' = M + Post[\blacksquare, t](f) - Pre[\blacksquare, t](f) = M + C[\blacksquare, t](f)$, denoted by $M \overset{t,f}{\to} M'$. For a general color condition, it is denoted as $M \overset{t}{\to} M'$ where f is implicit in a context.

The net in **Figure 2** represents a very simple CPN System $(\mathcal{N}, M_0)$ where:

- $P = \{p_1, p_2, p_3\}$,
- $T = \{t_1, t_2\}$,
- $B = o \cup r$, where $o = \{o_1, o_2\}$ and $r = \{r_1, r_2\}$ are variables,
- $F = \{f_1, f_2\}$,

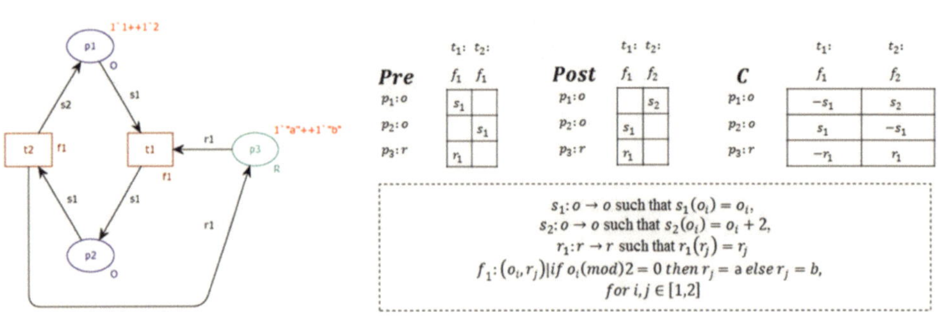

Figure 2. A CPN example.

- $C_p(p_1) = C_p(p_2) = o,\ C_p(p_3) = r,$
- $C_t(t_1) = f_1,\ C_t(t_2) = f_2,$
- *Pre* and *Post* are as depicted, and
- $M_0 = [\{o_1, o_2\}, \varnothing, \{r_1, r_2\}]'$, where $o_1 = 1, o_2 = 2, r_1 = a, r_2 = b.$

Notice that, at the initial condition, $M_0 \geq Pre[\blacksquare, t_1](f_1)$. That is $[\{o_1, o_2\}, \varnothing, \{r_1, r_2\}]' \geq [\{o_1, o_2\}, \varnothing, \{r_1, r_2\}] : \{(o_1, r_1)(o_2, r_2)\}$, thus, t_1 can be fired for any color binding $\{(o_1, r_2)(o_2, r_1)\}$ due to the condition in f_1. Suppose that, t_1 fires for color condition f_1 with (o_2, r_1), then $M_0 \xrightarrow{t_1, (o_2, r_1)} M_1$, with $M_1 = [\{o_1\}, \{o_2\}, \{r_2\}]'$, where $o_1 = 1, o_2 = 2, r_2 = b$, by $Post[\blacksquare, t_1](f_1) = \{(s_1)\}$ as detailed in the figure. Now, $M_1 \xrightarrow{t_1, (o_1, r_2)}$ and $M_1 \xrightarrow{t_2, (o_2)}$, in such a way, that if t_2 is fired, then $M_1 \xrightarrow{t_2, (o_2)} M_2$, with $M_2 = [\{o_1, o_2\}, \varnothing, \{r_1, r_2\}]'$, where $o_1 = 1, o_2 = 4, r_1 = a, r_2 = b$. However, if t_1 is fired from M_1 for the color condition (o_1, r_2), then $M_1 \xrightarrow{t_1, (o_1, r_2)} M_3$, with $M_3 = [\varnothing, \{o_1, o_2\}, \varnothing]'$, where $o_1 = 1$, $o_2 = 2$.

Roughly speaking, the CPN binds the even number in p_1 to the character "a" in p_3 and the odd number to character "b." This is defined by the guard function f_1 attached to t_1. The function s_1 discards the r element of the token bound to the firing of t_1, while the firing of t_2 adds two to the o element of the token and recovers the r element that is put back to the place p_3. Thus, the tones in p_1 changes to $o_1 = 1, 3, 5, \ldots$ and $o_2 = 2, 4, 6, \ldots$, while the characters "a" and "b" in p_3 remain the same all the time. The "R" in the place p_3 stands for "resources," which is the function intended for the characters in this CPN model.

Notice that, the bindings (o_1, r_1) and (o_2, r_2) are discarded by the function f_1. This is one of the advantages of the CPN modeling tool, since otherwise, the combinatorial explosion of possible bindings turns untreatable under some circumstances that typically arises in real applications. For more information about the CPN modeling formalism and related analysis and tools, see Ref. [36].

4. Modeling and simulation of task scheduling

The construction of a generalized model for a BDT based on CPN considers d different features and nT classes. The procedure includes the identification of the transitions and places of the model, the arcs and its labeling, as well as the multi-set of colored tokens. The remaining of this section is devoted to detail the methodology and illustrate it by short examples.

4.1. Structure of the task allocation as a CPN

Consider the following steps for the construction of a CPN model that captures the structure of a BDT. It is supposed that the BDT is a full binary tree with a complete set of tasks represented by a structure called Task Array. Thus, the size of the Task Array is 2^H, where the height of the tree is H.

Step 1. Labeling nodes in the BDT

Firstly, suppose that the DT is a full binary tree. Then, assign "0" to every left edge and "1" to every right edge. This labeling represents the result of the flip coin in the task allocation procedure of a BDT discussed in the previous section.

After that, some information is used to label every node with a pair $(depth, position)$, where *depth* is the level of the node, and *position* is the corresponding position from left to right. For example, consider the root node $(0, 0)$ in the section of the BDT depicted in **Figure 3**. It is a fraction of the tree of height $H = 3$ of **Figure 1**. Then, to label the children of the root node proceed as follows:

- Let be $depth = depth - of - the - parent + 1$ and $position = 2 * position - of - the - parent + h$, with $h = 0$ if this node is the left child, $h = 1$ otherwise.

Therefore, the label of the left child is $(depth = 0 + 1, position = 0 * 2 + 0) = (1, 0)$, while the label of the right child is $(depth = 0 + 1, position = 0 * 2 + 1) = (1, 1)$.

Step 2. Building the CPN System

Let $(\mathcal{N}, M_0)$ be a CPN System for a dynamic binary decision tree for nT classes and d features with $\mathcal{N} = \langle P, T, Pre, Post, B, F, C_p, C_t \rangle$ constructed as follows:

- $P = P_O \cup P_R \cup P_A$, where P_O is the set of places with assigned tokens of type O, P_R is the set of places with assigned tokens of type R, P_A is the place with assigned tokens of type A. $|P_O| = 2(H + 1)$, $|P_R| = H$ and $|P_A| = 1$, where $H = \log_2 nT$. Places of type O represent every level from the root to the leaves, forward, and backwards, i.e., a token in one of those place contains the information of *pos, depth, val*. Places of type R represent the state of every subtree from every node at that level, i.e., the value of the *data* function for every node of the same level given by *pos* and *depth*. Place of type A represent the *Task Array* state, i.e., the information of the availability of the task.
- T is the set of transitions with $|T| = |P_O|$.

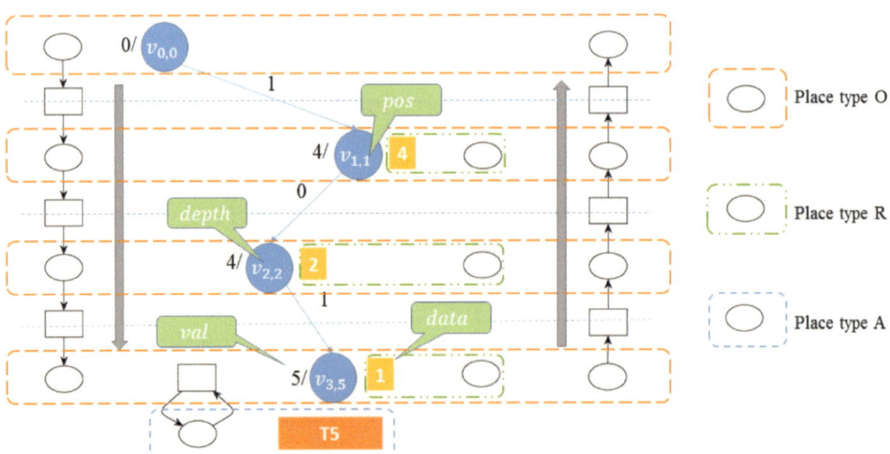

Figure 3. Relation BDT and CPN.

- $B = o \cup r \cup a$, for $o = \cup o_i$, $r = \cup r_j$, and $a = \cup a_l$ where $o_i = \langle depth_i, pos_i, val_i, success_i \rangle$, $r_j = \langle depth_j, pos_j, data_j \rangle$, $a_l = \langle pos_l, ready_l \rangle$ for $i \in [1, d]$, $j \in [1, 2^{H+1} - 2]$, and $l \in [1, nT]$, with $depth_i$, pos_i, val_i, $success_i$, $data_j$, $exist_l$ variables and $depth_j$, pos_j, pos_l constants.

- $F = \{f_1, f_2, f_3, f_4\}$, such that $f_1 : (o_i, r_j, r_k) | depth_i + 1 = depth_j = depth_k \wedge pos_i{*}2 = pos_j \wedge pos_i{*}2 +1 = pos_k$, $f_2 : (o_i, r_j) | depth_i = depth_j \wedge pos_i = pos_j$, $f_3 : (o_i, a_j) | pos_i = pos_j$, $f_4 : (o_j)$.

- $C_p(p_i) = o$ for all $i \in [1, |P_O|]$, $C_p(p_i) = r$ for all $i \in [|P_O| + 1, |P|]$ and $C_p(p_i) = a$ for $i = 2(H+1) + \mathrm{H} + 1$.

- $C_t(t_i) = f_1$ for $i \in [1, H]$, $C_t(t_i) = f_2$ for $i \in [H + 2, |P_O| - 1]$, $C_t(t_i) = f_3$ for $i = H + 1$ and $i = |P_O| + 1$.

- $Pre[p_i, t_i](f_1) = si_1 | f_1$, for $i \in [1, H]$, $Pre[p_i, t_i](f_2) = si_1 | f_2$, for $i \in [H + 2, |P_O| - 1]$, $Pre[p_i, t_i](f_3) = si_1 | f_3$, for $i = H + 1$, $Pre[p_i, t_i](f_3) = si_1 | f_4$, for $i = |P_O| + 1$, $Pre[p_i, t_j](f_3) = qi_1 | f_3$, for $i = |P_O| + |P_R| + 1$, $j = H + 1$, $Pre[p_{u+i}, t_i](f_1) = 2ri_1 | f_1$, for $i \in [1, H]$, $Pre[p_{u+i}, t_{u-i}](f_2) = 2ri_2 | f_2$, for $i \in [1, H]$, where:

  - si_1: $o \rightarrow o$, such that $si_1(\langle depth_i, pos_i, val_i, success_i \rangle) = \langle depth_i, pos_i, val_i, success_i \rangle$.

  - qi_1: $a \rightarrow a$, such that $i_1(\langle pos_l, exist_l \rangle) = (\langle pos_l, exist_l \rangle)$.

  - ri_1: $r \times r \rightarrow r$, such that $ri_1(\langle depth_j, pos_j, data_j \rangle, \langle depth_k, pos_k, data_k \rangle) = \langle depth_j, pos_j, data_j \rangle \langle depth_k, pos_k, data_k \rangle$.

  - $ri_2 : r \rightarrow r$, such that $ri_2(\langle depth_j, pos_j, data_j \rangle) = \langle depth_j, pos_j, data_j \rangle$.

- $Post[p_{i+1}, t_i](f_1) = so_1 | f_1$, for $i \in [1, H]$, $Post[p_{i+1}, t_i](f_2) = so_2 | f_2$, for $i \in [H + 2, |P_O| - 1]$, $Post[p_{i+1}, t_i](f_3) = so_3 | f_3$, for $i = H + 1$, $Post[p_1, t_i](f_3) = so_4 | f_4$, for $i = |P_O|$, $Post[p_i, t_j](f_3) = qo_1 | f_3$, for $i = |P_O| + |P_R| + 1$, $j = H + 1 Post[p_{u+i}, t_i](f_1) = ro_1$, for $i \in [1, H]$, $Post[p_{u+i}, t_{u-i}](f_2) = ro_2$, for $i \in [1, H]$, where:

  - $so_1 : o \rightarrow o$, such that $so_1(\langle depth_i, pos_i, val_i, success_i \rangle) = \langle depth_i + 1, pos_i{*}2 + h_i, val_i + (h_i){*} 2^{H - depth_i + 1}, success_i \rangle$, $with h_i = 0$ $if \alpha holds, otherwise$ 1. α is a decision function.

  - $so_2 : o \rightarrow o$, such that $so_2(\langle depth_i, pos_i, val_i, success_i \rangle) = \langle depth_i - 1, \frac{pos_i}{2}, val_i, success_i \rangle$.

  - $so_3 : o \rightarrow o$, such that $so_3(\langle depth_i, pos_i, val_i, success_i \rangle) = \langle depth_i, pos_i, val_i, success_i = 1 if Exist (pos_i, a_l) = 1$ $otherwise$ $0 \rangle$, where $Exist(pos_i, a_l)$ returns 1 if for a color class $a_l = pos_l, exist_l$ with $pos_l = pos_i$, $exist_l = 1$, otherwise 0.

  - $so_4 : o \rightarrow o$, such that $so_4(\langle depth_i, pos_i, val_i, success_i \rangle) = \langle 0, 0, 0, 0 \rangle$,

  - qo_1: $a \rightarrow a$, such that $qo_1(\langle pos_l, exist_l \rangle) = (\langle pos_l, exist_l = 0$ $if Exist(pos_l, a_l) = 1, otherwise 1 \rangle)$.

  - ro_1: $r \times r \rightarrow r$, such that $ro_1(\langle depth_j, pos_j, data_j \rangle, \langle depth_k, pos_k, data_k \rangle) = \langle depth_j, pos_j, data_j \rangle \langle depth_k, pos_k, data_k \rangle$.

  - ro_2: $r \rightarrow r$, such that $ro_2(\langle depth_j, pos_j, data_j \rangle) = \langle depth_j, pos_j, data_j - 1$ $if success_i = 1$, $otherwise data_j \rangle$.

- The initial marking, assuming that the Task Array is initially full, is M_0 defined as follows:
  - $M_0[1] = \{o_1, \ldots, o_d\}$, where $o_i = depth_i = 0, pos_i = 0, val_i = 0, success_i = 0 = 0, 0, 0, 0$ for $i \in [1, d]$.
  - $M_0[|P_O| + i] = {}_{\cup i=1H} {}_{\cup j=02^i-1} r_{2^i-2+j} = \langle i, j, 2^{H-i} \rangle$ assuming that the Task Array is initially full, as mentioned.
  - $M_0[2(\mathrm{H}+1) + \mathrm{H} + 1] = {}_{\cup i=1nT} a_i$ where $a_i = \langle pos_i = i, exist_i = 1 \rangle$.
  - $M_0[\mathrm{i}] = \varnothing$ for $i \in [2, |P_O|]$.

Figure 4 shows the relation of the tree structure with the proposed CPN as stated by the previous definition. Observe that places of type O represent every level from the root to the leaves, forward, and backwards, i.e., a token in one of those place contains the information of *pos*, *depth*, and *val*. Places of type R represent the state of every subtree from every node at that level, i.e., the value of the *data* function for every node of the same level given by *pos* and *depth*. Place of type A represents the *Task Array* state, i.e., the information of the availability of the task.

4.2. Dynamics of the task allocation as a CPN

Typically, in these tree structures, every reference to a task is allocated on the leaves. Thus, every internal vertex allows to a working process taking a decision based on a function over the number of tasks in every leaf of the subtrees from each child of the current vertex. Hence, the decision function, which could be a simple deterministic algorithm, or a sophisticated statistical or stochastic procedure, is a key element for which a process traverses through the tree structure, in this kind of allocation techniques. The following definitions allow capturing these dynamics aspects of the task allocation based on a BDT.

Definition 5. The *pos* is a position function defined from a set of vertexes V of a tree T to the set of natural numbers N as $pos : V \to N$, such that $pos(v) = j$, where j is the numeric position of vertex v with respect to all the vertexes in the same level and counting from left to right.

Definition 6. The *depth* is a function defined from a set of vertexes V of a tree T to the set of natural numbers N as $depth : V \to N$, such that $depth(v) = \#$edges from the root node to v.

Notice that, in **Figure 2**, the identification of a vertex v is given by $v_{i,j}$ where $i = depth(v)$ and $j = pos(v)$.

Definition 7. The w is a weight function defined from the set of edges E of a tree T to the set containing 0 and 1 as $w : E \to \{0, 1\}$, such that $w(e) = 0$ if e connects a parent vertex to its left child, and 1 if it connects to its right child. Let consider a vertex v of a tree T denoted as $v_{i,j}$ such that $i = depth(v)$ and $j = pos(v)$. Then, for $v_{i,x}$ parent of left child $v_{j,y}$ and right child $v_{j,z}$, with their respective edges $e_{i,j,y}$ and $e_{i,j,z}$, with $y < z$, by definition of *depth*, then $w(e_{i,j,y}) = 0$ and $w(e_{i,j,z}) = 1$.

Notice that, the weight function w provides a zero for an edge connecting a father with its left child and a one for the edge connecting it with the right child. In the modeling methodology here introduced, it is assumed that there exists a data structure called *Task Array*, which may have a reference to a task, if it is initially inserted, and the task has not been taken yet. This *Task Array* is mapped to the location of the leaves of a tree of height H from left to right, i.e., the array has a capacity for referencing a maximum of The quaternion semi – widel tasks. **Figure 1** shows a tree of height 3, with 8 leaves that are associated with the location in the *Task Array*, where references to task are $T0, T1..., T7$. Accordingly, the following functions are defined.

Definition 8. The *data* function is defined from the set of vertexes V of a tree T to the set of natural numbers N as $data : V \rightarrow N$, where $data(v) = \#$ of leaves in the subtree of root v with a task ready to be taken.

Definition 9. The *parent* is a function defined from the set of vertexes of a tree T to itself as $parent : V \rightarrow V$, such that $parent(v) = y$, if v is child of y.

Definition 10. The *val* is a recursive function defined from the set of vertexes V of a tree T of height H, to the set of natural numbers N as $val : V \rightarrow N$, such that:

- (Base): $val(v_{0,0}) = 0$.
- (Induction): $val(v_{i,j}) = val\left(parent(v_{i,j})\right) + w\left(e_{pos(parent(v_{i,j}), depth(v_{i,j}), j}\right) *2^{H-i}$, for every pair (i, j), where $1 \leq i \leq H, 0 \leq j < 2^i$.

In **Figure 2**, for example, $val(v)$ is shown in the left of every vertex v as $val(v)/$, e.g., $val(v_{2,3}) = val\left(parent(v_{2,3})\right) + w\left(e_{pos(parent(v_{2,3}), depth(v_{2,3}), 3}\right) *2^{3-2} = val(v_{1,1}) + w\left(e_{pos(v_{1,1}), 2, 3}\right) *2^1$ $= val\left(parent(v_{1,1})\right) + w\left(e_{pos(parent(v_{1,1}), depth(v_{1,1}), 1}\right) *2^{3-1} + w\left(e_{pos(v_{1,1}), 2, 3}\right) *2^1 = val(v_{0,0}) + = 0$ $+w(e_{0,1,1})*4 + w(e_{1,2,3})*2 = 0 + 1*4 + 1*2 = 6$.

Observe that function *val* generates the value of a node based on the value of his parent. Notice that, there are 8 leaves in level 3, and then, every node value is exactly one entry in the *Task Array*. For example, the value 4/ at $v_{3,5}$ points to the entry *T4*. Now, consider the nodes in level 2, which are 4, exactly the half of those at level 3. Every vertex at this level, points to the first entry in a range of 2, i.e., $v_{2,0}$ has a value of 0, $v_{2,1}$ and has a value of 2. Thus, every vertex at level 1, points to the first entry of the two partitions of the *Task Array*, and therefore, $v_{0,0}$ points to the first entry of the whole of the *Task Array*.

For illustration purposes, suppose that there is one node with two threads and eight tasks to be executed. Accordingly, $d = 2$ and $nT = 8$. The CPN System $(\mathcal{N}, \mathbf{M}_0)$ for modeling this problem is shown in **Figure 4**.

Notice that accordingly to the proposed method, a full binary tree is obtained when $nT = 2^n$ for some n, since, in this case, $H = \log_2 nT$ is exactly equal to $\log_2 nT$. In the particular example, $H = 3$, since $nT = 2^3 = 8$. Then, $|P_O| = 2(H + 1) = 8$, with $P_O = \{p_1, p_2, ..., p_8\}$; $|P_R| = H = 3$, with $P_R = \{p_9, p_{10}, p_{11}\}$; $|P_A| = 1$ with $P_A = \{p_{12}\}$; $|T| = |P_O| = 8$, with $T = \{t_1, t_2, ..., t_8\}$; $o = \{o_1, o_2\}$ since $d = 2$; $r = \{r_1, r_2, ..., r_{14}\}$, since $2^{H+1} - 2 = 2^3 - 2 = 14$, and $a = \{a_1, a_2, ..., a_8\}$.

The following functions complement the CPN model:

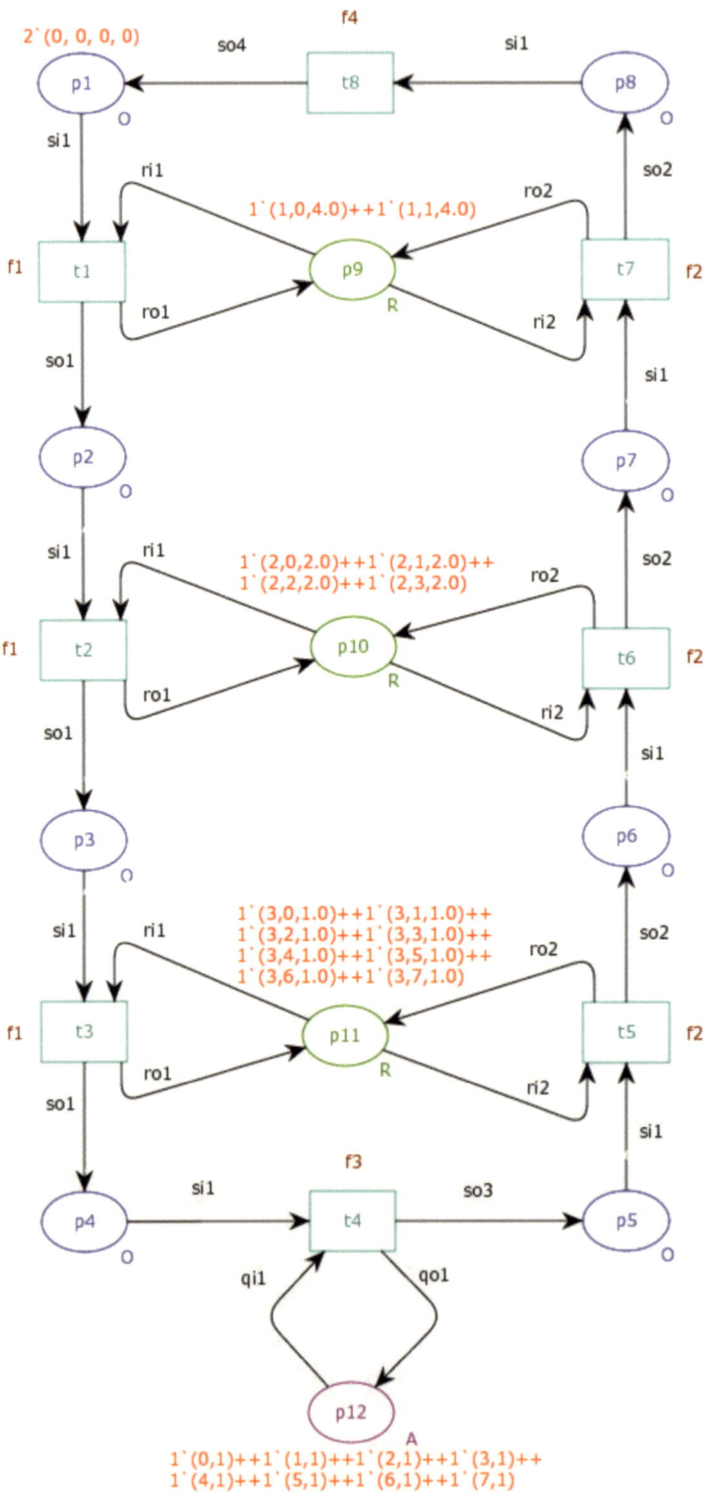

Figure 4. DS CPN with $nT = 8$.

- $o_i = \langle depth_i, pos_i, val_i, success_i \rangle = \langle 0, 0, 0, 0 \rangle$, for $i \in \{1, 2\}$. This marking represents the current state of every process, i.e., at the beginning, processes are at root node $v_{0,0}$ with a value 0. *Success* being 0 means that no task has been assigned to the current process.

- $r_j = \langle depth_j, pos_j, data_j \rangle$, such that $j \in [1, |r|]$, where: $r_1 = \langle 1, 0, 4 \rangle$, $r_2 = \langle 1, 1, 4 \rangle$, $r_3 = \langle 2, 0, 2 \rangle$, $r_4 = \langle 2, 1, 2 \rangle$, $r_5 = \langle 2, 2, 2 \rangle$, $r_6 = \langle 2, 3, 2 \rangle$, $r_7 = \langle 3, 0, 1 \rangle$, $r_8 = \langle 3, 1, 1 \rangle$, $r_9 = \langle 3, 2, 1 \rangle$, $r_{10} = \langle 3, 3, 1 \rangle$, $r_{11} = \langle 3, 4, 1 \rangle$, $r_{12} = \langle 3, 5, 1 \rangle$, $r_{13} = \langle 3, 6, 1 \rangle$, $r_{14} = \langle 3, 7, 1 \rangle$. These markings provide the information about the *data* available for every subtree constructed from the node identified as $v_{depth, pos}$.

- $a_l = \langle pos_l, ty_l \rangle$, such that $l \in [1, nT]$, where: $a_1 = \langle 1, 1 \rangle$, $a_2 = \langle 2, 1 \rangle$, $a_3 = \langle 3, 1 \rangle$, $a_4 = \langle 4, 1 \rangle$, $a_5 = \langle 5, 1 \rangle$, $a_6 = \langle 6, 1 \rangle$, $a_7 = \langle 7, 1 \rangle$, $a_8 = \langle 8, 1 \rangle$. These markings provide the information about the availability of the task located at *pos*, i.e., $ty = 1$ if the task is available, 0 otherwise.

The color mapping is $C_p(p_k) = o$ for $k \in [1, 8]$, $C_p(p_k) = r$ for $k \in [9, 11]$ and $C_p(p_{12}) = a$. That is, the places $p_1, \ldots, p_8$ accept tokens of type O, the places p_9, p_{10}, p_{11} accept tokens of type R, and p_{12} accept tokens of type A. The conditional color mapping is $C_t(t_k) = f_1$ for $k \in [1, 3]$, $C_t(t_k) = f_2$ for $k \in [5, 7]$, and $C_t(t_k) = f_3$ for $k = 4$ and $k = 9$. The *Pre-* and *Post* matrices for the net of this example are shown in **Figure 5**.

Thus, **Figure 4** represents a CPN that captures the structure of a BDT and the behavior of the working threads over the tree of height $H = \log_2 nT = \log_2 8 = 3$. They represents the places and transitions for the traveling from the root down to a leaf, and the reverse way from the leaf up to the root, on the left and right side of the CPN, respectively. Additionally, the central places, marked as "R," represent the "resources" in the system, i.e., the shared memory registers and the tasks.

Consider an initial token in place $p_1 = \langle 0, 0, 0, 0 \rangle$ as described by the initial marking M_0. Now, the binding for t_1 requires two tokens from p_9, besides one initial token in p_1, subject to

Pre	t_1: f_1	t_2: f_1	t_3: f_1	t_4: f_3	t_5: f_2	t_6: f_2	t_7: f_2	t_8: f_4
$p_1: \{o_1, o_2\}$	si_1							
$p_2: \{o_1, o_2\}$		si_1						
$p_3: \{o_1, o_2\}$			si_1					
$p_4: \{o_1, o_2\}$				si_1				
$p_5: \{o_1, o_2\}$					si_1			
$p_6: \{o_1, o_2\}$						si_1		
$p_7: \{o_1, o_2\}$							si_1	
$p_8: \{o_1, o_2\}$								si_1
$p_9: \{r_1, r_2\}$	ri_1						ri_2	
$p_{10}: \{r_3, \ldots, r_6\}$		ri_1				ri_2		
$p_{11}: \{r_7, \ldots, r_{14}\}$			ri_1		ri_2			

Post	t_1: f_1	t_2: f_1	t_3: f_1	t_4: f_3	t_5: f_2	t_6: f_2	t_7: f_2	t_8: f_4
$p_1: \{o_1, o_2\}$								so_4
$p_2: \{o_1, o_2\}$	so_1							
$p_3: \{o_1, o_2\}$		so_1						
$p_4: \{o_1, o_2\}$			so_1					
$p_5: \{o_1, o_2\}$				so_3				
$p_6: \{o_1, o_2\}$					so_2			
$p_7: \{o_1, o_2\}$						so_2		
$p_8: \{o_1, o_2\}$							so_2	
$p_9: \{r_1, r_2\}$	re_1						re_2	
$p_{10}: \{r_1, \ldots, r_4\}$		re_1				re_2		
$p_{11}: \{r_1, \ldots, r_8\}$			re_1		re_2			

Figure 5. Pre and postmatrices for CPN DS $nT = 8$.

conditions given by f_1: $(o_i, r_j, r_k)|depth_i + 1 = depth_j = depth_k \wedge pos_i * 2 = pos_j \wedge pos_i * 2 + 1 = pos_k$. Since in this case $o_i = o_1 = \langle pos_1 = 0, depht_1 = 0,\ val_1 = 0, success_1 = 0\rangle$ due to si_1, then the required tokens from p_9 are $r_j = r_1 = \langle depth_1 = 0, pos_1 = 1, data_1 = 2^{H-1} = 4\rangle$ and $r_k = r_2 = \langle depth_2 = 1, pos_2 = 1, data_2 = 2^{3-1} = 4\rangle$, where $data_1 = data_2 = 4$, assuming that the Task Array is full of tasks to be attended. Thus, the output of t_1 due to so_1 is $o_1 = \langle depth_1 = depth_1 + 1$, $pos_1 = pos_1 * 2 + h = 1,\ val_1 + h * 2^2 = 4, success_1 = 0\rangle = \langle 1, 1, 4, 0\rangle$, assuming $h = 1$.

The sketches of CPN in **Figure 6** show the three main marking evolutions in the CPN subject to the binding functions f_1, f_2, f_3. The marking evolution subject to f_1 from the current state is shown in (a). In (b), the tokens o_i, r_j, r_k are taken by the depicted transition, since f_1: $(o_i, r_j, r_k)|depth_i + 1 = depth_j = depth_k \wedge pos_i{*}2 = pos_j \wedge pos_i{*}2 + 1 = pos_k$, then $o_i =< 1, 1, 0, 0 >$, $r_j =< 2, 2, 2 >$, $r_k =< 2, 3, 2 >$. In (c), the transition has fired, then $o_1 =< 2, 3, 6, 0 >$, since $so_1(\langle depth_i, pos_i, val_i, success_i\rangle) = \langle depth_i + 1, pos_i * 2 + h_i, val_i + (h_i) * 2^{H-depth_i+1}, success_i\rangle$ assuming that $h_i = 1$. The tokens r_j, r_k remain the same, since $success = 0$. In (d), the marking evolution subject to f_3 from the current marking $< 3, 6, 6, 0 >$ is updated to the marking $< 3, 6, 6, 1 >$

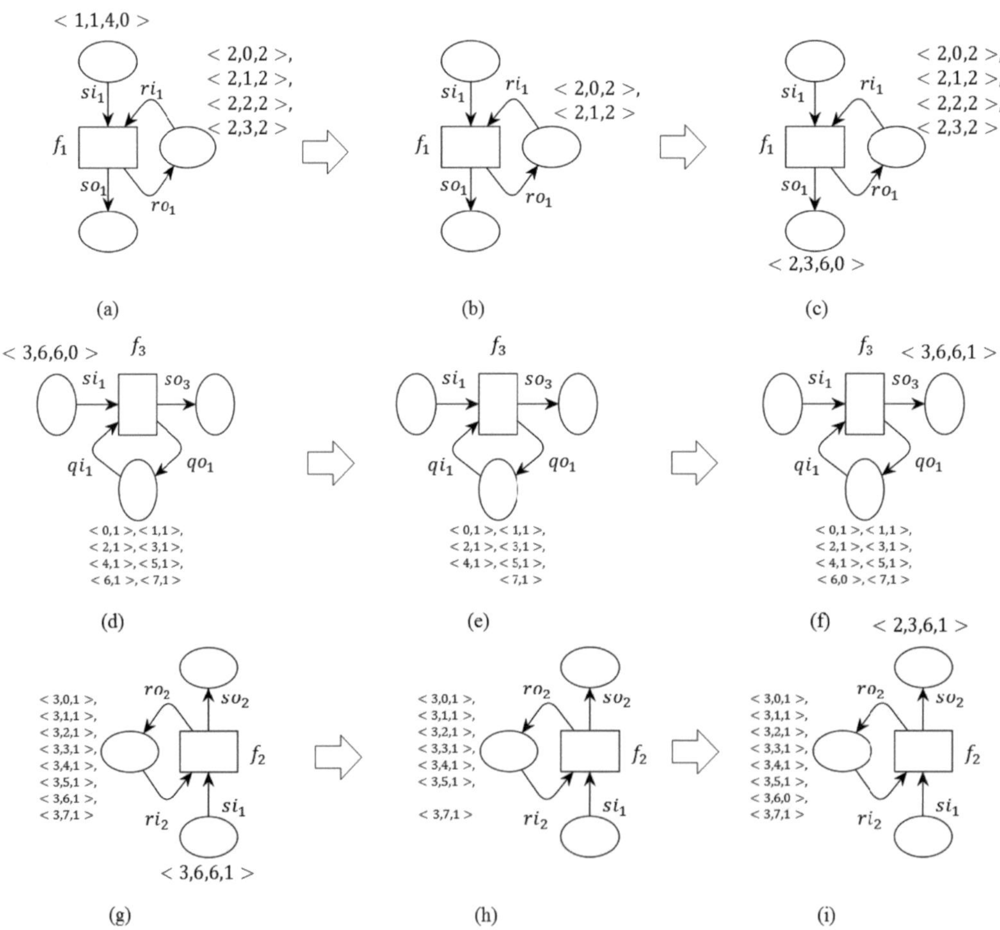

Figure 6. Binding and firing of a CPN transition.

as shown in (f), since the task reference represented by the marking $< 6, 1 >$ is available as shown in (e). Notice that, this marking is updated to $< 6, 0 >$ as shown in (f), as expected. In (g), the input state of the transitions subject to f_2 is represented with the marking $< 3, 6, 6, 1 >$. Then, it is binding by f_2 with the token $< 3, 6, 1 >$, as illustrated in (h). Thus, the input token $< 3, 6, 6, 1 >$ is updated to $< 2, 3, 6, 1 >$ by so_2, as well as, $< 3, 6, 1 >$ is updated to $< 3, 6, 0 >$ by ro_2, as shown in the section (i) of the figure.

One of the main advantages of modeling the task allocation problem by using CPN's is the possibility of varying the parameters during the simulation process, as well as the flexibility of the net structure in order to cope with a greater number of task to be attended. One of the key parameters for the simulation of the problem is the number of tokens of type O, which represents the number of processes or threads in a specific problem. The other important parameter is the decision function α, which is related to the spreading of processes or threads through the tree, by updating of *depth* and *pos* functions. It is clear, for example, that the distribution of the processes or threads at every level in the tree structure directly influences the contention at the acquisition of the tasks.

The next section explains the simulation process that is possible to execute with the proposed modeling methodology and how these simulations can help explore different parameters in order to optimize the task allocation problem.

5. Simulation of the CPN model

This section shows how to simulate a CPN model as that obtained by the methodology detailed in the previous subsection. The simulation process allows to investigate the performance of the model under parametric variations. First, the general characteristics of the simulation framework are introduced. Then, the simulation and results of a CPN model, representing a problem with 1024 tasks, are given.

In order to simplify the construction of the CPN model by using the herein proposed methodology, and thus, simulate its behavior, a CPN tool is used [43]. This environment allows editing, simulating and analyzing CPN models [36–42] and was successfully used for a variety of applications areas [44–48].

The model parameters that have to be considered are a number of initially available tasks $(nTasks)$, the height of the tree with respect to the number of tasks (H), and the decision function (α). For this example, those values are $nTasks = 1024$, $H = \log_2 1024 = 10$, and $\alpha = (r < data_j/(data_j + data_k))$ for a given o_i, r_j, r_k such that $depth_i + 1 = depth_j = depth_k \wedge pos_i * 2 = pos_j \wedge pos_i * 2 + 1 = pos_k$ and where r is a randomly generated number. These parameters are fixed during every simulation process. However, the number of threads is varying between simulations, with $d = 2^n$, $1 \leq n \leq nTasks$, for a total of 10 simulations runs.

In the simulation framework, there are different measurements of parameters that can be obtained. For illustrative purposes, in this example, the attention is focused on study the impact on the performance of the task allocation procedure when the number of processes, or working threads, is increasing.

Table 1 summarizes some results obtained from the simulations performed on the *CPN* tools framework for a model with model described previously. The number of tasks was constant, while the number of processes was increased by a power of two, represented in the first column. The second column represents the average of events required per process to complete all the tasks. It provides a measure of the speed by increasing the number of processes. The third column represents the total number of readings to the task array. The forth column represents the total number of read collisions, i.e., when a process reads a task that was previously attended by other process. The fifth column represents the average of the reads to the task array executed by each process. The sixth column shows the average of the failed reads or collisions executed by each process. The seventh column shows the proficiency of the execution by the total amount of processes. Finally, the eighth column represents the average of total reads, including the failed ones, to the task array required per task.

The plot in **Figure 7** shows the average of event, in the simulation framework, that each process required for completing all the tasks in the array. Notice that, as the number of processes increases exponentially, the number of events per processes decreases almost logarithmically.

The plot in **Figure 8** shows the average of reads that each process has performed to the task array for the completion of all the tasks. As in the previous figure, notice that the number of reads decreases almost logarithmically as the number of processes increases exponentially.

The plot in **Figure 9** shows the average of collisions, i.e., a process's read of a task that was previously attended by other process, as the number of processes increases. The figure shows that the maximum number of average collisions occurs when the number of processes is 32 in these experiments. The collisions, or failed reads, are highly influenced by the decision rule α.

The plot in **Figure 10** shows the proficiency of attending all the tasks in the array as the number of processes increases. The proficiency increases almost exponentially as the number of

Processes (d)	Average events	Reads	Collisions	Reads per process	Fails per process	Proficiency	Read per task
1	22528.00	1024.00	0.00	1024.00	0.00	1.00	1.00
2	11293.25	1027.00	3.00	513.50	1.50	1.99	1.00
4	5667.00	1030.67	6.67	257.67	1.67	3.97	1.01
8	2853.02	1038.00	14.00	129.75	1.75	7.89	1.01
16	1443.81	1051.33	27.33	65.71	1.71	15.58	1.03
32	743.34	1081.67	57.67	33.80	1.80	30.29	1.06
64	384.67	1117.33	93.33	17.46	1.46	58.65	1.09
128	202.77	1175.00	151.00	9.18	1.18	111.55	1.15
256	108.85	1265.67	241.67	4.94	0.94	207.12	1.24
512	55.39	1271.00	247.00	2.48	0.48	412.50	1.24
1024	27.70	1285.50	261.50	1.26	0.26	815.70	1.26

Table 1. Simulation results for $nTasks = 1024$.

http://dx.doi.org/10.5772/67950

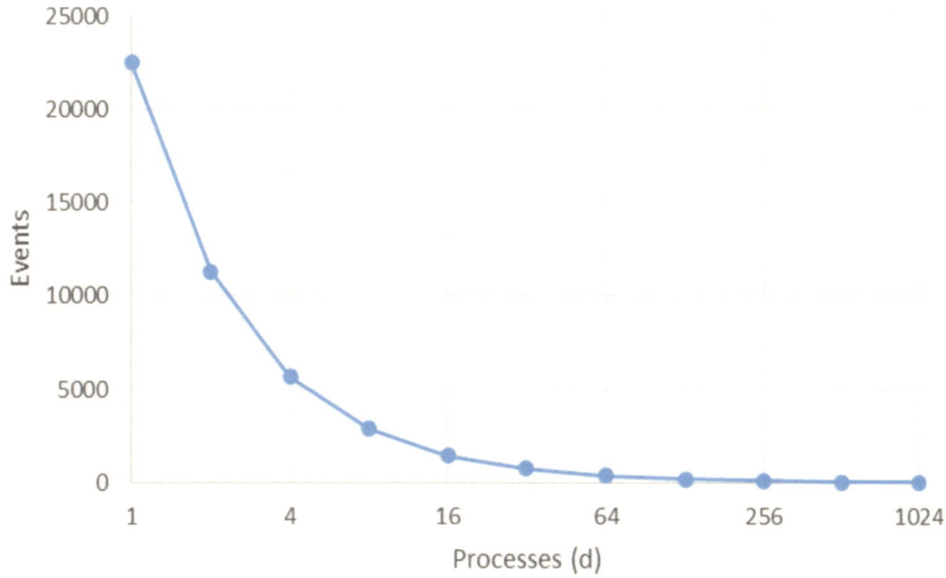

Figure 7. Average of events per process.

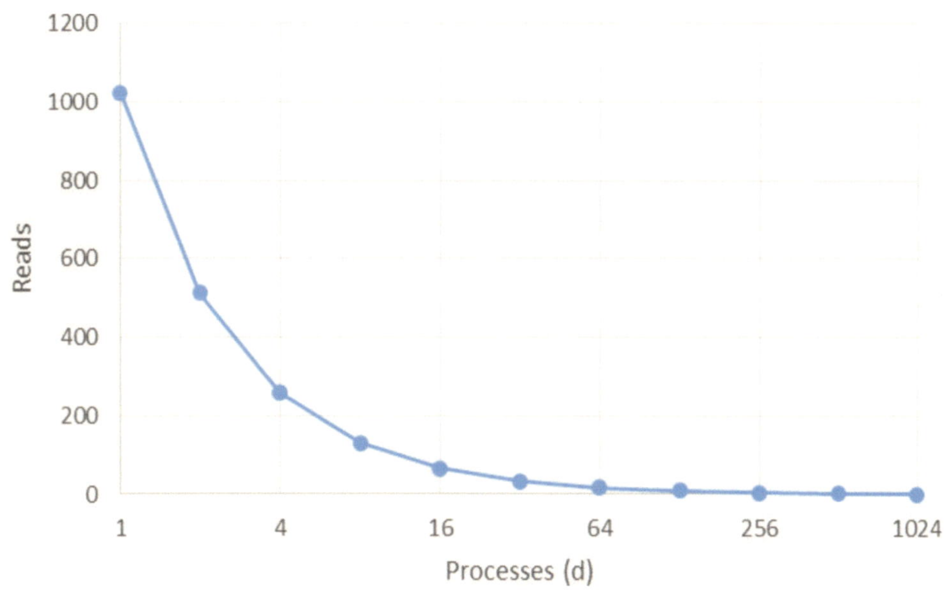

Figure 8. Average of reads per process.

processes increases to 256. The ideal behavior is to double the proficiency as the number of processes also double. However, the collisions at reading the tasks undermine this proficiency, as expected. Notice that, the plot is logarithmic.

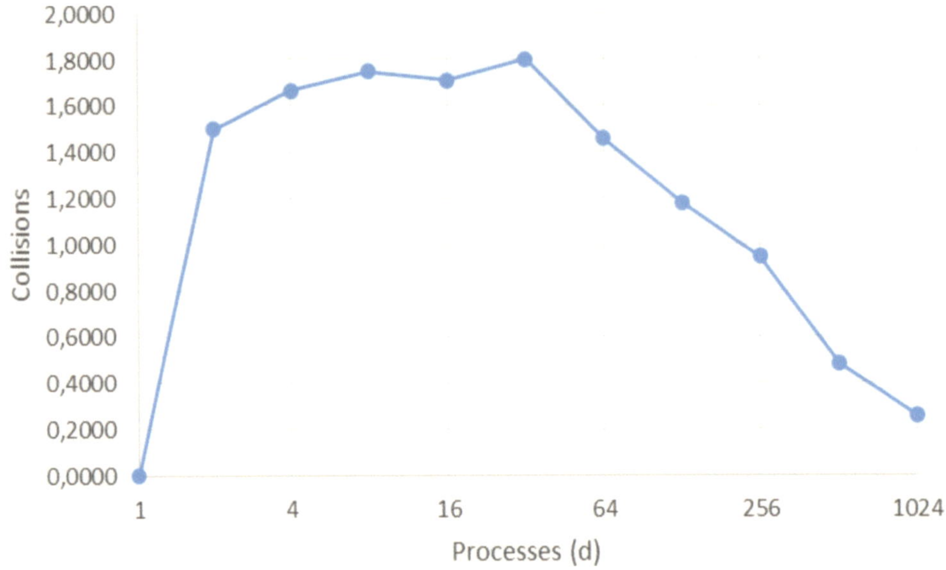

Figure 9. Average of collisions per process.

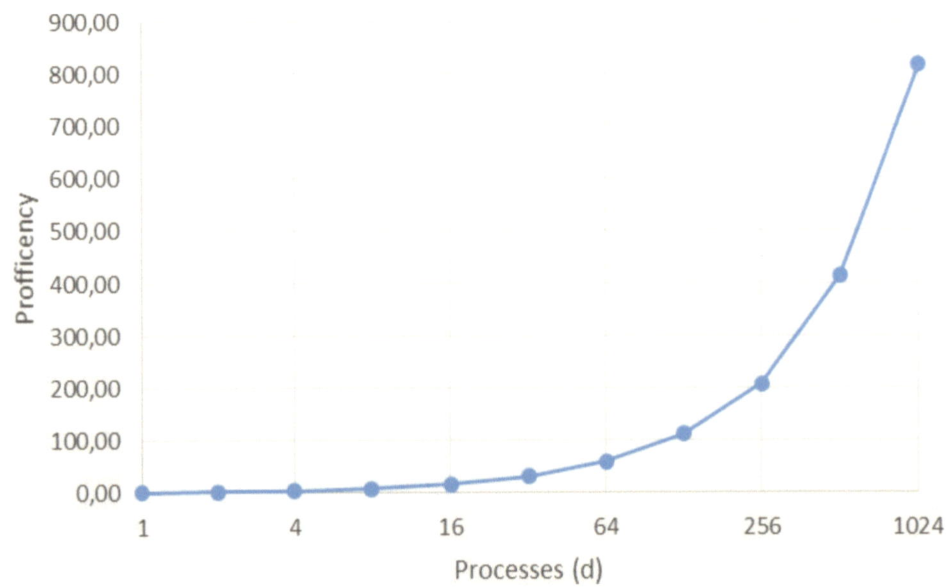

Figure 10. Average of proficiency.

The plot in **Figure 11** shows the average of work that each process has to do for completing a task, measured as the number of reads. This number slightly increases as the number of processes increases due to the growth in the number of collisions.

http://dx.doi.org/10.5772/67950

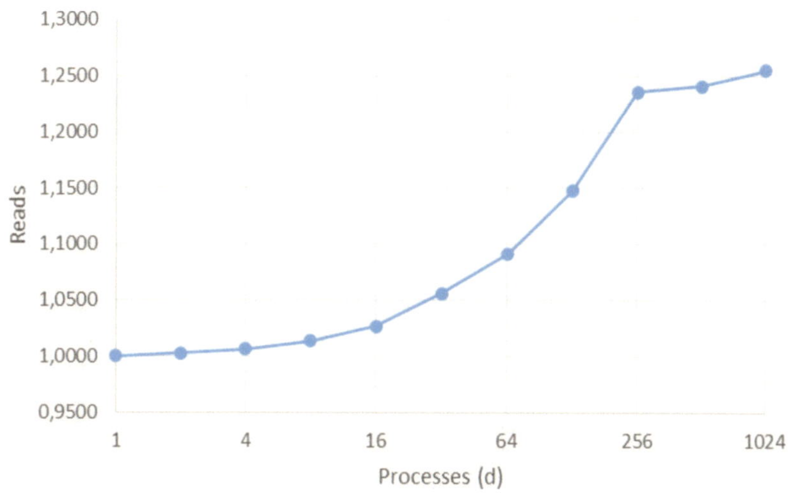

Figure 11. Average of reads per task.

6. Conclusions

This work presented a framework, based on Colored Petri nets, for the modeling and simulation of task allocation problems, which arises in environments such as grid or cluster of computers. The framework allows the construction of complex problems in a compact way. Additionally, a simulation process of the constructed models permits the study of different key aspects of the allocation strategies. Some analysis that could be performed includes the impact of different decision rules of the processes for allocating the tasks, the effect of a greater number of processes in the contention of the task's acquisition or the ration of the increased speed to the attention of tasks by a greater number of processes, among others. Additionally, the methodology allows with ease the construction of structures for an incremental model construction and its respective simulation process.

The proposed methodology allows with ease the extension to $n-ary$ tree structures as well as tree structures with a greater number of tasks and their respective simulation process.

Author details

Mildreth Alcaraz-Mejia*, Raul Campos-Rodriguez and Marco Caballero-Gutierrez

*Address all correspondence to: mildreth@iteso.mx

Electronics, Systems and Informatics Department, ITESO University, Tlaquepaque, Jalisco, Mexico

References

[1] Lee, E. Y. S., and Tsuchiya, M., A task allocation model for distributed computing systems. IEEE Transactions on Computers, 1982, vol 100, no 1, pp. 41–47.

[2] Han, Y., Jiang, C., and Luo, X., Resource scheduling model for grid computing based on sharing synthesis of Petri net, in Proceedings of the 9th International Conference on Computer Supported Cooperative Work in Design, Coventry, UK, 2005, pp. 367–372.

[3] Han, Y., Jiang, C., and Luo, X., Modelling and performance analysis of grid task scheduling based on composition and reduction of Petri nets, in Proceedings of the 5th International Conference on Grid and Cooperative Computing, Changsha, China, 2006, pp. 331–334.

[4] Zhao, X., Wang, B., and Xu, L., Grid application scheduling model based on Petri net with changeable structure, in Proceeding of 6th International Conference on Grid and Cooperative Computing, Los Alamitos, CA, 2007, pp. 733–736.

[5] Han, Y., Jiang, C., and Luo, X., Resource scheduling scheme for grid computing and its Petri net model and analysis, Parallel and Distributed Processing and Applications, Lecture Notes in Computer Science, vol. 3759, G. Chen et al., editors, Heidelberg: Springer, pp. 530–539, 2005.

[6] Hu, Z. G., Hu, R., Gui, W. H., Chen, J. E., and Chen, S. Q., General scheduling framework in computational grid based on Petri net, Journal of Central South University of Technology, vol. 12, no. 1, pp. 232–237, 2005.

[7] Shojafar, M., Barzegar, S., and Meybodi, M. R., A new method on resource scheduling in grid systems based on hierarchical stochastic Petri net, in Proceedings of the 3rd International Conference on Computer and Electrical Engineering, Chengdu, China, 2010, pp. 175–180.

[8] Buyya, R., and Murshed, M., GridSim: a toolkit for the modelling and simulation of distributed resource management and scheduling for grid computing, Concurrency and Computation: Practice and Experience, vol. 14, no. 13–15, pp. 1175–1220, 2002.

[9] Zhovtobryukh, D., A Petri net-based approach for automated goal-driven web service composition, Simulation, January 2007; vol. 83, 1: pp. 33–63.

[10] Haggarty, O. J., Knottenbelt, W. J., and Bradley, J. T., Distributed response time analysis of GSPN models with MapReduce, Simulation, August 2009; vol. 85, 8: pp. 497–509.

[11] Narciso, M., Piera, M. A., and Guasch, A., A methodology for solving logistic optimization problems through simulation, Simulation, May/June 2010; vol. 86, 5–6: pp. 369–389.

[12] Xiong, Z. G., Zhai, Z. L., Zhang, X. M., and Xia, X. W., Grid workflow service composition based on colored petri net. JDCTA: International Journal of Digital Content Technology and its Applications, 2011, vol. 5, no 5, pp. 125–131.

[13] Camilli, M., Petri nets state space analysis in the cloud. In 2012 34th International Conference on Software Engineering (ICSE). pp. 1638–1640.

[14] Longo, F., Ghosh, R., Naik, V. K., and Trivedi, K. S., A scalable availability model for infrastructure-as-a-service cloud. In 2011 IEEE/IFIP 41st International Conference on Dependable Systems and Networks (DSN), IEEE 2011. pp. 335–346.

[15] Wei, B., Lin, C., and Kong, X., Dependability modeling and analysis for the virtual data center of cloud computing. In 2011 IEEE 13th International Conference on High Performance Computing and Communications (HPCC), IEEE, 2011. pp. 784–789.

[16] Li, X., Fan, Y., Sheng, Q. Z., Maamar, Z., and Zhu, H., A petri net approach to analyzing behavioral compatibility and similarity of web services. IEEE Transactions on Systems, Man and Cybernetics, Part A: Systems and Humans, 2011, vol. 41, no 3, pp. 510–521.

[17] Muñoz, D. M., Correcher, A., García, E., and Morant, F., Stochastic DES fault diagnosis with coloured interpreted Petri nets. Mathematical Problems in Engineering, vol. 2015, Article ID 303107, 13 pages, 2015. doi:10.1155/2015/303107.

[18] Ghainani, A. T., Mohd Zin, A. A., and Ismail, N. A. M., Fuzzy timing Petri net for fault diagnosis in power system. Mathematical Problems in Engineering, vol. 2012, Article ID 717195, 12 pages, 2012. doi:10.1155/2012/717195.

[19] Alcaraz-Mejia, M., Lopez-Mellado, E., Ramirez-Treviño, A., Rivera-Rangel, I., Petri net based fault diagnosis of discrete event systems, In Proceedings of the IEEE International Conference on Systems, Man and Cybernetics. pp. 4730–4735, October 2003.

[20] Latorre, J. I., Jiménez, E., and Pérez, M., The optimization problem based on alternatives aggregation Petri nets as models for industrial discrete event systems, Simulation, March 2013; vol. 89, no 3: pp. 346–361.

[21] Latorre, J. I., and Jiménez, E., Simulation-based optimization of discrete event systems with alternative structural configurations using distributed computation and the Petri net paradigm, Simulation, November 2013; vol. 89, no 11: pp. 1310–1334.

[22] Alcaraz-Mejia, M., and Lopez-Mellado, E., Petri net model reconfiguration of discrete manufacturing systems. In Alexandre Dolgui Gerard Morel Carlos Pereira Editors: Information Control Problems in Manufacturing. 1st edition, Editorial Elsevier Science, 2006. pp. 517–552. eBook ISBN: 9780080478487, ISBN: 9780080446547, Page Count: 2480.

[23] Alcaraz-Mejia, M., and Lopez-Mellado, E., Fault recovery of manufacturing systems based on controller reconfiguration. In 2006 IEEE/SMC International Conference on System of Systems Engineering, IEEE, 2006. p. 6.

[24] Alcaraz-Mejia, M., Lopez-Mellado, E., and Ramirez-Treviño, A., A redundancy based method for Petri net model reconfiguration. In IEEE International Conference on Systems, Man and Cybernetics, 2007. IEEE, 2007. pp. 1382–1387.

[25] Chen, S. J., Zhan, T. S., Huang, C. H., Chen, J. L., and Lin, C. H. (2015). Nontechnical loss and outage detection using fractional-order self-synchronization error-based fuzzy petri nets in micro-distribution systems. IEEE Transactions on smart grid, 6(1), 411–420.

[26] Muñoz, D. M., Correcher, A., García, E., and Morant, F., Identification of stochastic timed discrete event systems with st-IPN. Mathematical Problems in Engineering, vol. 2014, Article ID 835312, 21 pages, 2014. doi:10.1155/2014/835312.

[27] Alistarh, D., Bender, M., Gilbert, S., and Guerraoui, R., How to allocate tasks asynchronously. 53rd Annual IEEE Symposium on Foundations of Computer Science, FOCS 2012, New Brunswick, NJ, USA, October 20-23, 2012, pp. 331–340, 2012.

[28] Jevtić, A., Gutiérrez, A., Andina, D., and Jamshidi, M., Distributed bees algorithm for task allocation in swarm of robots. IEEE Systems Journal, 2012, vol. 6, no 2, pp. 296–304.

[29] Delle Fave, F. M., Rogers, A., Xu, Z., Sukkarieh, S., and Jennings, N. R., Deploying the max-sum algorithm for decentralised coordination and task allocation of unmanned aerial vehicles for live aerial imagery collection. In 2012 IEEE International Conference on Robotics and Automation (ICRA). IEEE, 2012, pp. 469–476.

[30] Johnson, L., Choi, H. L., Ponda, S., and How, J. P., Allowing non-submodular score functions in distributed task allocation. In 2012 IEEE 51st Annual Conference on Decision and Control (CDC). IEEE, 2012, pp. 4702–4708.

[31] Zhao-Pin, S. U., Jiang, J. G., Liang, C. Y., and Zhang, G. F., A distributed algorithm for parallel multi-task allocation based on profit sharing learning. Acta Automatica Sinica, 2011, vol. 37, no 7, pp. 865–872.

[32] Macarthur, K. S., Stranders, R., Ramchurn, S. D., and Jennings, N. R., A distributed anytime algorithm for dynamic task allocation in multi-agent systems. In Proceedings of the 25th Association of the Advancement on Artificial Intelligence Conference (AAAI 2011), pp. 356–362, 2011. San Francisco, USA.

[33] Alistarh, D., Aspnes, J., Bender, M. A., Gelashvili, R., and Gilbert, S. Dynamic task allocation in asynchronous shared memory. In Proceedings of the Twenty-Fifth Annual ACM-SIAM Symposium on Discrete Algorithms. SIAM, 2014. pp. 416–435.

[34] Diestel, R., Graph Theory. Springer-Verlag, Heidelberg. Berlin. Graduate Texts in Mathematics, vol. 173, 3rd edition, 2005.

[35] Girault, C. and Valk, R., Petri Nets for Systems Engineering: A Guide to Modelling, Verification, and Applications, July 30, 2001, Springer-Verlag Berlin Heidelberg, Newyork, 2003. ISBN: 3642074472 9783642074479. Series ISSN: 1431–2654. vol. 2, no 1.

[36] Jensen, K., Coloured Petri nets: basic concepts, analysis methods and practical use. Springer Science and Business Media, 2013.

[37] Jensen, K., Kristensen, L. M., and Wells, L., Coloured Petri Nets and CPN Tools for modelling and validation of concurrent systems. International Journal on Software Tools for Technology Transfer, 2007, vol. 9, no 3–4, pp. 213–254.

[38] Ratzer A.V. et al. (2003) CPN Tools for Editing, Simulating, and Analysing Coloured Petri Nets. In: van der Aalst W.M.P., Best E. (eds) Applications and Theory of Petri Nets 2003. ICATPN 2003. Lecture Notes in Computer Science, vol. 2679. Springer, Berlin, Heidelberg.

http://dx.doi.org/10.5772/67950

[39] Wells, L., Performance analysis using CPN tools. In Proceedings of the 1st international conference on Performance evaluation methodologies and tools. ACM, 2006. p. 59.

[40] Westergaard, M., CPN Tools 4: Multi-formalism and extensibility. In Application and Theory of Petri Nets and Concurrency. Springer Berlin Heidelberg, 2013. pp. 400–409.

[41] Westergaard, M. and Slaats, T., CPN Tools 4: a process modeling tool combining declarative and imperative paradigms. Automatic Control and Computer Sciences, 2013, vol. 47, no 7, pp. 393–402.

[42] Dworzański, L. W., and Lomazova, Irina A., CPN Tools-assisted simulation and verification of nested Petri nets. Automatic Control and Computer Sciences, 2013, vol. 47, no 7, pp. 393–402.

[43] Cpntools.org, (2015). CPN Tools Homepage. [online] Available at: http://cpntools.org/ [Accessed 24 Jul. 2015].

[44] Machado, R. J., Lassen, K. B., Oliveira, S., Couto, M., and Pinto, P., Requirements validation: execution of UML models with CPN tools. International Journal on Software Tools for Technology Transfer, 2007, vol. 9, no 3–4, pp. 353–369.

[45] Vanderfeesten, I., van der Aalst, W., and Reijers, H. A., Modelling a product based workflow system in CPN tools. In Proceedings of the Sixth Workshop on the Practical Use of Coloured Petri Nets and CPN Tools (CPN 2005). 2005. pp. 99–118.

[46] Störrle, H., Semantics and verification of data flow in UML 2.0 activities. Electronic Notes in Theoretical Computer Science, 2005, vol. 127, no 4, pp. 35–52.

[47] Yi, X., and Kochut, K. J., A cp-nets-based design and verification framework for web services composition. In Web Services, 2004. Proceedings. IEEE International Conference on. IEEE, 2004. pp. 756–760.

[48] Rozinat, A., Wynn, M. T., van der Aalst, W. M., terHofstede, A. H., and Fidge, C. J., Workflow simulation for operational decision support. Data and Knowledge Engineering, 2009, vol. 68, no 9, pp. 834–850.

Chapter 11

Multi-Criteria Decision-Making in the Implementation of Renewable Energy Sources

Dejan Jovanovic and Ivan Pribicevic

Additional information is available at the end of the chapter

http://dx.doi.org/10.5772/67734

Abstract

The consideration of renewable energy sources as sources for the production of electricity, demands an approach that would enable an analysis which comprehends various factors and stakeholders. The *P*reference *R*anking *O*rganization *METH*od for *E*nrichment *E*valuations (PROMETHEE), as a mathematical model for multi-criteria decision-making, is one of the ideal methods used when it is necessary to rank scenarios according to specific criteria, depending on whom the ranking is applied. This chapter presents various scenarios whose ranking is done according to defined criteria and weight coefficients for each of the stakeholders. This model recognized and accepted according to the theory of decision-making could be used as a tool for so-called stakeholder value approach.

Keywords: renewable energy sources, PROMETHEE, the production of electricity, stakeholder value, multi-criteria decision-making proces, National Renewable Energy Action Plan (NAPOIE), mini hydros, biomass, wind, solar, geothermal energy

1. Introduction

The basis for this chapter was document which established the goals in usage of renewable energy sources until 2020 (National Renewable Energy Action Plan of the Republic of Serbia further on NAPOIE) [2], as well as the manner in which they are to be achieved. In addition, it has the goal to enhance investments in the field of renewable energy sources.

'According to article 20 of the Treaty Establishing Energy Community (further on: UOEnZ), the Republic of Serbia accepted the obligation to apply European Directives in the field of renewable energy sources (further on: OIE) —Directive 2001/77/EC on the promotion of the use of energy from renewable sources and Directive 2003/30/EC on the promotion of the use of biofuels and other renewable fuels for transport. Those Directives were gradually replaced since 2009, and in January 2012 abolished by the new Directive 2009/28/EC of the European Parliament and the Council of the 23rd of April 2009 on the promotion of the use of energy from renewable sources, amending and subsequently repealing Directives 2001/77/EC and 2003/30/EC CELEX No. 32009L0028'.[1]**

With the adoption of the 'Law of Ratification…',[2] [3] the Republic of Serbia internationally committed to create NAPOIE [2].

Data given in **Tables 1** and **2** were used as input data for this chapter.

Types of renewable energy sources taken in consideration in this chapter are as follows:

- Mini hydros (up to 10 MW).
- Wind energy.
- Solar energy.
- Biomass.
- Geothermal energy.

The National Renewable Energy Action Plan of the Republic of Serbia (NAPOIE) defined target values, that is, the amount of GWh expected to be produced from every renewable energy source and to be delivered in the system. The defined goal is 2252 GWh obtained from following renewable energy sources: mini hydros, biomass, solar, wind and geothermal energy (**Table 3**).

The *goal* is to verify the ranking sequence of renewable energy sources if only one of the listed renewable energy sources would be delivering the total expected amount of GWh into the system and to rank scenarios according to stakeholders[3], on the basis of previously defined criteria and calculated weight coefficients, and also to establish whether the sequence of renewable energy sources is identical for all stakeholders.

On the basis of ranking achieved this way, we may determine which type of renewable energy source is the priority, depending on the stakeholder, and also whether the participation of all listed types is justified.

A multi-criteria analysis will provide a clearly established sequence of renewable energy sources for the stakeholders, and according to clearly established criteria. This sequence is important for the establishing of priorities.

[1]Taken from introduction of document NAPOIE, Ministarstvo energetike, razvoja i zaštite životne sredine, strana 18, Beograd 2013 [2].

[2]Full name "Law on Ratification of the Treaty Establishing Energy Community between the European Community and the Republic of Albania, Republic of Bulgaria, Bosnia and Herzegovina, Republic of Croatia, Former Yugoslav Republic of Macedonia, Republic of Montenegro, Romania, Republic of Serbia and United Nations Interim Administration Mission on Kosovo in compliance with the Resolution 1244 of the UN Security Council" ("Službeni glasnik RS", no. 62/06).

[3]R. Edward Freeman. The stakeholder theory is a theory of organizational management and business ethics that addresses morals and values in managing an organization [1].

http://dx.doi.org/10.5772/67734

Type of renewable energy sources	(MW)	Estimated work hours (h)	(GWh)	(ktoe)	Participation (%)
HE (over 10 MW)	250	4430	1108	95	30.3
MHE (up to 10 MW)	188	3150	592	51	16.2
Wind energy	500	2000	1000	86	27.4
Solar energy	10	1300	13	1	0.4
Biomass: power plants with combined production	100	6400	640	55	17.5
Biogas (manure): power plants with combined production	30	7500	225	19	6.2
Geothermal energy	1	7000	7	1	0.2
Waste	3	6000	18	2	0.5
Landfill gas	10	5000	50	4	1.4
Total planned capacity	1092	–	3653	314	100.0

[1] Full name "Law on Ratification of the Treaty Establishing Energy Community between the European Community and the Republic of Albania, Republic of Bulgaria, Bosnia and Herzegovina, Republic of Croatia, Former Yugoslav Republic of Macedonia, Republic of Montenegro, Romania, Republic of Serbia and United Nations Interim Administration Mission on Kosovo in compliance with the Resolution 1244 of the UN Security Council" („Službeni glasnik RS", no. 62/06 [2].

Table 1. The production of electricity from renewable energy sources from new plants in 2020[1].

Type of renewable energy sources	(MW)	(GWh)	Specific investment costs* (€/kW)	Price according to planned installed capacity until 2020 (millions €)
HE (over 10 MW)	250	1108	1819	454.8
MHE (up to 10 MW)	188	592	2795	525.5
Plants powered by wind energy	500	1000	1417	708.5
Plants powered by solar energy	10	13	2500	25.0
Biomass: power plants with combined production	100	640	4522	452.2
Biogas (manure): power plants with combined production	30	225	4006	120.2
Geothermal energy	1	7	4115	4.1
Waste	3	18	4147	12.4
Landfill gas	10	50	2000	20.0
Total planned capacity	1092	3653	–	2322.6

[1] Full name "Law on Ratification of the Treaty Establishing Energy Community between the European Community and the Republic of Albania, Republic of Bulgaria, Bosnia and Herzegovina, Republic of Croatia, Former Yugoslav Republic of Macedonia, Republic of Montenegro, Romania, Republic of Serbia and United Nations Interim Administration Mission on Kosovo in compliance with the Resolution 1244 of the UN Security Council" („Službeni glasnik RS", no. 62/06 [2].

Table 2. Estimated finances for each of the technologies using renewable energy sources in the production of electricity needed to complete the planned share in energy production from new capacities until 2020 in electric energy sector[1].

Renewable energy type	Mtoe
Hydro	0.80
Solar	0.60
Biomass	2.25
Wind	0.20
Geothermal energy	0.20

Table 3. Available potentials [4].

For solving this type of problems, one of the mathematical models that can be used is the one developed by Jean-Pierre Brans in 1982, for a multi-criteria decision-making in a group of alternatives described with several attributes.

2. Theoretical overview of the PROMETHEE

The *P*reference *R*anking *O*rganization *METH*od for *E*nrichment *E*valuations (PROMETHEE)[4] is part of a group of methods for multi-criteria decision-making within a group of alternatives described with several attributes, used as criteria. This method enables a comprehensive structuring of quality and quantity criteria of different importance into a relation of partial organization in a unique result (PROMETHEE II), on the basis of which alternatives can be ranked in an absolute manner.

We will consider a multi-criteria problem:

$$\mathrm{Max}\left\{\left(k_1(a),\ldots,k_k(a)\right) \mid a \in A\right\}, \tag{1}$$

where A is a finite group of activities and $k_i = 1,\ldots, k$ are *usefulness criteria* which should be maximized or fulfilled according to the principle 'bigger is better' (this supposition enables a more simple presentation of the method—in cases when some of the criteria are *price criteria*, they can be transformed into usefulness criteria, or we can adjust the proceeding to those criteria as well).

The application of the PROMETHEE is characterized by two steps:

(1) constructing a preference relation within a group of alternatives A,

(2) using this relation to find an answer to the problem (1.1).

In the first step, a complex preference relation is formed (in order to stress the fact that this relation is based on the consideration of more criteria, this relation is called *outranking relation*), based on the generalization of the notion of the criteria. A *preference index* is then defined and a complex preference relation is obtained, which is shown in a graph representation. The essence of this step is that the decision maker (stakeholder) must express his preference

[4]Theoretical overview of the PROMEHTEE method is described in brief according to the "*Odlučivanje*", Milutin Čupić, Milija Suknović, Fakultet organizacionih nauka, Beograd 2010. All general theoretical formulas, functions and graphs are taken from Ref. [5].

between two alternatives (action and activity), according to every criterion, on the basis of the difference (differentiation) of criteria values of alternatives which are being compared.

PROMETHEE II can be a tool for 'Management philosophy that regards maximization of the interests of its all stakeholders (customers, employees, shareholders and the community) as its highest objective'.[5]

The preference relation obtained this way is used so that input and output flows are calculated for each alternative, in graphs or tables. On the basis of these flows, the decision maker can apply partial ranking (PROMETHEE I) or absolute ranking (PROMETHEE II) in the group of alternatives.

In this chapter, the absolute ranking method PROMETHEE II was used.

2.1. PROMETHEE preference relation

Let *k* be a real function used to express one of the attributes used as a criterion for comparing alternatives:

$$k : A \rightarrow \mathbf{R} \tag{2}$$

Let us assume that this is a usefulness criterion, that is, that alternatives (scenarios/models) are compared according to this criterion on the basis of the principle 'bigger is better'.

For every alternative a dA, $k(a)$ a criterion value is calculated according to criterion k. When two alternatives a, b dA are being compared, the result of that comparison is expressed as a preference.

With preference function P

$$P : A \times A \rightarrow [0, 1] \tag{3}$$

the intensity of preference for alternative a in relation to alternative b is expressed, with the following interpretation:

$P(a, b) = 0$ marks indifference between a and b, that is, there is no preference of a over b,

$P(a, b) \approx 0$ marks weak preference of a over b,

$P(a, b) \approx 1$ marks strong preference of a over b,

$P(a, b) = 1$ marks strict preference of a over b.

Preference function that is added to a given criterion is the difference function of criteria value of alternatives, and it can be written as

$$P(a, b) = P(k(a) - k(b)) = P(d) \tag{4}$$

$P(d)$ is a non-decreasing function that assumes value zero for negative difference values $d = k(a) - k(b)$, *if the functions should be maximized, that is,* $P(a, b) = P(k(a) - k(b))$, that is, $d = -(k(a) - k(b))$ if the criterion is minimized (**Table 4**).

[5]http://www.businessdictionary.com/definition/stakeholder-value-approach.html.

Criterion	Definition	Graph
Type 1. Common criterion	$P(d)=\begin{cases}0, & d=0\\ 1, & d\neq 0\end{cases}$	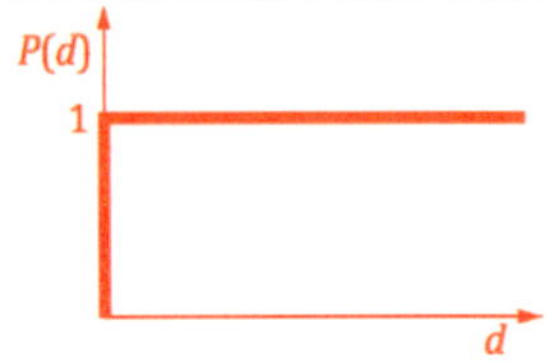
Type 2. Quasi criterion	$P(d)=\begin{cases}0, & d<m\\ 1, & d\geq m\end{cases}$	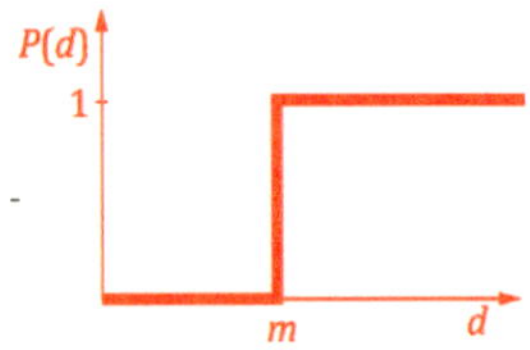
Type 3. Criterion with a growing linear preference	$P(d)=\begin{cases}\frac{d}{m}, & d<m\\ 1, & d\geq m\end{cases}$	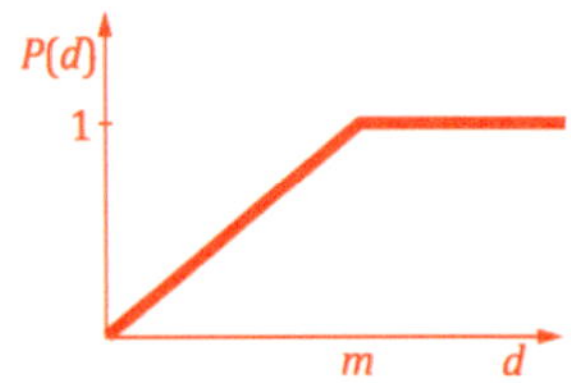
Type 4. Linear criterion with an indifference area	$P(d)=\begin{cases}0, & d\leq m\\ \frac{1}{2}, & m<d\leq n\\ 1, & d>n\end{cases}$	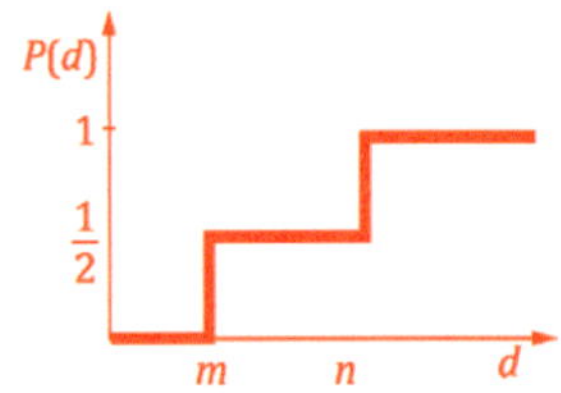
Type 5. Criterion with preference levels	$P(d)=\begin{cases}0, & d\leq m\\ \frac{d-m}{n-m}, & m\leq d\leq n\\ 1, & d>n\end{cases}$	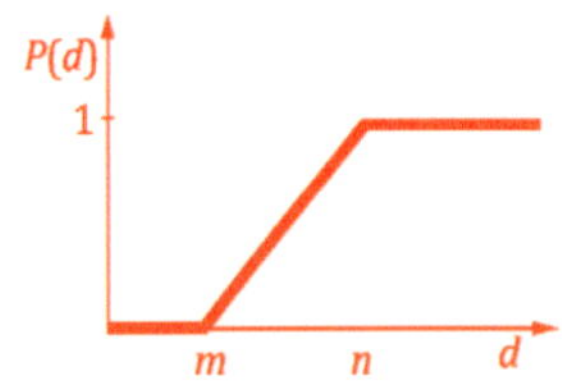
Type 6. Gauss' criterion	$P(d)=1-\exp\left\{-\frac{d^2}{2\sigma^2}\right\}$	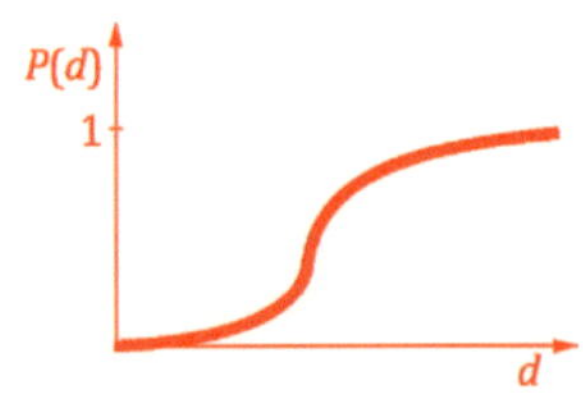

[1]Taken from Ref. [5].

Table 4. Types of functions in the application of the PROMETHEE[1].

2.2. Multi-criteria preference index

Let us assume that the decision maker sets preference function P_i and weight t_i; for every criterion k_i $(i = 1, \ldots, n)$ of the problem (2.2).

http://dx.doi.org/10.5772/67734

Weight t_i is the measure of relative importance of the criterion k_i. If all criteria have the same value for the decision maker, all weights are equal.

Multi-criteria preference index IP is defined as the medium of preference functions P_i:

$$IP(a, b) = \frac{\sum_{i=1}^{k} t_i P_i(a, b)}{\sum_{i=1}^{k} t_i}$$

IP (a,b) represents intensity, that is, the strength of decision maker's preference for activity a over activity b, when all criteria are compared at the same time. It varies between values 0 and 1.

$P(a, b) \approx 0$ marks weak preference of a over b for all criteria,

$P(a, b) \approx 1$ marks strong preference of a over b for all criteria.

This can also be shown in a graph. Between two nodes (two activities) a and b there are two arches with values IP(a, b) and IP(b, a). This relation is shown in **Figure 1**. There is no direct connection between IP(a, b) and IP(b, a).

Output and input flow:

Input and output flows can be defined for every node (shown in **Figure 2.**)

(a) Output flow is the sum of values of output flows:

$$T^{+}(a) = \sum_{x \in k} IP(a, x)$$

(b) Input flow is the sum of values of input flows (**Figure 3**):

$$T^{-}(a) = \sum_{x \in k} IP(a, x)$$

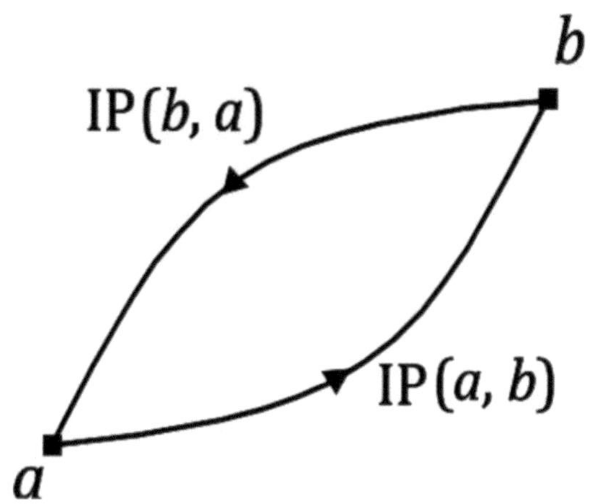

Figure 1. IP relation. Taken from Ref. [5].

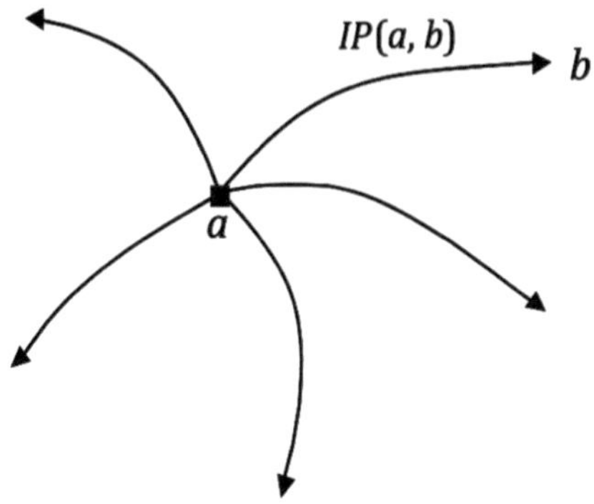

Figure 2. Output flow. Taken from Ref. [5].

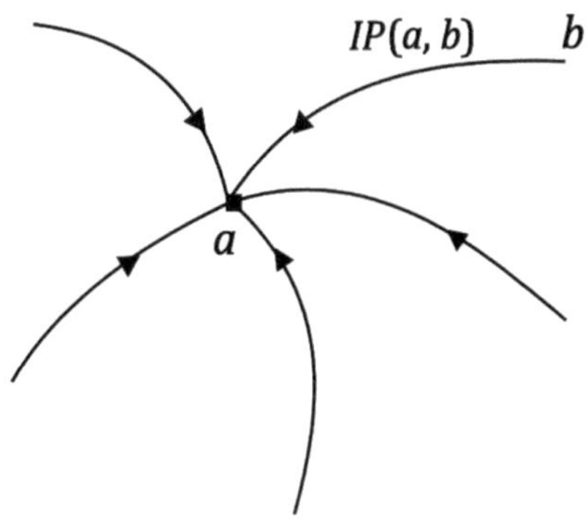

Figure 3. Input flow. Ibid 11, Ref. [5].

3. Absolute ranking: PROMETHEE II

If the decision maker wants an absolute ranking, the clear flow is considered:

Absolute ranking (PII, III) is defined in the following manner:

a PII b (a prefers b) if $T(a) > T(b)$.

a III b (a is indifferent to b) if $T(a) = T(b)$.

Elements of scientific research[6] are all the elements that have to be defined so that the aforementioned mathematical model could be applied. Those comprehend:

[6]This research paper gave initial idea for this chapter as well as for stakeholders and used criteria [6, 7].

http://dx.doi.org/10.5772/67734

- stakeholders
- criteria
- weight coefficients
- preference functions (for every criterion)
- suggested models.

Stakeholders considered in ranking are as follows:

- State (DR)
- Potential investors (PI)
- Local community (LZ).

3.1. Criteria

PRMOTHEE needs criteria to be defined, according to whom the ranking will be done. Criteria used in this study are presented in **Table 5**.

These 10 criteria can be divided into two categories:

(1) Empirical criteria, based on the data taken from NAPOIE (K1, K2, K3, K5, K9 and K10).

(2) Description criteria (K4, K6, K7 and K8).

Weight coefficients are calculated and given in **Table 4**.

Since each of the stakeholders treats each of those 10 criteria in a different manner, it is essential to define weight coefficients so that every criterion has a weight definition in relation to the stakeholder. For each of the stakeholders, the criteria were sorted into three categories:

K1	Maximal usage of available potentials
K2	Price according to planned installed capacity
K3	Incentive purchase price
K4	Technology development
K5	Supply safeness, expected work hours
K6	Possibility of combined production of electric and thermal energy
K7	Contribution to local development and welfare
K8	Social acceptability and sustainability of other influences on the environment
K9	Period of investment return
K10	Installed power

Table 5. Criteria for ranking scenarios.

- Very important,
- Important,
- Of little importance.

An assessment of weight coefficients was made on that basis, with values for K attributed on the scale of 1–10, starting from the categorization of the criteria. A representation of weight coefficients is given in **Table 6**.

Preference functions. A preference function is attributed to every defined criterion. Common functions according the PROMETHEE are presented in **Table 4**. For this chapter, the following allocation was adopted:

- Type 1. A common function is attributed to K6. Type 1 function is used when there are only two expected results, and it provides an obvious preference. Because of that it is attributed to criterion K6, since the combined production of electric and thermal energy is either possible or impossible.
- Type 3. A growing linear preference function is attributed to K2, K3, K5, K9 and K10. Type 3 function is used when the difference can be a constant value. The maximum value of difference is taken as decision threshold ($m = d$max)
- Type 4. A function with preference levels is attributed to K1, K4, K7 and K8. Type 4 function is used for discrete value differences and their outputs are discrete preferences 0, ½, 1 (m and n are decision thresholds). For criterion K1, assumed decision thresholds are m = 10% $d$max, and n = 30% $d$max, while for criteria K4, K7, K8 $m = 1$ and $n = 2$.

	Weight coefficient t_i	Σt_i	
State			
k1; k5; k10	(8 + 9 + 10)/3 = 9	0.1636	Very important: 16.36%
k2; k3; k6; k7; k8	(3 + 4 + 5 + 6 + 7)/5 = 5	0.0909	Important: 9.09%
k4; k9	(1 + 2)/2 = 1.5	0.02727	Of little importance: 2.72%
Investors			
k2; k3; k4; k9	(7 + 8 + 9 + 10)/4 = 8.5	0.154545	Very important: 15.45%
k5; k6; k10	(4 + 5 + 6)/3 = 5	0.0909	Important: 9.09%
k1; k7; k8	(1 + 2 + 3)/3 = 2	0.03636	Of little importance: 3.63%
Local community			
k6; k7; k8	(8 + 9 + 10)/3 = 9	0.1636	Very important: 16.36%
k1; k5	(6 + 7)/2 = 6.5	0.11818	Important: 11.818%
k2; k3; k4; K9; K10	(1 + 2 + 3 + 4 + 5)/5 = 3	0.0545	Of little importance: 5.45%

Table 6. Calculation of weight coefficients.

3.2. Suggested models

The following models (scenarios) were defined (**Table 6**):

- The first model (A1) represents allocation A1. This allocation fits the goals planned until 2020 according to NAPOIE.
- The second model (A2) represents allocation A2, in which the needed energy from renewable energy sources would be produced in mini hydros.
- The third model (A3) represents allocation A3, in which the needed energy from renewable energy sources would be produced from biomass.
- The fourth model (A4) represents allocation A4, in which the needed energy from renewable energy sources would be produced by the Sun.
- The fifth model (A5) represents allocation A5, in which the needed energy from renewable energy sources would be produced by the wind.
- The sixth model (A6) represents allocation A6, in which the needed energy from renewable energy sources would be produced from geothermal potentials.

N.B.: It is VERY important to point out here that, according to available potentials, as shown in **Table 7** (data taken from the document 'Politika Republike Srbije u oblasti OIE'), each of the renewable energy sources listed (mini hydros, biomass, solar, wind and geothermal energy) can deliver 2252 GWh of energy independently (**Table 8** presents coneversion of available resources presented in **Table 7** from Mtoe to GWh), which represents the remainder from the total of 3360 GWh, diminished by the amount delivered by hydro potentials >10 MW. The first model A1 of this chapter was given illustratively as the goal which was set to be reached and will be used in further researches as a continuation of this chapter.

Scenaria are treated according to the defined criteria. Values of criteria for each scenaria are calculated and presetned in **Table 9**.

	A1	A2	A3	A4	A5	A6
	GWh	**GWh**	**GWh**	**GWh**	**GWh**	**GWh**
Hydro potential						
>10 MW	**1108**	**1108**	**1108**	**1108**	**1108**	**1108**
<10 MW	592	2252	0	0	0	0
Biomass	640	0	2252	0	0	0
Solar	13	0	0	2252	0	0
Wind	1000	0	0	0	2252	0
Geothermal	7	0	0	0	0	2252
Total	3360					

Table 7. Scenarios A1–A6.

Type of renewable energy sources	Mtoe	GWh
Hydro	0.8	9304
Biomass	2.25	26,167
Solar	0.6	6978
Wind	0.2	2326
Geothermal energy	0.2	2326

Table 8. Available potentials of renewable energy sources.

		K1 (%)	K2 (€)	K3	K4	K5	K6	K7	K8	K9	K10
A1	PLAN	43.00	1,356,627,968	9.87	4	3564	1	3	4	6.1	799
A2	Hydro potential <10 MW	24.20	1,998,203,175	9.89	5	3150	0	2	4	9.0	715
A3	Biomass	8.61	1,591,178,750	10.74	4	6400	1	4	4	6.6	352
A4	Solar	32.27	4,330,769,231	18.45	3	1300	0	1	3	10.4	1732
A5	Wind	96.82	1,595,542,000	9.20	4	2000	0	1	3	7.7	1126
A6	Geothermal	96.82	1,323,854,286	8.30	4	7000	1	2	5	7.1	322

Table 9. Scenarios according to K criteria values.

4. Mathematical model

Criterion K4: Technology development	
Technologies in laboratory and research phases (laboratory)	1
Technologies in pilot programs (pilot)	2
Technologies demanding further improvements to enhance their efficiency (further improvement)	3
Commercially ready technologies with a reliable place in the overall local market (com_loc)	4
Commercially ready technologies with a reliable place in the supranational and European market (com_EU)	5

Criterion K7: Contribution to local development	
Without any influence on local economy (none)	1
Weak influence on local economy(weak)	2
Moderate influence on local economy (only a small number of permanent workplaces) (moderate)	3
Moderate to large influence on local economy (opening new workplaces and chains of companies in energy production sector)	4
Very large influence on local economy (strong incentive to local growth, creation of small industrial regions on wider areas)	5

Criterion K8: social acceptability and sustainability of other influences on the environment	
Most inhabitants are against any installations, regardless of their surroundings (no)	1
Inhabitants' opinion is split (split)	2
Most inhabitants accept installations, since they are far from inhabited areas and have no visible damaging effects (vis-res)	3
Most inhabitants accept installations, since they are far from inhabited areas, regardless of whether there is a visual contact (res)	4
Most inhabitants are pro installations (OK)	5

Mathematical model representation for the state as a stakeholder

	State	**Min**	**Min**	**Min**	**Max**	**Max**	**Max**	**Max**	**Max**	**Min**	**Max**
		K1%	**K2 €**	**K3**	**K4**	**K5**	**K6**	**K7**	**K8**	**K9**	**K10**
A2	Hydro potential <10 MW	0.2420	1,998,203,175	9.89	5	3150	0	2	4	9.0	715
A3	Biomass	0.0861	1,591,178,750	10.74	4	6400	1	4	4	6.6	352
A4	Solar	0.3227	4,330,769,231	18.45	3	1300	0	1	3	10.4	1732
A5	Wind	0.9682	1,595,542,000	9.20	4	2000	0	1	3	7.7	1126
A6	Geothermal	0.9682	1,323,854,286	8.30	4	7000	1	2	5	7.1	322

***d*(*a*2,*ai*)**	**Hydro potential <10 MW**	**Differentiation *d*: difference between scenario *a*2 and other suggested scenarios**									
		0.0000	**0**	**0.00**	**0**	**0**	**0**	**0**	**0**	**0.0**	**0**
	Biomass	−0.1559	−407,024,425	0.85	1	−3250	−1	−2	0	−2.4	363
	Solar	0.0807	233,266,056	8.56	2	1850	0	1	1	1.4	−1017
	Wind	0.7262	−402,661,175	−0.69	1	1150	0	1	1	−1.3	−411
	Geothermal	0.7262	−674,348,889	−1.60	1	−3850	−1	0	−1	−1.9	393

***P*(*a*2,*ai*)**	**Hydro potential <10 MW**	**Preference function *P*: scenario *a*2 versus other suggested scenarios**									
		0	**0**	**0**	**0**	**0**	**0**	**0**	**0**	**0**	**0**
*a*3	Biomass	0	0	0.099299	0.5	0	0	0	0	0	0.923
*a*4	Solar	0	1	1	1	1	0	0.5	0.5	1	0
*a*5	Wind	1	0	0	0.5	0.62	0	0.5	0.5	0	0
*a*6	Geothermal	1	0	0	0.5	0	0	0	0	0	1
	Ti	0.1636	0.0909	0.0909	0.02727	0.1636	0.0909	0.0909	0.0909	0.02727	0.1636

***d*(*a*3,*ai*)**	**Hydro potential <10 MW**	**Differentiation *d*: difference between scenario *a*3 and other suggested scenarios**									
		0.1559	**407,024,425**	**−0.85**	**−1**	**3250**	**1**	**2**	**0**	**2.4**	**−363**
	Biomass	0.0000	0	0.00	0	0	0	0	0	0.0	0
	Solar	0.2366	2,739,590,481	7.71	1	5100	1	3	1	3.8	−1380

$d(a3,ai)$ Hydro potential <10 MW	Differentiation d: difference between scenario $a3$ and other suggested scenarios								
	0.1559	**407,024,425**	**−0.85**	**−1**	**3250**	**1**	**2**	**0**	**2.4**	**−363**
Wind	0.8821	4,363,250	−1.54	0	4400	1	3	1	1.1	−774
Geothermal	0.8821	−267,324,464	−2.45	0	−600	0	2	−1	0.5	30

$P(a3,ai)$	Hydro potential <10 MW	Preference function P: scenario $a3$ versus other suggested scenarios									
		0.5	**0.148**	**0**	**0**	**0.637**	**1**	**1**	**0**	**0.63**	**0**
$a3$	Biomass	0	0	0	0	0	0	0	0	0	0
$a4$	Solar	0.5	1	1	0.5	1	1	1	0.5	1	0
$a5$	Wind	1	0.0016	0	0	0.862	1	1	0.5	0.289	0
$a6$	Geothermal	1	0	0	0	0	0	1	0	0.131	1
	ti	0.1636	0.0909	0.0909	0.02727	0.1636	0.0909	0.0909	0.0909	0.02727	0.1636

$d(a4,ai)$ Hydro potential<10 MW	Differentiation d: difference between scenario $a4$ and other suggested scenarios									
	−0.0807	**−2,332,566,056**	**−8.56**	**−2**	**−1850**	**0**	**−1**	**−1**	**−1.4**	**1017**
Biomass	−0.2366	−2,739,590,481	−7.71	−1	−5100	−1	−3	−1	−3.8	1380
Solar	0.0000	0	0.00	0	0	0	0	0	0.0	0
Wind	0.6455	−2,735,227,231	−9.25	−1	−700	0	0	0	−2.7	606
Geothermal	0.6455	−3,006,914,945	−10.16	−1	−5700	−1	−1	−2	−3.3	1410

$P(a4,ai)$	Hydro potential <10 MW	Preference function P: scenario $a4$ versus other suggested scenarios									
		0	**0**	**0**	**0**	**0**	**0**	**0**	**0**	**0**	**0.721**
$a3$	Biomass	0	0	0	0	0	0	0	0	0	0.978
$a4$	Solar	0	0	0	0	0	0	0	0	0	0
$a5$	Wind	1	0	0	0	0	0	0	0	0	0.43
$a6$	Geothermal	1t	0	0	0	0	0	0	0	0	1
	ti	0.1636	0.0909	0.0909	0.02727	0.1636	0.0909	0.0909	0.0909	0.02727	0.1636

$d(a5,ai)$ Hydro potential <10 MW	Differentiation d: difference between scenario $a5$ and other suggested scenarios									
	−0.7262	**402,661,175**	**0.69**	**−1**	**−1150**	**0**	**−1**	**−1**	**1.3**	**411**
Biomass	−0.8821	−4,363,250	1.54	0	−4400	−1	−3	−1	−1.1	774
Solar	−0.6455	2,735,227,231	9.25	1	700	0	0	0	2.7	−606
Wind	0.0000	0	0.00	0	0	0	0	0	0.0	0
Geothermal	0.0000	−271,687,714	−0.90	0	−5000	−1	−1	−2	−0.6	804

http://dx.doi.org/10.5772/67734

P(*a*3,*ai*)		Hydro potential <10 MW	Preference function *P* – scenario *a*5 versus other suggested scenarios									
		0	0.147	0.075	0	0	0	0	0	0.481	0.51	*a*3
Biomass	0	0	0.166	0	0	0	0	0	0	0.962	*a*4	Solar
0	1	1	0.5	1	0	0	0	1	0	*a*5	Wind	0
0	0	0	0	0	0	0	0	0	*a*6	Geothermal	0	0
0	0	0	0	0	0	0	1		*ti*	0.1636	0.0909	0.0909
0.02727	0.1636	0.0909	0.0909	0.0909	0.02727	0.1636						

d(*a*6,*ai*)	Hydro potential <10 MW	Differentiation *d* – difference between scenario *a*6 and other suggested scenarios									
		−0.7262	674,348,889	1.60	−1	3850	1	0	1	1.9	−393
	Biomass	−0.8821	267,324,464	2.45	0	600	0	−2	1	−0.5	−30
	Solar	−0.6455	3,006,914,945	10.16	1	5700	1	1	2	3.3	−1410
	Wind	0.0000	271,687,714	0.90	0	5000	1	1	2	0.6	−804
	Geothermal	0.0000	0	0.00	0	0	0	0	0	0.0	0

P(*a*6,*ai*)	Hydro potential <10 MW	Preference function *P* – scenario *a*6 versus other suggested scenarios									
		0	0.224	0.157	0	0.675	1	0	0.5	0.576	0
*a*3	Biomass	0	0.089	0.241	0	0.105	0	0	0.5	0	0
*a*4	Solar	0	1	1	0.5	1	1	0.5	1	1	0
*a*5	Wind	0	0.09	0.088	0	0.877	1	0.5	1	0.182	0
*a*6	Geothermal	0	0	0	0	0	0	0	0	0	0
	ti	0.1636	0.0909	0.0909	0.02727	0.1636	0.0909	0.0909	0.0909	0.02727	0.1636

IP(*a*2,*a*3)	IP(*a*2,*a*4)	IP(*a*2,*a*5)	IP(*a*2,*a*6)
0.1736	0.49084	0.369567	0.340835
IP(*a*3,*a*2)	IP(*a*3,*a*4)	IP(*a*3,*a*5)	IP(*a*3,*a*6)
0.398447	0.695355	0.5399	0.421672
IP(*a*4,*a*2)	IP(*a*4,*a*3)	IP(*a*4,*a*5)	IP(*a*4,*a*6)
0.117956	0.160001	0.233948	0.3272
IP(*a*5, *a*2)	IP(*a*5,*a*3)	IP(*a*5,*a*4)	IP(*a*5,*a*6)
0.116733	0.172473	0.386305	0.1636
IP(*a*6,*a*2)	IP(*a*6,*a*3)	IP(*a*6,*a*4)	IP(*a*6,*a*5)
0.29712	0.92625	0.613555	0.391871

N.B.: IP = (ai,as), $i,s = 2,3,4,5,6$; IP = $\sum tjPj(ai,as)$.

	*a*2	*a*3	*a*4	*a*5	*a*6	T+	T
*a*2	0	0.1736	0.49084	0.369567	0.340835	0.343711	0.111147
*a*3	0.398447	0	0.695355	0.5399	0.421672	0.513844	0.364169
*a*4	0.117956	0.160001	0	0.233948	0.3272	0.209776	−0.33674
*a*5	0.116733	0.172473	0.386305	0	0.1636	0.209778	−0.17404
*a*6	0.29712	0.092625	0.613555	0.391871	0	0.348793	0.035466
T−	0.232564	0.149675	0.546514	0.383822	0.313327		

The results for State are shown in **Figure 4**.

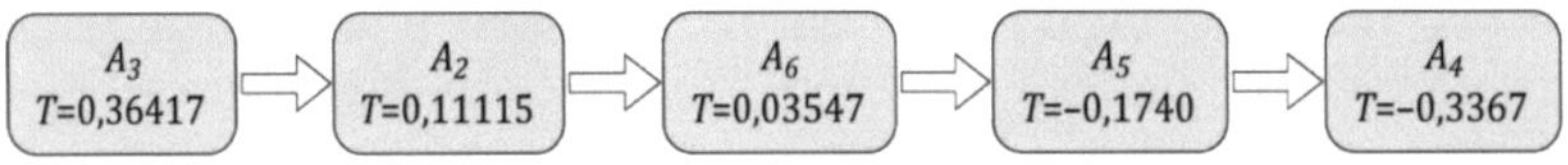

Figure 4. Chart representation of ranking results for the state as a stakeholder.

The same approach could be usd for detailed calculation for the investors and local community as stakeholders.

For the investors as stakeholders:

Determination of preference index			
IP(*a*2,*a*3)	IP(*a*2,*a*4)	IP(*a*2,*a*5)	IP(*a*2,*a*6)
0.1611	0.590895	0.272998	0.359078
IP(*a*3,*a*2)	IP(*a*3,*a*4)	IP(*a*3,*a*5)	IP(*a*3,a6)
0.377197	0.640883	0.402209	0.33841
IP(*a*4,*a*2)	IP(*a*4,*a*3)	IP(*a*4,*a*5)	IP(*a*4,*a*6)
0.195746	0.206178	0.21615	0.281805
IP(*a*5,*a*2)	IP(*a*5,*a*3)	IP(*a*5,*a*4)	IP(*a*5,*a*6)
0.143413	0.087446	0.477263	0.245445
IP(*a*6,*a*2)	IP(*a*6,*a*3)	IP(*a*6,*a*4)	IP(*a*6,*a*5)
0.294074	0.041479	0.622703	0.267196

N.B.: IP = (*ai*, *as*), *i*, *s* = 2,3,4,5,6; IP= ∑*tjPj*(*ai*,*as*).

	*a*2	*a*3	*a*4	*a*5	*a*6	T+	T
*a*2	0	0.1611	0.590895	0.272998	0.359078	0.346018	0.09341
*a*3	0.377197	0	0.640883	0.402209	0.33841	0.439675	0.315624
*a*4	0.195746	0.206178	0	0.21615	0.281805	0.22497	−0.35797
*a*5	0.143413	0.087446	0.477263	0	0.245445	0.238392	−0.05125

	*a*2	*a*3	*a*4	*a*5	*a*6	T+	T
*a*6	0.294074	0.041479	0.622703	0.267196	0	0.306363	0.000179
T-	0.2526075	0.124051	0.582936	0.289638	0.306185		

The reuslts for investors are shown in **Figure 5**.

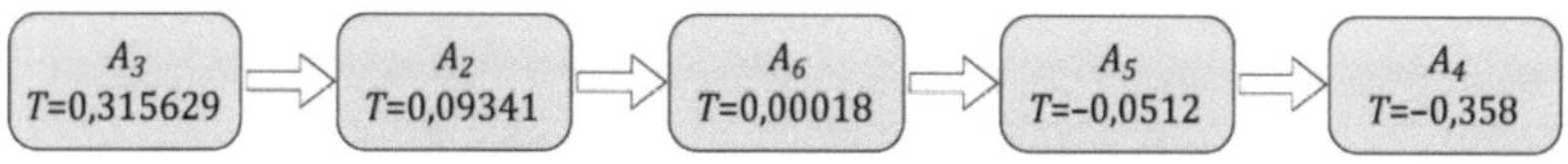

Figure 5. Chart representation of ranking results for the investors as stakeholders.

For the local community as a stakeholder:

Determination of preference index

IP(*a*2,*a*3)	IP(*a*2,*a*4)	IP(*a*2,*a*5)	IP(*a*2,*a*6)
0.082911	0.393418	0.316357	0.19993
IP(*a*3,*a*2)	IP(*a*3,*a*4)	IP(*a*3,*a*5)	IP(*a*3,*a*6)
0.436219	0.670658	0.553205	0.34342
IP(*a*4,*a*2)	IP(*a*4,*a*3)	IP(*a*4,*a*5)	IP(*a*4,*a*6)
0.039295	0.053301	0.141615	0.17268
IP(*a*5,*a*2)	IP(*a*5,*a*3)	IP(*a*5,*a*4)	IP(*a*5,*a*6)
0.066109	0.061476	0.202568	0.0545
IP(*a*6,*a*2)	IP(*a*6,*a*3)	IP(*a*6,*a*4)	IP(*a*6,*a*5)
0.305534	0.10103	0.611568	0.438984

IP = (*ai*, *as*), *i*,*s* = 2,3,4,5,6; IP= $\sum tjPj(ai, as)$.

	*a*2	*a*3	*a*4	*a*5	*a*6	T+	T
*a*2	0	0.082911	0.393418	0.316357	0.19993	0.248154	0.036365
*a*3	0.436219	0	0.670658	0.553205	0.34342	0.500876	0.426196
*a*4	0.039295	0.053301	0	0.141615	0.17268	0.101723	−0.36783
*a*5	0.066109	0.061476	0.202568	0	0.0545	0.096163	−0.26638
*a*6	0.305534	0.10103	0.611568	0.438984	0	0.364279	0.171647
T−	0.211789	0.0746795	0.469553	0.36254	0.192633		

The results for community are shown in **Figure 6**.

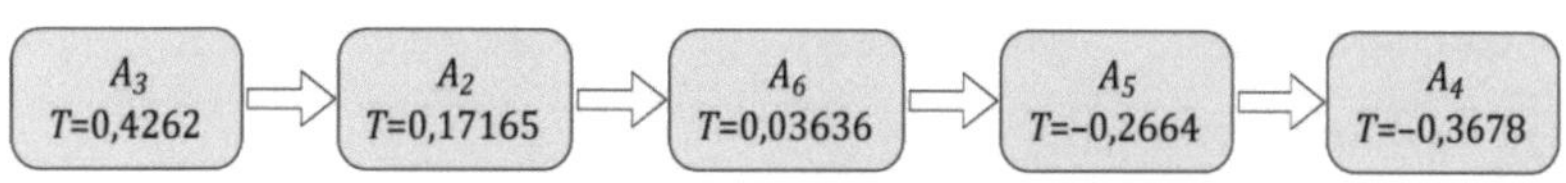

Figure 6. Chart representation of ranking results for the local community as a stakeholder.

5. Chart representation of results

After applying the PROMETHEE, as a tool for stakeholder value approach, and after the ranking, we can reach following conclusions on the basis of results obtained:

The results obtained and shown in the charts indicate, in fact, that, according to defined criteria and weight coefficients, the sequence of types of renewable energy sources is absolutely identical regardless of the stakeholder. The sequence of priorities in the application of renewable energy sources for the production of electricity goes as follows:

(1) Biomass

(2) Mini hydros

(3) Geothermal

(4) Wind energy

(5) Solar energy

Further activities of all stakeholders should be given to mini hydros and biomass, since they have the best relation toward the aforementioned criteria.

According to presented model, potentials of all the mentioned types of renewable energy sources are capable for achieving its goals, with the limitation that wind and geothermal energy would have, according to such a premise, a 96.82% usage, which is not a convenient circumstance, while biomass would have an 8.61% usage and mini hydros 24.20%.

The general conclusion is that the state as a stakeholder should focus its activities regarding the production of electricity from renewable energy sources on biomass and mini hydros, since, according to listed hypotheses, defined criteria and the application of the mathematical model, they proved to be the best solution. The same goes for investors and local community as stakeholders.

Methodology use in this chapter is taken into account the criteria and stakeholders which where possible to use according to the official available data. The final number of stakolders and criteria are endless and just make calculation model more comprehensive.

Author details

Dejan Jovanovic[1]* and Ivan Pribicevic[2]

*Address all correspondence to: deki.jovanovic@gmail.com

1 JP Zavod za udzbenike, Belgrade, Serbia

2 TMS CEE d.o.o Beograd, Belgrade, Serbia

References

[1] Edward Freeman, R. Univesity of Virginia. Faculty & Research. The Faculty Directory [Internet]. Available from: http://www.darden.virginia.edu/faculty-research/directory/r-edward-freeman/

[2] Radna Grupa.Ministarstvo energetike rudarstva i zastite zivotne sredine. Nacionalni akcioni plan za primenu obnovljivih izvora energije [Internet]. June 2013. Available from: http://www.mre.gov.rs/dokumenta-efikasnost-izvori.php

[3] Narodna Skupština Republike Srbije zakon o ratifikaciji. Zakon o ratifikaciji ugovora o osnivanju energetske zajednice i Republike Albanije, Rapublike Bugarske, Bosne i Hercegovine, Republike Hrvatske, Bivše Jugoslovenske Republike Makednoije, Republike Crne Gore, Rumunije, Republike Srbije, i privremene misije Ujedinjenih Nacija na Kosovu u skladu sa rezolucijom 1244 Saveta bezbednosti Ujedinjenih Nacija [Internet]. July 2006. Available from: http://www.parlament.gov.rs/narodna-skupština. 1.html

[4] Zorana Mihajlovic. Mistarstvo energetike rudarstva i zastite zivotne sredine. Politika Republike Srbije u oblasti obnovljivih izvora energije [Internet]. December 2012. Available from: http://www.serbio.rs/item/102-politika-republike-srbije-u-oblasti-obnovljivih- izvora-energije

[5] Milutin Čupić, Milija Suknović. Odlučivanje. 6th ed. Beograd: Fakultet organizacionih Nauka, Univerziteta u Beogradu; 2010.

[6] Available from: http://www.businessdictionary.com/definition/stakeholder-value-approach.html

[7] T. Tsoutsos T, Drandaki M, Frantzeskaki N, Iosifidis E, Kiosses I. Sustainable energy planning by using multi-criteria analysis application in the island of Crete. Energy Policy. 2009;**37**(2009):1587–1600.